Windows 98
Made Easy

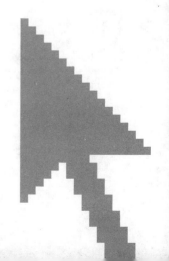

About the Authors

Tom Sheldon is the best-selling author of more than 25 computer books. He has worked as a computer consultant, programmer, and network administrator since the 1970s. His articles have appeared in *PC World*, *PC Magazine*, *BYTE*, and other publications.

Dan Logan is a book publisher, award-winning freelance writer, and journalist. He writes regional computer resource guides and is Webmaster of a regional Web-based magazine. Logan has published more than 600 articles in more than 40 magazines and newspapers including the *Los Angeles Times* and the *San Francisco Chronicle*.

Windows 98
Made Easy

Tom Sheldon
Dan Logan

Osborne McGraw-Hill

Berkeley New York St. Louis San Francisco
Auckland Bogotá Hamburg London Madrid Mexico City Milan Montreal
New Delhi Panama City Paris São Paulo Singapore Sydney Tokyo Toronto

Osborne McGraw-Hill
2600 Tenth Street
Berkeley, California 94710
U.S.A.

For information on translations or book distributors outside the U.S.A., or to arrange bulk purchase discounts for sales promotions, premiums, or fund-raisers, please contact Osborne/**McGraw-Hill** at the above address.

Windows 98 Made Easy

234567890 DOC DOC 90198765432109

ISBN 0-07-882407-9

Microsoft, Windows, the Windows logo, and Windows NT are registered trademarks of Microsoft Corporation.

Publisher
Brandon A. Nordin

Editor-in-Chief
Scott Rogers

Acquisitions Editor
Joanne Cuthbertson

Project Editor
Mark Karmendy

Editorial Assistant
Stephane Thomas

Technical Editor
Greg Guntle

Copy Editor
Claire Splan

Proofreader
Stefany Otis

Indexer
Jack Lewis

Computer Designers
Roberta Steele
Michelle Galicia

Illustrator
Brian Wells

Series Design
Peter F. Hancik

Cover Design
Woods & Woods
Design Communications

To new users everywhere, and experienced
users who want to learn more.

At A Glance

Part I
Getting Started

Part II
Personalizing Your System

Part III
File Systems: Local and Network

Part IV

Web Browsing and Communications

Part V

Configuration and Management

Contents

Part IV
Web Browsing and Communications

Acknowledgments

Thanks to everyone at Osborne/McGraw-Hill who made this book possible, including Joanne Cuthbertson, Mark Karmendy, Stephane Thomas, Michelle Galicia, Roberta Steele, Jani Beckwith, Lance Ravella, Ann Sellers, Peter Hancik, Brian Wells, Sylvia Brown and Jean Butterfield. Also thanks to Greg Guntle, who did a super job of checking everything for technical accuracy.

Introduction

Welcome to the age of the Internet, the Web, and of course, Windows 98. Today, powerful desktop computers are inexpensive and becoming as common as VCRs or microwave ovens. It's been over 20 years since the first desktop computers began to appear. Finally, we're at a point where they can do just about anything. Processing power and disk space are cheap, so graphics, sound, video, and other multimedia features are getting more exciting everyday.

Web-connected multimedia computers are luring people away from television and giving them the equivalent of a library in their own home or office. Entire newspapers can be downloaded via TV transmissions to your computer in time for morning coffee. People are meeting people around the world in chat rooms and videoconferences. Gamers are gaming with players on the other side of the planet. The Olympic Games are a Web-based, multimedia event!

Of course, Windows 98 fully supports the latest Web technologies and the latest hardware to make your computer system a lot more than you might have thought possible. In this book, you'll learn how to communicate and collaborate with people around the planet via email, Internet phone, or videoconferencing. You'll also learn about accessing the Web, doing searches, and receiving data broadcasts that are transmitted over television channels. We show you how to set up your computer as a Web server, how to manage your file system, how to take your work on the road, and how to optimize your system's performance. And, of course, we show you lots of tips and tricks along the way.

We hope you enjoy this book and Windows 98.

Tom Sheldon and Dan Logan

Check Out Our Web Site

The next few years are bound to bring many new and exciting innovations in the computer industry and in Windows 98. Our Web site will keep you informed and provide you with information about the following:

- Windows update information
- On-screen CD-ROM training
- Video training
- Additional training manuals

All you have to do is crank up your Web browser and visit the following Web site:

www.tec-ref.com

Getting Started

1

Windows 98 Visual Tour

BASICS

- Tour the Windows 98 Desktop
- Learn terminology used in the Windows environment
- Learn basic features of windows and dialog boxes
- Explore accessories and tools available in Windows 98
- Check out collaboration and communication tools

BEYOND

- Learn about the Windows 98 file system
- Explore the new Web-style interface
- Take advantage of the new Active Desktop
- Discover Windows 98 management tools

This chapter takes you on a visual tour of Windows 98. There is no hands-on here. Just sit back and let us show you what Windows 98 offers. This is a good chapter to read if you are on a flight or taking a commuter train to work.

You'll find numerous illustrations in this chapter which show you how Windows 98 works and introduce you to programs for writing, drawing, communicating, and managing your system. We also tell you which chapters in this book provide more information on the features we present.

The Windows 98 Desktop

Computer desktops, first introduced in the 1980s, are now so pervasive that it seems a bit ridiculous to explain what they are, sort of like describing the dashboard of a car. But there is terminology that we need to agree on, so stick with us while we go through the features.

The entire screen of your computer is called the *Desktop*. The Desktop is a metaphor for the top of a real desk. You run programs and open documents on the Desktop in the same way you open files and use tools like calculators on your desk. The first time you start Windows 98, your Desktop may not look exactly like the Desktop in Figure 1-1, but it should have the same basic features.

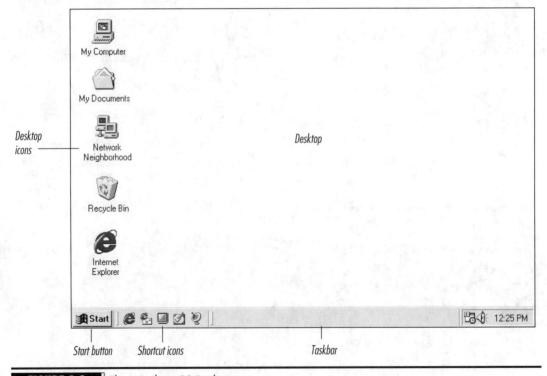

FIGURE 1-1 The Windows 98 Desktop

Note the *icons* on the Desktop. You click an icon to start a program or open a window that shows files on your local system, on a network, or on the Internet. The Internet Explorer icon opens a browser for exploring the World Wide Web

The Taskbar stretches across the bottom of the Desktop. It holds the Start button, the shortcut icons, and buttons for programs that are running in windows on the Desktop. The most important feature of the Taskbar is that it stays visible, no matter how many windows cover the rest of the Desktop. That way you can easily jump to other tasks or programs by clicking a button in the Taskbar.

You click the Start button to open the Start menu as shown next. Here is where you choose options to start programs, get help, find files, and access management features. The Programs *cascading menu* is open in this picture.

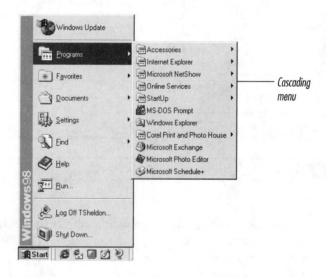

About "Windows"

Figure 1-2 shows what the Desktop looks like after opening a few Desktop tools like the Address Book, Phone Dialer, and Calculator. Each of these exist in a separate window.

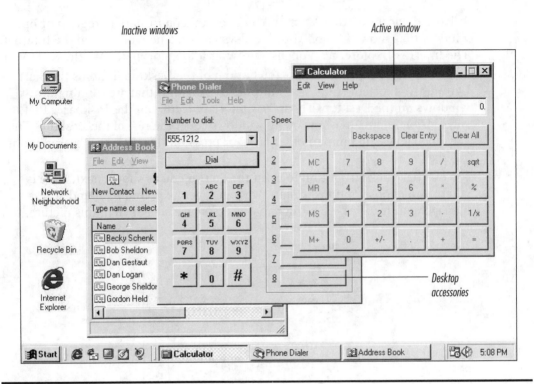

FIGURE 1-2 | Active and inactive windows on the Desktop

A *window* is a resizable and movable object that appears on your Desktop when you run a program or open a document. The important point is that you can have several windows open at the same time, as pictured in Figure 1-2.

Note the terminology used in Figure 1-2 to describe active and inactive windows. When you type, text appears in the active window. You can make any inactive window active by clicking it with the mouse.

Windows have active elements, such as borders, scroll bars, buttons, and menus as shown in Figure 1-3. For example, you can point to any border, then click and drag that border to make a window larger or smaller. You can also click any corner and drag to resize a window along two borders.

You use *scroll bars* to view content that won't fit in the "viewing area" of the window. Sometimes, you can expand a window's borders to make more content visible, but if the window has a lot of information, you'll need to scroll it into view.

Menus contain *options* that perform various actions. A dialog box may appear when you select some menu options. You make choices on dialog boxes about

Menu   Buttons

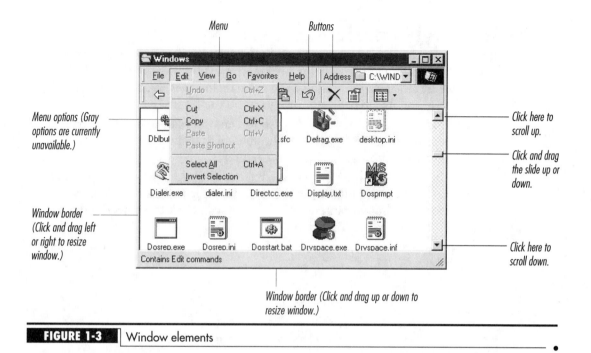

Menu options (Gray
options are currently
unavailable.)

Click here to
scroll up.

Click and drag
the slide up or
down.

Window border
(Click and drag left
or right to resize
window.)

Click here to
scroll down.

Window border (Click and drag up or down to
resize window.)

FIGURE 1-3   Window elements

how you want a command to execute. For example, on the following dialog
box, you set printing options, then click OK to print.

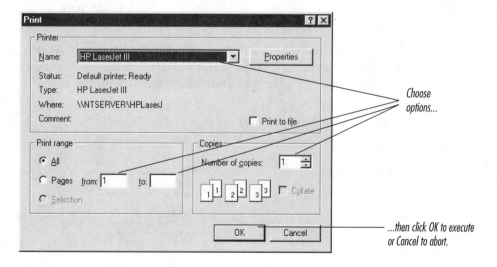

Choose
options...

...then click OK to execute
or Cancel to abort.

Web-Style Interface

If you've ever used a Web browser to explore the Internet, you know how easy it is to explore and search for information. Windows 98 now includes a Web-style interface so you can use the same techniques to access your local computer as you use to access information on the Internet.

Most important, Windows 98 now sports an optional single-click, Web-style interface (as opposed to the "classic" double-click technique used in Windows 95). We show you how to enable it in Chapter 2.

With the Web-style interface enabled, icons "light up" when you point at them with the mouse. This "hovering" technique helps you verify that you're pointing at the object you intended. Then you can click the object to open it or right-click it to get more information.

Just pointing at an object may present useful information. Two examples are shown below.

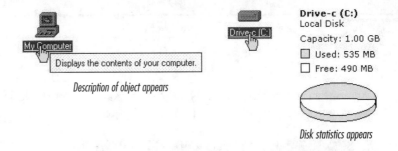

Description of object appears   Disk statistics appears

Right-clicking (pointing to an object and pressing the right mouse button) an icon will display a shortcut menu similar to the following where you can select options to rename, move, delete, or do other things with objects.

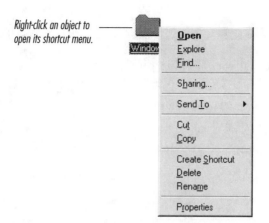

Right-click an object to open its shortcut menu.

You may need to double-click some objects in Windows 98. If the Web-style interface is enabled, you won't be double-clicki2ng as much as was required in Windows 95. Some applications still support double-clicking. For example, you double-click in Microsoft Word to select a word of text. You also double-click in some dialog boxes to select files and folders.

Personal Tools

Windows 98 includes some useful tools that may save you some money. You might not need to buy more elaborate and expensive software. You'll learn more about these tools in Chapter 5.

WordPad

WordPad is a writing accessory that lets you create, save, edit, and print text documents. As pictured in Figure 1-4, you can format text with a rich set of character fonts and insert pictures you have created in graphics applications such as Windows 98 Paint (discussed next).

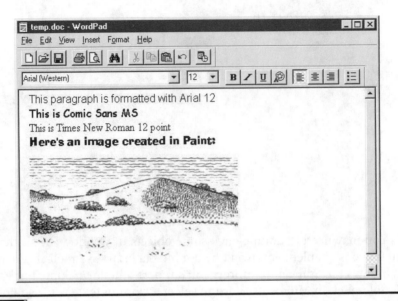

FIGURE 1-4 | WordPad

WordPad is not a full-featured word processing program like Microsoft Word, but it is easy to learn and has adequate formatting features that let you set paragraph indents, tabs, alignment (center, left justify, right justify), bulleted lists, and so on. It does not have advanced features such as spell checking, definable styles, and so on.

Paint

Paint is an accessory for creating and editing bitmap images A bitmap image is a picture consisting of dots (*pixels*) as shown in Figure 1-5. The image on Paint's "canvas" has been magnified to show the pixels.

Scanned photographs are examples of bitmapped images. You can use Paint to edit and touch up your pictures, or you can create your own images, such as a logo to insert as a letterhead in your WordPad documents.

Paint differs from vector-based *drawing* applications, where you create independent graphic objects that can be moved around and layered. Using Paint is like working with oils on a canvas—in other words, painting usually covers existing colors. In contrast, working with a drawing program can be compared to arranging paper cutouts of drawn objects (squares, circles, etc.) on some surface.

Magnified image showing pixels

Painting canvas

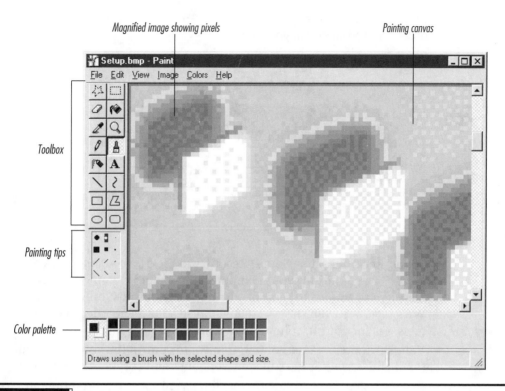

Toolbox

Painting tips

Color palette

FIGURE 1-5 Paint

Paint includes tools for freehand painting, brush painting, spray painting, and "spill" painting (color fills enclosed area). It also has tools for creating boxes, lines, and polygons, and an erasing tool to remove unwanted parts of the image. You can also select a specific part of the image (called a *cutout*) and move it to another location, stretch it, resize it, flip it, and do a number of other interesting things.

You can even use Paint to create interesting backgrounds to place on the Windows Desktop.

Multimedia Tools

Windows 98 includes some interesting multimedia tools for working with sound and video. These are described next:

- **CD Player**   Use CD Player to play your favorite music CDs. Just place the CD in your computer's CD-ROM drive and control the action with CD

Player's control panel, as shown next. You can play selected tracks in any order and repeat songs you like.

- **Sound Recorder** Use Sound Recorder to record voice messages or to create new sounds for your computer. For example, you can create messages or sounds to send in email messages or post on your personal Web page. We even show you how to use Sound Recorder to create messages for your telephone answering device.
- **Volume Control** Use Volume Control to control the volume of audio input and output devices like microphones and speakers.
- **Phone Dialer** The Phone Dialer stores your most important phone numbers and dials your telephone, assuming you have a modem attached to your system.

The File System, Windows Explorer, and My Computer

When you work at your computer, you'll create letters, work with spreadsheets, create pictures, and work with other types of information that you'll want to save for later. You save information in files on disks. For example, you can save your resume in a file called RESUME.DOC, where RESUME is the filename and DOC is a filename extension that *associates* the file with a word processor like Microsoft Word. Most applications add the extension, so you don't need to worry about it.

A typical hard disk drive may hold thousands or even millions of files. To keep track of all your files, you organize them into folders. You might have folders for personal files and folders for business files. This is not much different than a paper filing system as shown next, where file drawers contain folders that hold files just as your computer's drives contain folders that hold files.

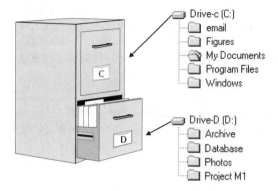

A folder may contain both files and other folders. For example, a folder called Photos may contain other folders called City, Country, Business, and Entertainment. A typical hard drive has a folder hierarchy similar to the following:

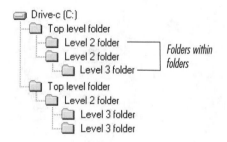

Identifying Disk Drives

As shown next, a typical PC will have at least one floppy drive called Drive A. If a second floppy drive is installed, it is called Drive B. The first hard drive is always called Drive C. Additional hard drives are called Drive D, Drive E, and so on. The first CD-ROM drive takes on the drive letter following the last hard drive letter (Drive E in the following example).

Exploring Your File System

There are two primary ways to explore your file system. The My Computer icon on the Desktop is one method. When you open it, a window appears that shows each of the disk drives on your system. You then open one of the drives to open yet another window that shows the files and folders on that drive. Then you can open a folder to view its list of files. This procedure is pictured in Figure 1-6.

TIP: When we say "open," we mean that you either click or double-click an object to open its window. Whether you click or double-click depends on whether the new Web-style interface is enabled (click) or whether you're using the Windows 95 style of double-clicking. Chapter 2 covers this further.

The other way to explore your file system is with Windows Explorer as pictured in Figure 1-7. Windows Explorer has two window panes. In the left pane, you see the hierarchical structure of your entire file system, including drives and folders on your local system and drives on other computers if you are connected to a network. The best thing about Windows Explorer is that you

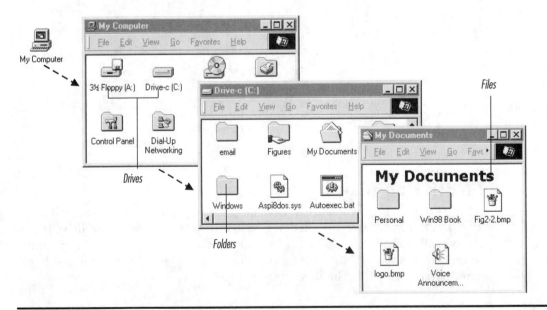

FIGURE 1-6 Exploring My Computer

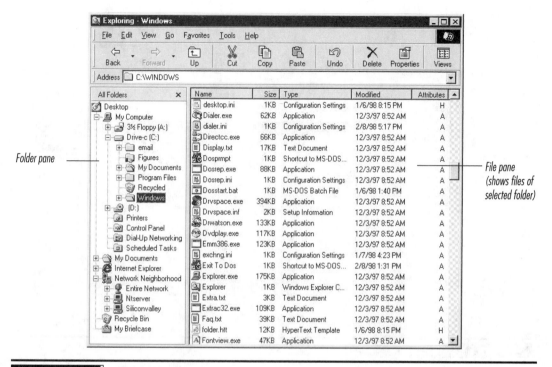

Folder pane

File pane
(shows files of
selected folder)

FIGURE 1-7 | Windows Explorer

can easily move or copy files in the file pane to any other drive or folder listed in the folder pane. Basically, Windows Explorer presents an arrangement that makes this kind of work easy.

TIP: Note that the file pane shows information about files such as their size, type, and creation date. You can sort on any of these columns by clicking the buttons at the top of the column. Refer to Part III for more information about working with files.

Exploring Your Network Neighborhood

If your computer is connected to a company network, you'll see the Network Neighborhood icon on the Desktop and in Windows Explorer. As shown in Figure 1-8, the Network Neighborhood displays icons for computers that have

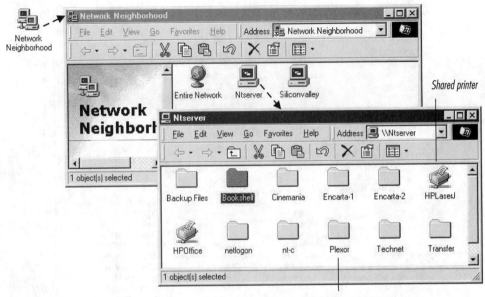

FIGURE 1-8 | Exploring Network Neighborhood

shared resources you can access, like files, CD-ROM drives, and printers. To open a file that has been shared on another computer, you open Network Neighborhood, find the computer that is sharing the resource, then open the shared resources.

Of course, shared resources on networks may be restricted to authorized users, so even though you can see a shared resource, you might not be able to access it unless you provide a password. Refer to Chapter 11 for more information about networks.

Exploring the Web

Windows 98 includes the Internet Explorer Web browser, Microsoft's advanced browser for exploring the Web. You can start Internet Explorer by clicking the Internet Explorer icon on the Desktop. The Internet Explorer is pictured in Figure 1-9 and is discussed in Chapter 12. If you are not already logged onto the Internet, Windows 98 will log you on so you can start exploring.

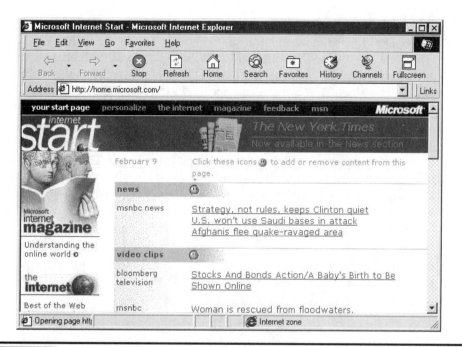

FIGURE 1-9   Internet Explorer

As mentioned, Windows 98 has many Web-like features that you can enable at any time. Microsoft refers to these features as the "Web view." You can access resources on the Web from almost any location. For example, look at the last two figures. The Address field normally displays the current drive and folder you are working with on your local system. But if you type a Web address in the address field, Windows 98 automatically connects to the Internet and displays a Web page as if the window were a Web browser.

Most people think of Web browsers as tools for accessing Web servers on the Internet. But most corporate networks today run the same network protocols that are used on the Internet and even make files and information available on their own internet Web servers. These internal Web-like networks are often called *intranets*. You can use Internet Explorer to explore your company's intranet and visit Web servers that have been set up by departments or even individual users.

You can even publish your own personal or business information on your intranet-connected Windows 98 computer. It's like setting up your own personal Web server. In fact, the software for doing it is called Personal Web Server or PWS! PWS is discussed later in this chapter and in Chapter 17.

Active Desktop

Active Desktop is the latest addition to Windows. It basically lets you convert your Desktop into something that looks like a bunch of Web browsers running at the same time. Take a look at Figure 1-10. Here, two channels have been added. The MSNBC Weather Channel shows the latest weather information. The Microsoft Investor channel shows the latest quotes for stocks that you select.

To understand Active Desktop, imagine that your Desktop has two layers. The top layer is a sheet of clear glass that holds your normal Desktop and its icons and windows. The lower layer is the Active Desktop, which displays information obtained from the Web. It's almost like the underlying Active Desktop has several small televisions that display the latest news, sports, and weather.

You pick the information you want displayed by *subscribing* to Web sites that provide just the information you need. Once subscribed, your computer periodically checks with the Web site to get the latest information and displays it in the appropriate window on the Active Desktop.

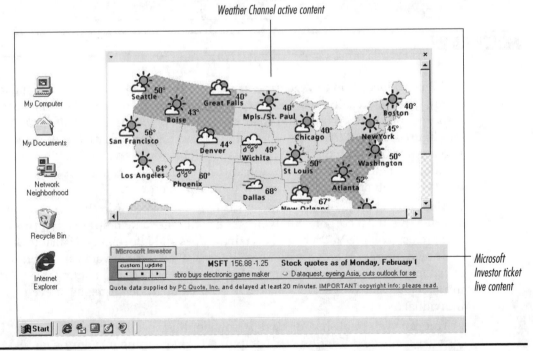

Weather Channel active content

Microsoft Investor ticket live content

FIGURE 1-10   Active Desktop is like another Desktop layer that runs Web controls and applets

TIP: Traditionally, the Windows Desktop has been a place to run Windows-specific applications. Active Desktop lets you run ActiveX controls and Java applets that were originally designed to run in Web browsers.

The Active Desktop is an important new feature in Windows and is discussed further in Chapter 13.

Channel Viewer and TV Tuner Technology

We've already used the analogy of a television to describe how information can be automatically retrieved from Web sites and displayed on your Desktop. Channel Viewer is a specialized version of Internet Explorer that could be compared to *TV Guide* for the Web. It helps you locate channels and subscribe to them.

Channel Viewer is pictured in Figure 1-11. When you click a category in the left pane, a list of available channels in that category appears in the right pane.

Channel groups

Click any logo to subscribe.

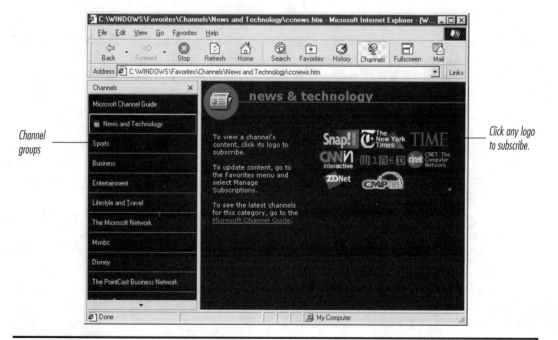

FIGURE 1-11 Channel Viewer

Windows 98 also supports new methods for broadcasting Web-like data transmissions over the television networks. The technology allows you to receive Web-like data that is embedded in a portion of TV transmissions called the Vertical Blanking Interval (VBI). All you need is a TV tuner card in your computer. No modem or Internet connection is required. Microsoft is working with WaveTop, a division of WavePhore, on this technology. WaveTop broadcasts are transmitted over 264 PBS member stations. Refer to "Data Broadcasting over TV Transmissions" in Chapter 13 for more details.

Collaboration and Communication

Windows 98 includes two important tools for communicating with other people over internal networks or over the Internet: Outlook Express and NetMeeting.

Outlook Express

Outlook Express is an electronic mail program that lets you exchange email with other people and manage your email archives. Figure 1-12 shows the Outlook Express window. You simply click an icon in the right pane to compose a message, read your mail, work with your address book, or find email addresses of people you know. The left pane contains mail folders that hold incoming mail, mail you are sending out, mail you have deleted (for archival purposes), and folders you create.

You can also use Outlook Express to work with newsgroups, which are basically email discussion groups that exchange messages related to specific topics such as archaeology, religion, computers, or just about anything.

NetMeeting

NetMeeting is a multimedia conferencing tool that lets you communicate and collaborate with other people over internal networks (intranets) and the Internet.

TIP: NetMeeting may sound like a business application, but it's also a great tool for family conferencing, especially if some family members are on the other side of the globe.

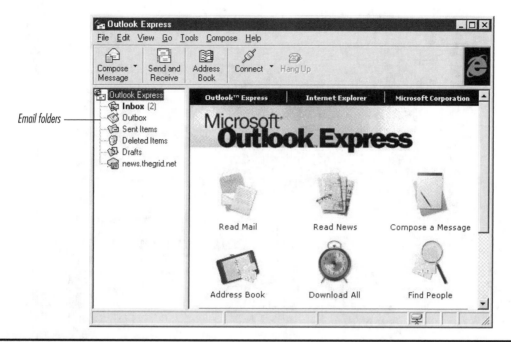

Email folders

FIGURE 1-12   Outlook Express

If you have a sound card, microphone, and speakers, you can use NetMeeting for voice conversation over the Internet in lieu of telephones. That will dramatically reduce your long-distance bills because you generally do not pay long-distance charges on the Internet. Of course, the parties you call will need similar equipment. If you have video cameras, you can use NetMeeting for videoconferencing. The NetMeeting window is pictured in Figure 1-13.

The interesting thing about NetMeeting is that, instead of dialing a phone number, you specify the email address or IP (Internet Protocol) address of the party you wish to reach. Multiple people can join in the conference.

Some additional features of NetMeeting include:

- **Chat**   A feature enabling conference members to exchange typed messages.
- **Whiteboard**   A Paint-like drawing application for creating images that all conference members can see and contribute to.
- **Application sharing**   A feature enabling any conference member to start an application that other members can see on their screens and control (one user controls the application at a time).

Microphone volume   Speaker volume   Video feed

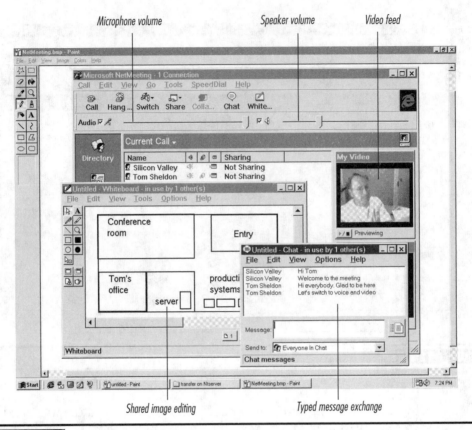

Shared image editing   Typed message exchange

FIGURE 1-13   NetMeeting

- **File Exchange** The ability to easily send and receive files among conference members.

FrontPage Express and Personal Web Server

You too can become a Webmaster with FrontPage Express and Personal Web Server (PWS). You use FrontPage Express to create and edit Web pages that you can post on your own Web server, a company Web server, or a Web site maintained by your Internet Service Provider. PWS is software that allows your personal computer to "serve up" Web pages just like any Web site on the Internet.

FrontPage Express makes it easy to create Web pages so you don't need to know a lot about HTML (HyperText Markup Language), which is the language of the Web. A setup wizard takes you step by step through the process of creating a home page and other hyperlinked Web pages. You can add hyperlinks to other pages or sites on the Web, design tables, create forms that collect information from users, and much more. FrontPage Express is discussed further in Chapter 16.

You can optionally install Personal Web Server if you want to publish Web pages from your personal computer. While you can connect your PC to the Internet and publish your pages worldwide, PWS is more practically used to publish Web pages on local intranets or to test Web pages before posting them with your Internet Service Provider. PWS is discussed further in Chapter 17.

Mobile and Remote Computing

Windows 98 includes extensive support for mobile and remote users. When you go on the road, you still need to keep in touch with your home or office computer as well as the resources available on your company network.

Mobile computers may be full-function portable computers or H/PCs (hand-held personal computers that do not include disk storage devices). You may need to connect these systems with your desktop computer in order to exchange files and other information. For example, before going on the road, you might move spreadsheets and other documents to your mobile computer. Windows includes software to make these moves.

An important consideration is that files on a mobile computer will become unsynchronized with files on desktop computers the moment you change them. A utility called the Briefcase tracks files that are stored in multiple locations and helps you keep them synchronized. When you go on the road, you copy files to the Briefcase and when you return, you copy from the Briefcase back to your desktop computer. In the process, Briefcase tracks changes to copied files, which helps you keep track of the most recent updates.

Windows 98 also includes support for dial-up networking, which allows mobile and remote users to dial into Windows 98 computers or Windows networks and operate on the network as if they were directly connected to it.

To improve communication and data transfer rates between remote users and home office systems, Windows 98 supports the ability to aggregate multiple dial-up lines and increase the bandwidth of a connection. For example, a remote office user could connect with the home office over four telephone lines using four 28.8 kilobits-per-second (kbps) modems to obtain a throughput of over 100 kbps, as shown in Figure 1-14.

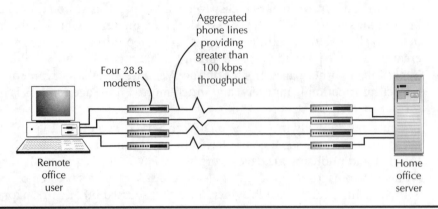

Four 28.8 modems

Aggregated phone lines providing greater than 100 kbps throughput

Remote office user

Home office server

FIGURE 1-14 | Modem aggregation in Windows 98

Mobile computing is discussed in Chapter 19 and modem aggregation is discussed in Chapter 20.

Management and System Performance Tools

Windows 98 includes a wide range of tools for managing your system, improving its performance, and troubleshooting problems. Most of these features are covered in Part V of this book. Some examples are listed next.

- **Windows Tune-Up Wizard** Allows you to schedule when Windows automatically starts utilities that tune and optimize your system. Some of the utilities that the Tune-Up wizard runs are discussed next.
  - **ScanDisk** Detects corrupted files on storage devices and corrects them.
  - **Disk Cleanup** Helps you locate files that are no longer needed and remove them to create more disk space.
  - **Disk Defragmenter** Automatically rearranges the way information is stored on a disk to improve access speeds. It moves fragmented files so they are stored in contiguous areas for faster access.
  - **Power Management** Advanced Power Management (APM) features shut down components such as the monitor and disk drives after a period of non-use.

• Other New Windows 98 Features

Some of the newest features in Windows 98 are outlined next:

- Universal Serial Bus (USB) support, which allows multiple devices like keyboards, mouse, and printers to be connected into a single port.
- Support for IEEE 1394 (Firewire) serial bus, which supports high-speed data transmissions from devices like video cameras. Firewire will spark a home video editing revolution.
- Support for new infrared interfaces that let you use peripheral devices without connecting wires. You can also transfer files and other information between computers using infrared interfaces.
- ActiveMovie video playback supports popular media types including MPEG audio and video, AVI video, and Apple QuickTime video playback.
- Support for DVD high-capacity optical disk storage devices.
- Last but not least, Windows 98 supports multiple displays. By installing more than one video adapter and connecting multiple monitors to your system, you can extend the size of the Desktop as pictured in the following illustration.

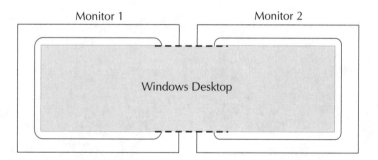

We hope you have a good overall picture of all the things you can do in Windows 98. It's like a trunk full of interesting gadgets, waiting to be explored. In the next chapter, you'll work hands-on with Windows 98.

Exploring the Windows 98 Interface

2

This chapter helps you explore the Windows 98 interface. Windows 95 users can skip some of the sections. However, you'll find Windows 98-specific information under some of the headings, including "Enabling the Web-Style Interface and Active Desktop," "Arranging Window Views," and "Instant Web Access."

Starting Windows 98

The first time you start Windows 98, you'll see one of the logon dialog boxes pictured next, depending on whether or not you are on a network. Type a password in the Password field and click OK. If this is the first time you've logged on, you may be asked to re-enter your password for verification.

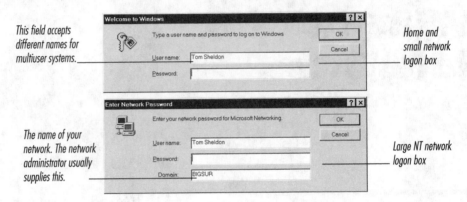

This field accepts different names for multiuser systems.

Home and small network logon box

The name of your network. The network administrator usually supplies this.

Large NT network logon box

Logging on may seem like a bother, especially if you are a home user, but there are some important reasons for it:

- Several people may use a single computer in your home or at your office. Windows 98 lets each user create a personalized Desktop, and then determines which Desktop to display from the information provided by the person logging on. See "Profiles for Multiple Users" in Chapter 6 for more information.

- If you are connected to a network, a password is required to access secure folders and files on other systems. Windows 98 will remember your password so you don't need to keep retyping it every time you try to log into a system that requires a password.

After you log on, the Windows 98 Desktop appears and you're ready to get started.

Techniques and Terminology

Just explore for now. You'll learn some techniques and we'll familiarize you with some Windows 98 terminology. Refer to Figure 2-1.

1. To make things happen, click the Start button.

2. Now drag the mouse up to the menu option called Programs.

3. Click Programs (or just hold the mouse there for a second). The Programs cascading menu opens, as shown in Figure 2-1.

4. Click Accessories on the cascading menu, then click WordPad on the next cascading menu.

T I P : If you don't see WordPad, it has not been installed. Refer to "Adding and Removing Windows 98 Components" in Chapter 6 to install it.

The WordPad window opens on your Desktop. We'll use it later in this chapter to experiment with windows and in Chapter 3 to get some real work done.

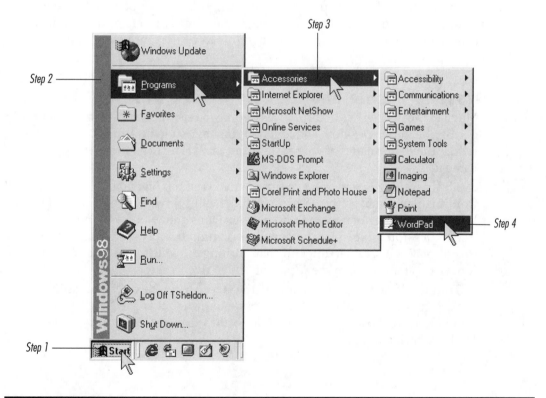

FIGURE 2-1 The Start menu and its cascading menus

Congratulations! You've just learned about 90 percent of what you need to know to work with Windows 98 (so you're wondering what the rest of this book is about?). In the process, we've introduced some important terminology. You clicked the *Start button* to open a *menu* that has *options*. You made a *selection* by clicking one of the options. Making selections opens menus, starts *programs*, or does a number of other things. Programs open in *windows* on the *Desktop*. As you'll see, you can open multiple windows and move or resize them on your Desktop, just like when you move papers around on your real desktop. When you're done with a program, you save your work and close the window.

Enabling the Web-Style Interface and Active Desktop

Now we need to do some housekeeping that will get your Desktop settings synchronized with the settings that we use in this book. We think they are the best settings for most people, so try them out for a while. You can always change them later. Note that the settings may already be enabled on your computer, but you should read through this to verify your configuration.

How to Enable and Disable Active Desktop

Much to the dismay of Microsoft, we're going to recommend that you temporarily disable the Active Desktop, and for good reason. Using the Active Desktop can reduce the performance of your system and there is no need to run it if you're not using it.

The best thing is that you can turn Active Desktop on and off in a jiffy. Recall from Chapter 1 that Active Desktop is like having a two-layer Desktop. The top layer is like a layer of glass that holds your icons and windows. Underneath, Active Desktop can display dynamic information from Web servers. Turning off this display is not much different than turning off your television. You can turn it back on at any time to see what's on the Active Desktop.

To turn off Active Desktop, follow the steps shown next. Note that View As Web Page is a *toggle* option; Active Desk is on when it is checked. Click the option to turn off Active Desktop. Follow these same steps to turn Active Desktop back on.

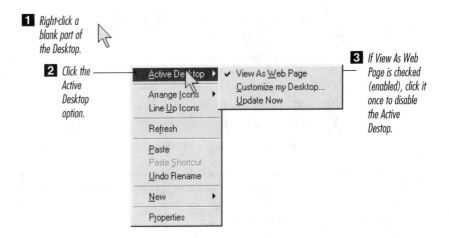

1 Right-click a blank part of the Desktop.

2 Click the Active Desktop option.

3 If View As Web Page is checked (enabled), click it once to disable the Active Destop.

Enable Web-Style Interface

Now enable the Web-style interface so you can single-click to open folders and documents or start programs just like you do when working on the Web.

Click Start, then choose Settings | Folder Options as shown here:

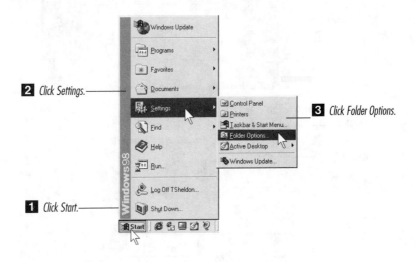

2 Click Settings.

3 Click Folder Options.

1 Click Start.

The Folder Options dialog box appears as shown in Figure 2-2. Notice that you can choose Web style (new for Windows 98), Classic style (like Windows 95), or set custom options. We're going to set a custom Web style.

1. Select the Custom option, then click the Settings button. The dialog box in Figure 2-3 appears.
2. Click the options on your dialog box so they match the settings we have.
3. Click OK when done and OK again to close the Folder options dialog box.

TIP: We're just recommending that you set the options as we have them. You might prefer to set the Browse folders option so it opens new windows when you click a folder. Try it both ways to see what you like best. A lot of what you will learn in this book is how to set options the way you like.

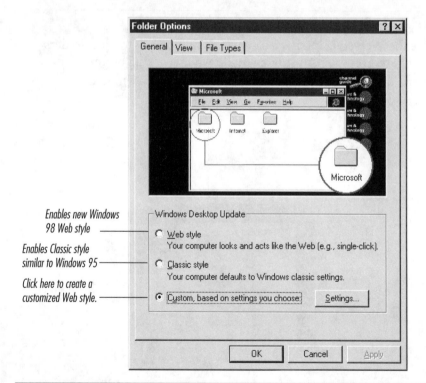

Enables new Windows 98 Web style

Enables Classic style similar to Windows 95

Click here to create a customized Web style.

FIGURE 2-2 | Choose a Desktop style

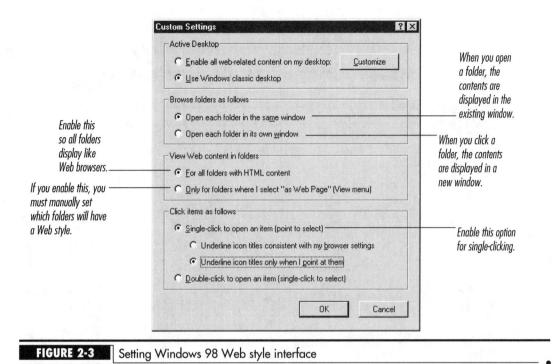

Enable this
so all folders
display like
Web browsers.

If you enable this, you
must manually set
which folders will have
a Web style.

When you open
a folder, the
contents are
displayed in the
existing window.

When you click a
folder, the contents
are displayed in a
new window.

Enable this option
for single-clicking.

FIGURE 2-3 Setting Windows 98 Web style interface

That's it for now. Now you can single-click to open folders, documents, and programs. We'll return to these custom settings again in Chapter 8.

Exploring My Computer

My Computer is an object on the Desktop that gives you access to resources on your own computer like disk drives and CD-ROM drives. It also provides information about your system hardware, as you'll see. Click the My Computer icon now. You'll see a window similar to the one shown in Figure 2-4.

Now open the first hard drive on your system (Drive C) and look at its contents. In Figure 2-4, Drive C has the name "Drive-c (C:)." On your system, the name may be different, but the name should contain "(C:)." Drive C may be the only hard drive in your system.

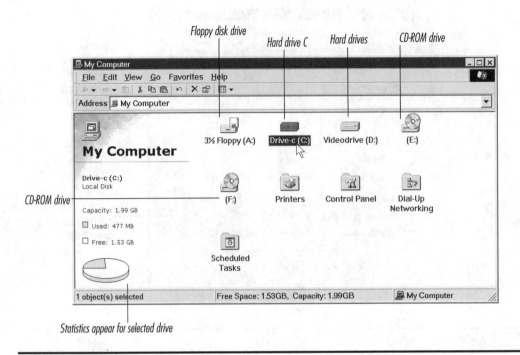

Floppy disk drive   Hard drive C   Hard drives   CD-ROM drive

CD-ROM drive

Statistics appear for selected drive

FIGURE 2-4 The My Computer window

Note that this example assumes your computer has a hard drive. Some companies use diskless workstations that access disk drives on corporate file servers. You may not see any drives in the My Computer window. See your network administrator for more details

Point to Drive C and click it. The contents of the drive appear in the window as pictured in Figure 2-5.

You may not have the same set of folders as shown in Figure 2-5, but your Drive C should have the Windows folder, which holds most of the Windows 98 program files.

TIP: As explained in Chapter 1, the files you create (letters, spreadsheets, pictures, etc.) are organized into folders and stored on disk drives.

Point to the Windows folder and click to open it. You'll see a message warning you not to delete or alter the contents of this folder. Good idea!

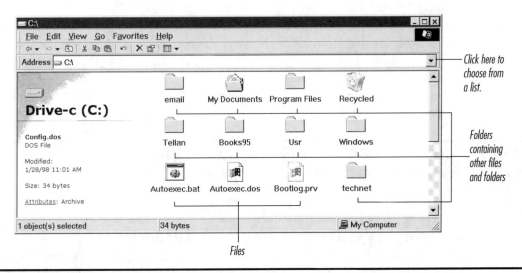

Click here to choose from a list.

Folders containing other files and folders

Files

FIGURE 2-5   The contents of a drive, including folders and files

We're just looking at it for now, so click Show Files in the warning message. Now you see a large list of folders and files as shown in Figure 2-6.

Click back arrow to go back one level.

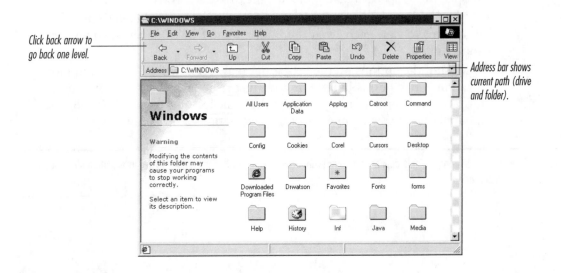

Address bar shows current path (drive and folder).

FIGURE 2-6   The Windows folder

Note the contents of the Address bar in Figure 2-6 compared to Figure 2-5. It illustrates that you are on Drive C in the Windows folder.

Now click the Back button to move back one level in the file system hierarchy to the "root" level of Drive C, as shown in Figure 2-5. This illustrates the way you can navigate through the file system on your computer in the same way you navigate on the World Wide Web.

Finally, for the next exercise, click the Back button again so that My Computer appears in the Address field.

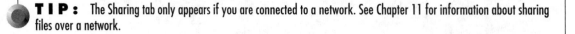 **TIP:** If you click the down arrow button on the right side of the Address field (see Figure 2-5), you see a list of drive and folder locations and you can choose any option to switch to that location.

Viewing System and Device Information

Now let's look at additional information about your computer. This exercise is not essential for beginners, but we thought you might be interested in knowing more about the storage devices and peripherals built into your computer.

You should have the My Computer window open on your Desktop. If not, click the My Computer icon on the Desktop.

Right-click (as opposed to left-click) the Drive C icon in the My Computer window. This opens the shortcut menu pictured in Figure 2-7. Click Properties to open the Properties dialog box for the drive as shown in the figure.

Click each of the "tabs" at the top of the dialog box (labeled General, Tools, and so on) to view each "page" of information. Click Cancel when you are done looking.

Most of the options on the Properties dialog box will be covered in more detail in Part V of this book. For now, just remember that these options exist for future reference. Once you learn the basic features of Windows 98, you'll no doubt be interested in exploring these options a little more.

TIP: The Sharing tab only appears if you are connected to a network. See Chapter 11 for information about sharing files over a network.

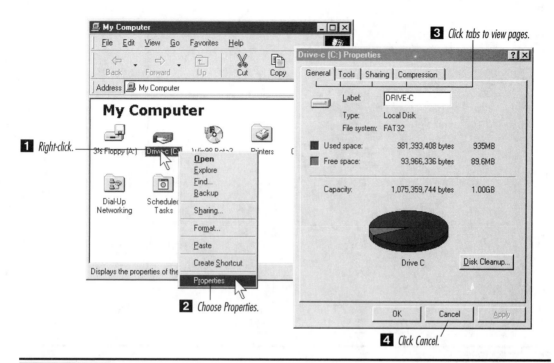

1 Right-click.

2 Choose Properties.

3 Click tabs to view pages.

4 Click Cancel.

FIGURE 2-7 | Viewing disk drive properties

There is one other place where you can view and change Windows 98 settings and options. Right-click the My Computer object on the Desktop to open the System Properties dialog box, shown in Figure 2-8. This is where you can get information about your system and the software running on it. For example, if you click the Performance tab, you'll see information about how your system is running.

Click Cancel to close the dialog box. As mentioned, you can refer to Part V of this book for more information on how to take advantage of these options.

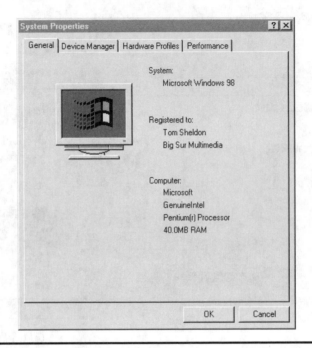

Getting information about your system

Exploring the Desktop and Taskbar

This section will demonstrate some of the most elemental techniques for working on the Windows 98 Desktop. You'll try some things that don't really accomplish anything except to show you how they work. Your job is to get familiar with the technique of clicking, selecting, and dragging. Sounds like dancing. Later chapters will illustrate useful methods for putting these techniques to work.

Click-and-Drag Techniques

First, try to "click and drag." Point to the My Computer icon, but this time when you click, hold the mouse button down and drag the icon to another location on the Desktop. When you release the mouse button, the icon assumes its new location.

You'll use click and drag for a variety of tasks. For example, you can rearrange the icons on your Desktop. Better yet, you can move files from one folder to another by simply dragging them to the new location. You can even print a file by dragging it on top of a printer icon.

Right-Click-and-Drag Techniques

Sometimes, click and drag can surprise you. You might accidentally drop a file into the wrong folder. A neat trick is to use the right mouse button when clicking and dragging in order to avoid mistakes.

As an example, open the My Computer window if you don't already have it open, then open Drive C. Right-click and drag the My Documents folder to the Desktop. When you release the mouse, a shortcut menu opens with a list of options, as shown in Figure 2-9. You can choose to move or copy the folder, create a shortcut, or cancel the operation, but for this example, just choose Cancel.

TIP: Move and Copy are quite different. Move removes an object from its original location and puts it in the new location. Copy duplicates the object so it exists in both locations.

Note that the Move Here option on the menu is bold, indicating that it is the default selection. The default selection is used when you click and drag with the left mouse button. There will be times when you want to copy an object or create a shortcut; right-clicking and dragging displays the shortcut menu so you can make that selection.

TIP: When clicking and dragging, always right-click. That way, you see a menu that gives you options for how to dispense with the object(s) you are dragging.

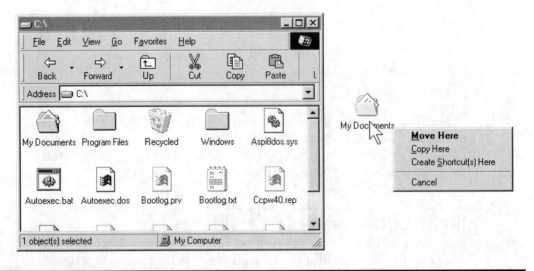

FIGURE 2-9 Clicking and dragging with the right mouse button displays a menu of options

Selecting Multiple Items

There will be times when you need to select multiple files, folders, or objects at the same time. When you select objects, they "light up" or reverse their color. Once you've selected icons, you can perform operations like moving or copying them to another location or deleting the objects. There are three techniques for selecting multiple objects:

- Hold the CTRL key and click the items you want to select. Keep holding the CTRL key as you select other items.
- Hold the SHIFT key and click the first item. Keep holding the SHIFT key and click the last item. All the items in between are selected.
- Click and drag a box around the objects (assuming the objects are grouped next to each other).

Try these methods now by selecting objects on your Desktop or inside the My Computer window. When using the SHIFT key method, make sure to press the SHIFT key first; otherwise, you may open an object rather than select it. The third method "box" may take a few tries. Just click near the objects to select and drag the mouse to the opposite corner of the objects.

Once the objects are selected, just click on any of the selected objects and drag. All the objects drag together or right-click to see the shortcut menu.

Move the Taskbar

Now try clicking and dragging one more object—the Taskbar. Click on any blank portion of the Taskbar, then drag to one of the side borders or even the top border. When you release the mouse, the Taskbar moves to the selected location.

Rearranging Icons

At this point, your Desktop may look a little disorganized since you've been moving icons around. There is an easy way to get things reorganized.

Right-click the Desktop to open the Desktop shortcut menu, then click the Arrange Icons option to see the cascading menu shown next. This is where you can choose to rearrange icons according to names and dates and other information. Choose the Line Up Icons option to straighten up your desktop now.

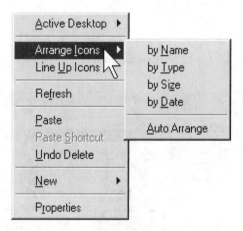

The Auto Arrange option is a toggle. When you set it on, icons are automatically rearranged whenever they get out of place or when you add a new icon. This can be annoying if you are trying to reorganize your desktop, so set this option off for the Desktop.

TIP: Auto Arrange can be set on for folders. Then when you resize a folder window, icons in the window automatically rearrange to fit the new folder dimensions. This is covered in the next section under "Automatic Arrangements."

• Working with Windows

The way you work with windows on the Desktop is analogous to the way you manage papers and other things on your real desk. You move some papers to the top of the stack and place temporary work to the side. This section explores techniques for managing windows.

You probably have the My Computer window open on your Desktop along with the WordPad window. If not, open them now.

The terminology for windows is as follows: the window in front is called the *active window* and all underlying windows are the *inactive windows*. The *Title bar* of the active window is a distinctive color while the underlying inactive window's Title bar is gray, as shown in Figure 2-10. All actions including typing take place in the active window.

Click the inactive WordPad window now. It jumps to the top and becomes the active window.

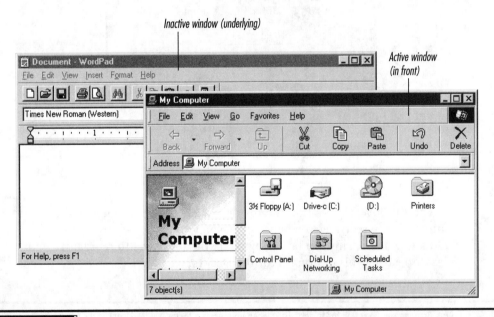

FIGURE 2-10 Active and inactive windows

Minimizing and Maximizing

With two or more windows open, your Desktop might be getting crowded. To clean things up, try minimizing the inactive windows as follows.

1. In one of the open windows, click the Minimize button as shown here:

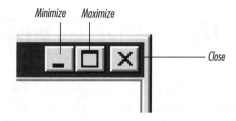

   The WordPad window is reduced to a button on the Taskbar.

2. Click the WordPad button on the Taskbar to *restore* the WordPad window.

3. Now click the Maximize button.

   Maximize makes the WordPad window as large as your entire screen. When a window is maximized, the Maximize button converts to a Restore button.

4. Click the Restore button to restore the window to its original size.

   The X button closes a window, but don't click the Close button because we're going to use both WordPad windows for the next few exercises.

T I P : Some applications run faster in maximized windows.

Switching Windows

If you have a lot of windows open or if a window is maximized, it's not easy to click the window you want to make active. There are three alternative ways to make a window active:

• Click the button for the window in the Taskbar.

- Press ALT-TAB to display the Task Switcher and keep pressing ALT-TAB until the window you want is selected.
- Press ALT-ESC to cycle through each window until the one you want appears.

The two keystroke methods are probably worth posting on a sticky note next to your computer along with some other shortcuts we'll show you later.

Resizing and Arranging Windows

There will be many times when you want to change the size of a window. That's easy to do with the *click-and-drag* technique.

Point with the mouse to any border of the active WordPad window. A double-headed arrow appears similar to the following. Click and drag the window border in or out to shrink or expand the window size.

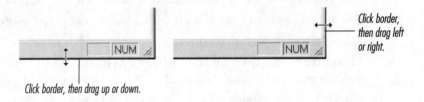

Click border, then drag left or right.

Click border, then drag up or down.

TIP: Point to a corner, then click and drag to resize a window in two directions at the same time.

Automatic Arrangements

If you don't like to fiddle around with window borders, you can have Windows 98 automatically resize and arrange windows for you. There are three options to choose:

1. Point to a blank portion of the Taskbar as shown next and right-click the mouse. The Taskbar menu appears as shown here:

Options for arranging windows

2. Choose Cascade Windows, Tile Windows Horizontally, and Tile Windows Vertically.

Each of these arrangements is pictured in Figure 2-11. Experiment with the options to see how they work.

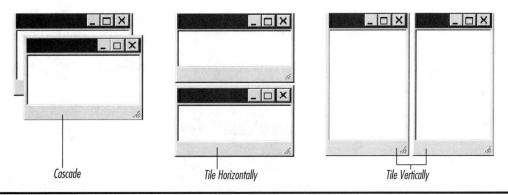

Cascade   Tile Horizontally   Tile Vertically

FIGURE 2-11 | Different ways to arrange windows on the Desktop

 T I P : If you're trying to compare two documents or copy text from one document to another, the Tile Windows Vertically option is definitely the best one to choose, assuming you have enough room on your Desktop to put the windows side-by-side.

The Minimize All Windows option is really useful. It minimizes all the windows so that you can see the Desktop. A quicker way to minimize all windows is to click the Show Desktop button in the Taskbar as shown here:

Show Desktop button

Arranging Window Views

While programs run in windows, you'll also work with windows that display lists of folders and files. In the latter case, you'll need to know techniques for changing and rearranging the views.

Open the My Computer window and then open Drive C. A window similar to Figure 2-5 appears with a list of folders and files. Now you can set the options described next.

Toolbars

Toolbars provide convenient single-click access to options and commands. While you probably already have most toolbars enabled, this section will show you how it's done.

Click View on the Menu bar, then click the Toolbars option. You'll see the cascading menu pictured here:

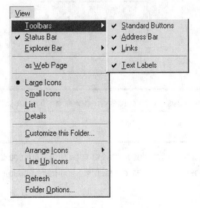

If an option is checked, the toolbar is already on. The Toolbars option on the View menu are toggles, so you click an option to either turn it on or turn it off. Each of the toolbars is shown here:

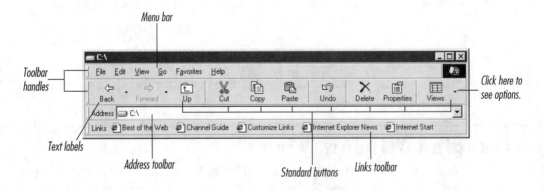

Note that if you enable all toolbars, your window might not look exactly like the one shown here. For example, the Links toolbar may appear to the right of the Address toolbar. Click the toolbar handle and drag the toolbar down to its own line on the window.

We recommend enabling the Standard Buttons and Address toolbars. Text Labels add a text reminder under the buttons in the Standard Buttons toolbar.

TIP: Disabling Text Labels makes the Standard Buttons toolbar smaller and gives you more room inside the window to display objects, which is important if you have a small Desktop.

Arranging Toolbars

Here's something you can try. Move the Address toolbar into the right side of the Menu bar and clicking the Address toolbar handle and dragging it up just to the right of the Help option. The Address toolbar then appears as shown here:

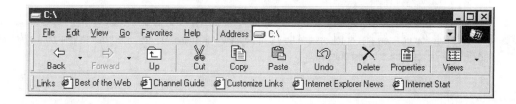

Changing Views

Some of the buttons on the Standard toolbar provide an instant change of the folder and file views. Try the following to see how you can change the view:

• Click the Views button repeatedly to switch among Large Icon, Small Icon, List, and Detail views.

• Click the down arrow button next to the Views button to choose one of these views from a list. These same view options are available by choosing View on the Menu bar.

• Choose Details from the View drop-down menu to see the view pictured in Figure 2-12. This view lets you see file information, such as dates and sizes. You can also click the buttons above the columns to sort the columns. Click once for ascending order; click again for descending order.

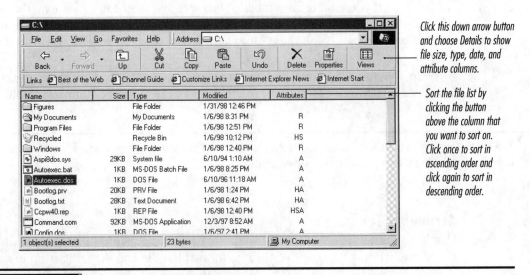

Click this down arrow button and choose Details to show file size, type, date, and attribute columns.

Sort the file list by clicking the button above the column that you want to sort on. Click once to sort in ascending order and click again to sort in descending order.

FIGURE 2-12 Detailed view of file listing

TIP: If you add new files or folders and they don't appear immediately in the folder, choose View on the Menu bar and click the Refresh option or just press F5.

Chapter 8 provides more information about customizing and arranging the look of folders.

Keyboard Techniques for Navigating Windows

Keyboard techniques provide an alternative way to access the Windows interface. They are presented for two reasons. You might find them faster than using a mouse in some cases and they can bail you out if your mouse freezes (or runs away).

Here are the basic keyboard techniques for accessing the Windows 98 interface. For more information, look up "shortcut keys" in the Help system and print the information for future reference.

- When working in a window, press ALT to access the Menu bar, then type the underlined letters in the menu options you want to access.
- As mentioned earlier, press ALT-TAB or ALT-ESC to jump between windows.
- Press TAB to move among fields in open windows or dialog boxes.

- Press ALT-SPACEBAR to open a window's Control menu. The Control menu has options for manually moving, sizing, minimizing, maximizing, and closing a window.

If you choose Move on the Control menu, a four-headed arrow appears over the window's Title bar. Just press the arrow keys to move the window. To resize a window, choose Size, press the arrow key that points to the border you want to adjust, then press the appropriate arrow key to resize it.

Try these techniques now on your own.

Menus

So far, you've been opening and making selections from quite a few menus. It's important to realize that each different type of object has its own set of right-click menu options as illustrated in Figure 2-13.

The main thing for now is to be aware of the differences in types of objects and their menu options. For example, choosing Find on the My Computer menu lets you search across all the drives in your system while choosing Find on a folder menu lets you search through just that folder. Another interesting option is Send To, which lets you "send" a file to a printer, another disk, or to a specific application.

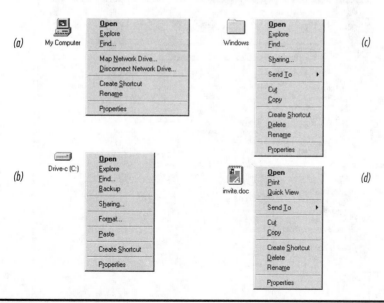

FIGURE 2-13 Right-click menu options for My Computer (a), a disk drive (b), a folder (c), and a file (d)

If you right-click a drive and choose Sharing, every folder and file on the drive will be shared and accessible to network users. That is not a good idea unless you trust everyone on your network. A safer option is to right-click just the folder you want to share and choose Sharing on its menu. As you work through this book, you'll learn more about these subtle options, so stay tuned.

Windows Explorer

Windows Explorer is a utility that helps you explore the folders and files on your computer or on your local network. It also has a Web-style interface so you can access Web sites while working in the utility.

You can start Explorer by clicking the Start button, then Programs | Windows Explorer. Alternatively, you can right-click My Computer, any drive, or any folder, and choose Explore on the shortcut menu that appears.

The Explorer window is pictured in Figure 2-14. It is very similar to any other window, except for the addition of the folder pane, which lists all the drives and folders that are accessible from your system. If you select a folder in the left pane, the contents of that folder appear in the right pane.

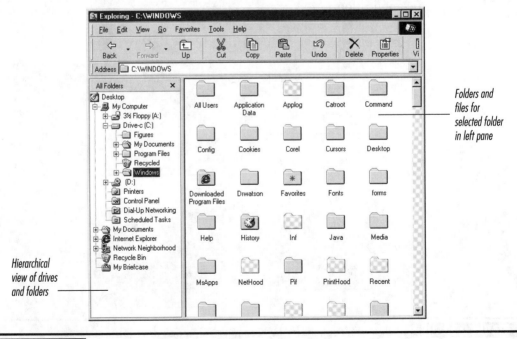

Hierarchical view of drives and folders

Folders and files for selected folder in left pane

FIGURE 2-14 | Windows Explorer

Putting It To Work

Clicking and Dragging to Copy Files in Explorer

Explorer makes it easy to work with files in Windows 98. This section will show you how to create a copy of the WordPad program in the My Documents folder using the click-and-drag techniques you learned earlier. Starting WordPad from My Documents is easier than opening all those cascading menus from the Start button. Follow the steps you see in Figure 2-15.

Now you can click the My Documents folder in the left pane to see the results. You can also click the My Documents folder on the Desktop to see the results.

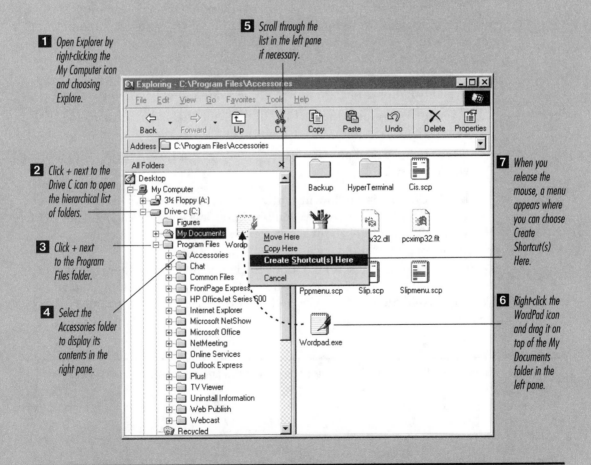

1 Open Explorer by right-clicking the My Computer icon and choosing Explore.

2 Click + next to the Drive C icon to open the hierarchical list of folders.

3 Click + next to the Program Files folder.

4 Select the Accessories folder to display its contents in the right pane.

5 Scroll through the list in the left pane if necessary.

7 When you release the mouse, a menu appears where you can choose Create Shortcut(s) Here.

6 Right-click the WordPad icon and drag it on top of the My Documents folder in the left pane.

FIGURE 2-15 Working with files in Explorer

Explorer lets you see all the drives and folders on your system in a single window, which makes it easy to copy and move folders and files around. For example, looking at Figure 2-14, to copy the Cookies folder in the right pane to a floppy disk, you simply click and drag the Cookies folder on top of the floppy disk icon in the left pane. The files in the folder are then copied to the floppy disk.

Instant Web Access

Folder windows have Web-browser features that let you access information on the Internet in the same way you access files on your own computer. Try the following example, assuming you have an Internet connection (connecting to the Internet is covered in Appendix B).

1. Open My Computer.
2. Type **http://home.microsoft.com** in the Address field and press ENTER.
3. If you are not online, the Dial-Up Connection dialog box appears to ask if you want to go online. Click Connect.
4. Once you're logged on, Microsoft's Web page appears in the My Computer window!

The My Computer window instantly converts to a Web browser so you can explore the World Wide Web. When Microsoft talks about Web integration in Windows 98, it's talking about accessing the Web from any folder or application as you just did.

You can also choose several options to change the look of the window. On the View menu, choose Explorer options. This opens a cascading menu where you can enable such options as Search Favorites, History, and Channels. These and similar options are discussed further in Part IV of this book.

TIP: You can also click Favorites on the Start menu to jump to Internet favorites and other links on the Web.

• Getting Help

Windows 98 provides a complete Help system that you can search to find answers to specific problems. Choose Help on the Start menu to display the Windows Help window shown in Figure 2-16. Help in Windows 98 now has a Web-like interface, so using it is not much different than using a Web browser. The Contents tab displays topics in book form while the Index tab displays topics in alphabetical order. You can also click the Search tab to search for topics by keyword.

You'll also find help options in the programs you use. For example, most programs have a Help option on the Menu bar where you can choose to display help topics or search for specific help information.

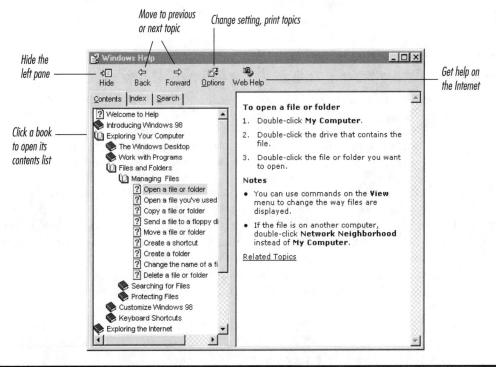

FIGURE 2-16 The Windows Help system

When working with dialog boxes, right-click any field title to display the What's This? option as shown here. Click it and you'll see a short description for the field.

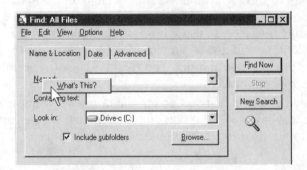

Closing Programs and Shutting Down

You've learned a wide range of Windows 98 features and techniques. Now it's time to learn one rule:

Always use the Windows 98 Shut Down routine before turning off the power to your computer.

There are a number of reasons for this rule, but one important point is that you may have forgotten you have unsaved documents open. You would lose the documents if you turned the computer off. Another reason is that Windows may be doing some important work, like writing information to disk. Turning the power off might cause a disk error that would need to be corrected the next time you start the system. Windows will make the corrections automatically, but it takes time and you might lose some important information or system settings.

Closing Open Programs

Before shutting down your system, close all programs. If any documents are still open in the programs, you'll be asked if you want to save them.

1. Click the Close button on all open windows. If you have unsaved information in the windows, the program will ask you if you want to save the information.

2. Some programs may be minimized to the Taskbar. Click the buttons for any running programs in the Taskbar, then click the Close button.

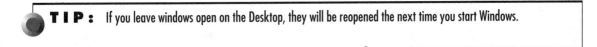

TIP: If you leave windows open on the Desktop, they will be reopened the next time you start Windows.

Shutting Down Windows 98

Now you're ready to shut down Windows 98.

1. Click the Start button, then choose Shut Down. The Shut Down Windows dialog box appears.

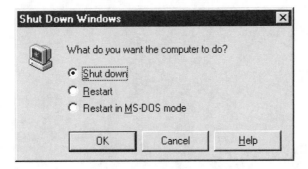

Note that you can choose to shut down the computer, restart the computer, or restart in MS-DOS mode. You may need to restart your computer after installing new software, or because it has become unstable and is exhibiting strange behavior. Some software applications may cause your system to become unstable.

2. Choose Shut down on the dialog box and click OK.

Windows 98 will either turn your computer off for you or display a message that it is OK to turn the computer off.

Performing Everyday Tasks

3

BASICS

- Day-to-day activities for using Windows 98
- Start programs
- Organize your work area
- Open, edit, save, and print documents

BEYOND

- Create font sample sheets
- Find documents on your disk storage system
- Create document templates

In this chapter you get two lessons in one. You'll learn how to perform some of the most common tasks in Windows 98, such as starting programs, working with files, and printing. At the same time, you'll learn about features of the Windows 98 interface.

We want you to do some interesting and useful things while you learn techniques that are required to work in a skillful way with Windows 98. As you work through this chapter, think about how you can apply these techniques to your everyday activities.

• Starting a Program

Programs are the tools you use to perform tasks, like writing a letter, creating a spreadsheet, sending electronic mail, drawing a picture, or updating your schedule. In this section, we'll show you how to start WordPad, a writing application that comes with Windows 98. Note that some of you may have other writing applications installed on your computer, but this chapter will largely use WordPad to explain the features of Windows 98. Keep in mind, however, that the techniques discussed here apply to almost every Windows application.

Follow the steps in Figure 3-1 to start WordPad. When you're done, the WordPad window will appear on top of the Desktop.

Take a few moments to experiment with the Start button and its cascading menus. Notice that when you highlight a menu option that has a right-pointing arrow, a cascading menu appears in about one second. You can also just click the option to open its menu.

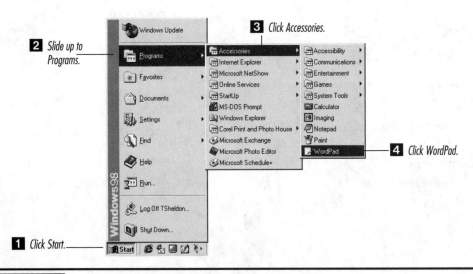

FIGURE 3-1 Starting a program from the Start menu

There will be times when you'll want to work on two different documents at the same time. Perhaps you need to transfer text from an earlier document to a new document. Also, with two copies of WordPad open at the same time, you can easily make notes in one window while you create an important document in the other.

Try this now. Open a *second* copy of WordPad by following the steps just given in Figure 3-2.

When the new copy of WordPad opens, it exactly overlaps the first copy. You'll need to drag it off as outlined by the steps shown in Figure 3-2.

Ah ha! There is a second window under the first. Keep both windows open for now. We'll use them in the next few exercises to help you learn how to organize your work area.

Remember how to move windows. You'll do that often as you work with Windows 98.

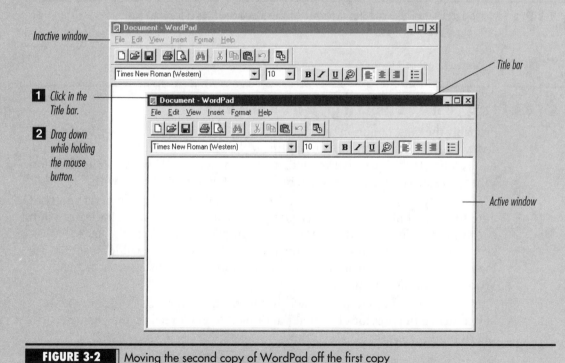

Inactive window

Title bar

1 Click in the Title bar.

2 Drag down while holding the mouse button.

Active window

FIGURE 3-2 Moving the second copy of WordPad off the first copy

Organizing Your Work Area

In this section, you'll learn the techniques and tricks for moving among windows and organizing your work area. In the next section, you'll type some text.

Remember that the top window on the desktop is called the *active* window. Its title bar is highlighted, and any keyboard activities appear in this window. Other windows are called *inactive* windows.

Click the inactive WordPad window now. It jumps to the top and becomes the active window. Minimize one of the windows now by clicking its Minimize button. It doesn't matter which window you minimize at this point; the window minimizes to a button on the Taskbar and the other window becomes active.

Now try resizing the window on your desktop. Point with the mouse to any border of the active WordPad window. A double-headed arrow appears when you're pointing at the border. Click and drag the window border in or out to shrink or expand the window size.

TIP: Point to a corner, then click and drag to resize a window in two directions at the same time.

Creating and Editing Documents

Probably the most common thing people do with their computer is write and edit documents. This section explains editing techniques in WordPad, but they are the same editing techniques that you will use in almost every Windows 98 application. What you learn here can be applied in most applications you work with.

Start by typing your name and address in the WordPad window. As you type, note that the blinking cursor precedes your characters. This just indicates your current typing location. If you type the wrong character, press the BACKSPACE key to remove it. When you're done, the WordPad window will look similar to Figure 3-3. We've pointed out some of the more important features of the WordPad window in this figure.

Use the arrow keys to move back and forth in the text. Use the BACKSPACE key to delete the previous character and the DEL key to delete the character to the right of the cursor.

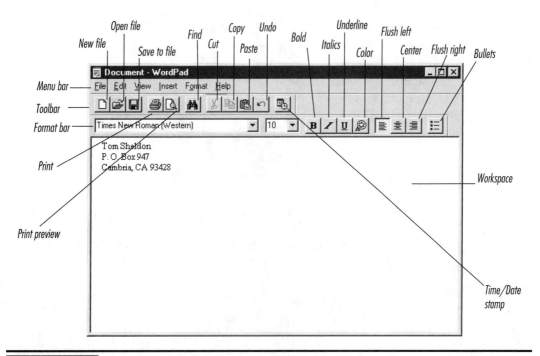

New file
Open file
Save to file
Find
Cut
Copy
Paste
Undo
Bold
Italics
Underline
Color
Flush left
Center
Flush right
Bullets

Menu bar
Toolbar
Format bar
Print
Print preview

Workspace
Time/Date stamp

FIGURE 3-3 The WordPad window's toolbars and buttons

Selecting Text

Now try changing the font and style of the text you just typed. You first need to *select* the text you want to change. Try the following exercises. As you do them, keep in mind that the reason you select text is to change its style, copy it to another location, or delete it. You will use these same techniques when working in Windows 98 dialog boxes and most other Windows 98 programs.

1. Put the "I-beam" cursor in front of any character, then click the mouse and drag to the right. Characters on the line are *highlighted*, as in the example shown here:

Tom Sheldon
P.O. Box 947
Cambria, CA 93428

2. Click anywhere outside of the highlighted area to remove the highlighting.

3. Now try the same thing again, but click and drag down to the bottom line. This extends the highlight through multiple lines, as shown here. Remove the highlight again as mentioned in step 2.

4. Now point to the white area next to the window border at the extreme left of a line. This area is called the *Selection bar*. The cursor will turn into an arrow that points to the text. Click the mouse button to highlight just the line you pointed to, as shown here:

Selection bar

5. Now drag the pointer downward to highlight all of the lines, as shown here:

That's how easy it is to select text. In the next few sections, you'll see how to format the text you have selected and how to copy it to another location.

Formatting Text

You can change the font and style of the text you have selected. In the previous steps, you highlighted the entire block of text. Now try changing its style.

Experiment with the formatting buttons on the Format bar as pictured in Figure 3-3. For example:

1. Click the Bold button to make the text bold, then click the button again to turn boldfacing off.

2. Click the Center button to center the text, then click the Flush Right button, then the Flush Left button.

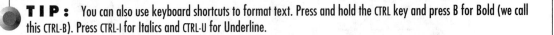

TIP: You can also use keyboard shortcuts to format text. Press and hold the CTRL key and press B for Bold (we call this CTRL-B). Press CTRL-I for Italics and CTRL-U for Underline.

Now let's change the font of the selected text. This will give you a chance to work with Windows 98 dialog boxes.

- Select only the first line of text, which should be your name. We're going to make its font different from the other lines.
- Point to the Format option in the Menu bar and click to open the Format menu. Slide the mouse pointer down and choose Font. The Font dialog box appears as shown in Figure 3-4.
- Choose a font by following the steps outlined in Figure 3-4.

You don't need to open the Font menu every time you want to change fonts. You can choose a font and font size in the Format bar. Just click the down arrow button to drop the list down as shown in Figure 3-5, then choose a new font. Keep in mind, however, that the Font menu has a few extra formatting options that don't appear on the Format bar.

1 Select a new font from the font list.

4 Click OK when done.

2 Choose a different font size here.

3 A sample appears in the sample window.

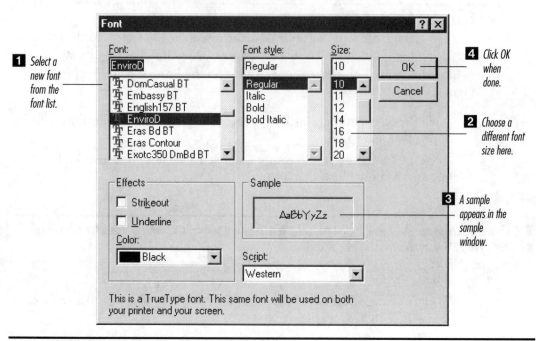

FIGURE 3-4   Choosing Fonts on the Font menu

1 View styles here.   **2** Select a style here.   **3** Select a size here.

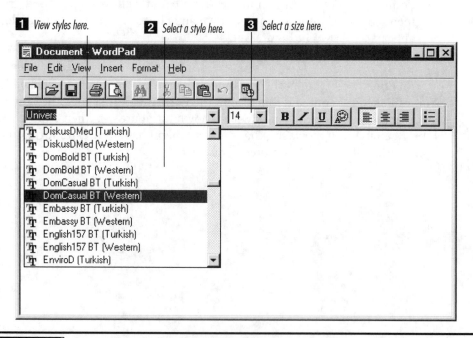

FIGURE 3-5   The Font drop-down menu makes it easy to change fonts

Windows 98 applications provide you with quite a few fonts to choose from. In this exercise, we show you how to create a font sample sheet that you can print. When you're done, your font sample document will look something like the following, with a sample and title of each font on a separate line.

1. Start by opening a new version of WordPad as outlined in the "Starting a Program" section earlier in this chapter. This will keep the name and address in the other WordPad window intact for later.

2. When the new WordPad window opens, open the Font drop-down menu as previously illustrated in Figure 3-5.

3. Scroll to the top of the font list and choose the Arial font.

4. Now select a larger font size. Click the font size down arrow button and choose a font size of 18.

5. Now type "Arial" on the first line of the document and press the ENTER key.

6. Now repeat step 2 and choose a different font such as Bookman.

7. Type Bookman in the document.

8. Repeat the previous steps for each major font style in the font drop-down list box that you think you might use (or until you get tired of doing this exercise!).

9. To print the font samples, click File in the Menu bar, then choose Print. Click the OK button when the Print dialog box appears.

If you don't get a printout, your printer may not be set up in Windows 98. Refer to the printer section in Chapter 20.

We'll show you how to save the font samples in the section called "Saving Your Work," later in this chapter.

The Character Map

People frequently ask how they can get special characters, such as characters with accent marks, into their documents. The Character Map is designed just for that.

Open the Character Map by clicking the Start button, then choose Programs | Accessories | System Tools | Character Map on the cascading menu. The Character Map appears, as shown in Figure 3-6.

To use a character from the Character Map:

1. Select a font from the drop-down font list (try Webdings).

2. Click any character to see it up close.

3. Double-click the character(s) to copy (you can select more than one). It will appear in the Characters to copy box.

4. Click Copy to copy the characters.

5. Switch to your working document window and position the cursor.

6. Press CTRL-V to paste the character(s) into your document.

The Character Map is so useful that it seems foolish to have to open all those cascading menus every time you want to use it. We're going to show you how to create a *shortcut* for Character Map on the Desktop. One more time, click the Start button, then open Programs | Accessories | System Tools. This time, however, right-click the Character Map option and keep holding the mouse button while you drag it out to a blank part of the desktop. Release the mouse

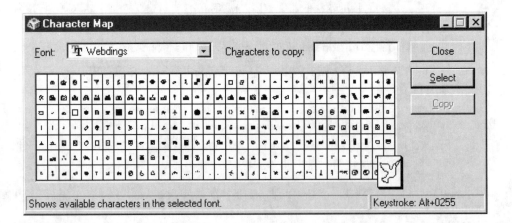

FIGURE 3-6 Working with the Character Map

and choose Create Shortcut(s) Here from the menu that appears. A Character Map icon appears on the desktop; now you can click it any time you want to start Character Map. You'll learn more about creating these shortcuts in the next few chapters.

Copying, Cutting, and Pasting

This exercise will show you some of the most important and often used editing features in Windows 98: copying, cutting, and pasting. You cut or copy information to an invisible *Clipboard*, then paste it to another location. The Cut, Copy, and Paste options are on the Edit menu, or you can use the shortcut keys mentioned in parentheses here. Write these down on a sticky note!

- *Cut* (CTRL-X) removes the selection and puts it on the Clipboard so you can paste it elsewhere.
- *Copy* (CTRL-C) copies the selection to the Clipboard (and does not delete the selection) from its current location.
- *Paste* (CTRL-V) puts the information you cut or copied at the location you select in the same document, or in another document.

Follow the steps here to cut and paste a line of text to a new location. This illustrates how the text is cut to the Clipboard and how you can paste it elsewhere.

1. Highlight the text you want to cut.
2. Use any of the following methods to cut the text (as you work with Windows 98, you'll eventually find a method you prefer):

   - Choose Cut from the Edit menu.
   - Press the CTRL-X shortcut key.
   - Click the Cut button on the toolbar (see Figure 3-3).
   - Right-click the highlighted text and choose Cut from the shortcut menu.

3. Position the blinking cursor to where you want to paste the text.
4. Use any of the following methods to paste the text at the insertion point:

   - Choose Paste from the Edit menu.
   - Press the CTRL-V shortcut key.
   - Click the Paste button on the toolbar.
   - Right-click near the insertion point and choose Paste from the shortcut menu.

The information you placed on the Clipboard is still there so you can paste it again. In fact, it stays on the Clipboard until you cut or copy some other information to the Clipboard. You can even start up another application and paste the text into that application. Now try this:

1. Position the cursor and press CTRL-V to paste another copy into the document.

2. Now click the other WordPad window. Recall that it contains the name and address you typed earlier.

3. Click on a blank portion of the document, then press CTRL-V again to paste the text that is stored on the Clipboard.

This illustrates that the Clipboard can be used to transfer information between documents!

 T I P : Remember to choose Cut if you want to remove the text from its current location and paste it somewhere else. Choose Copy if you just want to copy and paste it to another location.

Undoing Mistakes

Now assume that you pasted some text by mistake or made some other kind of mistake. You can easily recover by using the Undo command. Choose any of the following options to remove the text you pasted in the last step:

- Choose Undo from the Edit menu.
- Press CTRL-Z to undo.
- Click the Undo button on the toolbar.

Click and Drag Editing

Now let's try a different editing technique. Go back to the other WordPad window, the one that contains the font samples. You used cut and paste techniques to move a line of text to another location. Now click and drag to move the same text back to its original location.

T I P :   You can also click and drag selected text from one document window to another. Just drag the text across the window borders to a location in the other document as shown in Figure 3-7. Note that when you drag between documents, a copy is made. The selected text in the original document is not removed.

Creating a Scrap on the Desktop

A scrap is a block of text, copied to the Desktop, that you can reuse over and over again. From the Desktop, you can drag the scrap into any other document. The name and address you typed earlier is a good example of a scrap you might want to place on the Desktop. Windows uses the first few words in the scrap to name it. Follow these instructions to rename the scrap to something more

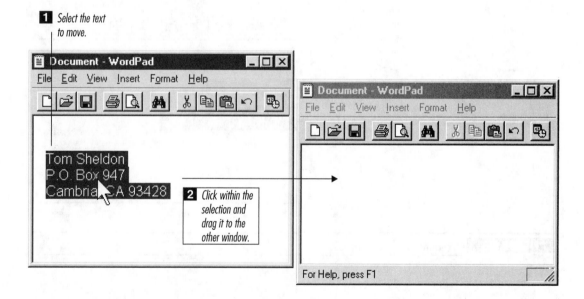

FIGURE 3-7   Dragging text between documents

meaningful like "Address." Then try dragging the scrap into the other WordPad window. You'll see how scraps can save you from a lot of excess typing.

1. Select the text.
2. Click within the selection and drag to the Desktop, as shown in Figure 3-8.
3. Rename the scrap by right-clicking it and choosing Rename, then type **address**.
4. Press ENTER.
5. Try dragging the scrap into another document.

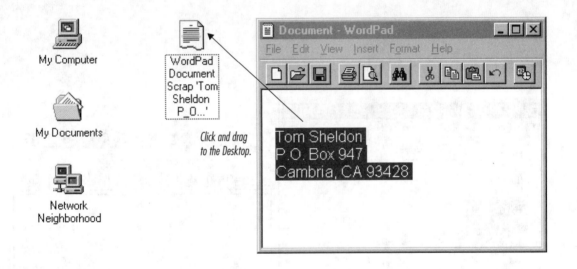

FIGURE 3-8 | Creating Desktop scraps

You will no doubt be sending out letters to friends and clients on a regular basis. Why not create a custom letter now that has a unique design and your company logo? This section will show you how to create a document that you can use over and over again as a template for writing new letters. It will save you from having to retype redundant information and apply formatting. It will also give your letters a consistent look.

An example template and the instructions for creating it are shown in Figure 3-9. Change the font and size of any of the elements to suit your needs. Notice that placeholder instructions are typed where body text is supposed to be typed. When you use the template, you'll just type over this text and your typing will obtain the formatting of the placeholder text. That way you don't need to set format options everytime you create a new letter.

1 Insert the "Address" scrap, then select it and click the Right Align button on the Format bar. Change the font to fit your needs.

2 Choose a special character from the Character Map, then press CTRL-V multiple times to insert it as a border.

3 Type your company name on the next line, then highlight it and select a font and font size that fits your company profile.

4 Type some short instructions to serve as placeholders and format the placeholders with the font you want to use.

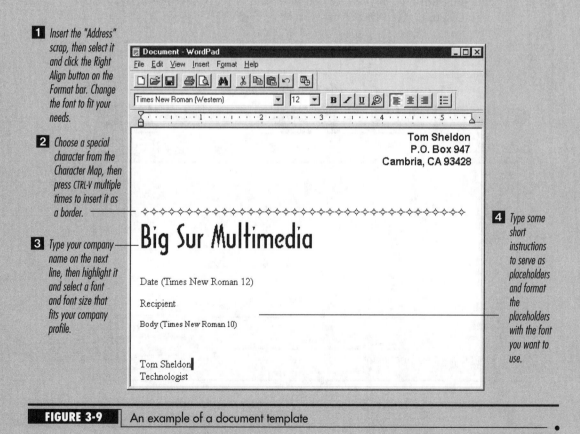

FIGURE 3-9 An example of a document template

Saving Your Work

Saving documents is a critical aspect of working with computers. When you finish a document, you should save it to disk so you can access it the next time you start your computer. In fact, you should save periodically while you are creating a document, just in case the power goes out and your system abruptly shuts down. If you don't save, you'll need to redo your work.

To save a file:

1. Click File on the Menu bar.

2. Click Save As to save with a new filename. The Save As dialog box appears as pictured in Figure 3-10.

3. Type **template** in the File Name field if you are saving the document template created in the previous exercise.

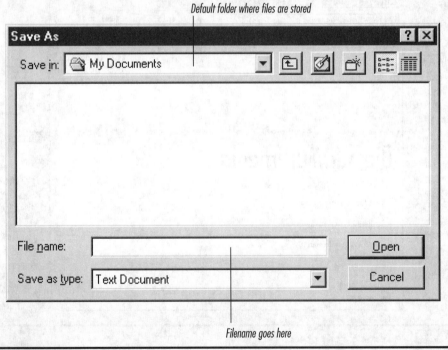

Default folder where files are stored

Filename goes here

FIGURE 3-10 Saving a file with a new name and file type

T I P :   WordPad suggests that you save the file in a folder called My Documents. Later, you'll see how to create custom folders to hold and organize your personal and business documents.

After you save a file for the first time, you can choose the Save option on the File menu to save any subsequent changes. If you want to save a file that already has a name with a different filename (thus preserving the original), use the Save As command. The Save As option also lets you save a copy of a file to a different location.

Be careful using Save. It's important to understand the behavior of the Save and Save As options. If you choose Save and your document has not already been saved, the Save As dialog box appears so you can type a new filename and storage location. If you open an existing document that already has a name and make changes to the document, then choose Save, the changes are saved to the existing document. This can be a problem if you wanted to keep the original intact and save your changes to a new file. Make sure you choose Save As in this case.

T I P :   If you work with templates and make changes to the template, be sure to use the Save As option so you can save your changes to a new file and not the template.

Printing Your Documents

Now that you have a document template to work with, write us a letter to show us your new template and tell us what you think of the book so far. Our mailing address is P.O. Box 947, Cambria, CA 93428.

To print the letter, choose Print from the File menu. The dialog box in Figure 3-11 appears.

If your computer is connected to a network, you might be able to print on printers that are attached to other computers in your office. Click the down arrow button in the Name field to see if other printers exist. Your Network Administrator can help you with this.

Print dialog boxes will differ depending on the application you use, but most have the same basic features. Click the Properties button to view special settings for your printer. Figure 3-12 shows two pages for an HP LaserJet printer. While you probably don't need to set any of these options for this example, you should remember that this is where you set important options like the type of paper and graphics mode.

Click here to choose another printer if you have one available.

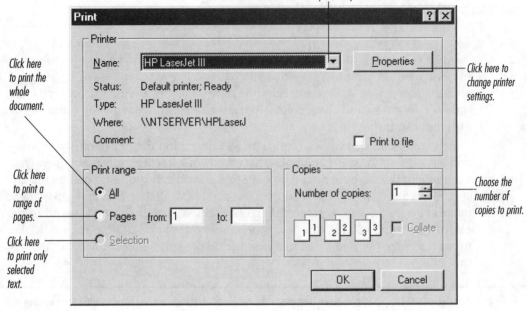

Click here to print the whole document.

Click here to change printer settings.

Click here to print a range of pages.

Click here to print only selected text.

Choose the number of copies to print.

FIGURE 3-11 | The Print dialog box

Click here to set paper options.

Choose paper type.

Print sideways.

Click here to set graphics options.

Choose Fine for the best graphics.

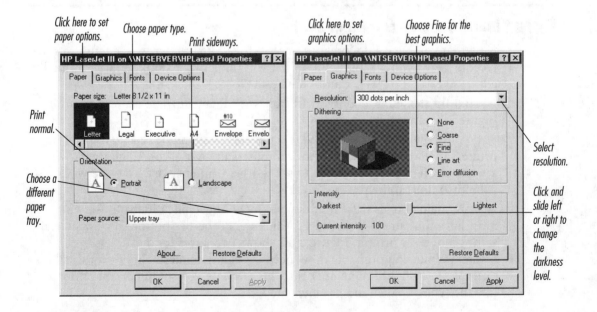

Print normal.

Choose a different paper tray.

Select resolution.

Click and slide left or right to change the darkness level.

FIGURE 3-12 | Access special print options on the properties dialog box

As mentioned, if you open and change the template, make sure you save it with a different filename to preserve the original. However, accidents will happen, so it's a good idea to create a backup copy of the file and store it in a safe place.

In this section, you'll create a new folder and copy a backup of TEMPLATE.txt to the folder. Then if you loose the original template, you can open the backup and re-save it as your new template.

This exercise also shows you some tricks for working with folders. Folders are essential for organizing your documents. Follow the steps shown on Figure 3-13. If you ever need to access the backup copy of TEMPLATE, choose Open on WordPad's File menu, then open the Backup folder and open TEMPLATE.

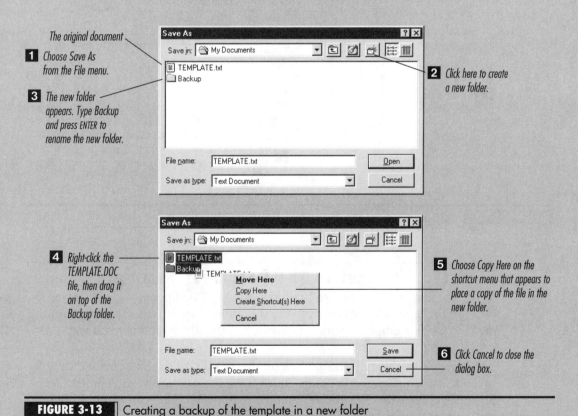

FIGURE 3-13 Creating a backup of the template in a new folder

About Files and Folders

When you saved the template in the previous exercise, Windows 98 suggested the My Documents folder as the place to save files. You might be wondering where that folder and your files are located. Follow the steps in Figure 3-14 to find out.

You can see the template file and the Backup folder you created in the My Documents window. At this point, you can just click on TEMPLATE.txt to open it. You don't need to first open WordPad to access this file.

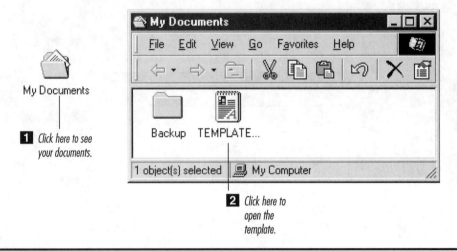

My Documents

1 *Click here to see your documents.*

2 *Click here to open the template.*

FIGURE 3-14 | Look inside the My Documents folder on the Desktop

Create a Shortcut to the Document Template

In the last exercise, you had to first open the My Documents folder in order to click on the template file and open it for editing. If you create a shortcut on the desktop for the template, you can easily open the file every time you want to create a letter.

To create the shortcut, right-click on the TEMPLATE.DOC icon and drag it to a blank portion of the Desktop. Release the mouse button and choose Create Shortcut(s) Here on the shortcut menu that appears. Now you can just click the shortcut on the Desktop to open the template.

Assume you're starting a new project and you want to organize all the files for that project in a single folder. After all, why mix letters to your relatives with important business correspondence? We'll create a new folder inside the My Documents folder. The steps are outlined in Figure 3-15.

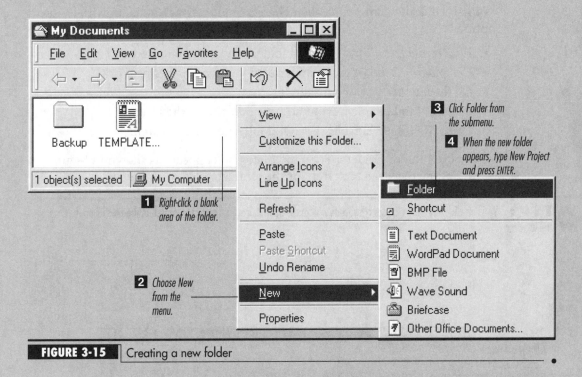

1 Right-click a blank area of the folder.

2 Choose New from the menu.

3 Click Folder from the submenu.

4 When the new folder appears, type New Project and press ENTER.

| FIGURE 3-15 | Creating a new folder |

Now when you save new documents, you can choose to save them in the New Project folder. The folder will appear in the Save As dialog box (see Figure 3-10) and you can double-click it to open it as a place for saving your files.

Finding Documents

So far, we've created multiple copies of the template and put them in different places. Can you recall all the places where you put them? Will you remember next week? If not, Windows 98 comes with a handy search utility that can help you find files that you may have stuffed away in some hidden folder. Give it a try now just to see how it works.

First, click the Start menu, then choose Find to display a menu with these options:

- *Files or Folders*   Find files and folders on your computer.
- *Computers*   Find other computers on your company's network.
- *On the Internet*   Search on the Internet.
- *People*   Find people in your address book or on the Internet.
- *Using Microsoft Outlook*   Use Outlook's Advanced Search.

Choose Files or Folders. The Find dialog box appears as shown in Figure 3-16. Follow the steps to search for the template files you created.

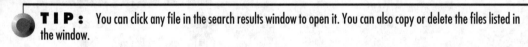

T I P :   You can click any file in the search results window to open it. You can also copy or delete the files listed in the window.

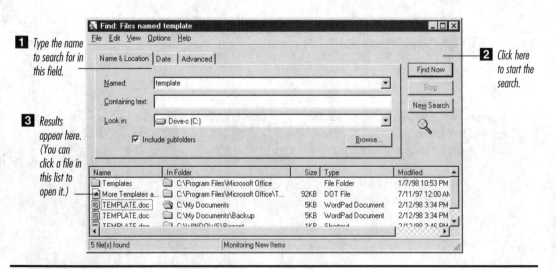

1 *Type the name to search for in this field.*

2 *Click here to start the search.*

3 *Results appear here. (You can click a file in this list to open it.)*

FIGURE 3-16 | Finding files

Learning More About Windows 98

B A S I C S

- Special techniques for running programs and opening documents
- Quick-viewing documents
- How to create shortcuts to programs and documents anywhere
- Special printing options
- Automatically start programs when Windows 98 starts
- How to schedule tasks
- How to recover deleted files

B E Y O N D

- Create shortcuts on the fly
- Set up folders for special projects
- Use Find to organize your files
- Create Send To options that appear on shortcut menus

This chapter presents a collection of tricks and techniques to help you improve your skills with Windows 98. Previous chapters demonstrated some useful techniques, but this section takes you beyond the basics and helps you master the operating system, not only by showing special techniques but by leading you through practical exercises.

Running Programs and Opening Documents

The usual way to start a program is to click the Start button, choose Programs, and then select a group on the Programs menu that holds your program. There are other startup methods, some of which are faster or more convenient.

Rummaging Through Windows

Not all the programs available on your system are conveniently listed on the Start menu. You might need to go browsing for them. One technique is to look in the folder where those programs are located. Try this technique now:

1. Open My Computer.
2. Click on Drive C.
3. Click on the Windows folder, then, if you are in Web view, click Show Files to display the contents of the folder.
4. On the View menu, choose Arrange Icons, then choose By Type to group program files together.
5. Scroll down the list past the folders until you see the program icons like Calculator, CD Player, Dialer, and so on.
6. Click any of these icons to start the program.

   The point of this exercise is to demonstrate where actual program files are stored—i.e., in the Windows folder (or other folders, as you'll see). The Start menu provides quick access to programs, but programs are actually stored in folders at many different locations on your computer.

The Run Dialog Box

Another way to start programs is with the Run command. Click Start, then choose Run to open the Run dialog box pictured next.

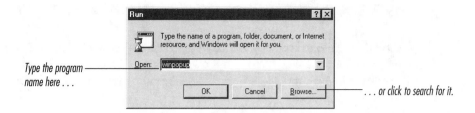

Type the program
name here . . .

. . . or click to search for it.

If you know the name of the program you want to start, you simply type its name in the Open field and click OK. Here are some interesting programs you can start by typing the command on the left in the Run dialog box. Note that you won't find these programs on the Start menu.

WHAT YOU TYPE IN RUN	WHAT YOU GET
welcome	Opens the Windows 98 Welcome screen that includes tutorials and instructions. This program may show up every time you start Windows, but if you disabled it, type **welcome** to reopen it.
clipbrd	Opens the normally invisible Clipboard. You see information that was recently copied or cut and you can save it to a file for later retrieval, as discussed under "Saving Clipboard Information" later in this chapter.
taskman	The Task Manager is a utility for switching between programs (it was actually the precursor to the Taskbar and is not often used today, although it is still available).
winpopup	A simple messaging program for exchanging messages between other network users. Other users must also be running the program to receive your popup messages. This utility is explained in Chapter 11.
winver	This pops up a window that displays version information about your copy of Windows.

The Run dialog box will automatically look in the Windows folder for the programs you specify. But if the program is located in some other folder, you will need to specify the folder name along with the program name. The best way to do this is by browsing for the folder, as discussed next.

This section demonstrates methods you can use to browse for and locate programs and documents on your computer. We'll use Browse from the Run dialog box that was just shown, but keep in mind that the Browse button exists on many different dialog boxes to help you search for programs and documents.

1. Open the Run dialog box by choosing Run on the Start menu. Click the Browse button to open the Browse dialog box pictured in Figure 4-1.

2. The Look in field indicates your starting point. Click the down arrow button to choose a different location. This drop-down list appears:

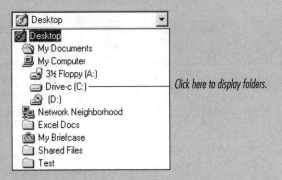

Click here to display folders.

3. Click the Drive C icon to display a list of folders on that drive. Double-click the Windows folder.

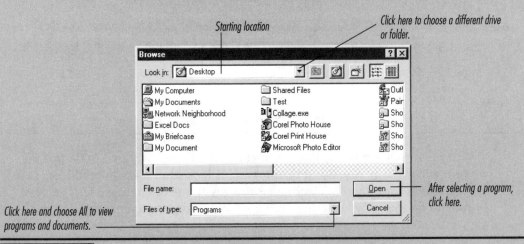

Starting location

Click here to choose a different drive or folder.

After selecting a program, click here.

Click here and choose All to view programs and documents.

FIGURE 4-1   The Browse dialog box

4. The Browse dialog box now contains a list of programs you can run. You may need to scroll right in the file list. Programs have the EXE or COM filename extension.

5. Scroll to the right until you see the Explorer program icon and click it once. The name appears in the File name field.

Before clicking the Open button to start Explorer, try one interesting trick. You can access folders and files in the Browse dialog box like you would in any folder. While the box is open, right-click and drag the Explorer icon onto the Desktop as shown in Figure 4-2, then choose Create Shortcut(s) Here from the menu that appears.

What does this demonstrate? You can start programs by browsing for them from the Run dialog box, but once you locate the icon, make a shortcut so you can easily start the program from the Desktop the next time you want to run it.

From now on, you can start Windows Explorer by clicking the shortcut on the Desktop instead of choosing it from a menu.

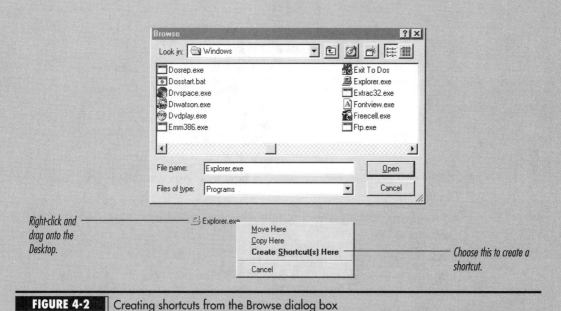

Right-click and drag onto the Desktop.

Choose this to create a shortcut.

FIGURE 4-2 Creating shortcuts from the Browse dialog box

Opening Documents

You can open any document by simply clicking its icon. If you worked through the exercises in the last chapter, you created a document in WordPad and stored it in the My Documents folder. Open the folder now and click on the document to open it.

You can also open and create a new document on the Desktop or in a folder. The following exercise will show you how to create a new document without first opening a particular program.

1. Right-click a blank part of the Desktop, or open the My Documents folder and right-click a blank area inside the folder window.

   A menu for creating new objects appears similar to what you see next. Note that you can create a new folder, a shortcut, a bitmap image (Paint file), and other types of files.

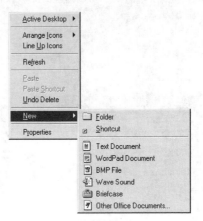

2. Click the Text Document option. A new icon appears called New Text Document.

3. Before doing anything else, rename the new object by typing **Test.txt** and pressing ENTER.

4. Click the new icon to open Notepad.

   Text files are associated with Notepad, so the program opens when you click the document. Clicking other types of documents will open the programs that are associated with them.

5. Type some text in the document such as your name and then close the Notepad window. Click Yes to save the changes.

Now try an interesting trick. Click the Start button, then choose Documents. A list of your most recently opened documents appears as pictured next. Now you can open a recent document by choosing it from this list. The Documents menu is a great help if the document you need to open is buried in a folder or was pulled up from a remote network computer.

Quick-Viewing a Document

Quick View is a tool you can use to quickly look at a document without fully loading it into its associated application. This is especially helpful if you're cleaning out old files or trying to locate a file with some specific content. Quick View will show you the contents of almost any file. If you are scanning a folder that contains text files, spreadsheets, or other types of files, you don't need to open a separate application to look at each—just use Quick View to look at the contents of any of the files.

To open any file in Quick View, simply right-click the file's icon, then choose Quick View. Figure 4-3 illustrates this process.

You can't edit a document in Quick View, but you can click the Open File for Editing button to launch the associated application if you need to edit the file.

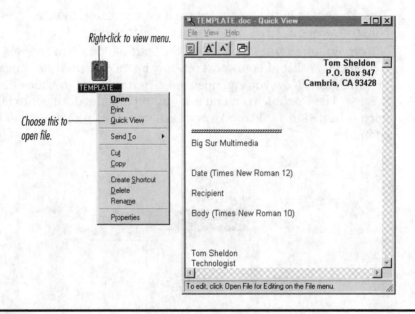

FIGURE 4-3 Quick-Viewing a file

Shortcuts

You're probably familiar with shortcuts by now. They are icons, usually on the Desktop for starting a program or opening documents that are stored elsewhere in the filing system. Earlier in this chapter, you created a shortcut for Windows Explorer on the Desktop by dragging the program icon from the Windows folder out to the Desktop. Using the drag-and-drop technique to create shortcuts is easy if you are already in the folder that holds the object you want to create a shortcut to.

The "official" way to create shortcuts is described here:

1. Right-click a blank portion of the Desktop, click New on the menu, then choose Shortcut. The Create Shortcut wizard appears as shown in Figure 4-4.

If you know the name of the program or document, you can type it directly in the Command line field. If not, you can click the Browse button to scan your system. In this example, we'll create a shortcut for the Calculator by using the Browse method.

2. Click Browse to open a dialog box similar to the one pictured in Figure 4-1.

3. Click the down arrow button in the Look in field, then select Drive C.

4. Double-click the Windows folder.

5. Scroll through the list of programs and double-click the Calc icon. You are returned to the Create Shortcut wizard with the program name in the Command line field.

6. Click the Next button, change the name to **Calculator**, and click Finish.

The new shortcut appears on the Desktop. Click it to open the Calculator. Much easier than clicking the Start button and choosing Programs | Accessories | Calculator, isn't it?

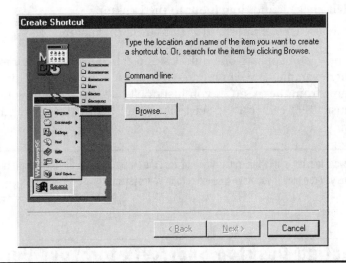

FIGURE 4-4 The Create Shortcut wizard

Folder Shortcuts

Not every folder is easily accessible on the Desktop. Some folders are "hidden" in the hierarchy of the file system. You must open My Computer and Drive C, then "drill down" through the folder hierarchy to access the folders. To make these folders more accessible, you can create a shortcut for them on the Desktop.

As an example, let's create a shortcut to the Favorites folder, which is located in the Windows folder. Favorites is the place where your favorite Web sites are stored. When you click a favorite, Windows 98 takes you immediately to the Web site. Note that Favorites is already a selection on the Start menu. This exercise will also create a shortcut on the Desktop and illustrate the technique for creating a folder shortcut.

1. Open My Computer, then open your Drive C.
2. Open the Windows folder (if the files are not listed, click Show Files in the left window pane)
3. Scan through the list to locate the Favorites folder, then right-click (not left-click) it and drag it out to the Desktop.
4. Choose Create Shortcut(s) Here from the menu.

A new icon appears on your Desktop called "Shortcut to Favorites." As a further example, you can rename the shortcut by right-clicking it and choosing Rename from the menu. If you just don't like this icon on your Desktop because it's already on the Start menu, right-click the icon and choose Delete.

 TIP: If you want to have a little fun, right-click and drag the Media folder to the Desktop. It contains some interesting sound files you can play if you have a sound card in your system.

Creating Desktop Shortcuts for Your Personal Programs

If you've installed your own programs, such as Microsoft Office, the startup icons for your programs are located in folders other than the Windows folder. Creating a Desktop shortcut for these programs is easy:

1. Click the Start button, then Programs.

2. Locate the Startup option for the program on the Programs menu (or one of its cascading menus).

3. Right-click the program option and drag it to the Desktop.

4. Choose Create Shortcut(s) Here.

Finding Files

The Find utility can help you locate files that might be scattered across different folders. Files with similar names, dates, or other information are listed in the Find window where you can quickly open them for viewing or select groups of files and copy them to other folders or disks. You can use Find to help organize the files on your system into more manageable groupings. To see how this works, follow these steps:

1. Click Start and choose Find, then click Files or Folders on the cascading menu. The Find dialog box appears as shown here:

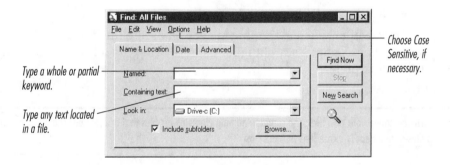

Type a whole or partial keyword.

Type any text located in a file.

Choose Case Sensitive, if necessary.

2. Type **txt** in the Named field to list all files that contain "txt" in their filename.

3. Click the down arrow button in the Look in field and choose your Drive C.

4. Click Find Now to start the search.

This should produce a large list of text files similar to that shown in Figure 4-5. By the way, many of these files contain information about Windows 98 features. You may want to open and read them while they are listed in the Find window.

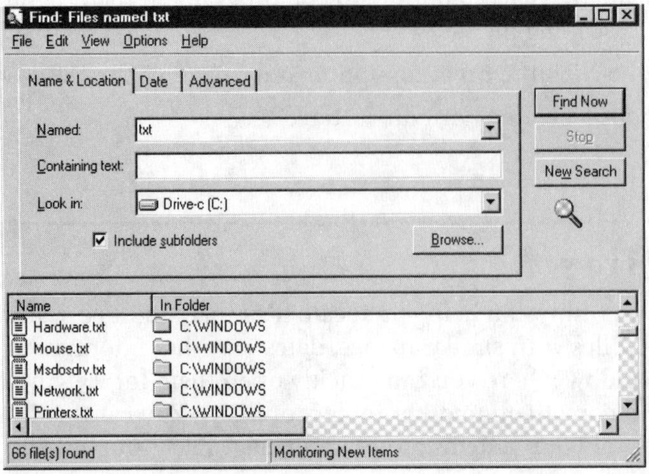

FIGURE 4-5 Find results

Try your own searches for files you know to be on your system or files that you create often, such as graphic images. Try searching for common character strings. For example, searching for **explore** brings up a list of files related to Internet Explorer.

TIP: When creating your own files, use common naming elements for files that are related. That way, you can use Find to group files or more easily locate files that are "lost."

One of the best things about Find is that it groups files so you can do the following:

- Right-click any file and choose options such as Print, Copy, Delete, and Rename. You can also choose Properties to see information about a file.
- Click and drag one or more files from the Find window to another folder, to a disk, or to other locations, such as into email messages.

- Locate the most recent version of a file that is stored in multiple locations by comparing the modified dates of files in the list.
- Clean unnecessary or old documents off your system by copying them to a disk or some other backup medium.

T I P :   If you know a file contains some text such as a recipient name, a company name, your name, and so on, enter the text in the Containing text field.

The Name & Location page on the Find dialog box lets you enter keywords for your search. If you click the Date tab, you can search for files by date. For example, you could search for files within a specific time period during which you were working on a special project:

Choose type of file.

Choose a time range.

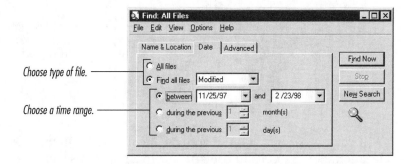

Click the Advanced tab to display the following page. Here, you can search for files by type, such as all video files or all document files:

Click here to choose a file type.

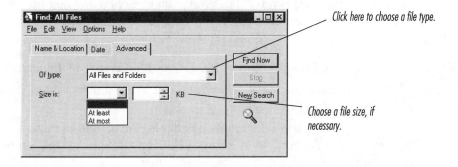

Choose a file size, if necessary.

You can save the information you find to view again at a later time. Choose Save Results on the Options menu, then choose Save Search on the File menu. This creates an icon on the Desktop that you can open at any time.

• The Send To Option

There is a fast way to copy or print files. It's called the Send To option and it exists on the shortcut menus of folders and files.

To check out the Send To option, right-click one of the objects you created earlier in this chapter, such as the Special Project folder or one of the files within the folder, then click Send To. You see a menu similar to the one shown here:

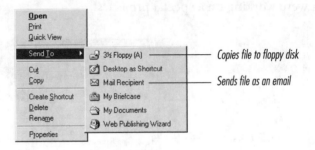

If you choose one of these options, the file is sent to the selected device or location. For example, to copy the file to a floppy disk, choose 3½ Floppy (A). To send the file in an email message to someone else, choose the Mail Recipient option.

You can add your own options to the Send To menu. We'll add two now: Notepad and your printer. That way, you can open any text file for editing by sending it to Notepad or you can print the file by sending it to your printer. We'll do this by opening two separate windows.

1. Open My Computer, then Drive C and the Windows folder.

2. Scroll down the list of folders and open the SendTo folder. We'll copy shortcuts to this window.

3. Now open a second window by clicking My Computer again. This time, click the Printer folder. Right-click (don't left-click) the icon for your printer and drag it to the Send To folder.

4. Now add the Notepad shortcut by using the Create Shortcut wizard. Right-click a blank part of the SendTo folder window, then choose New and Shortcut from the menu.

5. Type **notepad** in the Command line field, then click Next and Finish.

When you're done, the Send To menu should include the Notepad and Printer options as shown next.

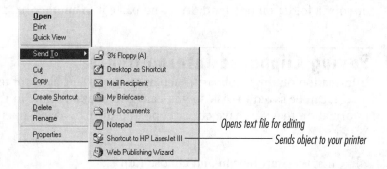

Cut, Copy, and Paste

One of the most important and useful features of Windows is the ability to cut or copy information from one location and paste it in another location:

- Cut removes the selected information from the current location
- Copy duplicates the selected information
- Paste places the information you either cut or copied at a selected location

Information you cut or copy is placed on the invisible Clipboard. You can cut or copy and paste within the same document or paste the information in a different document. Information stays on the Clipboard until you cut or copy something else. Only one item of information may be on the Clipboard at a time, so make sure you finish pasting before you cut or copy something else.

Copying or Moving Files and Folders

You can copy or move files and folders from one location to another using these same techniques. Try copying one of the files in your My Documents folder to the Desktop. To cut or copy multiple files, hold down the CTRL key, then click each file:

1. Right-click the document and choose Copy from the menu.
2. Right-click the Desktop and choose Paste from the menu.

That was simple. Consider using these same techniques when copying and moving entire folders from one location to another. For example, you might cut or copy a folder on one hard drive and paste it to another hard drive.

Saving Clipboard Information

Information on the Clipboard, such as an important block of text or graphic image, can be saved to disk so you can paste it at any time in the future. To save information that you have cut or copied to the Clipboard, open the Clipboard Viewer:

1. Click the Start button and choose Run.
2. Type **clipbrd** and click OK.

The Clipboard Viewer appears with the most recent information you have cut or copied. In the following illustration, the Clipboard shows some text we recently copied:

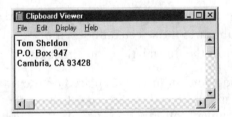

To save the information, choose Save As on the Clipboard File menu. To recover saved Clipboard information, choose Open on the File menu.

TIP: You may end up saving a lot of Clipboard information in different locations. Clipboard files are stored with the CLP extension. Open Find and type *.**CLP** in the Named field to locate these files.

• Printing Options

Almost every Windows application has a Print option on its File menu. When you choose Print, a dialog box opens similar to Figure 4-6. Note that Printer dialog boxes differ quite a bit among printers. The options we picture here are for a Hewlett-Packard laser printer. However, most Print dialog boxes have the general options we discuss here. Note that if your printers are not yet installed, refer to Chapter 20.

You can click the Properties button to set special options for printing. A dialog box similar to Figure 4-7 appears. Note the different tabs for choosing options. The options on the Graphics tab are pictured in Figure 4-8. The contents of other tabs will differ depending on your system or type of printer. To get information about an option or field, right-click the field name to open the What's This? help option.

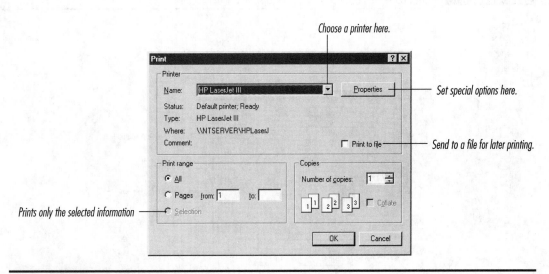

FIGURE 4-6 | The Print dialog box

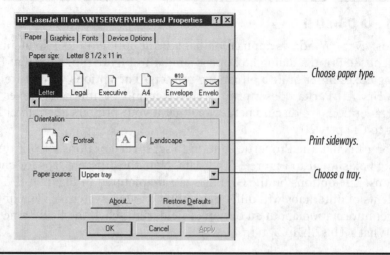

Choose paper type.

Print sideways.

Choose a tray.

FIGURE 4-7 Print Properties dialog box paper options

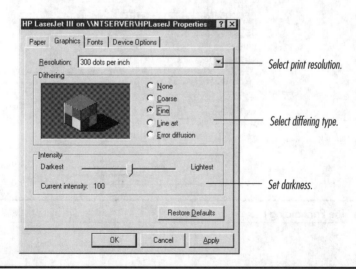

Select print resolution.

Select differing type.

Set darkness.

FIGURE 4-8 Print Properties dialog box graphics options

When a file is sent to a printer, the printer icon appears on the right side of the Taskbar. Click it to see a list of print jobs and their current status. You'll see a dialog box similar to the one shown here:

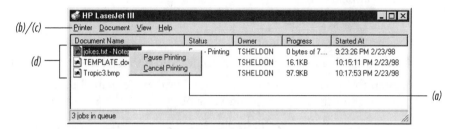

Here are some of the things you can do with print jobs in this dialog box:

- Right-click any document in the list, then choose to pause or cancel the printing of that document. (a)
- Pause all print jobs by choosing Pause Printer on the Printer menu. (b)
- Delete all print jobs by choosing Purge Print Jobs on the Printer menu. (c)
- Rearrange the order of jobs being printed by clicking and dragging a print job either up or down. (d)

Using Printers Offline

If you own a portable computer and are temporarily disconnected from your printer, you can still send print jobs to the print queue. When you reconnect, Windows 98 will automatically send the documents to the printer. To avoid annoying messages that tell you the printer is not working, open the Print job dialog box and choose Use Printer Offline from the Printer menu.

Automatic Program Startup

You can have programs automatically start up when you start your computer by adding them to the Startup folder. You can view the contents of this folder now by clicking Start, choosing Programs, and clicking Startup. It may be empty, which means that no programs start up automatically.

To add startup items to the Startup menu, follow these steps.

1. Right-click the Start button, then click the Open option on the menu that appears.
2. Open the Programs folder.
3. Open the Startup folder.
4. Right-click a blank part of the folder and choose New, then Shortcut.
5. Step through the Create Shortcut wizard as described under "Shortcuts" earlier in this chapter to add your program to the Startup folder.

As an example, type **Calc** in the Command line field. The next time you start Windows 98, the Calculator will be open and ready to use.

Scheduling Tasks

The Task Scheduler is a new Windows 98 utility that lets you schedule tasks to run on your computer at selected times. For example, you can schedule to run programs that optimize the performance of your disk drive during the night, or you can schedule the backup program to back up your files to tape. These tasks usually take a lot of time and tie up your computer.

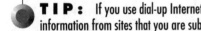

T I P : If you use dial-up Internet connections, you can have Task Scheduler dial the Internet at night and download information from sites that you are subscribed to. See Chapter 13 for more information.

To start Task Scheduler, click Start | Programs | Accessories | System Tools. Finally, choose Scheduled Tasks on the System Tools cascading menu. You'll see a window similar to the one shown next. The currently scheduled tasks are listed in the Name column and the scheduled run time is listed in the Schedule column.

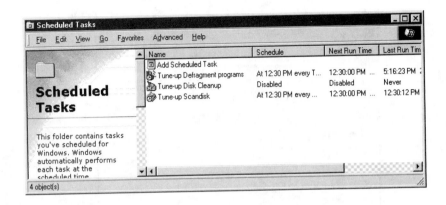

TIP: Right-click any scheduled task and choose Properties from the menu to change scheduling options.

Scheduling a New Task

Click the Add Scheduled Task option in the window to create a new scheduled task. This opens the Scheduled Task wizard which guides you through the scheduling process. Just fill out the dialog boxes as instructed and click the Next button to work your way through the wizard.

As an experiment, try running a simple program such as Calculator or Character Map in two or three minutes from your current time. That way you can see the Task Scheduler in action.

Task Scheduler is discussed in more detail in Part V of this book.

Recycle Bin

The Recycle Bin holds files that you have recently deleted. As you delete new files, the oldest files in the Recycle Bin are permanently purged. The Recycle Bin basically gives you a chance to recover deleted files if necessary.

Click the Recycle Bin icon on the Desktop to display a window similar to Figure 4-9.

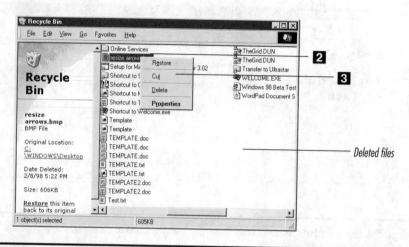

The Recycle Bin

| **FIGURE 4-9** | The Recycle Bin |

To recover a deleted file:

1. Open the Recycle Bin by clicking the Recycle Bin icon.
2. Find the file in the list and right-click.
3. Choose Restore on the menu.

That's it. The file is restored to its original location. You'll learn more about the Recycle Bin in Chapter 10.

Windows 98 Programs and Accessories

5

BASICS

- Create logos, maps, illustrations and other art with Paint
- Perform calculations with Calculator
- Dial your phone automatically with Phone Dialer
- Connect with online services using HyperTerminal
- Play music CDs on your computer
- Use multimedia accessories like Sound Recorder and Media Player

BEYOND

- Use special effects to create unique art
- Add pictures to your Desktop
- Create graphics for your personal Web pages
- Create your own voice recordings and sounds to insert in email messages or to play on your telephone answering device

This chapter will help you use the accessories that come with Windows 98 to produce pictures and sounds or take advantage of equipment attached to your computer such as multimedia equipment and modems.

• Paint

Paint is a bitmap painting program with a full set of painting tools and a wide range of editing tools that you can use to create business graphics, company logos, illustrations, maps, and artwork in general. Once you've created a picture, you can copy all of it or part of it to other documents. You can even create pictures for display on the Windows 98 Desktop.

Start Paint now by clicking Start, then choose Programs | Accessories | Paint. Figure 5-1 illustrates an open Paint window with a logo painted on the canvas.

TIP: If you are going to use Paint often, create a shortcut on the Desktop as described under "Shortcuts" in Chapter 4.

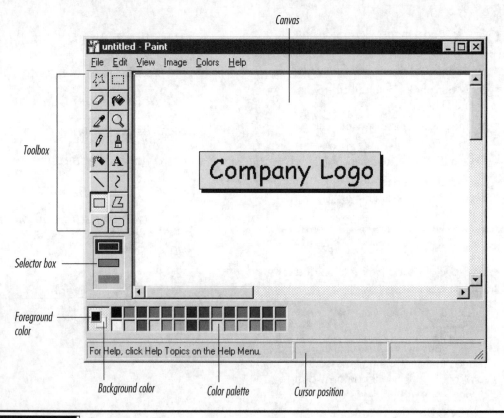

FIGURE 5-1 The Paint window

To begin painting, you choose a painting tool from the toolbox, select a color, then click and drag the mouse in the canvas. It's really just about that simple, except that some tools have special options that you can select in the Selector box as outlined later.

The table below describes Paint's primary tools. Note the following:

- You really must experiment with Paint's tools to get a feel for how they work. The Free-form select tool and the Select tool are used to select a *cutout*.
- Cutouts can be dragged to other parts of the canvas or you can copy cutouts and paste them in other documents. You can also flip, rotate, and stretch cutouts by choosing options on the Image menu.
- Generally, you use the left mouse button to select or work with the foreground color and the right mouse button to select or work with the background color.

ICON	TOOL	DESCRIPTION
	Free-form select	Selects an irregularly shaped cutout. Two options appear in the Selector box: Opaque and Transparent. If you drag an *opaque selection*, nothing underneath shows through. If you drag a *transparent selection*, objects underneath show through.
	Select	Selects a square or rectangular cutout. This tool has opaque and transparent options, just like the Free-form select tool.
	Eraser	Converts all colors to the currently selected background color. Right-click and drag to erase only the currently selected foreground color.
	Fill	Fills an enclosed area with the currently selected foreground color. Right-click to fill with the background color.
	Eyedropper	"Picks up" a color on your painting that you want to use somewhere else. The color you left-click becomes the foreground color and the color you right-click becomes the background color. This tool is useful for picking a color on pictures with hundreds or thousands of colors.

ICON	TOOL	DESCRIPTION
	Magnifier	Lets you zoom in to any part of your painting to view or edit the pixels (dots) that make up the painting. The Selector box will show different zoom options, including 1x so you can quickly return to normal view.
	Pencil	Works just like a pencil. Use this tool in zoom mode for detail work.
	Brush	Works just like a brush. Choose a brush tip in the Selector box.
	Airbrush	Works just like spray paint. Choose a spray width in the Selector box.
	Text	Lets you type text in the canvas. After selecting this tool, drag a box in the canvas where you want to type. The Fonts dialog box then appears where you can choose a font, size, and style.
	Line	Lets you paint lines in the text. Choose a line width in the selector box. Hold down the SHIFT key to restrict lines to 45 degree increments.
	Curve	Creates curved shapes. This tool uses an "anchor and pull" technique that you'll need to experiment with. Think of pulling a rubber band between two posts. First, you set down the posts, then you stretch the rubber band. For example, paint a line, then click above it and drag up to stretch the line.
	Rectangle	Paints square or rectangular shapes with borders or no borders, depending on what you click in the Selector box.

ICON	TOOL	DESCRIPTION
![Polygon icon]	**Polygon**	Creates irregularly shaped triangles, boxes, and other multisided objects.
![Ellipse icon]	**Ellipse**	Creates circles and ellipses. Hold down the SHIFT key while painting to create circles.
![Rounded Rectangle icon]	**Rounded Rectangle**	Creates squares and rectangles with rounded corners.

When you click Rectangle, Polygon, Ellipse, or Rounded Rectangle, the Selector box has the following options:

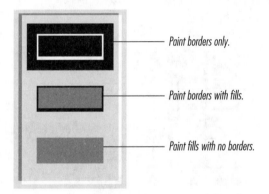

Paint borders only.

Paint borders with fills.

Paint fills with no borders.

Painting Exercise

The following exercise will lead you through the most common painting techniques.

1. *Paint boxes.* The illustration shown next contains the steps to create a blank box with thin borders and a filled box with fat borders.

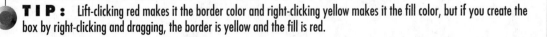

T I P : Lift-clicking red makes it the border color and right-clicking yellow makes it the fill color, but if you create the box by right-clicking and dragging, the border is yellow and the fill is red.

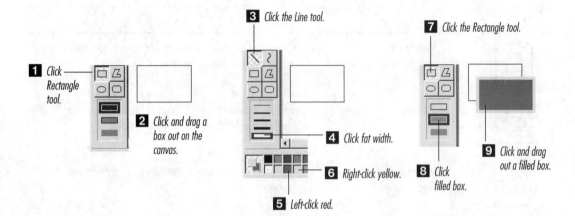

1 Click Rectangle tool.

2 Click and drag a box out on the canvas.

3 Click the Line tool.

4 Click fat width.

5 Left-click red.

6 Right-click yellow.

7 Click the Rectangle tool.

8 Click filled box.

9 Click and drag out a filled box.

2. *Select a cutout.* Click the Select tool, then click and drag a box around the boxes you just painted, as shown here.

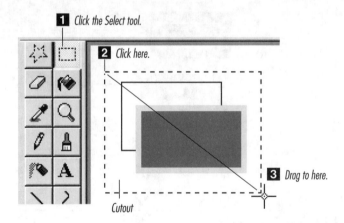

1 Click the Select tool.

2 Click here.

3 Drag to here.

Cutout

3. *Copy and move the cutout.* Choose Copy, then Paste on the Edit. This places a duplicate cutout on the canvas. Click the cutout and drag it around on the canvas, then release the mouse to position it. Now press CTRL and drag off a copy of the original as shown in the middle illustration next, then hold SHIFT and drag off a "streaming" copy as shown on the right.

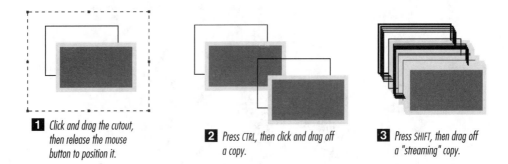

1 *Click and drag the cutout, then release the mouse button to position it.*

2 *Press CTRL, then click and drag off a copy.*

3 *Press SHIFT, then drag off a "streaming" copy.*

4. *Transparent and opaque cutouts.* Click the Select tool and drag a box around part of your picture to create a new cutout. Click the Transparent box as shown next, then drag the cutout over other parts of your picture. Notice how underlying art shows through. Click Opaque and drag some more, and notice how the underlying art is covered up.

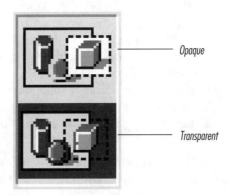

Opaque

Transparent

5. *Erase a cutout.* Choose the Select tool, then drag a box around part of the drawing to erase. Press the DELETE key to erase the cutout.

6. *Create a filled polygon.* Click the Line tool and choose a fat line, then left-click red and right-click yellow in the color palette. Now click the Polygon tool and make sure the filled box is selected; then paint a polygon by clicking each point of the polygon. To complete it, connect the first point with the last point.

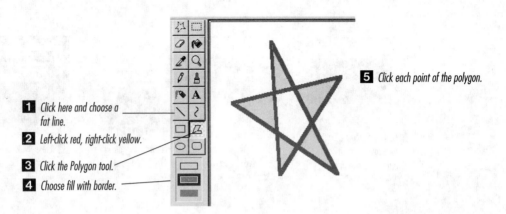

1 Click here and choose a fat line.

2 Left-click red, right-click yellow.

3 Click the Polygon tool.

4 Choose fill with border.

5 Click each point of the polygon.

7. *Fill an area.* If you created a star in the last example, the middle of the star is not filled. Click the Fill tool, then try both left-clicking and right-clicking inside the center of the star. This fills the area with either the foreground or background color.

8. *Undo mistakes.* You can click the Undo command to undo any changes you made since picking the last tool from the toolbox. Try the following experiment. The canvas color is the currently selected background color, but you might sometimes make the mistake of dragging a cutout when the wrong background color is selected. Right-click green now, then select any part of your picture and drag it somewhere else. Notice how green shows through. Choose Undo on the Edit menu, then right-click white in the color palette and drag the cutout again. Notice how the previous mistake is avoided.

9. *Erase selected parts of the painting.* Click the Eraser tool and drag over part of your painting to erase. Choose a different eraser size in the Selector box. Right-click a color in the Color Palette to erase with a different color.

10. *Erase only a selected color.* You can use the Eraser tool to change an existing color to a new color without changing other colors. In the color palette, left-click the color you want to change, then right-click the color you want to change it to. Click the Eraser tool, then right-click the mouse and drag over the color you want to change on the canvas. All other colors under the Eraser path are not affected.

Believe it or not, you have just learned the most important techniques for working with Paint. You can continue to experiment on a new canvas by choosing New from the File menu.

Special Effects and Techniques

This section describes techniques for manipulating cutouts. You must first select a cutout, then choose one of the flip, rotate, stretch, skew, or invert options from the Image menu.

- **Flip/Rotate**   After selecting a cutout, choose Flip/Rotate from the Image menu. The dialog box in Figure 5-2 appears where you can choose the option you want.

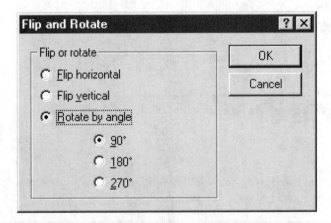

FIGURE 5-2   Options for flipping and rotating the current cutout

- **Stretch/Skew**   Select a cutout, then choose Stretch/Skew on the Image menu to display the dialog box in Figure 5-3. Type in appropriate values and click OK. If you don't get the results you like, click Undo on the Edit menu and try again.

Now let's create something really useful with Paint: a company logo that you can insert in your document, your email messages, or your personal Web pages. You can even designate it as a background picture for your Desktop.

1. If you already have Paint open, clear the canvas by choosing New from the File menu.
2. Click the Text tool and drag out a fairly large box on the canvas in which to type your company name.
3. A small Fonts window should appear above the canvas (if not, choose Text Toolbar from the View menu). Select a font and font size from the Fonts menu.
4. Click the light gray color in the color palette.
5. Type your company name. This will be the drop shadow.
6. Now repeat steps 2 through 5 on a different part of the canvas to create the text to place over the drop shadow. This time, choose black in the color palette and make sure you use the same font and size.

TIP: We recommend black and gray for this round, but you can try this again with different colors.

At this point, your canvas should look similar to the one shown here. Now all you need to do is drag the black text over the gray shadow.

1 Click Select tool

2 Click transparent.

Gray drop shadow

Black upper text

7. Now click the Select tool and choose the transparent option in the Selector box, then drag a selection box around the black text you just typed.

8. Click and drag the cutout over the gray text and position it so it looks like this:

Big Sur Multimedia

At this point, you can continue spiffing up your logo by adding a box around the text or a line under it. You might also add a symbol or some other art.

When you finish the logo, click the Select tool and draw a selection box around the logo (leaving any unnecessary parts out), then choose Copy To from the Edit menu. A dialog box appears that lets you save just the selected text to a file. Save it on your Desktop for easy access, then you can open it and insert it into your documents whenever you want.

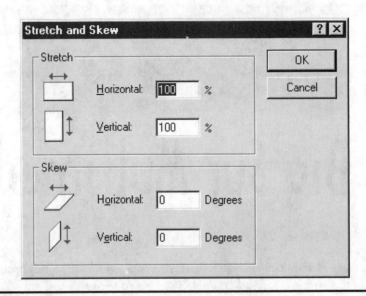

FIGURE 5-3 Options for stretching and skewing the current cutout

- **Invert Colors**   You can invert the colors of a selection by choosing Invert Colors from the Image menu. One use of this feature is to reverse text—that is, change black text against a white background into white text against a black background.

Coordinates and Canvas Attributes

The Paint window has a status bar that you can enable by choosing Status Bar from the View menu. The coordinates of the cursor appear in the status bar to help you position elements and make exact selections. You can also create objects such as same-size boxes by watching the coordinates.

You can change the attributes of the canvas by choosing Attributes from the Image menu. The dialog box in Figure 5-4 appears.

Initially, Paint opens with a default canvas size but it may increase in size if you paste a large image.

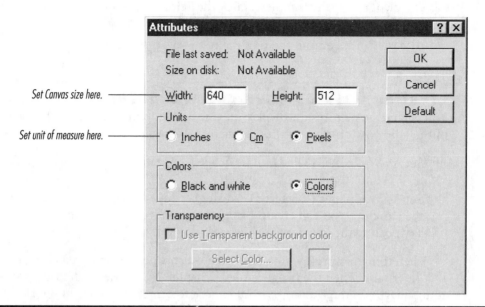

Set Canvas size here. ──────

Set unit of measure here. ──────

FIGURE 5-4 | Options for adjusting canvas size and Paint attributes

Saving Cutouts to Reduce File Size

The smaller an image, the less disk space it takes. This is important if you are transmitting images as well, since it will take less time to send the image. You can set the canvas size before you start a painting, but this is inconvenient since you often need some extra canvas to move things around. The best method is to start with a large canvas, which you can specify in the Attributes dialog box pictured in Figure 5-4. Then after you complete your picture, cut out just the part you need and save the cutout. This will help you remove any extraneous white space. Here are the steps:

1. Set up a large canvas by specifying large values in the Attributes dialog box.

2. Create your painting, using extra canvas space to move objects around or hold them for later.

3. Once your image is complete, click the Select tool and drag a box around just the part you want to save.

4. Choose Copy To from the Edit menu to save just the cutout.

Creating Desktop Tiles and Wallpaper

You can create pictures for display on your Desktop in Paint, then choose one of the following options on the File menu to set them in place on the Desktop:

- **Set As Wallpaper (Tiled)**   The image is repeated over the Desktop like a tiled countertop.
- **Set As Wallpaper (Centered)**   A single copy of the image is centered on the Desktop. You can create a single large image to fill the entire Desktop. Try posting the logo you created earlier in this way.

When tiling pictures, you usually create a small image with matching edges that intermesh when the image is tiled. Chapter 7 discusses techniques for tiling images on the Desktop. If you choose to center an image on the Desktop, you can make it as large as the Desktop or small enough to fit in the center of the Desktop (such as a company logo).

 T I P :   The image you create for the Desktop can include really useful information like birth dates, important phone numbers, and other information you reference daily.

Calculator

The Windows 98 Calculator is both a standard calculator and a scientific calculator. To start the Calculator, click Start, then choose Programs | Accessories | Calculator. The Calculator appears on your Desktop as shown in Figure 5-5.

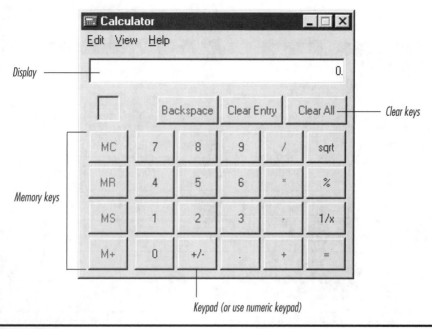

Display ——

Clear keys

Memory keys

Keypad (or use numeric keypad)

FIGURE 5-5 | The standard Calculator

To switch between standard and scientific calculator views, choose either Scientific or Standard on the View menu. The scientific Calculator is shown in Figure 5-6.

The Calculator uses standard calculator techniques. You will find a full description in Calculator's help system.

TIP: To get a description of any key and its keyboard equivalent, right-click the key and click "What's This?".

Number conversions

Trigonometric input mode

Logical operators

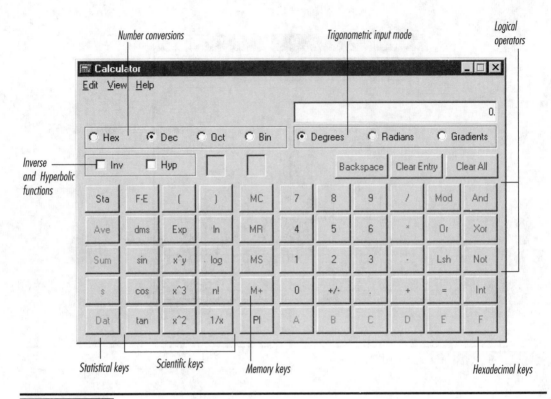

Inverse and Hyperbolic functions

Statistical keys

Scientific keys

Memory keys

Hexadecimal keys

FIGURE 5-6 The scientific Calculator

Some of the finer points of the Calculator are described here:

- You can use standard copy and paste functions in the Calculator's display. For example, you can paste in values you copied from other documents or you can copy and paste values from the display into your documents.

- You can use the mouse to click buttons on the Calculator, but it may be easier for you to enter values from the numeric keypad. Make sure the NUM LOCK key is on.

- To clear current entries, click the Clear All button or press ESC on the keyboard. To clear only the current entry without clearing previously entered numbers, click Clear Entry or press DELETE on the keyboard. Click Backspace to remove the most recent digit or press BACKSPACE on the keyboard.

- The Memory buttons store and accumulate values for later use. The memory buttons are outlined here:

  - **MS (Memory Store)**   Clears memory and places the value in the display into memory.
  - **M+**   Sums the value in the display with the value in memory.
  - **MR (Memory Recall)**   Displays the current memory value.
  - **MC (Memory Clear)**   Clears memory.

Phone Dialer

Phone Dialer is an accessory that dials phone numbers for voice telephone calls. You must have a modem attached to your computer to use the accessory since it uses the modem's dial tones to place a call. When the call starts ringing, you pick up the handset and continue with the call as if you had dialed it on your phone. Best of all, calls made with Phone Dialer can be logged to create a record for billing or accounting purposes.

To start Phone Dialer, click Start, then choose Programs | Accessories | Communications | Phone Dialer. Phone Dialer is illustrated in Figure 5-7. You might want to create a shortcut on the Desktop for this accessory, or if you use

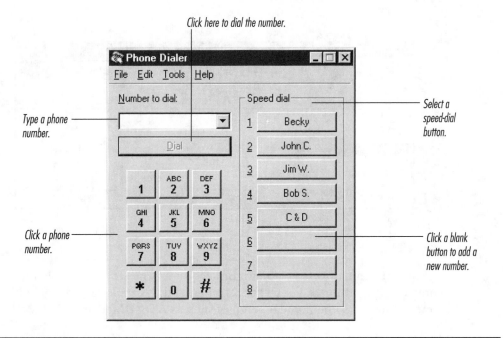

| **FIGURE 5-7** | Phone Dialer |

it everyday, have it start automatically when Windows starts as described under "Automatic Program Startup" in Chapter 4.

As you can see, Phone Dialer is easy to use. You can either type a phone number, click it out on the number pad, or click one of the speed-dial buttons. Here are some other things to know:

- To enter speed-dial entries, just click a blank button, then type a name and a number.
- To edit speed-dial entries, choose Speed Dial from the Edit menu.
- To view a log of your phone calls, click Show Log on the Tools menu. You can use the log for call accounting purposes.

HyperTerminal

HyperTerminal is a communication application that you can use to connect with another user or an online service with a modem connected to a telephone line. It can operate in the background to download files from bulletin boards or other services while you do other tasks.

To start HyperTerminal, click the Start button, then choose Programs | Accessories | Communications | HyperTerminal. The following window opens on your Desktop.

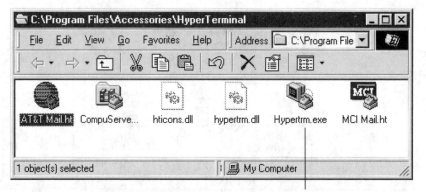

Click Hypertrm to create a new connection.

You must initially create a new connection for the service you plan to connect with, although the HyperTerminal window includes predefined connections for some popular services such as AT&T Mail and MCI Mail.

Creating a New Connection

To create a new connection, click the Hypertrm.exe icon. This opens a dialog box where you can type a name for the new connection and choose an icon to represent the new connection in the HyperTerminal window.

When you click OK, the following dialog box appears where you can edit the dial-up settings. Enter the phone number for the service you are dialing in the Area code and Phone number fields and make sure the correct modem is selected in the Connect using field, then click OK.

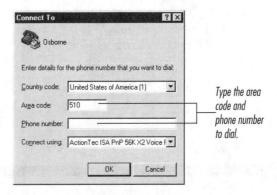

Type the area code and phone number to dial.

Next, the Connect dialog box appears as shown next. This is where you can verify your settings. Click Modify to change the phone number, modem type, and other settings if necessary. You can also click the Dialing Properties button to change dialing features. Refer to "Telephony Settings" in Chapter 6 for more details about these telephone settings.

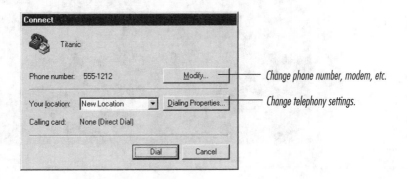

Change phone number, modem, etc.

Change telephony settings.

Click the Dial button to call the service. Even if you click Cancel at this point, HyperTerminal will give you a chance to save the settings before you exit HyperTerminal so the session is available for future use.

A new session icon will appear in the HyperTerminal window for this connection. You can click it at any time to dial the service.

Connecting and Working Online

If you're not already connected, click the connection icon in the HyperTerminal window for an online service you want to connect to. A dialog box appears that displays the status of the connection. When you connect, the HyperTerminal window appears and displays messages from the service you are connecting to similar to what you see in Figure 5-8. Sign on to the service as instructed on the screen.

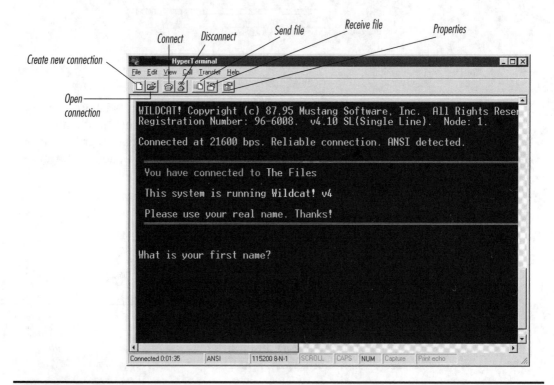

FIGURE 5-8 | Online with HyperTerminal

Here are some things you can do while working in the HyperTerminal window:

- Use the scroll bars to move back through the text that has scrolled offscreen.
- Choose Font on the View menu to change the size of the onscreen text.
- Choose Disconnect from the Call menu to hang up the connection.
- Choose Capture to Printer from the Transfer menu to print text as it scrolls down the screen.

Transferring Files

If you need to send and receive files while online, choose options in the Transfer menu as follows:

- To send a file, initiate a file upload procedure with the online service, then choose Send File from the Transfer menu. A dialog box appears where you can type the name of the file you want to send.
- To receive a file, first initiate a file download with the online service, then choose Receive file on the Transfer menu. A dialog box appears where you can type a name for the file you are about to receive.
- You can capture text that scrolls by on the screen by choosing Capture Text on the Transfer menu. On the dialog box that appears, type a filename and click the Start button.

Multimedia Tools

Windows 98 includes a selection of accessories for editing and listening to sound, watching movies, and playing music CDs. You access these accessories by clicking Start, then choosing Programs | Accessories | Entertainment. The accessories include CD Player, Media Player, Sound Recorder, and Volume Control, all of which are covered here.

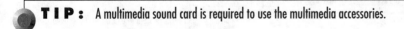

T I P : A multimedia sound card is required to use the multimedia accessories.

To create shortcuts to the multimedia devices, right-click on the Desktop, choose New | Shortcut. In the command line field, type the following command names:

MULTIMEDIA ACCESSORIES	COMMAND LINE ENTRY
CD Player	CDPLAYER.EXE
Media Player	MPLAYER.EXE
Sound Recorder	SNDREC32.EXE
Volume Control	SNDVOL32.EXE

For more information about multimedia in Windows 98 and how to control multimedia devices, refer to Chapter 20.

CD Player

The CD Player lets you control music CDs in your computer's CD-ROM drive. It has standard start, stop, and pause controls, as well as play list capabilities. You can put just the tracks you want to play in a play list. CD Player remembers information about CDs such as song titles (you must initially type them in) and play lists. The next time you insert a CD, CD player displays the information.

The CD Player is pictured here. If yours doesn't look the same, make sure the Toolbar, Disc/Track Info, and Status options are checked on the View menu. Point to each button on the dialog box to see the pop-up description of what it does.

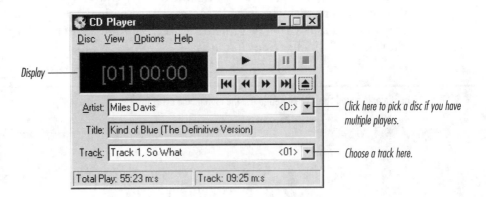

Display —

Click here to pick a disc if you have multiple players.

Choose a track here.

To use CD Player, just slip a music CD into your CD-ROM drive, then start CD Player. You can just start playing music, or you can edit the play list as discussed under "Creating and Editing a Play List."

The display shows the track time elapsed, time remaining, or disc time remaining, depending on which button you have pressed on the toolbar.

If you have multiple CD-ROM drives, put a disc in each drive and click the Multidisc Play button. If you click the Random Track Order button, CD Player will randomly pick tracks from all the discs available. Note that you can click the Intro Play button to play a short introduction for each track so you can preview a CD.

Setting Options

Choose Preferences on the Options menu to open the Preferences dialog box pictured here. In most cases, the default options are the best, but you might want to extend the period of the intro play time. If you want to continue to hear music but close the CD Player window, disable the Stop CD playing on exit option.

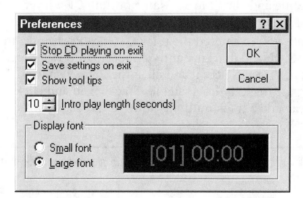

Creating and Editing a Play List

You can catalog your CDs by typing in the CD names and the track names, then create play lists by arranging the play order for tracks. Every CD has an identification number that CD Player uses to associate your entries with the CD when you put it back in the drive. It then reloads the track information you previously entered.

Click the Edit Play List button to open the dialog box pictured here.

Select a track and click Add or Remove.

Drag entries up or
down to rearrange
play order.

Enter track titles here, then click Set Name.

Fill in the Artist and Title fields, then in the lower Track field, type in the track title and click the Set Name button. CD Player will lead you through typing a name for each track.

Once you've entered the tracks, you can rearrange the entries in the Play List field. Click and drag any entry either up or down to rearrange its order. To remove a track, select it and click the Remove button. To add a track back in, select the track in the Available Tracks field and click the Add button. Note that you can add a track multiple times to the Play List.

CAUTION: Be sure to click OK when done to save your changes for the next session.

Media Player

Media Player is an accessory for playing multimedia files and devices. You can use it to open and play WAV sound files, MIDI files, and video files. You can even use it to play music CDs (although not with the same control as CD Player).

NOTE: MIDI (Musical Instrument Digital Interface) is a command system for controlling digital music synthesizers and playback devices.

If you receive files that include sound and video, Media Player will typically open when you select the files for playback.

Keep in mind that Media Player provides basic controls for playback of multimedia files and equipment. Most multimedia software and hardware includes its own media controls that you may prefer over Media Player. However, Media Player is included with Windows 98. If you send media clips to other Windows 98 users, you can reasonably expect that they will have this player available to run the clips.

Media Player is pictured next playing a music CD. Note that the scale shows six tracks of music and the pointer indicates the current playback position. You can click and drag this slider to move forward or backward in the playback of the media. The Scale menu option lets you choose among time, frames, or tracks in the scale, as appropriate. Point to each button to see a pop-up description of what it does.

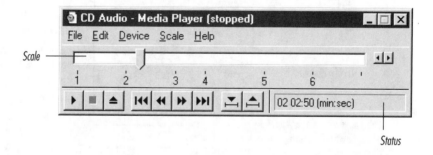

In most cases, Media Player appears when you open a multimedia file for playback. However, you can open Media Player and choose Open from the File menu to display a standard File Open and Browse dialog box. To open a particular type of media, choose an appropriate option on the Device menu, such as ActiveMovie, Video for Windows, Sound, MIDI Sequencer, and so on.

Marking and Copying Selections

You can mark part of your media file with in and out points, then easily jump back and forward to those points by clicking the Previous Mark and Next Mark buttons. You also mark a selection that you want to copy to another location as discussed in a moment.

Move the slider to the starting point, then click the Start Selection button. Next, move the slider to the ending point and click the End Selection button. Now play the selection and click Previous Mark and Next Mark to jump to the in and out points respectively.

You can also fine-tune your in and out points on the Set Selection dialog box. Choose Selection on the Edit menu to specify numeric values for the selection.

Copying and Pasting a Selection

After you have made a selection, click Copy Object on the Edit menu to copy the selection to the Clipboard. You can paste the selection in just about any Windows 98 document. An icon appears that plays the selection when double-clicked.

To control the playback options and appearance of selected objects, choose Options from the Edit menu after marking the selection. The following dialog box appears.

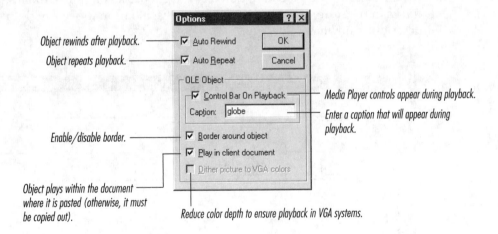

Object rewinds after playback.

Object repeats playback.

Media Player controls appear during playback.

Enter a caption that will appear during playback.

Enable/disable border.

Object plays within the document where it is pasted (otherwise, it must be copied out).

Reduce color depth to ensure playback in VGA systems.

Change the options to fit your requirements, then choose Copy Object from the Edit menu. Now paste the object in a document, an email message, on the Desktop, in a folder, or elsewhere. When the object is opened, it will play using the options you have set.

Sound Recorder

The Sound Recorder accessory is a handy digital recorder. In fact, it is a critical tool that helps you communicate in today's computer world. Here are just a few ideas for the sounds you can create with Sound Recorder:

• An announcement for your telephone answering device
• An audio welcome message for your Web site

- A message to add to email messages, such as a short greeting or a voice "calling card" that introduces you or your company
- Voice instructions to include in an instructional document
- New system sounds for your computer that sound off at a particular event (i.e., "Johnny, don't format the hard drive")

The Jungle, Musica, and Utopia sound schemes that come with Windows have some interesting sounds that you can copy and paste into your own recordings.

Sound Recorder, as its name implies, is a sound recording device. All you need is a microphone to record your own sounds. You can also record from other sources such as a CD player or tape recorder. Sound Recorder records analog sound waves (like your voice) and converts the sound to digital data that can be easily stored on disk. The filenames for wave files have the WAV filename extension.

TIP: Refer to Chapter 20 for more information about multimedia.

The Sound Recorder is pictured here with a description of its primary controls.

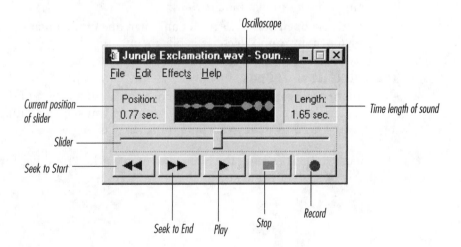

Sound Recorder has some interesting editing and mixing capabilities. For example, you can copy pieces out of existing sounds and combine them into a new sound file using copy and paste techniques. You can even add special effects to sounds before or after you copy and paste. Special effects include:

- Adding echo
- Mixing two or more sounds
- Slowing down or speeding up sounds
- Reversing sounds

Playing Pre-recorded Sounds

To play some pre-recorded sounds, look inside the Media folder, which is inside the Windows folder. You should see at least a few WAV files in the folder if your sound card was installed properly.

T I P : You can install additional pre-recorded sounds by adding custom sound schemes as outlined in Chapter 6 under "Customizing Event Sounds."

To play a file, just click it. The Media player appears to play the file. You can also right-click the file and choose Record to open the file in Sound Recorder. If you open an existing sound in this way, you can use some of Sound Recorder's interesting features to manipulate the sound.

You can also open Sound Recorder and then open individual sound files by choosing Open on Sound Recorder's File menu.

Recording New Sounds

As mentioned, all you need is a microphone to record a new sound, or a patch from an audio source such as a CD player. Before you start recording a new sound, you'll need to set its recording properties, as follows:

1. Choose Properties from the File menu to open the Properties for Sound dialog box as shown next.

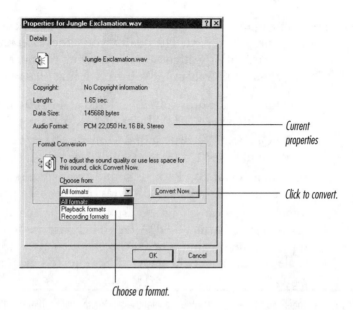

Current properties

Click to convert.

Choose a format.

2. To set the recording quality, choose Recording formats on the Choose from drop down list, then click the Convert Now button.

The Sound Selection dialog box appears as shown here.

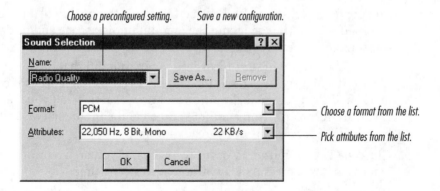

Choose a preconfigured setting.   Save a new configuration.

Choose a format from the list.

Pick attributes from the list.

The Name field has three preset options, or you can choose a custom setting as described next. The quality you choose depends on your requirements, with the highest quality taking up more disk space and requiring longer to transmit if you are sending files to someone else.

- **CD Quality** Records sound in stereo at 44,100 samples/sec. The resulting file uses 172,000 bytes of disk space per second of sound.
- **Radio Quality** Records sound (non-stereo) at 22,050 samples/sec. The resulting file uses 22,000 bytes of disk space per second of sound.
- **Telephone Quality** Records sound (non-stereo) at 11,025 samples/sec. The resulting file uses 11,000 bytes of disk space per second of sound.
- **Custom** You can choose a custom setting by clicking the down arrow button in the Format field. After you choose an option, its attributes appear in the Attributes field. You can then give the setting its own name in the Name field and click Save As to save it for later use.

> **TIP:** If you are sending voice messages to other people, use telephone quality. There is little need to use CD quality (stereo) for single channel voice recording. Note that a three-second telephone-quality voice recording requires 36,000 bytes of disk space while a three-second radio-quality voice recording requires over 75,000 bytes of disk space.

3. Choose a preset quality in the Name field, or choose a custom property in the Format field, then click OK.

   The previous steps can also be used to reduce the quality of an existing recorded sound, thus reducing the amount of disk space and/or data transmission time it requires.

   Now you are ready to start recording. Keep in mind that the longer you record, the bigger your sound file will be. Even your silence is recorded and takes up disk space, so make sure you know exactly what you want to say. If you are recording from another source via the input jack on your sound board, make sure the device is ready to play.

4. Click the Record button to begin recording. If you are recording from an external source, press its Play button at the same time.

5. When you finish recording, click the Stop button as soon as possible to prevent overruns.

6. After recording, click the Play button to listen to your recording. If you like the recording, choose Save As from the File menu to save it. If you don't like the recording, start over by choosing New from the File menu. You can reduce the size of your sound files by clipping unnecessary silence as described later under "Clipping Sounds."

You can also append new sounds at the end of your recording by positioning the slider where you want to start recording and clicking the Record button. Note that any sounds after the insertion point are recorded over if you use this technique.

Sound Editing Techniques

You can edit a recording to delete unwanted parts of the sound (to save disk space), to append more sound, or to insert sounds at any location within the recording.

One of the first things you will need to learn how to do is position the slider so you can edit the sound. Here are some tricks to help you position the slider, a task that is slightly inexact:

1. Listen to the sound and note the time in the Position field where you want to position the slider.
2. Position the slider near the place you noted and press Play again to make sure you're in the correct position.
3. Reposition the slider if necessary and repeat these steps until you get it in just the right spot.

Once you've positioned the slider, you can take advantage of the options on the Edit menu as discussed in the following sections.

TIP: You need to know the difference between inserting and mixing. When you *insert* sound, the sound after the insertion point is moved further out in the time scale. When you *mix* a sound, the pasted sound is added to (mixed with) the current sound.

The usual editing technique is to have two or more versions of Sound Recorder running at the same time. One holds the master sound file you are working on. The other windows are used to record new sounds or to edit existing sound files. You then copy and paste sounds between windows. For example, take a look at Figure 5-9.

Assume you are creating an announcement for your telephone answering device. You start by recording your voice message in a master window, then start other Sound Recorder windows to record or edit sounds that you will insert or mix into the master window. The important difference between inserting and mixing is discussed in the following sections.

As mentioned, Windows 98 comes with some interesting jungle, music, robot, and "utopia" sound files (but you must install the multimedia sound

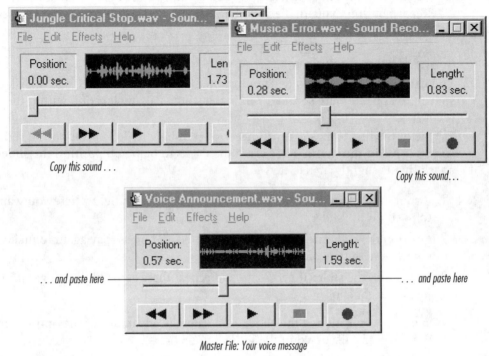

Working Copies: For recording and editing other sounds

Copy this sound . . .

Copy this sound . . .

. . . and paste here

. . . and paste here

Master File: Your voice message

FIGURE 5-9 | Working with multiple copies of Sound Recorder

schemes as discussed in Chapter 6). You can open any of these sounds files and use them as they are or cut out specific parts of the sound, such as the screech of a monkey or the slam of a door, to use in your own sound file. Once you get the sound you need, you copy it, then paste it at just the right spot in your master sound file.

> **TIP:** While editing, you can choose Revert from the File menu at any time to remove your changes. But, keep in mind that all changes you have made since the last time you saved are reverted, so be sure to save immediately after making important changes that you want to keep.

Clipping Sounds

Before we tell you about inserting and mixing sounds, you need to know how to extract sounds from existing files. Of course, you can just record your own sounds, but if you have difficulty imitating a toucan, you might want to pull that sound out of a pre-recorded file.

You can browse the available sound files in the Media folder (in the Windows folder) by right-clicking a sound and choosing Play. If the As Web Page option on the View menu is enabled, playback controls appear on the left side of the menu when you point to a sound file. After you find a sound file you want to work with, follow these instructions to extract the part of the sound you want:

1. Position the cursor to just before the target sound, then choose Delete Before Current Position from the Edit menu.

2. Now position the cursor after the end of the target sound and choose Delete After Current Position from the Edit menu.

3. Choose Copy from the Edit menu so you can paste it into another sound, or choose Save As from the File menu to save your new sound to disk.

Now you've got a sound to either insert or mix into your master sound file. Refer to one of the following sections for instructions.

Before going further, you might want to apply special effects to your sound as discussed under "Special Effects." For example, you can reduce the volume of a sound you plan to mix so it doesn't overwhelm the master sound.

Inserting Sounds

When you insert a sound, the sound after the insertion point is moved further out in the time scale. There are two ways to insert sounds. You can either paste a sound that you have copied onto the Clipboard, or you can insert a sound that has been saved as a file. Choose the appropriate option listed here from the Edit menu.

- **Paste Insert**   This inserts a sound clip that you have copied to the Clipboard into the current sound at the slider position.
- **Insert File**   This inserts a sound file into the current sound at the slider position.

To create a repeating sound, copy a sound onto the Clipboard, then choose Paste Insert several times.

Mixing Sounds

Mixing allows you to combine existing sounds with new sounds. There is very little loss of quality when mixing, but you must be careful to adjust volumes before mixing so that one sound is not too loud. See the next section, "Special Effects," for details. Note that "loss of quality" is relative. Repeatedly mixing into the same sound will eventually cause some loss of quality.

After positioning the slider at the point where you want to mix in a sound, choose one of the following options from the Edit menu:

- **Paste Mix**   This option mixes a sound you have copied onto the Clipboard into the current sound at the slider position.
- **Mix with File**   This mixes a sound file into the current sound at the slider position.

When you insert a sound, there is often an unpleasant gap between the existing sound and the new sound. To create a smooth transition, mix in the new sound just a little before the previous sound ends. Position the slider at the end of the sound, drag it left just a little, then choose Paste Mix or Mix with File from the Edit menu.

Special Effects

As mentioned, you might want to apply special effects to a sound in a separate Sound Recorder window before you insert or mix it into your master sound. Remember to choose Revert from the File menu if you don't like the changes you make. Note also that you can apply an effect multiple times to obtain even more interesting special effects.

Here are some of the interesting special effects Sound Recorder offers:

- **Volume**   Choose Increase Volume or Decrease Volume on the Effects menu to change the volume of a sound. Make sure to do this before you insert or mix it into another sound. Alternatively, you can mix sounds, then check the volume and revert your changes to try again if you don't like it.
- **Speed**   Choose Increase Speed or Decrease Speed from the Effects menu to change the speed of a sound. Experiment with this option by increasing or decreasing speed multiple times.
- **Echo**   Choose Add Echo to add an echo effect to a sound. You may need to repeat this command a number of times.
- **Reverse**   Choose Reverse to play a sound backwards.

As an example, try the following to obtain some interesting sounds from the Chimes sound file (in the Media folder). Open the file, then choose Decrease

Speed from the Effects menu. Listen to the new sound, then cut out the last "gong" in the sound. Now decrease its speed again and try adding effects like Echo. You can also mix in several gongs that overlap at different intervals or you can reverse the sound.

Volume Control

The Volume Control is an accessory for controlling the amplitude of sound on multimedia devices. It serves as a master control where you can adjust the stereo balance and volume of the input and output devices attached to your system. You can open the Volume Control by double-clicking the speaker on the right side of the Taskbar. The Volume Control is shown in Figure 5-10. It may look a little different on your system, but the controls are generally the same.

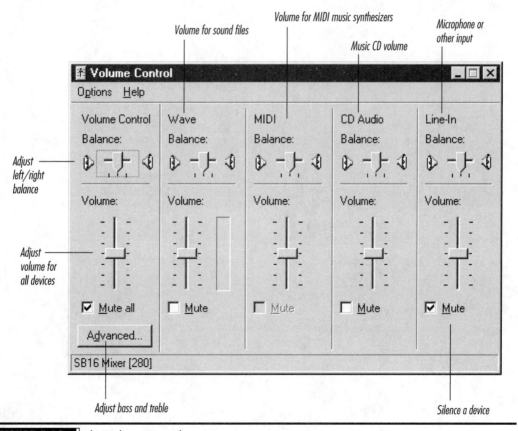

FIGURE 5-10 The Volume Control

Personalizing Your System

Basic Settings

6

This chapter is about changing the settings on your system— much as you would adjust the color, sounds, and other settings on your television. But while you're learning about configuring your computer in this chapter, you'll also refine your skill at working with the Windows 98 interface.

Have some fun. You're going to explore some areas that a lot of computer users never bother to learn about. Those are the same users that get completely lost when something goes wrong. A little time spent learning new features now will save you more time in the future.

Where to Change Windows 98 Settings

There are a number of places where you can set Windows 98 configuration options. The most likely place is the Settings cascading menu. Click the Start button and choose Settings to see the following menu.

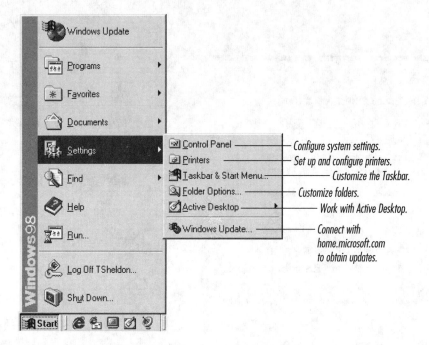

The Control Panel is the primary place to change Windows 98 settings. Click Control Panel on the Settings menu now. The Control Panel is pictured in Figure 6-1.

To see the information on the left side of the Control Panel window, select View | As Web Page. Now you can point to a Control Panel icon to see a description of what it does. Depending on your system configuration, you may not have all the icons illustrated in Figure 6-1. This chapter and other chapters in this book will discuss the options in the Control Panel.

Enable "As Web Page" on View menu to display left pane.

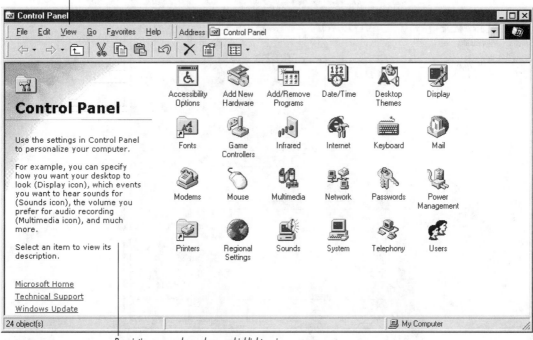

Descriptions appear here when you highlight an icon.

FIGURE 6-1 The Control Panel

Another way to change settings is to right-click the Desktop and choose Properties. The Display Properties dialog box appears as shown in Figure 6-2. This is the same dialog box you see if you open the Display option in the Control Panel.

Still another place to change settings is on the System Properties dialog box. Right-click the My Computer icon and choose Properties, then click the Performance tab to display the dialog box shown in Figure 6-3. This is the same dialog box you see if you choose System in the Control Panel. The settings on this dialog box are covered further in Part V of this book.

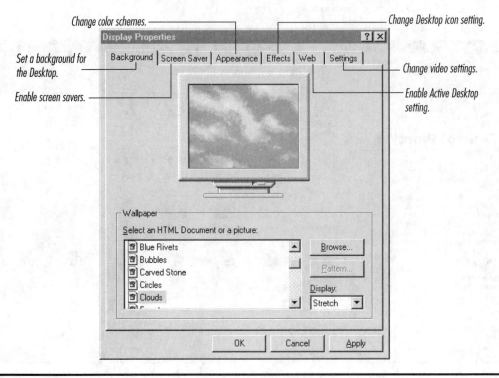

Change color schemes.

Set a background for the Desktop.

Enable screen savers.

Change Desktop icon setting.

Change video settings.

Enable Active Desktop setting.

FIGURE 6-2 | Display Properties dialog box

Profiles for Multiple Users

Many homes and offices have computers that are shared by multiple users. Windows 98 has built-in features that allow each user to log onto the computer and see his or her own files and Desktop settings. For example, when John logs on, he sees only the files that he has stored in the My Documents folder and the arrangement that he has given the Desktop. When Sue logs on, she sees only her files in the My Documents folder and her own personal Desktop arrangements. You can skip this section if you don't need multiple users.

TIP: You can create multiple profiles for yourself that display different Desktops and settings, depending on the type of work you need to do. For example, you can set up a Desktop for mobile use.

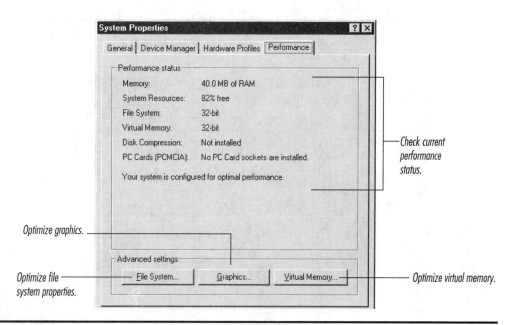

System Properties

General | Device Manager | Hardware Profiles | Performance

Performance status

Memory: 40.0 MB of RAM
System Resources: 82% free
File System: 32-bit
Virtual Memory: 32-bit
Disk Compression: Not installed
PC Cards (PCMCIA): No PC Card sockets are installed.

Your system is configured for optimal performance.

Check current performance status.

Optimize graphics.

Advanced settings

[File System...]   [Graphics...]   [Virtual Memory...]

Optimize file system properties.

Optimize virtual memory.

FIGURE 6-3   Viewing and setting performance options

Figure 6-4 illustrates the parts of Windows 98 that each user can customize to fit his or her own needs. These features are elaborated on here.

- **Desktop folder and Documents menu**   Each user can make customized changes to the Desktop that are not visible to other users. Users see only their own recently opened documents on the Start/Documents menu.

- **Start menu**   Each user can make changes to the Start menu and see only the changes that he or she has made.

- **Favorites folder**   Each user can create his or her own favorites (i.e., Internet sites they like to visit).

- **Downloaded Web pages**   A separate cache is maintained for each user to hold Web pages he or she has visited.

- **My Documents folder**   Each user sees only his or her own documents in the My documents folder.

If you plan to customize settings for each user, you should enable multiuser settings before continuing with this chapter. Some of the features discussed in the following sections can then be personalized for each user.

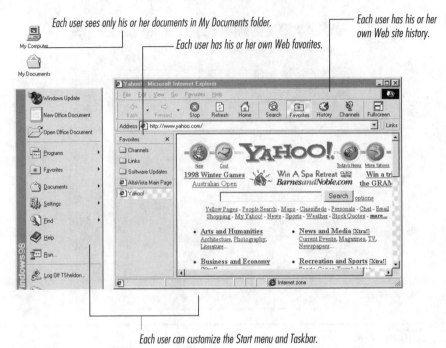

Each user sees only his or her documents in My Documents folder.

Each user has his or her own Web favorites.

Each user has his or her own Web site history.

Each user can customize the Start menu and Taskbar.

FIGURE 6-4 | Features that can be personalized on multiuser systems

Enabling Multiuser Mode and Creating a New User

The following steps lead you through the process of enabling multiuser mode and creating the first user.

1. Open the Control Panel and choose Users.

   A wizard appears to guide you through the process of setting up the first user.

2. Click the Next button on the opening dialog box and type in a user name on the next box.

3. Click Next again, then type in a password for the new user.

   Initially, one person can set up each user's profile and assign a password. Then, each user should log on and immediately change his or her password.

4. Click Next to move on to the Personalized Items Settings dialog box as shown in Figure 6-5.

   This is where you can select the items that will be personalized for the user. Each item was described earlier. In addition, you can choose one of the following options:

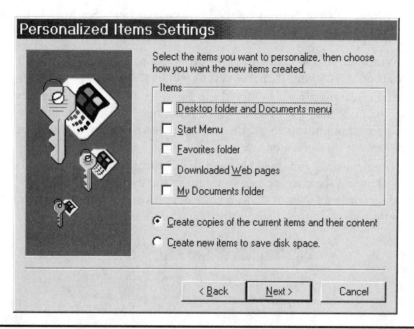

Personalized Items Settings

Select the items you want to personalize, then choose how you want the new items created.

Items
☐ Desktop folder and Documents menu
☐ Start Menu
☐ Favorites folder
☐ Downloaded Web pages
☐ My Documents folder

⦿ Create copies of the current items and their content
○ Create new items to save disk space

< Back   Next >   Cancel

FIGURE 6-5 | Choosing Personal Settings

- *Create copies of the current items and their contents*   If you choose this option, Windows 98 copies the existing computer settings into the new user profile, including the current Desktop configuration, all the documents in the My Computer folder, all the Web favorites, and all the existing downloaded Web pages.

- *Create new items to save disk space*   If you choose this option, Windows 98 creates a brand new fresh Desktop, Start menu, Favorites folder, and My Documents folder for the new user. The My Documents folder will be empty.

Click the second option if new users do not need to share any of the Desktop settings or files that are already set up on the computer. Even if some files must be shared, you can create a separate folder to hold these files and make that folder available to all users. Choose the first option only if you must. It duplicates all the configuration files, documents in the My Documents folder, and downloaded Web files into a new profile for the user and may use up quite a bit of disk space.

5. After choosing options on the Personalized Items Settings dialog box, click Next and then Finish to complete this process.

Windows 98 will create the new profile, copy configuration information and files if necessary, and then ask you to reboot your system.

Since you presumably entered the password for the new user, you should try logging in as that user. You can then rearrange the Desktop and perform other configuration options to get the computer ready for the new user or you can just leave it up to him or her.

The next time you open Users in the Control Panel, you see a dialog box showing the current users, similar to the following illustration. You can delete a user or make a copy of an existing user profile. New users should also open this dialog box to change their password.

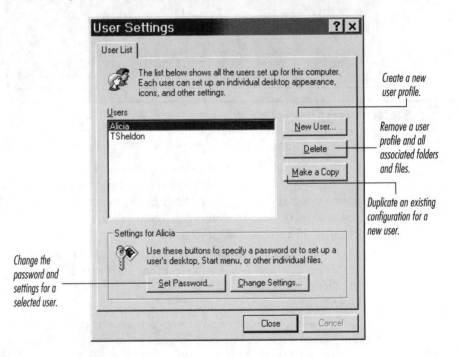

Create a new user profile.

Remove a user profile and all associated folders and files.

Duplicate an existing configuration for a new user.

Change the password and settings for a selected user.

Profile Folders

You might be interested in knowing where configuration information is stored for each user. Windows creates a folder called Profiles in the Windows folder and adds a folder in Profiles for each user, as shown in the following directory tree. Note that each user's personal folder contains subfolders that hold personal information, such as Desktop settings, favorites, documents (in My Documents), and downloaded Web files (in Temporary Internet Files).

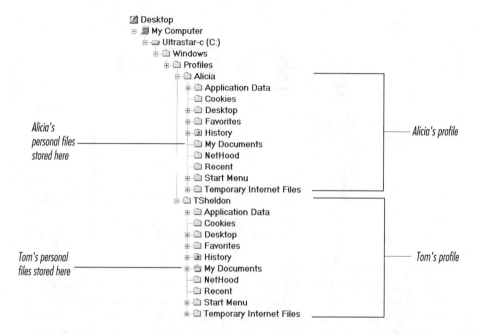

TIP: When you delete a user, all the user's profile folders and the files they contain are deleted.

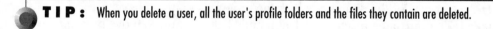

• Adding and Removing Software

This section describes how to add and remove programs from your system, such as the following:

- Windows 98 components that exist on the Windows 98 CD-ROM
- Popular off-the-shelf programs such as word processors, games, and accounting packages
- Utilities and programs you obtain from other sources

You install components by opening Add/Remove Programs Properties in the Control Panel. Choose it now to open a dialog box similar to the following:

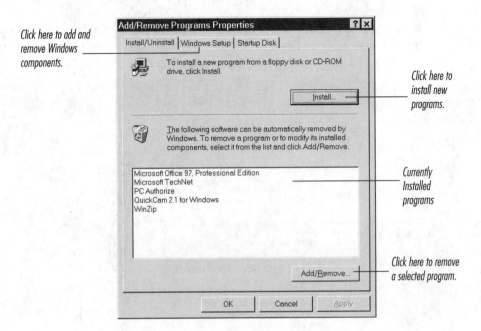

Click here to add and remove Windows components.

Click here to install new programs.

Currently Installed programs

Click here to remove a selected program.

The Install/Uninstall tab is where you go to install off-the-shelf software or any programs you may have obtained from other sources. Click the Install button and Windows 98 leads you through a browse process to locate the SETUP or INSTALL utility for installing the program. It first looks for a floppy disk, then a CD-ROM. If it doesn't find a setup program, you can browse your disks.

The lower part of the dialog box lists the programs that you have already installed. To uninstall a program, select it and click the Add/Remove button.

Adding and Removing Windows 98 Components

Your system may have the minimum Windows 98 installation, which means you may not have all of the utilities and accessories installed on your system that are discussed in this book. This section will help you install other Windows 98 components that may not be on your system.

TIP: The reason some components may not be installed is because you may not have hardware (such as a sound card) to support them or you have limited disk space. If you have appropriate hardware and plenty of disk space, we recommend installing all the components and trying them out.

Click the Windows Setup tab to view a list of Windows 98 components and determine which components are installed on your system. You'll see a dialog box similar to the one shown in Figure 6-6.

The components listed in this box may consist of several subcomponents. For example, the Description field indicates that the highlighted Accessibility option has two components and both are installed. A check mark in a white box indicates that all components are installed. If a box is gray or unchecked, you can choose to install components that are not currently installed.

Highlight a component and click the Details button (or just double-click the component). You now see a dialog box similar to the following where you can

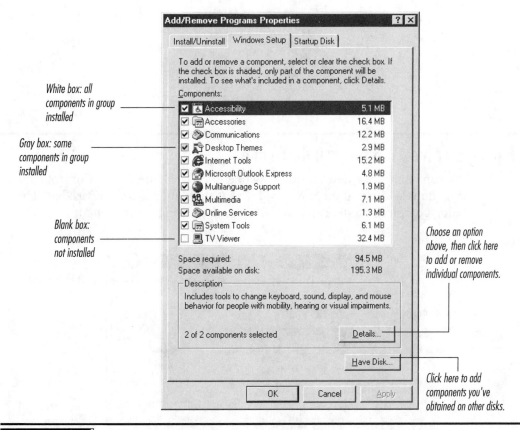

White box: all components in group installed

Gray box: some components in group installed

Blank box: components not installed

Choose an option above, then click here to add or remove individual components.

Click here to add components you've obtained on other disks.

FIGURE 6-6 | Adding and removing Windows components

click the components you want to add (or remove). Note in this example that Document Templates and Imaging accessories are not installed. After selecting components, click the OK button.

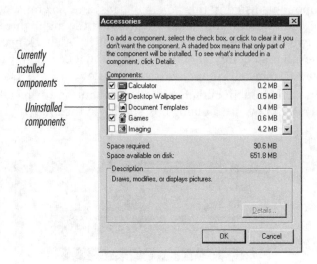

Currently installed components

Uninstalled components

Change the Date and Time

You can change the date and time by opening Date/Time in the Control Panel, or by double-clicking the time displayed at the right side of the Taskbar. The dialog box pictured here appears. Change the settings as indicated.

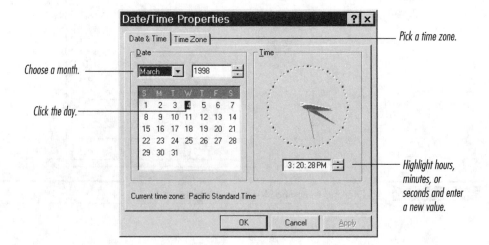

Choose a month.

Click the day.

Pick a time zone.

Highlight hours, minutes, or seconds and enter a new value.

• Customize Your Mouse

Choose Mouse in the Control Panel to change the settings of the mouse. You'll see the dialog boxes pictured in Figure 6-7 on this page and the next. Changing mouse settings is as simple as following the instructions on the figure. You can also test your settings in the dialog boxes.

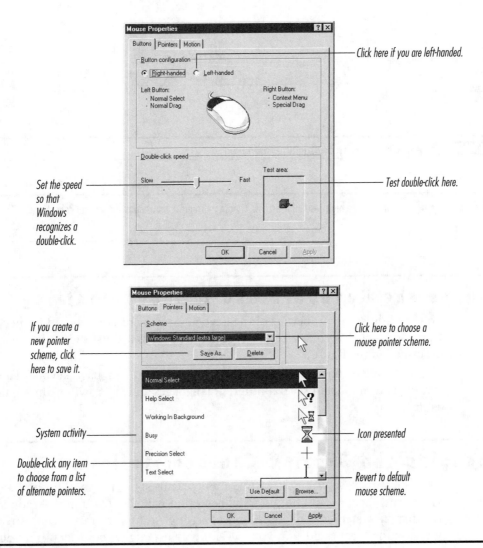

Click here if you are left-handed.

Set the speed so that Windows recognizes a double-click.

Test double-click here.

If you create a new pointer scheme, click here to save it.

Click here to choose a mouse pointer scheme.

System activity

Icon presented

Double-click any item to choose from a list of alternate pointers.

Revert to default mouse scheme.

FIGURE 6-7   Changing mouse settings

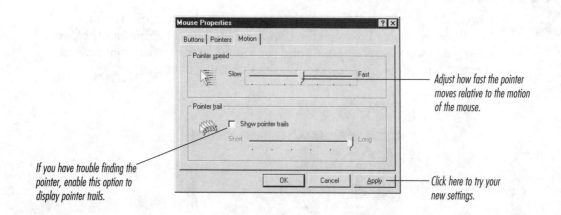

Adjust how fast the pointer moves relative to the motion of the mouse.

If you have trouble finding the pointer, enable this option to display pointer trails.

Click here to try your new settings.

FIGURE 6-7 | Changing mouse settings (*continued*)

TIP : If you work with a large high-resolution screen, choose extra large mouse pointers on the Pointers tab.

Change the Keyboard and Language Settings

You can adjust the properties of the keyboard by opening Keyboard in the Control Panel. The dialog box in Figure 6-8 appears. Adjust the settings as described in the figure.

Click the Language tab if you need to use a foreign language keyboard and layout. You can install several different languages and then switch among them as necessary.

Changing the Display Characteristics

The video display system of your computer consists of the monitor and a video card inside your computer. This section will show you how to adjust the display system and choose the best settings to fit your taste. You can increase the "real estate" on your Desktop or use higher color depth if you are working with high-resolution graphics.

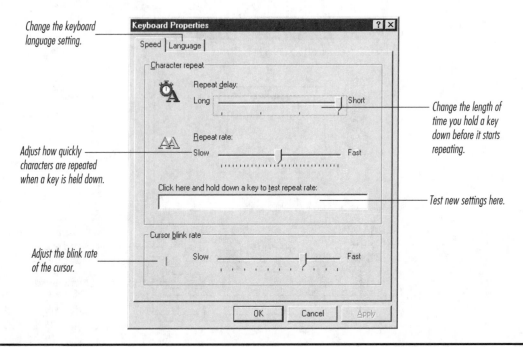

Change the keyboard language setting.

Change the length of time you hold a key down before it starts repeating.

Adjust how quickly characters are repeated when a key is held down.

Test new settings here.

Adjust the blink rate of the cursor.

FIGURE 6-8 Changing keyboard properties

There are many different types of video display systems, just like there are many different sizes and types of televisions, so the screenshots in this section may not match your system exactly. However, you should be able to follow the general discussion with little problem.

NOTE: Settings related to Desktop backgrounds, pictures, window color schemes, and other effects are covered in Chapter 7.

To change display settings, choose Display in the Control Panel, or right-click a blank portion of the Desktop and choose Properties. When the Display Properties dialog box appears, click the Settings tab to see the dialog box pictured in Figure 6-9.

The Settings page is the primary place to adjust video resolution and color depth. The quality of your video equipment will determine the settings you can make in the Colors and Screen area fields. On low-resolution equipment,

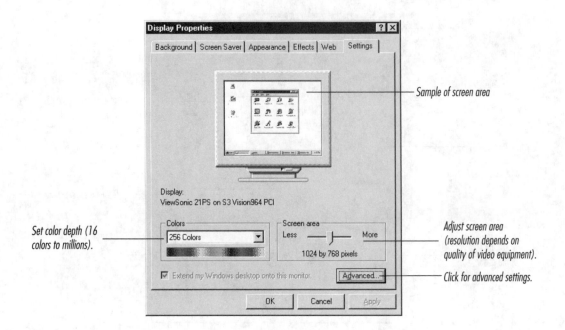

Sample of screen area

Set color depth (16 colors to millions).

Adjust screen area (resolution depends on quality of video equipment).

Click for advanced settings.

FIGURE 6-9 | Changing the settings of your display

increasing the screen area will automatically reduce the color depth and increasing the color depth will reduce the screen area. Adding more memory to your video card will help you achieve higher color and screen area settings. Setting these values lower will allow you to achieve higher video refresh rates on the Adapter page—which removes flickering and reduces eyestrain and headaches.

Click the Advanced button to set additional options as described here.

- **General page**   Click the General tab to adjust the font size to match the screen area you have selected. If you are using a high-resolution screen, choose larger fonts for easier reading.
- **Adapter page**   Click the Adapter tab to view information about the current video adapter, choose a new adapter driver, and change the refresh rate.

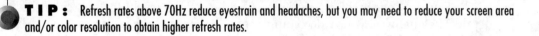

TIP: Refresh rates above 70Hz reduce eyestrain and headaches, but you may need to reduce your screen area and/or color resolution to obtain higher refresh rates.

- **Monitor page** Click the Monitor tab to change your monitor type or set specific options for the type of monitor you are using.
- **Performance page** Click the Performance tab to change the acceleration level for your video equipment. Lowering acceleration may help you avoid mouse and computer system problems. Refer to Chapter 22 for more information.

Saving Power

If your monitor is Energy Star compatible, you may be able to adjust its power down settings. Click the Screen Saver tab on the Display Properties dialog box, then click the Settings button in the Energy Star field. The Power Management Properties dialog box appears as shown in Figure 6-10.

Choose a power scheme in the Power schemes drop-down list, or create your own by setting options in the System standby and Turn off monitor fields. The time settings you make in these fields is the amount of time the system waits before shutting down, assuming there is no keyboard or mouse activity.

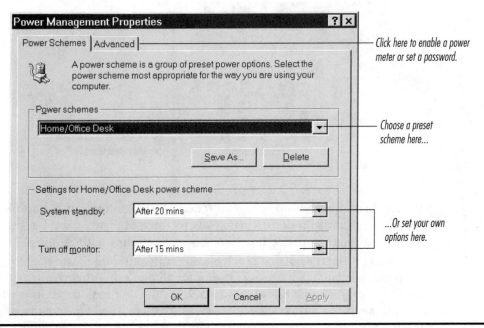

FIGURE 6-10 Setting monitor power down features

CAUTION: Save all your work and test these options with the lowest time settings. Some systems may lock up when using these settings and you may need to reboot and disable the settings.

If you click the Advanced button, you can enable a power meter on the Taskbar and require a password to recover the computer from standby mode.

Telephony Settings

Telephony settings are used with all of the telephone-related equipment that is connected to your computer. For example, telephony settings are used when dialing the Internet, to make remote dial-up connections, and to connect with bulletin boards.

You only need to configure telephony settings once but you can edit them at any time or add new configurations to match the settings you use on the road. The telephony settings dialog box appears when you're getting ready to dial into the Internet or some online service, as shown here:

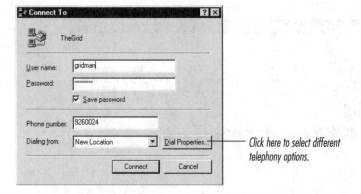

Click here to select different telephony options.

You can change the dial-up settings by clicking the Dial Properties button. This opens the Dialing Properties dialog box pictured in Figure 6-11, but the normal way to open this dialog box is to choose Telephony in the Control Panel.

The Dialing Properties dialog box lets you create different location settings. For example, you could create dial settings for a hotel room that requires you to dial 9 for local calls and 8 for long-distance calls. After making appropriate settings on the dialog box, you click New to save them, then type a name such as **Mobile Office** in the I am dialing from field. When you're in your office, use the normal settings; when you go on the road, choose the mobile settings.

If you use calling cards, enable the calling card check box and choose a calling card in the drop-down list. You can also create your own calling card

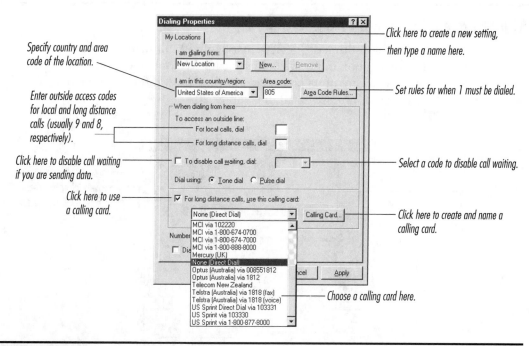

Specify country and area code of the location.

Enter outside access codes for local and long distance calls (usually 9 and 8, respectively).

Click here to disable call waiting if you are sending data.

Click here to use a calling card.

Click here to create a new setting, then type a name here.

Set rules for when 1 must be dialed.

Select a code to disable call waiting.

Click here to create and name a calling card.

Choose a calling card here.

FIGURE 6-11 Changing the telephony settings

settings by clicking the Calling Card button. The dialog box pictured next appears. The steps are simple: click New to specify a new card name, then enter a PIN and the phone numbers you must dial to gain domestic and international access. Finally, click the Long Distance Calls and/or International Calls buttons to specify the dialing steps.

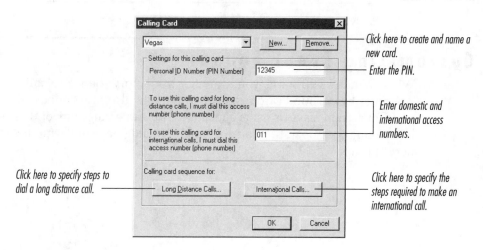

Click here to create and name a new card.

Enter the PIN.

Enter domestic and international access numbers.

Click here to specify steps to dial a long distance call.

Click here to specify the steps required to make an international call.

Multimedia Control Panel

You can control multimedia devices by opening Multimedia in the Control Panel. The dialog box in Figure 6-12 appears. We only mention Multimedia now so you are aware of its presence. Multimedia and the Multime dia control panel are covered in more detail in Chapter 20.

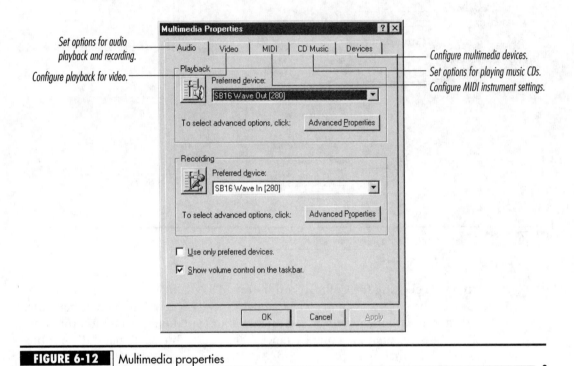

Set options for audio playback and recording.

Configure playback for video.

Configure multimedia devices.

Set options for playing music CDs.

Configure MIDI instrument settings.

FIGURE 6-12 | Multimedia properties

Customizing Event Sounds

When Windows 98 starts, you hear an introductory sound, assuming your computer has a sound card installed. You might also hear sounds when you perform certain tasks or make a mistake. You can change any of these sounds by opening Sounds in the Control Panel. A dialog box similar to the one shown here appears.

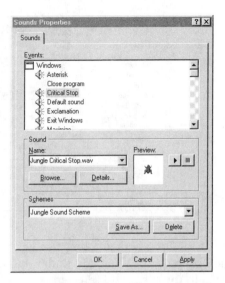

Explore the dialog box as follows, then set the options to fit your own needs:

1. Click an event in the Events window, then click the Play button to see what it sounds like.

2. Scroll down the list of events in the Events field and notice that there are groups of sounds, such as Windows, Power Management, Windows Explorer, and so on.

3. Install a preassigned sound scheme by clicking the down-arrow button in the Schemes field and choosing one of the available sound schemes, such as Musica or Utopia.

T I P : If other sound schemes are not available, refer to "Adding and Removing Windows 98 Components" earlier in this chapter and install the sound schemes that are listed in the Desktop Themes and Multimedia components.

4. After choosing a new sound scheme, select an event and click the Play button to see what it sounds like.

5. To change the sound of any event, click the event and click the Browse button. This opens the Browse dialog box pictured next, with a listing of the sound files in the Media folder.

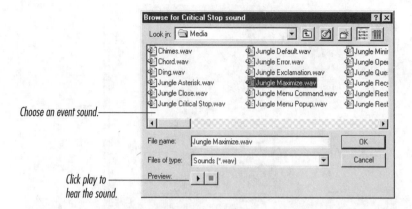

Choose an event sound.

Click play to hear the sound.

6. Notice that the Browse dialog box also has a Play button. Click a sound and click the Play button. When you find a sound you like, click OK. The sound is assigned to the event you selected.

You can continue reassigning sounds to different events. When you're happy with your new scheme, you can save the scheme by clicking the Save As button. This opens a dialog box where you can type a name for your new scheme.

Fonts

Fonts are collections of letters that have a special style. Some fonts are formal while others are designed for fun, personal correspondence. Windows 98 includes a set of fonts, but many applications such as Microsoft Office come with their own set of fonts that you can choose to install when you set up the application.

The Fonts folder in the Control Panel is where you can examine the fonts that are installed on your system, print font sample sheets, and add new fonts. Open the Fonts folder now to see a window similar to this one:

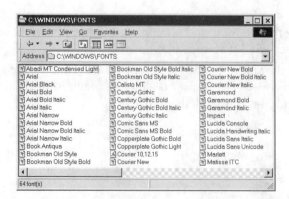

Try the following now:

- Double-click any font in the window to view a sample.
- Click the Print button to print a full-page sample of the font.
- In particular, open the Wingdings font. Instead of letters, it contains symbols and objects that you can use in your documents, pictures, personal Web pages, and so on.
- To see only the base font and not variations (bold, italic, etc.), choose Hide Variations from the View menu.

As mentioned, many applications will add fonts to your system during the installation process, or you can install fonts that you have obtained from different sources. To install a new font, open the Fonts folder and choose Install New Font from the File menu. The Add Fonts dialog box appears as shown here:

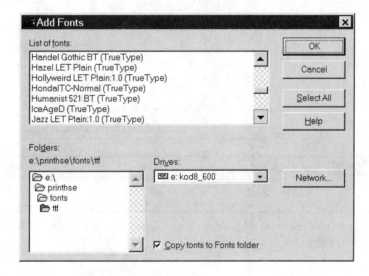

Choose the drive and/or folder where the new fonts exist in the Folders and Drives field. When the available fonts appear in the List of fonts field, select the fonts to install. You can hold the CTRL key and select multiple fonts or click the Select All button. Click OK to install the fonts. The fonts are immediately available in your applications that use fonts.

• Accessibility Options

If you have a physical disability or know someone who does, you will be interested in the Accessibility options. Open Accessibility in the Control Panel to display the dialog box pictured in Figure 6-13.

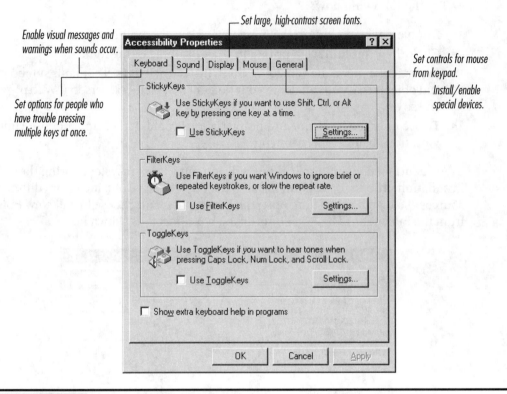

Enable visual messages and warnings when sounds occur.

Set large, high-contrast screen fonts.

Set options for people who have trouble pressing multiple keys at once.

Set controls for mouse from keypad.

Install/enable special devices.

FIGURE 6-13 | Setting accessibility options

T I P : If Accessibility options are not available, refer to "Adding and Removing Windows 98 Components" earlier in this chapter for information on installing the components.

The Accessibility Properties dialog box has five tabs where you can set various types of options. The dialog box does a good job of explaining each option and you need to determine which settings will be best for your situation.

For example, the StickyKeys keyboard option allows single-click use of the keyboard, even for keystrokes that normally require pressing two or three keys. For example, for a key combination such as ALT-TAB, where normally both keys must be pressed at the same time, you can press ALT, then TAB.

This is the kind of chapter you might need to refer back to occasionally when you have a need to change your Windows 98 configuration. Take one last look through the chapter to review what you've read, and make some mental notes about the kinds of changes you can make and where you can go in this book to get information. In the next chapter, we continue our discussion about configuring Windows 98 by covering Desktop settings.

Customizing the Desktop, Start Menu, and Taskbar

7

BASICS

- Customize the Desktop
- Add pictures to the Desktop
- Customize the Start menu
- Customize the Taskbar
- Create your own toolbars
- Create custom Desktop icon arrangements

BEYOND

- Create color, text, and window schemes for large, high-resolution monitors
- Put a control on the Active Desktop
- Create custom floating toolbars on the Desktop
- Set up password-protected screen savers

Everybody likes to have an organized Desktop. Well, almost everybody. In this chapter, we show you how to keep your Desktop organized and interesting by adding background pictures or changing the color schemes. As you'll see, there are also practical reasons for doing this.

Changing Desktop Settings

The first thing you'll need to know is where to change settings for the Desktop. You can right-click any blank portion of the Desktop and choose Properties to open the Display Properties dialog box as pictured in Figure 7-1.

Note the following tabs, which we will work with in this chapter:

- **Background** Add patterns and pictures to the Desktop. See "Changing Desktop Backgrounds" next.
- **Screen Saver** Screen savers blank out your screen after a period when you've not used your computer. You can set up a password-protected screen saver to prevent other people from accessing your system while it is running a task. Refer to "Setting Up Screen Savers" at the end of this chapter.
- **Appearance** Change the color schemes, border widths, font sizes, and other features of windows. See "Changing Window Schemes" later.

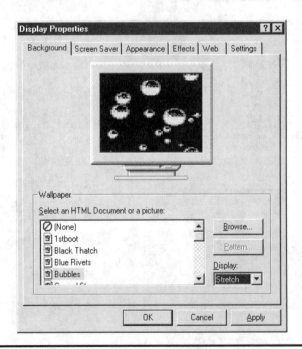

FIGURE 7-1 | Setting Display Properties

- **Effects** Specify settings for icons on the Desktop. See "Changing Icon Settings" later.

There are two other tabs as well which are not covered in this chapter. The Web tab is where you control the Active Desktop, a topic covered in Chapter 13, and the Settings tab is where you control video display settings, as discussed in Chapter 6.

Another way to change Desktop settings is to select themes in the Desktop Themes utility, as discussed under "Desktop Themes" later in this chapter.

WEBLINK: Leviathan Press has hundreds of downloadable wallpaper images, themes, screens, and screen savers. Go to http://www.themesplus.com/.

Changing Desktop Backgrounds

The default setting for the Windows Desktop is a solid green color, but you can add patterns or pictures to the Desktop.

Open the Display Properties dialog box as described previously and make sure the Background tab is selected. You see the dialog box pictured in Figure 7-1. Click a pattern in the Wallpaper list and then click Center, Tile, or Stretch in the Display field. Most of the items in the list are meant to be tiled (repeated over the Desktop).

The computer screen in the dialog box is supposed to let you see what the wallpaper looks like, but it doesn't display the results well. Click Apply to see what the pattern looks like on the real Desktop. The dialog box stays open so you can continue making other selections.

If you choose a picture, click Center in the Display field, then click the Pattern button. This opens the Pattern dialog box where you can choose a pattern to fill in the part of the Desktop that is not covered by the picture. You can even edit a selected pattern by clicking the Edit Pattern button in the Pattern dialog box.

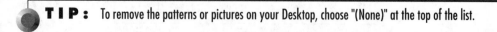
TIP: To remove the patterns or pictures on your Desktop, choose "(None)" at the top of the list.

Changing Window Schemes

Click the Appearance tab on the Display Properties dialog box to show the page pictured in Figure 7-3. The options on this page help you change the way windows appear on the desktop.

The first thing to do is try some of the predefined schemes. Click the Scheme field to open its drop-down list box, then press the DOWN ARROW key to start scrolling through the selections. Each entry will appear in the sample window on the dialog box. If you find one you like, click Apply to see what it looks like on the desktop and OK to accept it.

To create your own scheme, start by choosing one of the existing schemes that has colors and text sizes closest to what you want. Then change individual elements to suit your taste by selecting items in the Item field. For example, if you choose Menu in the Item field, you can change the font, font size, and font color of menus.

Once you create a custom scheme, click the Save As button and save your scheme with a unique name.

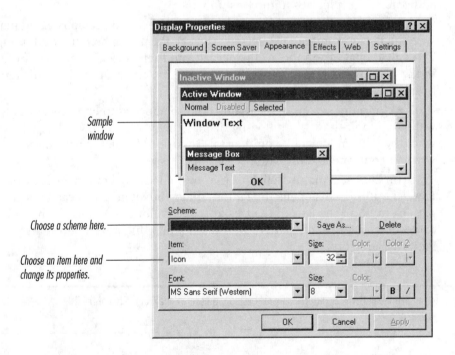

Sample window

Choose a scheme here.

Choose an item here and change its properties.

FIGURE 7-2 | Changing window appearances

While pictures and patterns have some aesthetic appeal, they aren't really that practical. Look at the Desktop in Figure 7-2. Here we're used Paint to create some empty labeled boxes that will help us organize icons on the Desktop. In addition, we've typed in some information that we need to refer to often.

To create a similar Desktop picture, follow these steps:

1. First, right-click a blank part of the Desktop and select Properties from the shortcut menu. Click the Settings tab in the Display Properties dialog box. In the Screen area field, make note of the screen size settings.

2. Start Paint, then choose Attributes on the Image menu and enter the screen size settings into the Width and Height fields, making sure that "pixels" is selected in the Units field. This creates a canvas that is the same size as your Desktop.

3. Now create the boxes and add the text, similar to what you see in Figure 7-2, or be creative and create your own custom Desktop image.

4. Installing the image on the Desktop is easy because you can do it directly from Paint. Just choose Set As Wallpaper (Centered) from the File menu.

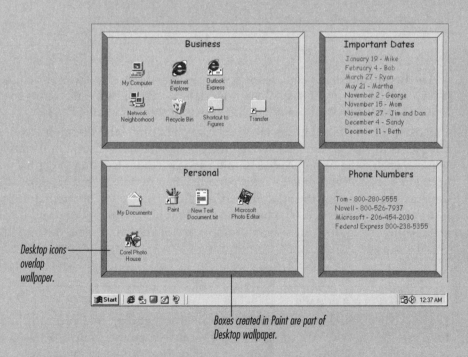

Desktop icons overlap wallpaper.

Boxes created in Paint are part of Desktop wallpaper.

FIGURE 7-3   Our custom wallpaper (we've placed Desktop icons over the boxes)

Changing Icon Settings

Click the Effects tab on the Display Properties dialog box to view the following page, where you can change some of the properties of Desktop icons.

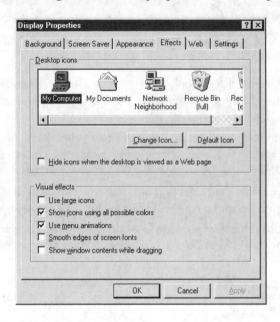

The first item called "Hide icons when the desktop is viewed as a Web page" is an Active Desktop setting. When it is enabled, this option hides icons so you only see the Active Desktop when the Active Desktop is enabled.

Most of the settings on this tab are self-explanatory, but you might be curious as to why you are even given the options in some cases. For example, you can enable the option called "Show window contents while dragging" for aesthetic reasons (you drag an empty frame when disabled), but on older systems, the effect may be affected by slow performance. Menu animation may also reduce performance. The best thing to do is set all the options and try them for a while. If you don't like them or notice a slow-down, disable the options you don't want.

Desktop Themes

Desktop Themes are an optional Windows 98 component that you can choose to install during the Windows 98 setup process. Open the Control Panel and choose Desktop Themes now. You see a dialog box similar to Figure 7-4.

Tuning It To Work

Creating a Custom Scheme for High-Resolution Monitors

If you have a big monitor running at high-resolution, you can choose one of the schemes that is described as "large" and "extra large." These schemes use larger than normal fonts that are easier to read.

However, you might want to create your own custom scheme as described here. We point out some of the more important items to change in the following set of steps:

1. Start by choosing the scheme you want to work with. For this example, we chose Windows Standard (extra large).

2. Choose Icon in the Item field, then increase the value in the Size field (just to the right of the Item field) to enlarge Desktop icons. Click Apply to see the changes and adjust the value further if necessary.

3. With Icon still selected in the Item field, change the Font and Font Size values to fit your needs. Click Apply to review the changes.

4. If the icons are too close together after resizing, choose Icon Spacing (Horizontal) and/or Icon Spacing (Vertical) in the Item field and increase the size of the spacing between icons.

5. Choose Menu in the Item field and change the values so that the font's type and size match the settings you made for icons.

6. Choose Scrollbar in the Item field and increase the value in the Size field. You can see this change in the upper viewing window.

7. Optionally, choose Active Windows Border in the Item field and increase the size of the border for the active window.

8. When you're done, click the Save As button and give your new scheme a name.

Choose a theme here.

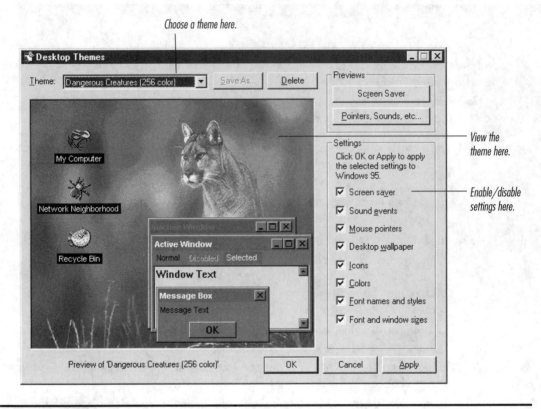

View the theme here.

Enable/disable settings here.

| **FIGURE 7-4** | Choosing new Desktop Themes |

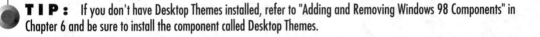

T I P : If you don't have Desktop Themes installed, refer to "Adding and Removing Windows 98 Components" in Chapter 6 and be sure to install the component called Desktop Themes.

With Desktop Themes, you install predesigned Desktop, icon, and sound arrangements such as Dangerous Creatures (pictured), Baseball, Space, and others. Each theme includes a picture that covers the Desktop, unique icons related to the theme, and sounds related to the theme.

Any theme can be customized by changing options in the Settings field. For example, you can disable the background picture (which covers the entire Desktop) if you find it distracting, but you can keep the unique icons and sounds of the scheme.

W E B L I N K S :   There are three great Web sites for Desktop Themes:

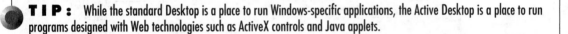

Desktop Themes Unleashed	http://themes.tierranet.com/
Galt Software	http://www.galttech.com/
Connectix (list of theme links)	http://www.quickcam.com/html/more_ themes.html

---

• Configuring the Active Desktop

As mentioned in Chapter 1, the Active Desktop is like a second Desktop where you can display information from Web sites on the Internet, such as the MSNBC Weather Channel or the Microsoft Investor stock ticker. In this section, we give you a brief introduction to the Active Desktop. You'll find more details in Chapter 13.

T I P :   While the standard Desktop is a place to run Windows-specific applications, the Active Desktop is a place to run programs designed with Web technologies such as ActiveX controls and Java applets.

Besides subscription services that provide updated information from sites on the Web, you can also install stand-alone controls and applets that are available from various sources. In this section, we show you how to install the rotating 3D Java clock pictured here on your Desktop. It doesn't look like much as a still image, but it's interesting to watch the time snake around an invisible globe.

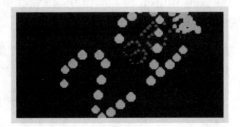

WEBLINK: Microsoft's gallery of active items is at http://home.microsoft.com/ie/ie40/gallery.

Follow the steps below to obtain the Java clock from Microsoft's Internet Explorer Active Desktop Gallery and install it on your Active Desktop. Note that these steps assume you have access to the Internet. Refer to Appendix B for information about getting wired.

1. Right-click the Desktop and choose Properties, then click the Web tab to see the following dialog box.

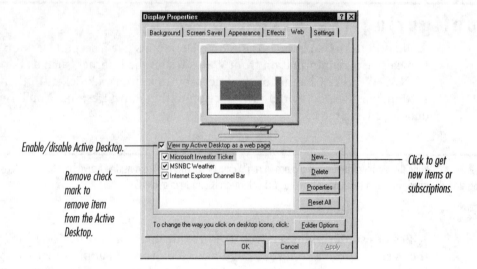

Enable/disable Active Desktop.

Remove check mark to remove item from the Active Desktop.

Click to get new items or subscriptions.

2. Make sure the option called "View my Active Desktop as a web page" is checked.

3. Click the New Button to obtain the new content. You see the following dialog box:

4. Click Yes to log onto Microsoft's Internet Explorer 4.0 Gallery, then click Cool Utilities. Finally, click 3D Java Clock.

TIP: By the time you read this, Microsoft may make extensive changes to its gallery site. If the Java Clock is no longer available, just pick some other utility to install on your Desktop for this example.

You are asked whether you really want to download the utility and install it on your Active Desktop. Choose Yes and in a moment, you see it running.

Some Active Desktop items can reduce the performance of your computer while they are running, so you should disable them if they are not needed. To disable an item, open the Desktop Properties dialog box pictured earlier and click the Web tab, then remove the check mark from the item you want to turn off. You can always turn it back on using this same method.

You can also turn off the Active Desktop at any time to disable all its items. Right-click the Desktop, choose Active Desktop from the menu, then click View As Web Page (if it is checked). Refer to Chapter 13 for a continuation of this discussion.

Customizing the Start Menu

You use the Start menu constantly to start programs, access utilities, open files, and do many other things. Why not customize it to make it even more useful? In this section we show you how.

You can easily add options to the Start menu at any time. For example, if windows are always covering an icon you want to access on the Desktop, you might just want to add that icon to the Start menu. You can add a startup icon for just about anything to the Start menu, including documents, videos, and pictures. We show you two methods for customizing the Start menu in the following sections.

Dragging and Dropping Items on the Start Menu

Once you get used to it, the drag-and-drop method is the easiest way to customize the Start menu. In this example, we'll show you how to add a shortcut icon to start the Welcome program. Welcome appears the first time you start Windows and it includes tutorials and Help information. You may have closed it or even disabled it. Adding a Welcome option to the Start menu will make it easy to start Welcome any time you want to use it, not just when Windows 98 starts. (You don't need to add Welcome. Substitute any program you want to add to the Start menu in the following procedure.)

Follow the steps here to add the Welcome options:

1. Start by locating the Welcome program icon. Open My Computer, then Drive C, then the Windows folder. Scroll to the bottom of the list until you see Welcome.

2. Click the Welcome options, and while holding the mouse, drag it over the Start button and hold it there until the Start menu opens.

   You need to keep holding the mouse button during this operation. What you're going to do is drag the icon to where you want Welcome to appear on the menu.

3. Drag the icon up and hold it over Programs until the Programs cascading menu appears, then drag it down the Programs cascading menu.

   Notice the black line following the icon. This tells you where the new option will be inserted.

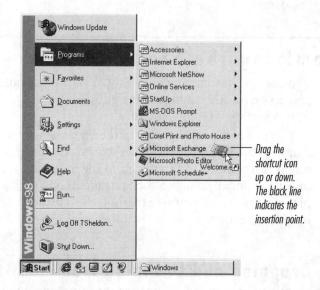

Drag the shortcut icon up or down. The black line indicates the insertion point.

4. Position the icon near the bottom of the menu and release the mouse button. The new Welcome menu option appears on the menu.

Note the following:

- If you don't like this new location, just click and drag the menu option to another location. It's that easy.
- You can copy or move any icon currently on your Desktop to the Start menu using these methods. Doing so may help reduce clutter on your Desktop.
- To remove the menu option, right-click it and choose Delete from the shortcut menu.

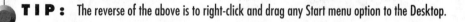

T I P :   The reverse of the above is to right-click and drag any Start menu option to the Desktop.

The Start Menu Wizard

Now we're going to add a menu option by using the Start Menu Wizard. Once again, we'll add Welcome, but you can substitute any program you want to add to the Start menu. If you follow our example and add Welcome, delete the Welcome option you created in the previous section before continuing (i.e., right-click the option and choose Delete). Note that we actually prefer the previous drag-and-drop method, but some people prefer to be guided by wizards. Also, this technique may be better for locating programs that are buried deep in folders.

1. To open the Start Menu Wizard, choose Settings on the Start menu, then choose Taskbar & Start Menu. Next, click the Start Menu Programs tab.
2. Click the Add button to start the Create Shortcut Wizard.
3. Click the Browse button to search for the Welcome program.

4. Open the Windows folder on Drive C and double-click WELCOME.EXE at the end of the file list.

5. You are returned to the Create Shortcut Wizard where you click Next to display the following dialog box. Choose the menu where you want to place the new menu option. In this example, we chose Programs.

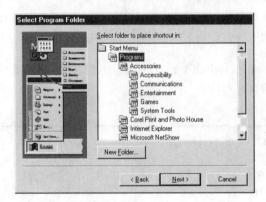

6. Click Next, then type a name for the menu option ("Welcome" in our example) and click the Finish button.

   The new menu option is added to the bottom of the menu you selected. Use the click-and-drag technique to move it up to another location on the menu.

Exploring the Start Menu Folders

Options on the Start menu are actually organized into folders that you can explore. In fact, you can manage Start menu options by working with these folders rather than using the method described in the two previous sections. Take a few seconds to explore these options and then keep them in mind for future reference.

1. To explore the Start menu folders, right-click the Start button and choose Open. This opens the Start Menu folder as shown in Figure 7-5. The icons in the Start menu folder are the same icons that you see on the Start menu.

2. Next, open the Programs folder, which shows you all the icons and folders on the Start | Programs menu.

3. Next, open Accessories. The window that appears contains all shortcut options on the Accessories menu.

What can you do with this window view of the Start menu options? One trick is to add shortcuts like you did in the previous examples. Simply right-click in the window and choose New | Shortcut to open the Create Shortcut Wizard. When you're done, the shortcut appears on the menu. You can also drag-and-drop icons into the windows to add new menu options or drag items out of the windows to the desktop to create a duplicate startup option on the desktop. Finally, you can remove any menu option by deleting its icon in a window.

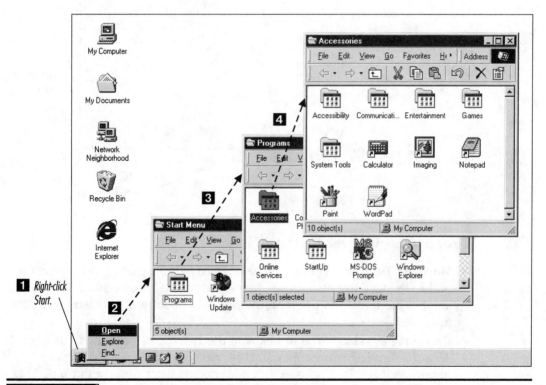

FIGURE 7-5 Exploring Start menu folders

Customizing the Taskbar

The Taskbar is specifically designed to make it easy to switch among applications. The best thing about the Taskbar is that, by default, it's always visible (on top). You can always click the Start button or Quick Launch buttons, no matter how many windows are piled on the Desktop.

Here are the Taskbar's most important features:

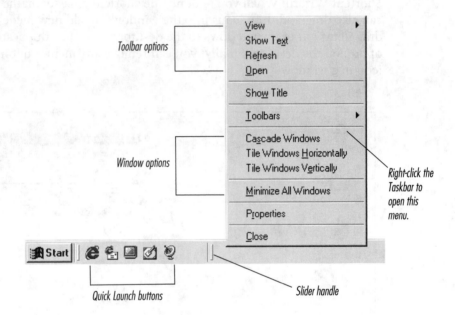

Toolbar options

View
Show Text
Refresh
Open

Show Title

Toolbars

Window options

Cascade Windows
Tile Windows Horizontally
Tile Windows Vertically

Right-click the Taskbar to open this menu.

Minimize All Windows

Properties

Close

Quick Launch buttons

Slider handle

You can also move and resize the Taskbar:

- **Move the Taskbar**   You can move the Taskbar to a side border or the top of the Desktop. Just click in any blank part of the Taskbar and drag it to another border. If you put it on the side, you might want to resize it as discussed next.

- **Resize the Taskbar**   You can expand the Taskbar by pointing to its edge. A double-headed arrow appears. Click and drag to resize. Resizing is important if the Taskbar is on the side and you can't read the buttons. The next illustration shows the Taskbar located on the right border before and after resizing.

Assume you work on a special project that requires its own set of applications and has its own set of files. You can group all of the programs and documents into a Start menu folder and they will appear as a group option on the Start menu. We're going to create a special group called Secret Project that will appear on the Start menu as shown here. You can, of course, create a group that is more practical for your needs.

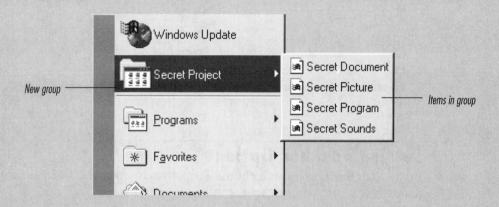

New group —

Items in group —

1. Right-click the Start button, then choose Open. The Start Menu window opens.
2. Right-click a blank area of the window and choose New I Folder. A new folder appears.
3. Type a new name before doing anything else and press ENTER to accept the new name.

   At this point, the new group should appear on your Start menu. Click Start to see it.

Now you can add program shortcuts and documents to the new group. Right-click the Start button and choose Open, then open the folder you created in the last step. Use drag-and-drop techniques to add programs and documents to the folder. Alternatively, you can add new items by running the Shortcut Wizard. Right-click and choose New I Shortcut to start it.

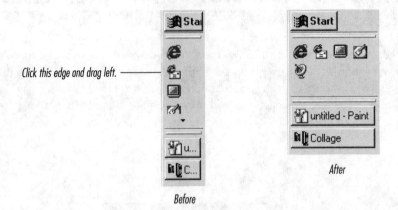

Click this edge and drag left.

Before

After

The following sections describe some other interesting ways to customize the Taskbar.

Setting Taskbar Options

Right-click the Taskbar and choose Properties to open the Taskbar Properties dialog box where you can set the following options:

- **Always on top**   The Taskbar always stays above any open windows on the Desktop.
- **Auto hide**   When this option is checked, the Taskbar hides and then reappears when you point to the edge of the Desktop.
- **Show small icons in Start menu**   Enabling this option basically reduces the size of the Start menu by reducing the size of its icons.
- **Show clock**   This option displays the clock on the right side of the Taskbar.

Adding Quick Launch Buttons

The Quick Launch buttons let you start your most important programs right from the Taskbar. If the Taskbar is set to be always on top, this is the best place to start applications. You can add your own applications to the Quick Launch toolbar by using simple drag-and-drop techniques.

To copy your favorite startup icon on the Desktop to the Quick Launch toolbar, follow these steps:

- Make the Quick Launch toolbar larger by clicking and dragging the slider handle on the right.
- Click your favorite Desktop icon and drag it over the space you created in the Quick Launch toolbar as shown here:

The new icon appears immediately. If in the future you decide to remove the button, right-click it and choose Delete.

There are several other ways to add Quick Launch buttons. You can open My Computer and find the folder on a drive that contains a startup icon for a program, then drag that startup icon to the Quick Launch toolbar. You can also open Windows Explorer and use the same technique.

Still another method is to open the Start menu and locate a menu option that you access often, then click and drag that option to the Quick Launch toolbar.

Working with Toolbars

In addition to adding your own options to the Quick Launch toolbar, you can create your own toolbars. Try the following exercise now to see how this works. You'll add My Computer as a toolbar to the Taskbar, then remove it (unless you want to keep it).

Click the My Computer icon on your Desktop and drag it over a blank portion of the Taskbar, then release the mouse. The icons you normally see in the My Computer window now appear as tiny icons on the Taskbar as shown next. Note the arrow on the right that you click to scroll right in the toolbar.

Click here to scroll right.

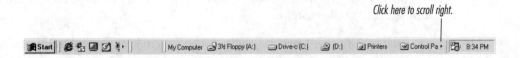

The only problem with toolbars is that it can get crowded with icons when you start opening program windows, as shown here:

Open window buttons are crowded.

To solve this problem, you can slide the toolbar's handle to the right to make more room for buttons, but another solution is to remove the text from the buttons as follows:

1. Right-click the title for the toolbar (My Computer, in this example).
2. Disable the Show Text option (remove the check mark from the option).
3. Slide the toolbar handle to the right so the Taskbar is a little more organized as shown here:

ToolTip (point to a button to see its description)

Still, we have a problem. There are icons, but no descriptions. What if you forget what an icon does? One solution is to "hover" over the icon with the mouse pointer until its "ToolTip" appears as shown in the previous illustration, but a better way is to make more room on the Taskbar for your toolbars and then enable the text descriptions. Here's how:

1. Resize the Taskbar by clicking its top border and dragging up.
2. Click the My Computer toolbar handle and drag it down. Now the toolbar appears below the buttons.

3. Right-click the My Computer toolbar and enable the Show Text option so you can once again see the button descriptions. Now the Taskbar looks something like this:

Rearrange toolbars by clicking and dragging handles.

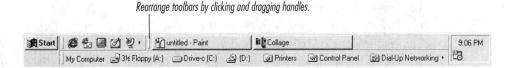

There are a number of other toolbars that you can add to the Taskbar. Right-click the Taskbar and choose the Toolbars option to display the following menu.

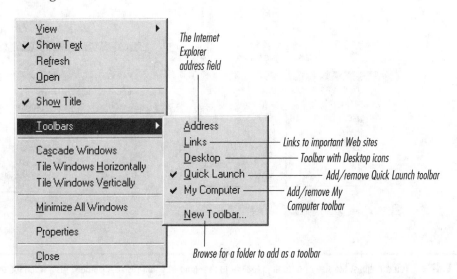

Note the following:

- Enable the Address field and the Links field if you want Internet Explorer features on the Taskbar.
- Enable Desktop to put all the Desktop icons on the Toolbar.
- Choose New Toolbar to open a browse window so you can search for folders to add to the Taskbar.

It's up to you to explore these options. Make sure you go through the previous exercises to get familiar with customizing the Taskbar, then decide on the style you like.

Floating Toolbars

One more cool thing you can do is "float" your toolbars on the Desktop. An example is pictured below. First, you must install a toolbar on the Taskbar. You then drag the toolbar to the Desktop to create a floating toolbar. In this example, My Computer and My Documents were added as toolbars to the Taskbar. Then, both toolbars were dragged out to the Desktop. The toolbars on the left were dragged out separately. The toolbars on the right were joined by dragging the second toolbar out on top of the first.

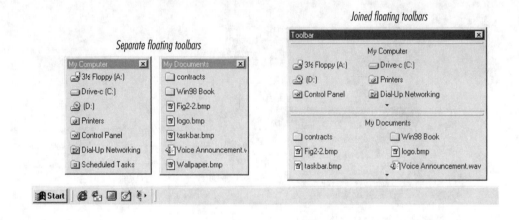

Joined floating toolbars

Separate floating toolbars

T I P : You can adjust the size of a floating toolbar in the same way you resize a window. Also, when toolbars are joined, handles appear that help you adjust the size of each toolbar.

Figure 7-6 is an example of how you can customize a floating toolbar. We started with the toolbar on the right in the previous illustration. The Address field and Quick Launch toolbar were then added by right-clicking the toolbar and choosing Address and Quick Launch from the menu. Next, large icons were selected for the My Computer icons by right-clicking the My Computer toolbar and choosing View | Large. Then, text labels were added to the Quick Launch icons (right-click and choose Show Text). Finally, the joined floating toolbars were resized and adjusted as you see it in Figure 7-6.

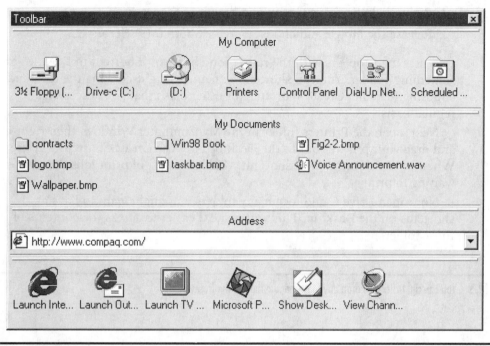

FIGURE 7-6 Setting up floating toolbars

Organizing and Managing Desktop Shortcuts

You've already worked with shortcuts. A shortcut is an icon, usually located on the Desktop, that starts a program or opens a document. Usually, the actual program or document is buried in some folder that is hard to get to, or may even be located on another computer attached to your company's network. The shortcut is a reference to the program or document. It uses only a small amount of disk space because it does not hold the program code or document content it references.

Let's start by creating some more useful shortcuts on your Desktop. We start by putting disk drives on the Desktop, then some important folders. Remember that we are just giving you some ideas. You can always try these for a while and if you don't like them, just delete the shortcuts.

1. Open the My Computer window.

2. Right-click the Drive C icon and drag it to the Desktop.

3. Release the mouse and choose "Create Shortcut(s) Here."

A new icon appears with the rather long name of "Shortcut to Drive-c" or something similar. You can shorten the name by right-clicking the icon and choosing Rename. Create shortcuts for other disks that you access on a regular basis.

Next, open the Printers folder in the My Computer Window, then right-click and drag your printers out to the Desktop. Choose Create Shortcut(s) Here. When you click the printer shortcut, you'll see a list of print jobs that are waiting to print.

Now open Drive C and locate any folders you might want to have as shortcuts on the Desktop. This will make it easier to access the contents of those folders.

TIP: You can right-click and drag any Start menu option to the Desktop.

Shortcuts can help you consolidate related files into a single folder. For example, assume you are working on a project that requires both text files and graphics files. The text files are stored in the Drafts folder and the graphics files are stored in the Pictures folder. You can leave the actual files where they are, but still create a folder that consolidates access to the files. Start by creating a folder on the Desktop called "Project" or some similar name. Now create shortcuts for the files you need to access that are located in the Drafts and Pictures folders.

Editing Shortcuts

You can change some of the settings of shortcuts by right-clicking the shortcut and choosing Properties. A dialog box similar to the one in Figure 7-7 appears where you can make the changes noted.

Setting Up Screen Savers

Screen savers were once used to protect monitors from "burn-in," which occurred when an unchanging image burned itself onto the phosphor of the screen. This is usually not a problem on modern monitors, but screen savers are still around because they are useful in other ways, and because they are

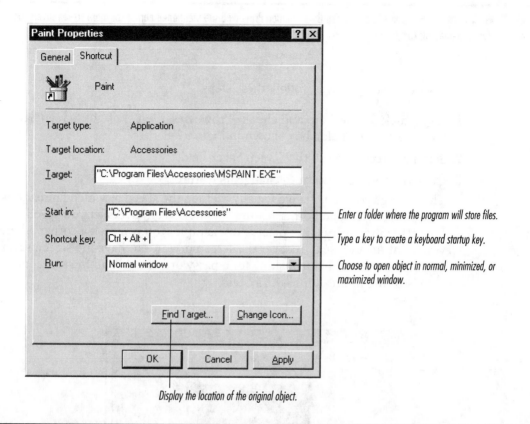

FIGURE 7-7 Setting shortcut properties

aesthetically appealing. A screen saver typically blanks the screen or turns on some moving image like a shark swimming across the screen after a few minutes of nothing being done on the computer.

Today, the most practical use of a screen saver is to blank your screen and require a password to restore it. With password protection, you can leave your computer while you go to lunch and no one will disturb it (unless they turn it off). This is especially useful if you need to "crunch some numbers" or run a program while you're away and you don't want anybody to accidentally or intentionally disturb the process.

Windows 98 comes with a number of screen saver schemes and you'll find even more if you install Desktop Themes as discussed earlier in this chapter.

> ⚡ **WEBLINK:** Don't forget to visit the Leviathan Press Web site mentioned earlier for more screen savers. Go to http://www.themesplus.com/. Another source for screen savers is http://www.softsea.com/.

To set up a screen saver, follow these steps:

1. Right-click the Desktop and choose Properties, then click the Screen Saver tab. You see the dialog box shown in Figure 7-8.

2. Select a screen saver in the Screen Saver field.

3. Click the Settings button to change its features.

   The settings you can change usually include the speed at which animations take place, colors, and other features. Some screen savers let you specify how screen recovery takes place. For example, you can pick a corner where you point the mouse to recover the screen or you can have the screen saver wait a few seconds before asking for a password as a way to foil someone who is trying to break into the system.

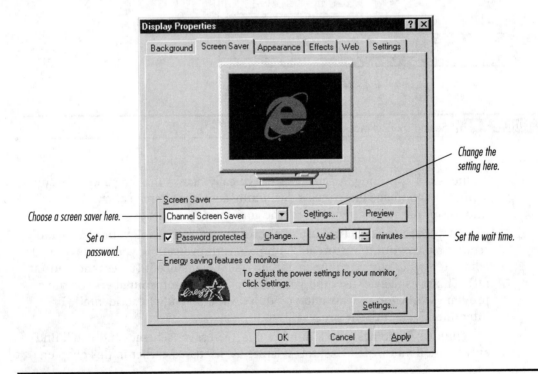

Choose a screen saver here.

Set a password.

Change the setting here.

Set the wait time.

FIGURE 7-8 | Setting up a screen saver

4. After changing settings, click the Password protected box if you need this type of security, then click the Change button to specify a password.

5. In the Wait field, specify the number of minutes of non-activity that the computer waits before enabling the screen saver.

You must try out the Scrolling Marquee screen saver. It scrolls a message across your screen. For example, the message could say "Out to lunch. Back at 1:00." If you set up a computer as a kiosk, you can create a message that invites people to use the system, such as "press a key to see the latest travel specials." Choose Scrolling Marquee in the Screen Saver list, then click the Settings button to display the following dialog box. Fill out the fields as shown.

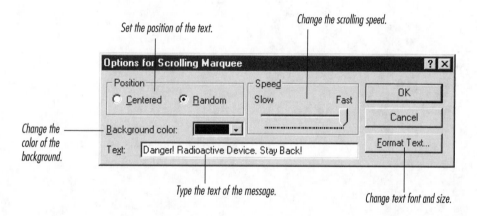

TIP: Computer cameras used for videoconferencing such as the Connectix QuickCam have screen savers that display the image being captured by the camera. You can even purchase software that starts recording video when someone starts tinkering with your computer.

As we mentioned, many of the settings and options discussed in this chapter are not critical to running Windows faster or better. However, if you like to periodically reorganize your office and your desk to make things more efficient, then you'll appreciate why Windows 98 offers the features discussed in this chapter. Return to this chapter from time to time to review these options; eventually you'll come up with a desktop scheme that is just right for you.

Customizing Folders

In this chapter, we show you different ways to customize the view and the way you work with folders. In the next chapter, you learn more about the filing system and the way folders are used to organize the filing system.

My Computer vs. Windows Explorer

You can browse the file system by opening My Computer or Windows Explorer. Before going further, it's worth exploring the difference between My Computer and Windows Explorer and discussing why you would use one over the other.

Windows Explorer presents a two-pane view of the file system with a hierarchical view of folders on the left and files on the right as shown in Figure 8-1. If you open My Computer, you will not see the hierarchical folder view.

The folder view pane in Windows Explorer is a significant feature. When you click any drive or folder in the left pane, a list of files and folders appears in the right pane. Since all your drives and folders can be displayed in the left pane, Windows Explorer provides an easy way to browse your file system. More important, you can click and drag any file or set of files in the right pane to a drive or folder object in the left pane. That makes it easy to copy and move files and folders to other folders, other drives, or even other computers attached to your network.

Now consider the My Computer folder window. It doesn't have a hierarchical folder view, but if you click the down arrow button in the Address field, a drop-down list appears similar to the one shown on the next page. Here you can choose to view the contents of another drive or folder.

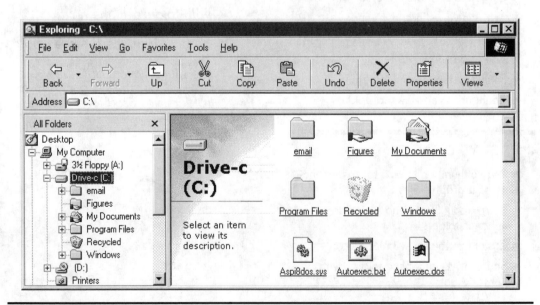

FIGURE 8-1 | Windows Explorer

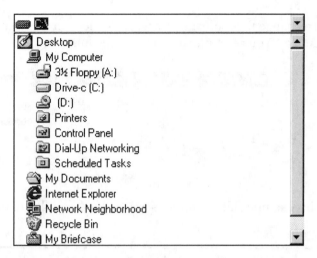

If you plan to copy and move files between folders and drives, we recommend using Windows Explorer because the hierarchical folder list simplifies the process as you'll see in Chapter 10. You can open multiple copies of Windows Explorer to help with copying and moving files. The program can be opened from almost anywhere, as follows:

- Click Start | Programs and choose Windows Explorer.
- From the Desktop, right-click My Computer and choose Explore.
- In any My Computer window, choose Explore from the File menu.
- Right-click any folder and choose Explore. Windows Explorer opens with a view of the selected folder.

Try each of these now to become familiar with the locations where you can start Explorer. In addition, you can create a Quick Launch button for the program on the Taskbar as follows:

1. Click Start | Programs, then right-click (not left-click) and drag the Windows Explorer option to the Quick Launch toolbar.
2. Choose Copy on the shortcut menu that appears.

Configuring Toolbars and Window Features

Now let's look at ways that you can customize the look of folder windows. The toolbars for My Computer and Windows Explorer are the same but you can change them independent of one another, so the techniques described next apply to either Windows Explorer or any folder window.

To change the toolbar settings, click View on the Menu bar or right-click the Menu bar. You see a menu similar to the following:

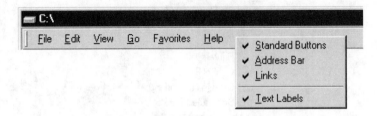

In this example, all the options are enabled as indicated by the check marks.

TIP: You can also enable or disable the status bar by choosing Status Bar from the View menu.

Here's an example of Windows Explorer with all of the toolbar features and the status bar enabled:

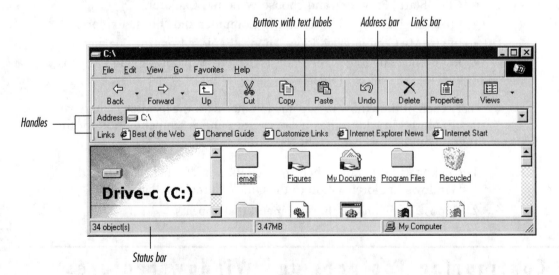

Notice that the buttons and toolbars take up quite a bit of room. This may take up too much real estate on small Desktops, so we often configure windows with the more efficient layout shown here:

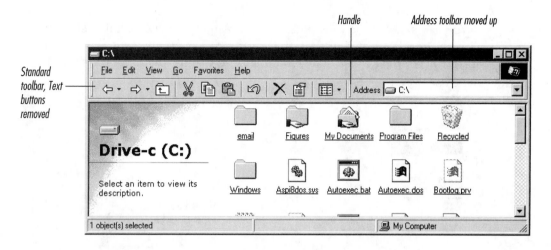

To set these options, disable the Links toolbar (unless you really need it), then disable Text Labels (to make the buttons smaller). Next, move the Address toolbar up to the Standard toolbar by clicking and dragging its handle. You can also remove the status bar if you don't need to see the information it displays.

Arranging Folder Views

You can arrange the view of objects in a folder window by changing the type of icon displayed and by arranging the order in which icons are displayed. Options are located on the View menu as shown here:

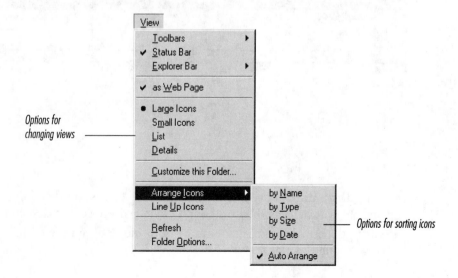

You can also choose view options by clicking the View button as shown here on the left, or by right-clicking a blank part of an open window, which opens the shortcut menu shown on the right. Use the method that is most convenient.

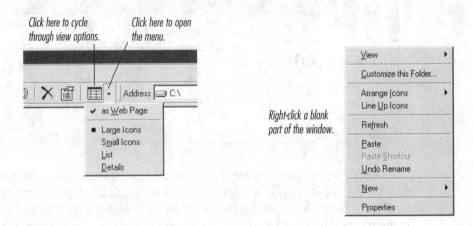

Click here to cycle through view options.

Click here to open the menu.

Right-click a blank part of the window.

Try each of the view options now to see which you prefer. The Details view is probably the best because it shows useful information about files. It displays a window like the following that has folder and file details in separate columns.

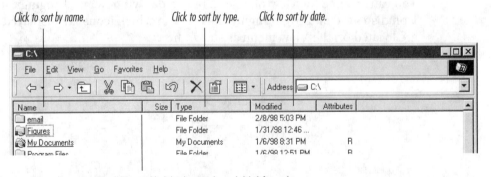

Click to sort by name.

Click to sort by type.

Click to sort by date.

To adjust column width click a button edge and slide left or right.

Note the following:

- Click the button above a column to sort the file list on that column. Click once to sort in ascending order and click again to sort in descending order.
- Change the width of the column by pointing between the buttons and dragging left or right.

Sorting and Arranging Icons

In Detail view, you can sort files by simply clicking the button above each column. If a window is arranged with another view (Large icon, Small icon, or List view), you can sort icons by choosing one of the Arrange Icons options on the View menu: By Name, By Type, By Size, and By Date.

TIP: Choose By Type to sort files according to their filename extension. For example, all files with the DOC extension would be sorted together.

Occasionally, you may want to organize the icons in a folder according to your own taste rather than in some order. Make sure Auto Arrange is not enabled, then rearrange icons as you like. Now choose Line Up Icons on the View menu to align the icons.

TIP: Choose Refresh on the View menu to update the list of files and folders in a folder window. Newly created folders and files may not appear or be sorted properly until you click this option.

Auto Arrange

The Auto Arrange option on the View | Arrange Icons menu is a toggle option that will automatically arrange the icons in a window as new icons are added or as you change the size of a window. Try this now:

1. Open the Drive C folder window.

2. Make sure Auto Arrange is enabled.

3. Resize the window and notice how icons automatically rearrange themselves to fit the new window size.

As you add new files and folders, they are automatically sorted into the list of files and folders.

Thumbnail Views

Thumbnails provide a unique way to view the contents of files without actually opening the files. An example is pictured in Figure 8-2. Here, we see thumbnail

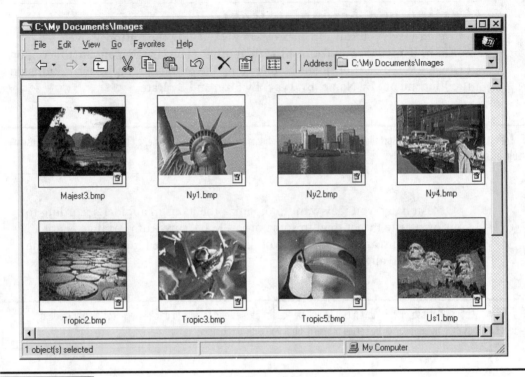

C:\My Documents\Images

File   Edit   View   Go   Favorites   Help

Address C:\My Documents\Images

Majest3.bmp   Ny1.bmp   Ny2.bmp   Ny4.bmp

Tropic2.bmp   Tropic3.bmp   Tropic5.bmp   Us1.bmp

1 object(s) selected   My Computer

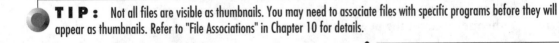

FIGURE 8-2   Folders can display thumbnail views of file contents

views for a folder that holds graphics images. You can also use thumbnail views to view other types of documents, although text files are usually not readable in thumbnail view.

TIP: Not all files are visible as thumbnails. You may need to associate files with specific programs before they will appear as thumbnails. Refer to "File Associations" in Chapter 10 for details.

You enable thumbnail view for each folder individually rather than for all folders at once. The steps are outlined next.

Find the folder for which you want to enable thumbnail view. Right-click the folder and choose Properties. If the folder window is already open, right-click a blank part of the window and choose Properties. The Properties dialog box appears as shown next:

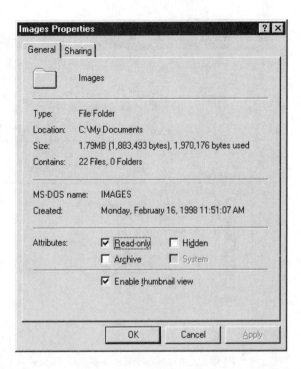

1. Place a check mark by the option called "Enable thumbnail view" and click OK.

2. If the folder window was already open, you will need to close it and then reopen it before the Thumbnail option appears on the View menu.

3. Click Thumbnail on the View menu to see thumbnail views of the files in the folder.

Setting Special Folder Options

There are some specific options that you can set on the Folder Options dialog box. Open the folder you want to configure, then click Folder Options on the View menu. When the Folder Options dialog box appears, click View to see the dialog box in Figure 8-3.

Note the top box called Folder views. If you click the Like Current Folder button, all the Windows 98 folders will take on the settings of the current folder. To use this option, set up a folder the way you like and change the Advanced settings discussed next, then click this button. To revert back to the default settings, click the Reset All Folders button.

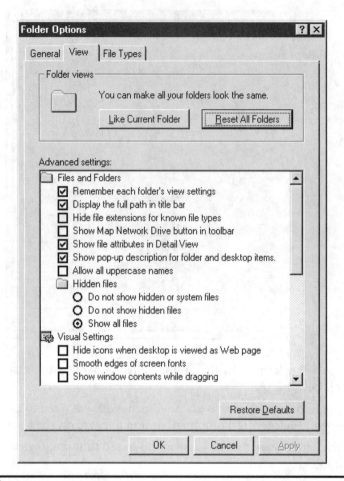

FIGURE 8-3 | Setting special folder options

Advanced Settings for Folders

The Advanced settings pictured in Figure 8-3 are described here. The Advanced settings affect all folders, so keep that in mind when deciding how you want to set these options.

- *Remember each folder's view settings*   If enabled, the folder settings you have selected while working in a folder are retained and used the next time you open the folder. If disabled, the folder returns to its default view settings the next time you open it. The setting of this option is a matter of

personal preference and you may need to work with windows a while
before you decide what you like.

- *Display the full path in title bar*   Enable this option to see in the window's
  Title bar the names of the drive and folders that hold the current folder.
  Recommended setting is enabled.

- *Hide file extensions for known file types*   This option can help reduce clutter
  in file lists by not showing filename extensions. We recommend not using it
  (disabled).

- *Show Map Network Drive button in toolbar*   Enable this option to show
  buttons for mapping network drives. Mapping a network drive assigns a
  drive letter to a shared folder on a network-connected computer. Our
  recommendation is to disable this option to reduce the number of buttons
  on the toolbar.

- *Show file attributes in Detail View*   Enable this option to view the attributes
  of files when Detail view is enabled. We recommend enabling this option.

- *Show pop-up description for folder and desktop items*   Enable this option to
  see descriptions of folders and Desktop items in small pop-up windows.
  When enabled, pop-up descriptions appear similar to what you see when
  Web View is enabled. We recommend enabling this option.

- *Allow all uppercase names*   Enable this option to display filenames in all
  uppercase characters (i.e., FILENAME.DOC) if the file was originally
  named in uppercase characters. When this option is disabled, filenames
  are changed to lowercase characters with initial caps (i.e., Filename.doc).
  The setting of this option is a matter of personal taste. Windows 98 does
  not distinguish between uppercase and lowercase letters. It sees
  FILENAME.DOC as being the same file as Filename.doc.

- *Do not show hidden or system files*   Some files are used only by the
  operating system and are normally marked as hidden and system. If you
  enable this option, you won't see the hidden and system files. This is
  appropriate if someone might accidentally delete the files, but we are going
  to make changes to some hidden files later in this chapter, so for now,
  enable the Show all files option described next.

- *Do not show hidden files*   See previous option.

- *Show all files*   When this option is enabled, all files will be visible in folder
  windows. Enable this option for now in order to make changes described at
  the end of this chapter, but later you can enable *"Do not show hidden or
  system files"* to protect these files from accidents.

- *Hide icons when desktop is viewed as Web page*   The Active Desktop can be
  turned on or off at will. If you prefer to have the Active Desktop on all the
  time, disable this option so you can work with the normal Desktop at the

same time. If you like to turn Active Desktop on and off, enable this option so the Desktop icons disappear while you're viewing the Active Desktop.

- *Smooth edges of screen fonts*   Enable this option to make screen fonts appear smoother (jagged edges are filled in). However, doing so may affect the performance of your system. Your decision about the setting of this option will depend on the speed of your system. Try it both ways.

- *Show window contents while dragging*   You set this option for aesthetic reasons. When enabled, the full contents of a window appear as you move the window. When disabled, only an empty frame appears while dragging the window.

Add Folders to Favorites

Favorites is a list of places you like to visit on the Internet, on your local computer, and on your company's intranet. When you click a Favorite, the window quickly displays the contents of the favorite location. If it is a Web site, you see a Web page. If it is a folder on your own computer, you see a list of files in that folder. The Favorites menu for a folder window is pictured here:

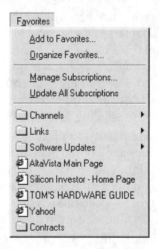

Notice the Web favorites such as AltaVista and Yahoo! More important to this discussion, notice the folder at the bottom called Contracts. When I click

Contracts, the contents of a folder on my own computer called Contracts appear in the current folder window. You can add your own folders to the Favorites list to gain instant access to the folders.

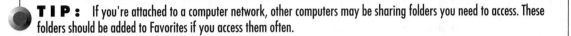

T I P : If you're attached to a computer network, other computers may be sharing folders you need to access. These folders should be added to Favorites if you access them often.

You can add your own folders to the Favorites list as follows:

1. Open the folder that you want to add to Favorites. It can be anywhere on your own computer or on a network computer.

2. Open the Favorites menu in the folder window and choose Add to Favorites. The following dialog box appears:

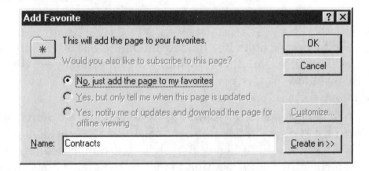

3. The name of the folder appears in the Name field. Optionally, you can type a new name or some descriptive text in the Name field, then click OK to create the new favorite selection.

Open the Favorites menu again to see the new selection. The Favorites menu has an option called Organize Favorites. You can click this option to add, remove, or move Favorites. An easy way to remove a Favorite from the menu is to simply right-click it and choose Delete from the shortcut menu.

• Setting Folder Browse Options

When you open the My Computer window, it appears on the Desktop with a view of file system objects. You can browse through folders using one of the methods illustrated here:

The contents of the selected drive or folder appear in the existing window.

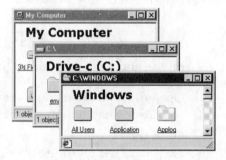

The contents of the selected drive or folder appear in new overlapping windows.

Some people don't like the second option because it tends to clutter the Desktop with a lot of folder windows. The advantage of the second option is that windows you've opened stay open in case you want to copy or move files among them or open other folders.

To choose one of these browse options, click the Start button, then select Settings | Folder Options. When the Folder Options dialog box appears as shown on the left in Figure 8-4, click "Custom, based on settings you choose," then click the Settings button to display the dialog box on the right.

In the "Browse folders as follows" field, choose the option you want. The first option displays new folders in the currently open window and the second option opens new windows as you browse.

• Configuring Web View Features for Folders

Because Web features are integrated into Windows 98, folder windows have most of the same features as Internet Explorer and can be used to view either local files or Web content. For example, you can open a folder window to look at local files, then type a Web address into the Address field and quickly view information on the Internet. Then you can click the Back button to jump back to your local file system.

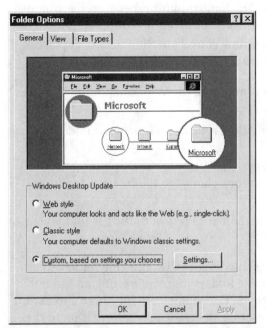 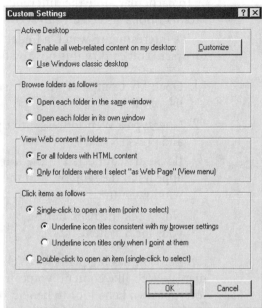

FIGURE 8-4 | Setting folder options

The Windows 98 user interface knows what type of information is being displayed in the window and changes the toolbar options on the window to match. For example, in the following illustration, the top image is a folder window showing a view of Drive C. The bottom image is the same window after typing a Web address in the Address field. Basically, the window has converted to Internet Explorer. However, you can click the Back button to return to the file view as seen in the top window.

Folder window viewing Drive C

Same window after typing in a Web address

In particular, note the difference in the toolbar buttons between the windows. Menu options also change to accommodate the current window content.

It's interesting to watch a folder window convert to the Internet Explorer browser. You can try this now by following these steps:

1. Open My Computer, then Drive C and then the Windows folder. You see a list of files.

2. Now type a Web address into the Address field, such as **home.microsoft.com** and press ENTER.

   If you are connected to the Internet, the Web page at this Internet address appears in the window and the buttons change to the Internet Explorer window buttons.

3. Now click the Back button on the toolbar to return to the file folder view on your local system.

Microsoft has big plans for Web-enabled folders. By allowing folders to display Web-like content, you can make folders more interesting and useful for your own benefit or to benefit others. For example, if you share a folder on your computer with other network users, you can display information in the folder about its contents or include hyperlink buttons that display files in a Web browser or ask users if they want to copy the file to their systems. The next section shows you how to customize folders in this way. You can also use editors like FrontPage Express to create HTML Web pages for folders, as discussed in Chapter 16.

Enabling Web View for Folders

The ability to enable Web views in folders is one of the best new features in Windows 98. When Web view is set for a folder, Web content (HTML, ActiveX controls, Java applets, and scripts) can appear in that folder. To see how Web View works, follow these steps:

1. Open My Computer.

2. Enable the option called "as Web Page" on the View menu (it may already be enabled).

Putting It To Work

With Web view still enabled, you can point at files in a folder and see an image of the files' contents on the left side of the folder. You can try this now by working with the collection of Paint files that comes with Windows 98. These files are located in the Windows directory.

Try this:

1. Open My Computer, then Drive C, and the Windows folder.
2. If the files don't appear right away, click "Show Files" in the left pane (this is a protective feature).
3. On the View menu, choose Arrange Icons, then By Type on the cascading menu to arrange all the Paint files together.
4. Scroll down or right until you see the Paint files with the BMP extension (clouds.bmp, forest.bmp., etc.)
5. Point at any of these files, but don't click. An image of the file appears in the left pane.

Most graphics, text, and Web files can be viewed in this way. For example, locate the files with the GIF extension in the Windows folder such as cloud.gif, content.fig, and hlpbell.gif, then view them using this technique.

3. Point to an object to see information about the object in the left window pane as shown here.

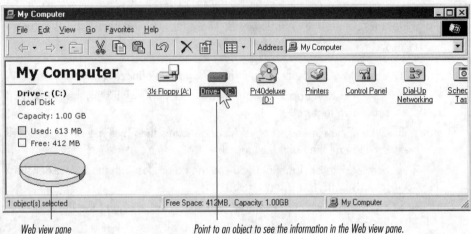

Web view pane

Point to an object to see the information in the Web view pane.

The window may display the contents of certain types of files in the left pane when you point to them. For the remainder of this chapter, make sure the "as Web Page" option is enabled.

If you want to see the Web view in all folder windows, you can set the Web view option on the Custom Settings dialog box pictured previously in Figure 8-4. Follow these steps:

1. Click Start, then choose Settings | Folder Options.
2. Click the Custom option as shown in Figure 8-4 and click the Settings button.
3. In the "View Web content in folders" field, choose the option called "For all folders with HTML content" and click OK to close the windows.

Now all of your folders will be Web view-enabled by default.

Customizing Folders with Web Content

It's easy to customize folders with HTML content, as you'll see. You can add HTML to spruce up a folder to suit your own taste, to provide information about files for your own future reference, or to provide other people with file information.

If your Windows 98 computer is attached to a company network, you can share a specific folder on your computer with other people on the network. When they access the folder, they can open and/or download the files you have shared. For example, assume you organize a company golf tournament and you want to share information about the tournament. You can create a folder called Golf and share it on the network. Then you can add files related to the golf tournament that other people can access. You can even add HTML content so your shared folder appears to other people just like a Web page on the Internet.

The following illustration shows a "normal" shared folder that lists four files that other users on the network can open or copy to their own system. It's really not a very exciting view and people might have trouble trying to figure out what the files are since the file names are not very descriptive.

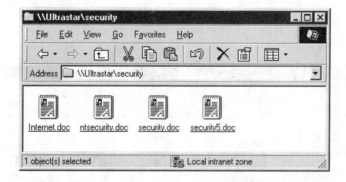

Figure 8-5 shows the same shared folder after it has been spruced up with HTML. Look closely at the toolbar—this is a folder, not Internet Explorer! Instead of the dull and boring icons with eight-character filenames, it has a description of each file and a hyperlink that users click to open or download the files. Best of all, it contains a picture so coworkers can associate the page with its author. The window even has hyperlinks to favorite Web sites.

One of the most important reasons for adding HTML content to a folder is to provide information to other people. This might be someone who sits down at your computer, but more likely, it is someone on your company's network who accesses a folder you have shared on your computer.

You can put hyperlinks in your shared folders that do any of the following:

- Open another folder or a personal Web page.
- Open a file for viewing. The file opens in the folder window.
- Download a file to the user's computer. In this case, a dialog box appears similar to the following that asks the user if they want to save the file on their computer.

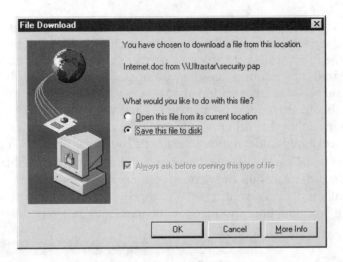

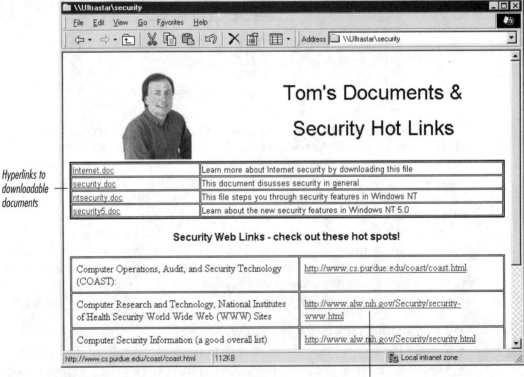

Hyperlinks to downloadable documents

Web links

FIGURE 8-5 An HTML-enhanced shared folder

Keep in mind that you are basically setting up a Web site on your computer that other users can access to get information you publish. You might want to use a combination of all the above methods to provide this information. You can include hyperlinks to other folders or HTML pages that contain information about yourself and projects you are working on, or you might just want to display a list of files that people can open or download as shown in Figure 8-6. Basically, by sharing HTML-customized folders, you can provide many of the same services as a professional Web server.

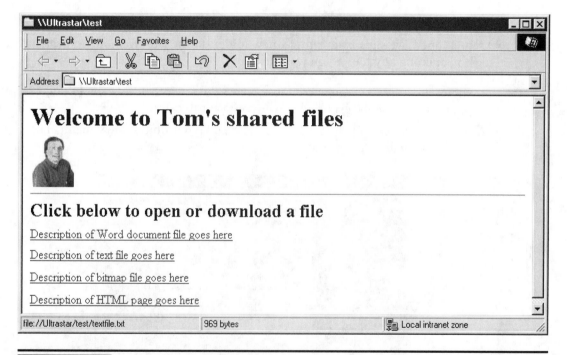

FIGURE 8-6 Sample HTML folder window

Creating a Basic HTML File Listing

In this section, we show you how to create a very simple but useful HTML file to display files in a folder. You can use Notepad to create it. This will be a very simple exercise that won't require a lot of typing on your part. Then you can expand on the ideas presented here. Note that you can also create Web pages with FrontPage Express, as explained in Chapter 16.

The steps we'll go through are outlined here:

- Create a new folder and enable it to display HTML.
- Create the HTML file that will display information in the folder.
- Share the folder so other network users can access it.

The following exercise has you create a new folder on the Desktop and add some dummy files so you can quickly test these techniques. However, you can just as well apply these techniques to any folder on your system that contains files you want to share.

Enabling HTML in a Folder

As mentioned, we start by creating a new folder on the Desktop, but you can start by opening any folder you want to work with.

1. Right-click the Desktop and choose New | Folder. When the new folder appears, rename it Test or whatever you want to call it.

2. Open the folder and choose Customize this Folder on the View menu. The following dialog box appears:

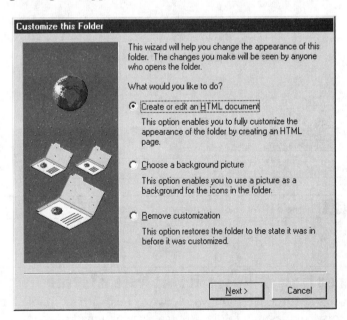

3. Choose Create or edit an HTML document and click the Next button. Some instructions appear on the next box and you can click Next again to continue.

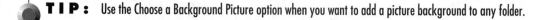

TIP: Use the Choose a Background Picture option when you want to add a picture background to any folder.

A Notepad window appears with some HTML code already defined. This code is what enables the two-pane folder windows that display information about objects in the left pane.

4. We're not going to use this code, so close the Notepad window and click the Finish button on the Customize this Folder dialog box.

At this point, you should see two new files in the folder called DESKTOP.INI and FOLDER.HTT. If you don't see these files, choose Folder Options from the View menu, then click the View tab and enable the Show all files option.

5. Now delete the file called FOLDER.HTT. As mentioned, we're not going to use it. We're going to create a new custom file called FOLDER.HTT.

Create a New FOLDER.HTT File

Now you can create a new FOLDER.HTT file for the folder. Figure 8-6 illustrates how this folder will appear to other users who access this folder over the network.

Of course, you can insert your own picture and create your own file descriptions. You should consider the file you create here as a template that you can use for other folders. If you are not familiar with HTML, consider this section a quick introduction to writing HTML code.

Note that some of the text in this listing should be replaced with your own text. For example, put your own name in the third line and put your own descriptions in the seventh through tenth lines.

1. Right-click a blank area in the Test folder window, then choose New and Text Document. When the icon appears, type **FOLDER.HTT** and press ENTER to rename it.

2. Double-click the new file and type in the HTML code shown here:

```
<HTML>
<BODY>
<H1>Welcome to Tom's shared files</H1>
<p><img src="photo.gif"></p>
<HR>
<H2>Click below to open or download a file</H2>
<P><A HREF="Wordfile.doc">Description of Word document file goes here</A></P>
<P><A HREF="textfile.txt">Description of text file goes here</A></P>
<P><A HREF="picture.bmp">Description of bitmap file goes here</A></P>
<P><A HREF="page2.htm">Description of HTML page goes here</A></P>
</BODY>
</HTML>
```

3. Choose Save on the File menu to save the file, then close the Notepad window.

4. On the Folder menu, choose View | as Web Page to activate the new code.

The last step should display a Web page similar to Figure 8-6, but with an X box where the picture should be. That is because you need to add a file into the folder called PHOTO.GIF. If you have a scanner and scanning software, you are in luck. Just scan the image, crop and edit it any way you like, then save the image with the filename PHOTO.GIF in the Test folder. If you don't have access to a scanner, have your local copy shop do it for you, or substitute some other image for now. You can use Find to search your system for GIF files. You're bound to find some, especially if you've been browsing the Internet.

Now we'll give you a brief overview of the HTML code. For more detailed information about HTML, refer to any of the HTML-specific books on the market.

The first two lines and the last two lines set up the HTML page. The third line is the title that you can change to fit your needs. The fourth line inserts the picture. Replace "photo.gif" with the name of any picture you like or just remove it if you don't want a picture.

The code <HR> in the fifth line inserts a horizontal line, and the sixth line is the instructional sentence on how to open or download a file. The next few lines are hyperlinks to files or other HTML pages. The name of the linked files appears between the quotes and the description follows. You can change any of these to fit your needs.

Note the last hyperlink. It opens another HTML page called PAGE2.HTM. You can create this second HTML page in your folder by following these steps:

1. Right-click a blank area in the Test folder window, then choose New and Text Document. When the icon appears, type **PAGE2.HTM** and press ENTER to rename it.

2. Double-click the new file and type in the following HTML code, replacing the comments with your own text. Type in as much text as you want. The eighth line is hyperlink that returns to the original page.

```
<HTML>
<BODY>
<H1>Put your title here </H1>
<HR>
<P>Type paragraph text here. </P>
<P>Type more paragraph text here. </P>
<HR><BR>
<P><A HREF="folder.htt">Return to top</A></P>
</BODY>
</HTML>
```

3. Choose Save on the File menu to save the file, then close the Notepad window.

Now you're ready to test your changes, as outlined in the next section.

Testing the New Folder

Test your new Web page by opening the folder. If icons are showing, choose View | as Web Page. You can switch back to icon view by choosing Large Icons on the View menu. You'll need to switch back to this view to add new files or make other file system changes.

If you created the hyperlinked HTML file in the last three steps, click the hyperlink on the main folder window. The hyperlinked page should appear. Click Return to top to return to the main folder window.

If you've made it this far, you can congratulate yourself. What you have done is create the beginning of a Web site without any special Web server software.

Editing FOLDER.HTT

You'll probably want to edit FOLDER.HTT periodically to add new file listings or change the files that are listed.

1. First, open the folder and then choose Large Icons on the View menu to view icons on the page instead of HTML.

2. Now open Notepad and drag the file to edit into its document area.

3. Make the changes and save the file.

Notepad is a good editor for these short simple files. Notepad may be an option on the Send To menu. If so, right-click FOLDER.HTT and choose Send To, then Notepad to open the file in Notepad. If not, refer to "The Send To Option" in Chapter 4 for instructions on how to add Notepad to the Send To option.

Sharing the Folder

Once your HTML-enabled folder is ready for public presentation, you can share it with other network users. Right-click the icon for the folder and choose Sharing (if the folder is already open, right-click the icon in the upper-left corner of the window). One of the following Properties dialog boxes will appear where you can set sharing options.

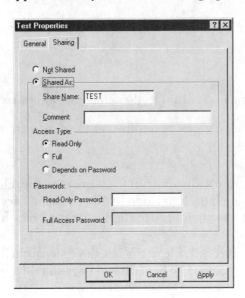 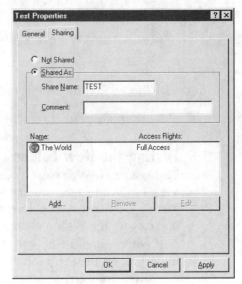

The left box typically appears if your network is small and local. The right box appears if your network is connected to a Windows NT Server that keeps track of user accounts.

- If you see the left box, click Shared As, then click Read-Only and OK.
- If you see the right box, click Shared As, then click the Add button. A dialog box appears where you choose to let everybody access the folder by selecting The World or where you can select specific users. After clicking The World or a user, click the Read Only button. Click OK when done.

Now you should be able to call other users and let them know that you have a shared folder. Other Windows users can then find your shared folder by opening Network Neighborhood and locating your computer.

You'll learn more about networking in Chapter 11.

File Systems: Local and Network

The Windows 98 File System

It's important that you learn about the Windows filing system and how to manage it. You've already learned some basic concepts by simply working with folders and files in previous chapters. This chapter shows you detailed filenaming and file organization techniques to help you master your filing system.

· File System Hierarchy

Computer systems are all about storing and retrieving digital information on disk storage devices. You store information in files that have unique filenames, then organize files into folders. A file may hold the text of a letter, spreadsheet information, accounting data, digitized photos, recorded voice message, and so on. A typical file system may hold thousands or even millions of files, so folders are essential to organizing information.

The Windows 98 file system is a hierarchical structure of folders as shown next. Each drive has a set of top-level folders that can contain multiple levels of subfolders. In previous operating systems like DOS (Disk Operating System), folders were called directories and subfolders were called subdirectories. The terms are still used interchangeably today.

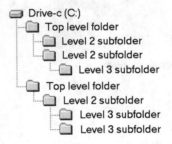

A default folder hierarchy is created on your hard drive when Windows 98 is installed. This hierarchy is pictured in Figure 9-1. The folders called My Documents, Program Files, and Windows are at the *root* level of the disk drive. Other folders branch from these default folders.

Note that we are not showing all the subfolders within Program Files and Windows, only the most important or interesting folders. For example, the Media folder under Windows has some interesting multimedia files you can play. The folder called Temporary Internet Files is a buffer that holds information downloaded from Web pages.

TIP: Windows Explorer is the best tool to use to "explore" the folder hierarchy of your system.

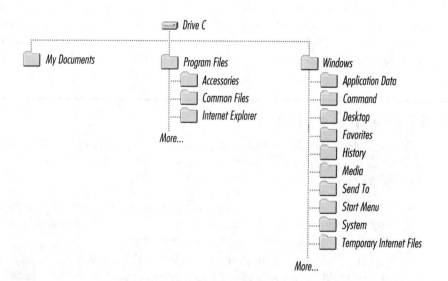

FIGURE 9-1 | Initial folder hierarchy (not all subfolders shown)

Organizing Folders

We've mentioned before that it is a good idea to come up with a folder hierarchy of your own that fits your needs. Don't rename or remove any of the default root-level folders previously described, however.

Use the My Documents folder as a starting place for building your own folder hierarchy. Most Windows applications will suggest that you save files in this folder. The Program Files folder is the usual place where program files are stored when you install new programs.

Create a folder hierarchy that fits your needs. For example, you could create a folder called Personal and a folder called Business within My Documents. Then you could create folders within these folders that hold files related to family matters, special projects, and so on.

Organizing files into specific folders makes backing up files a snap. You can copy an entire folder to a floppy disk (if it will fit), or to another drive in your computer. We now prefer to back up our files to CD-R (Compact Disc Recordable) instead of traditional backup media like magnetic tape. CD-R drives are now very inexpensive and also very convenient. If your computer breaks down, you can take your CD-R disks to any other Windows computer that has a CD-ROM drive and access the files. That way, you're not out of business while your computer is being repaired.

File System Basics

Files contain information like text, graphics, and numeric data. You initially create files in computer memory, then save them to disk. Follow these guidelines as you work with files in Windows 98:

- Files within the same folder cannot have the same name. If you try to move or copy a file into a folder that already has a file with that name, Windows 98 will ask if you want to replace the existing file.

- Copying and moving files are two different things. When you copy a file, the original file remains intact and a copy is made in the new location you specify. Moving a file removes it from its original location and puts it in the new location you specify.

- Deleted files can be *recovered* by opening the Recycle Bin. This is useful if you accidentally delete a file. However, as the Recycle Bin gets full, the oldest files in it are removed and are no longer recoverable. You can adjust the size of the Recycle Bin as a percentage of the drive space. The Recycle Bin is discussed in Chapter 10.

- Moving and deleting files that belong to programs may prevent the program from starting. While you can move your own documents, moving or renaming program files and folders is not a good idea. You may need to reinstall a program if you need to move it to another location.

- Windows 98 supports 256 character filenames and upper- and lowercase characters. You can create descriptive filenames like "CONTRACT REVISION FOR PROJECT X."

- The drive and folder location of a file is important. In some cases, you will need to tell a program or a user where a file is located by describing its path. A *path* is the name of the drive, folder, and subfolders where a file "lives," as explained next.

Types of Files

Now lets look at the types of files that you are likely to encounter while exploring your file system.

Program Files

Program files contain computer-readable code written by programmers. If you viewed a program file, you would see a garbled set of characters that make no sense to you, but make a lot of sense to your computer. Program files have the filename extension COM or EXE. When you click a program file, the program starts up. Program icons are usually somewhat descriptive as you can see here:

Calc.exe   Cdplayer.exe   Defrag.exe   Explorer   Freecell.exe   Hwinfo.exe   Ftp.exe

Support Files

Some programs store information in auxiliary *support files*, but these files don't start any program. Common support files have the extensions INI (initialization file), CFG (configuration), DAT (configuration data), DLL (dynamic link library), BIN (binary), OVL (overlay), SYS (system), and DRV (driver). Some typical support files are shown here:

Control.ini   Ctpnp.cfg   Oplimit.dat   Snmpapi.dll   W98setup.bin

Text Files

Text files contain readable, alphanumeric characters that typically comply to the ASCII (American Standard Code for Information Interchange) format. Such files have readable text that is accessible by a wide range of programs, even programs that run on non-Windows computers. That means you can share them with other users. Note that some text files may contain unreadable control codes before or after the actual text. These control codes define text formatting and other features. Here are examples of text file icons:

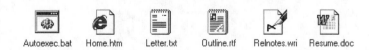

Autoexec.bat   Home.htm   Letter.txt   Outline.rtf   Relnotes.wri   Resume.doc

Graphics Files

Graphics files contain visual or graphic information. A *bitmap graphic file* contains the actual dot information you see on your screen. You can create bitmap files with Paint. Bitmap files have the BMP extension. Scanned images may also contain bitmap images. In contrast to bitmap files, *vector graphics files* contain the actual series of commands to recreate the image. Some examples of graphics files are listed here:

Paint1.bmp   Paint2.bmp   Kodak.dcx   Photo.jpg

Multimedia Files

Multimedia files hold sound and video information in digital form. Common icons are shown below. The file with the MID extension is a MIDI (Musical Instrument Digital Interface) file that holds instructions for playing a song on a MIDI-compatible sound board or device. The file with the MPG extension is a movie file, and the file with the WAV extension is a sound file.

Music.mid   Movie.mpg   Sound.wav

Other Data Files

Data files contain numbers, names and addresses, and other information created by database and spreadsheet programs. The most popular data file formats are readable by a variety of different programs.

Using Find to Locate Files by Type

You can use the Find command to locate files on your system by type of file. Click Start, then choose Find | Files and Folders. When the Find dialog box appears, click the Advanced tab, then click the down arrow button in the Of type field. You see a dialog box similar to this:

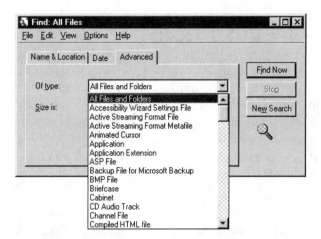

Choose the type of file you want to locate and click Find. Note that this method searches files by association. More than one type of filename extension may be associated with a particular type of application. For example, searching for movie clips will find files that have the filename extensions MPG, MP2, MPE, MPEG, and M1VM. File associations are discussed further in Chapter 10.

DOS Filenaming Conventions

Once you understand filenaming conventions and filenaming strategies, you are well on your way to mastering Windows 98. Windows 98 supports the filenaming conventions used in DOS and previous versions of Windows, and also supports the long filenaming conventions in which you can create filenames up to 256 characters long that are very descriptive.

TIP: Even though DOS filenaming conventions are becoming outdated, they are still used. If you still run older applications, you might need to deal with such files on your own system or you might need to create files for use on systems that only support DOS filenaming conventions.

8 + 3 = DOS Filename

A DOS filename is limited to a maximum of eight characters for the filename and three characters for the filename extension. This calls for special filenaming strategies since you're limited in the number of characters you can use. While filenaming strategies are less important in Windows 98 (since you can name files with up to 256 characters), it's still a good idea to learn about filenaming strategies because they can help you organize your files.

Here's an example of a DOS filename with an eight-character name and a three-character extension:

NEWSINFO.TXT

Of course, you can use fewer characters in the name and extension if you like. If you type more than the supported number of characters, the extra characters will be removed if copied to a DOS system.

Paths for Filenames

Another important aspect of a filename is its location, or path. In DOS, a path specifies the drive and directory (folder in Windows) where a file exists. For example, if the NEWSINFO.TXT file is in the RESEARCH folder on drive D, its complete path is

D:\RESEARCH\NEWSINFO.TXT

The backslashes separate the folder and filename information, and a colon always follows the drive letter. If you're working in one folder and you want to access a file in another folder, you'll need to specify its path. Fortunately, this is easy in Windows 98 because you do so by browsing with a dialog box, but if you're working at the DOS level, you'll need to type a path like the one pictured previously.

Filename Extensions

The filename extension associates a file with a particular application and also gives you a good idea of the file's general contents.

Note that filename extensions are hidden by default in folder windows and Windows Explorer. If you want to see filename extensions, choose Folder Options from the View menu, then click the View tab and disable the option called Hide file extensions for known file types.

Table 9-1 lists some commonly used filename extensions. Most programs automatically add an extension when you save a file, unless you specifically type a different extension.

FILENAME EXTENSION	DESCRIPTION
AVI	Audio Video Interleave file
BAK	A backup file automatically created by some applications when you edit a file
BAT	Batch file used in the MS-DOS environment to automate routines
BMP	Bitmapped file created in Windows 98 Paint or other program
COM	Command file (executable program file)
DAT	A generic extension for files that contain data in some form
DLL	Dynamic Link Library file (program file)
DOC	Document file
DRV	Driver file (to support printers, modems, etc.)
EXE	Executable program file
FON	Font file
GIF	Graphic Image file
HLP	Help file
HTM or HTML	HyperText Markup file (a Web file)
HTT	HyperText Template
INF	Information file
JPG or JPEG	JPEG image file
MID	MIDI (Musical Instrument Digital Interface) file
MMF	Microsoft Mail file
MPG or MPEG	MPEG graphic image file
RTF	Rich Text Format (a standard for formatting text documents)
SCR	Screen saver file
TTF	True Type Font file

TABLE 9-1 Some of the most common filename extensions

FILENAME EXTENSION	DESCRIPTION
TXT	Text file
WAV	Wave file created by Sound Recorder or other sound application

TABLE 9-1 Some of the most common filename extensions (*continued*)

TIP: Filename extensions are useful when listing files. When files are listed by extension, you see all the program files grouped together, and all the document files grouped into categories related to the applications that created them.

Try the following example to see how filename extensions can be used to organize file listings.

1. Open the Windows folder by clicking My Computer, then Drive C, and Windows. If Web View is enabled, click Show Files under the warning message.

2. On the View menu, choose Arrange Icons | by Type.

3. Now choose Details on the View menu.

4. Scan through the list and notice that all files with the same extension are listed together.

Arranging files by extension is useful when you're looking for specific types of files or when you want to select a group of files and copy them to another drive or delete them.

DOS Filenaming Strategies

This section describes a filenaming strategy you might find useful if you create a lot of similar files with the same application. It is especially suited for the eight-character filename limitation of DOS. If you're using applications that support Windows 98 long filenames, you'll still find this information useful if you are copying files to DOS systems. It also provides background information on filenaming strategies that you can adapt for use with Windows 98 long filenames.

Always create filenames that describe and categorize the contents of the file. Try to create filenames that make sense to you and others. Simple names like

NOTE1.TXT, NOTE2.TXT and NOTE3.TXT are meaningless if you create dozens of notes. You'll soon forget the contents of each file and need to open them to find out what's inside.

Let's consider a filenaming strategy for a set of report files. A name like JANREPRT.TXT certainly indicates that the file is a report for January, but if you have several report files for January, you'll need more specific filenames. Here are some examples that use a filenaming strategy to organize monthly report files created with Microsoft's Excel spreadsheet program. At first, this file list might look intimidating, but if you study it, you'll find it makes a lot of sense and you might want to imitate it for your own file system.

        RA980830.XLS
        RB980830.XLS
        RC980830.XLS
        RA980928.XLS
        RB980928.XLS
        RC980928.XLS

The *R* designates that the files are reports. Budget files might start with *B*. The second letter indicates reports for departments *A*, *B*, and *C*. The remainder describes the reporting year, month, and day. The filename extension XLS is added by Microsoft Excel. We'll work more with these example files in a moment.

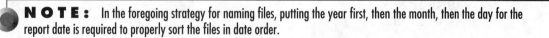

N O T E : In the foregoing strategy for naming files, putting the year first, then the month, then the day for the report date is required to properly sort the files in date order.

Listing Files with Wildcards

There are different methods you can use to list files. When files follow a common filenaming strategy like that previously described, you can narrow down file listings so that only files you might be interest in are displayed. You can then quickly locate the exact file or files you want to open, copy, move, or delete.

Wildcard characters help you narrow file lists. They are characters you can use as substitutes for any letter or group of letters when specifying filenames, as follows:

- The asterisk (*) substitutes for any set of characters.
- The question mark (?) substitutes for any single character.

T I P : You can also use wildcard characters when working with Windows 98 browse dialog boxes and when working with the Windows 98 Explorer.

Here's an example of using the asterisk character when listing the report files described in the previous section. Let's say you start Microsoft Excel and choose the Open option on its File menu. The following dialog box appears:

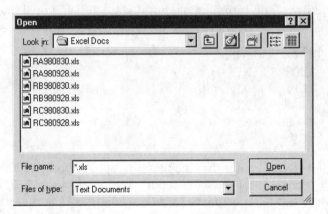

If we type **RA*.*** in the File name field and press ENTER, only these files are listed in the file window:

    RA980830.XLS
    RA980928.XLS

If we type **R???08*.*** in the File name field and press ENTER, only these files are listed:

    RA980830.XLS
    RB980830.XLS
    RC980830.XLS

Finally, if we type **RA??08*.*** and press ENTER, only this file is listed:

    RA980830.XLS

Of course, this strategy works best when there are many more files than the six examples shown here. Notice how the question mark serves as a placemarker; that is, any character may occupy its position. The asterisk, on the other hand, is used to represent any *group* of characters in the filename or the extension.

Windows 98 Filenaming Conventions

Windows 98 allows filenames of up to 256 characters in length. Applications designed for Windows 98 can access and save files with long filenames. Older DOS and Windows applications can still access the files, but the filenames are truncated to the eight-character filename, three-character extension format. You'll need to keep this conversion in mind when copying files to DOS systems.

Here are the filenaming rules for Windows 98:

- You can have a maximum of 256 characters in file and folder names.
- You can use multiple period-separated extensions, if necessary, to create filenames like the following:

    REPORT.SALES.SMITH.JUNE98

- Names cannot include these symbols:

    ? \ * " < > |

- Windows 98 preserves the uppercase/lowercase format of the name you specify but does not use case to distinguish between filenames. For example, *Myfile.doc* and *MYFILE.DOC* are considered to be the same filename by Windows 98.
- You can use wildcard characters (? and *) when searching for and listing filenames.

Folder View Settings for Files

You may need to change the Advanced Setting on the Folder Options dialog box before continuing. Click the Start button, then choose Settings | Folder Options. When the Folder Options dialog box appears, click the View tab. Set the following options on the dialog box:

- Enable "Display the full path in the title bar."
- Disable "Hide file extensions for known file types."
- Enable "Allow all uppercase names."

How Windows 98 Long Names Are Sliced into Short DOS Names

Table 9-2 shows 11 Windows 98 file or folder names. You can use these as examples for your own filenames. The right column lists the conversion of the Windows 98 long filename to the DOS filenaming convention (eight-character filename, three-character extension).

WINDOWS 98 FILENAME	DOS CONVERSION
REPORTS.SALES.SMITH.JUN98	REPORT~1.JUN
REPORTS.SALES.SMITH.JUL98	REPORT~1.JUL
REPORTS.SALES.SMITH.AUG98	REPORT~1.AUG
REPORTS.SALES.JONES.JUN98	REPORT~2.JUN
REPORTS.SALES.JONES.JUL98	REPORT~2.JUL
REPORTS.SALES.JONES.AUG98	REPORT~2.AUG
ThisIsALongFileName	THISIS~1
ThisIsALongFileName.TXT	THISIS~1.TXT
Lecture notes on history conference	LECTUR~1
Cairo conference notes	CAIROC~1
My Documents folder	MYDOCU~1

TABLE 9-2 Windows 98 file conversion to DOS filenames

Notice that the first six Windows 98 names use periods to separate the long filenames into four parts. Study the DOS conversion of these filenames.

- In the first three examples, the first six characters of the long filename are used in the DOS filename and ~1 is added to the end. Windows 98 then assigns an extension using the first three characters after the last period in the long filename.
- In the fourth through sixth long filenames on the list, the first six characters are used and ~2 is added to the end in order to avoid duplicating the DOS filenames. If another set of files with similar long filenames existed, it would increment the number at the end, so you would see DOS filenames like REPORT~3.JUN and REPORT~4.JUN.
- In the last five long filenames, notice how Windows 98 allowed uppercase and lowercase characters, but the DOS filename equivalents were converted to uppercase. Also notice how Windows 98 handles period separators and spaces. Periods are used to separate filenames and extensions, as seen in the DOS filename THISISAL.TXT. Spaces are dropped, as seen in the last three examples.

If you're working in a DOS application and you need to access a Windows 98 folder that has spaces in its filename, just drop the spaces and specify only the first eight characters of the filename.

N O T E : Be sure to take filename conversion techniques into consideration if you plan to move Windows 98 files to a DOS computer.

Filenaming Strategies for Long Filenames

The filenames you see in the previous list illustrate a practical way to name your own files, assuming you plan to keep them on your Windows 98 system. You can use the period separator in place of a space, but the period is much more than that. The period separates different parts of the filename to help you create a filenaming strategy to fit your own needs or those that your company has dictated.

The first six filenames have four "subnames," each separated by periods. The first subname describes the type of file—in this case REPORTS. The second component describes the type of reports—SALES. The third component holds the name of the person for whom the report was written. The last component holds the date for the file. You might create a fifth component for a filename extension to describe the program used to create the file, such as XLS (Excel) or DOC (Word for Windows).

The period separators are critical when it comes to listing files. If you open a Browse dialog box as pictured next, you can use wildcard characters (* and ?) to list specific files. In this example, we typed **REP*** in the File name field to list all the files that have the first three characters REP.

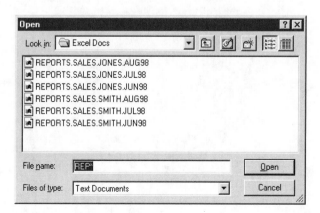

If we had typed **REPORTS.*.JONES.*** in the File name field, we would get this listing, which shows all the report files for Jones instead of Smith and Jones:

    REPORTS.SALES.JONES.AUG98
    REPORTS.SALES.JONES.JUL98
    REPORTS.SALES.JONES.JUN98

To see all the report files for August of 1998, type **REPORTS.SALES.*.AUG98**, or just *AUG98 and see this listing:

    REPORTS.SALES.JONES.AUG98
    REPORTS.SALES.SMITH.AUG98

As an example of using the question mark wildcard character, you could type ***.JONES.???98**. The Browse window would then show any file for Jones in 1998.

In the next chapter, you'll learn more about the file system and how to implement the filenaming strategies you learned here.

10

Working with the Windows 98 File System

This chapter helps you explore the Windows 98 file system further by working with folder windows and the Windows Explorer. First, we cover creating, copying, and moving files. Then we cover folders and drives. In later sections, you learn advanced techniques for using the Find command to locate files and managing and recovering deleted files.

Windows Explorer

You've already worked with Windows Explorer in previous chapters and you've been introduced to many of its features. You'll use it extensively in your day-to-day activities to manage your file system. We recap its features here and show you some additional tips and tricks.

Recall that you can open Windows Explorer in the following ways:

- Click the Start button, then choose Programs | Windows Explorer.
- From the Desktop, right-click My Computer and choose Explore.
- In any My Computer window, choose Explore from the File menu.
- Right-click any folder and choose Explore. Windows Explorer opens with a view of the selected folder.
- If you have a keyboard with a WINDOWS key (under the Z), press it and E at the same time.

If you haven't already done so, we also recommend adding Windows Explorer to your Quick Launch toolbar so it is always easily accessible. Click Start | Programs, then right-click and drag the Windows Explorer option to the Quick Launch toolbar and choose Create Shortcut(s) Here from the shortcut menu.

Start Windows Explorer now. Refer to Figure 10-1 and try some of these basic steps to become more familiar with Windows Explorer.

The most important feature of Explorer is that it simplifies copying and moving objects between drives and folders, as you'll see later. The basic procedure is simple: you select a drive or folder in the left pane to display its files in the right pane. This view of files stays intact while you scroll in the left pane to locate a destination drive or folder. Once the folder is in view, you click and drag files from the right pane to the destination drive or folder in the left pane.

Working with Files

Files are the basic unit of information storage with Windows 98 and most operating systems. This section explains how to work with files in general, how to copy and move files using various mouse and keyboard techniques, and how to use special tricks for managing files.

Click + to expand subfolders.   Files in right pane belong to the open folder.

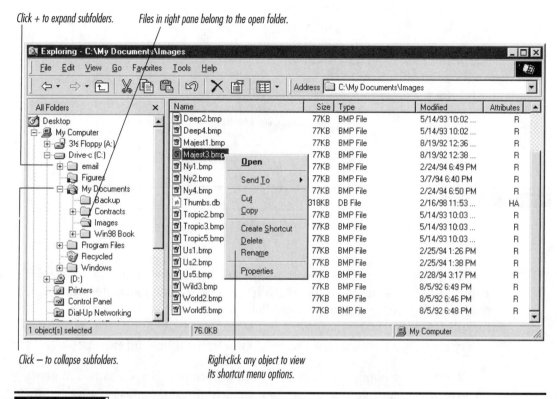

Click – to collapse subfolders.   Right-click any object to view
its shortcut menu options.

FIGURE 10-1 | Windows Explorer

Creating Files

Normally, you create new files while working in your applications as follows:

- Open the application and choose New from its File menu.
- Open an existing document and save it with a new name by choosing Save As from the File menu.

Another way to create new documents is to right-click in any folder and choose the New option. A menu appears (similar to the one shown in Figure 10-2) where you can choose the type of document to create.

The file options that appear on this menu will depend on the type of applications you have installed on your computer. Text documents are

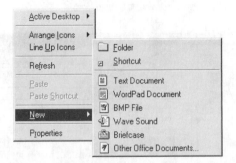

FIGURE 10-2 Creating new files

normally associated with Notepad, bitmapped files are normally associated with Paint, and wave sound files are normally associated with Sound Recorder. You may see other options on this menu. For example, if Microsoft Word is installed, you will see "Microsoft Word Document."

Try creating a new file now that you'll use in the following exercises:

1. Right-click a blank part of the Desktop and choose New | Text Document.
2. When the new object appears, its name will be highlighted. Rename it by typing **TEST.TXT** and pressing ENTER.

TEST.TXT now appears on your Desktop as an icon. The file is empty at this point and it won't need any text for the following exercises.

Creating Files via Duplication

You can also create new files by duplicating existing files. The contents of the existing file are copied to the new file and you can edit the contents in any way you like. Here's how to duplicate a file using copy and paste techniques:

1. Right-click the file you want to duplicate and choose Copy on the shortcut menu.
2. Locate the folder where you want to copy the file.
3. Right-click the destination folder (or a blank area in the folder if it is open) and choose Paste.

This procedure puts a copy of the file on the Clipboard and holds it so you can paste the file elsewhere. As you'll see later, you can select multiple files to copy and paste. Note that you can also "cut" files from their current location and paste them in a new folder, thus moving the files.

Selecting Multiple Files

Most of the time, you will need to copy or move multiple files. This section shows you some tricks for selecting multiple files and then copying or moving them with a single operation.

One trick is to organize your file lists before you start selecting. For example, you could sort by file type to group all your Excel documents together or sort by date to locate all the files created in June.

To group documents in a folder window or in Windows Explorer, choose Details from the View menu, then click the Type button to sort by file type or the Modified button to sort files by date.

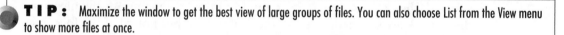

T I P : Maximize the window to get the best view of large groups of files. You can also choose List from the View menu to show more files at once.

Open any folder window and experiment with the following selection techniques, which are also pictured in Figure 10-3. Keep in mind that if Web View is enabled, you only need to point to files you want to select. If it is not enabled, you single-click files to make selections.

- **Select contiguous files.** If you've sorted a list of files, all the files you want to select are in a contiguous row (presumably). Point to or click the first file in the list. It is highlighted. Now hold down the SHIFT key and point to or click the last file in the list. All the files in between are highlighted.

- **Select non-contiguous files.** It may not be possible to select all the files as a contiguous group. To add any file to a selected group, hold down the CTRL key and point to or click the files you want to add.

- **Box them in.** If all the files you want to select are grouped together, click and drag a box around the items with the mouse. When you release the mouse, the items are highlighted.

Once you've selected a group of files, you can right-click anywhere in the highlighted area to open a shortcut menu, then choose Cut, Copy, Delete, Rename, or Properties. You can also click anywhere in the group and drag it to another location. Refer to the next few sections for details.

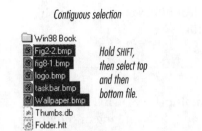 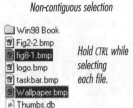 

FIGURE 10-3 | File selection techniques

Experiment with these techniques to become more familiar with how they work. Here are some other selection tricks:

- Choose Select All from the Edit menu to select all the files in the window.
- Create an inverted selection. Start by selecting the files you don't want selected, then choose Invert Selection from the Edit menu. All the files you didn't click are selected. Use this method if most but not all of the files in a list should be selected.

TIP: As mentioned earlier, you can use the Find command to create a list of files based on filenames, creation dates, or other criteria, and then perform operations on those files from within the Find dialog box.

Copying and Moving Files

Now we get into more detail about copying and moving files. At some point, you'll need to put a file in another folder or on another disk. You may want to rearrange the way files are organized into folders or copy and move files to other disks as mentioned earlier. This section will show you a few more tricks for copying and moving files.

TIP: Keep in mind that most of the techniques discussed here can be used to copy folders as well.

Here are the methods you can use to copy and move folders and files:

- **Copy, Cut, and Paste**   Use this technique if drag-and-drop is difficult because the destination is not visible on the Desktop. You copy the files in one window, then go to the other window and paste. You may still need to open windows, but at least you don't need to arrange them on the Desktop like you do with drag-and-drop.

- **Drag-and-Drop**   Use this technique if both the source objects and destination objects are accessible. This is easy to do in Windows Explorer but not so easy on the Desktop because you may need to open and rearrange windows before you can even start dragging and dropping. That's too much trouble to copy a single file, but appropriate if you're rearranging a lot of files.

- **Send To**   When you right-click a file and choose Send To, you can choose to copy an object to a floppy disk or other location.

- **DOS Commands**   Some veterans of DOS prefer copying and moving files by using the COPY and MOVE commands at the MS-DOS prompt. Click Start then choose Programs | MS-DOS Prompt. Refer to a suitable DOS manual for instructions on using these commands, or type COPY /? and MOVE /? at the DOS prompt for instructions.

Copy, Cut, and Paste

You can use the invisible Clipboard to copy and move files to different locations. Cutting translates to moving a file because you are removing it from its current location and pasting it somewhere else.

The basic technique is to right-click a file to copy or cut, then choose Copy or Cut on the menu that appears. Go to the place where you want to copy the file, right-click a blank area, and choose Paste from the menu.

T I P : You can select multiple files for these operations as discussed earlier under "Selecting Multiple Files."

Copying and Moving with Drag-and-Drop

Drag-and-drop is natural and intuitive. So why discuss it further? There are some subtle details that you need to know about. For example, move is the default drag-and-drop action if you are clicking with the left mouse button, but you can change this on the fly to fit your needs. Note the following:

To copy or move on the same drive:

- Left-click and drag to *move* an object (this is the default).
- To force a copy, press CTRL, then left-click and drag.

To copy or move between different drives:

- Left-click and drag an object to *copy* it between drives (just the opposite of what happens when you left-click and drag to the same drive).
- To force a move, hold down the SHIFT key, then left-click and drag.

N O T E : An exception to these rules is when you drag a program file. The default is to create a shortcut in the destination. Moving a program out of its registered location would disable it.

It's easy to forget all these rules, so we recommend that you use the right-click and drag method, which pops up a menu of choices for dispensing with the item(s) you've dragged.

As a side note, there is a reason for the strange behavior when copying and moving files using drag-and-drop as described in the previous list. Windows assumes you never want to copy on the same drive because that would create a lot of duplicate files. Likewise, the default is to move files between drives because Windows assumes you want to make file backups or duplicate files to another disk. Also, for safety reasons, it's not good to delete original files until you are sure they have been successfully copied to another location.

Try experimenting with drag-and-drop to become more familiar with its behavior. Try the following with the TEST.TXT file you created earlier:

1. Click TEST.TXT with the left mouse button (yes, left button) and drag it to the My Documents folder.
2. Release the mouse button to complete the move.

   The file vanishes from the Desktop. *You're not even asked to confirm the operation and you're not shown a menu of different options.* Think about how this could get you into trouble if you drag files to the wrong place by accident. That's why we recommend right-clicking to drag files so you can choose copy or move from the shortcut menu.

3. Open My Documents, and while holding the CTRL key, left-click and drag the file back to the Desktop.

This procedure creates a duplicate. Now you have a file in My Documents and a duplicate on the Desktop. Think about how you would use this technique. For example, if you use templates (documents with prewritten text and/or formatting that you use to create other documents), you could keep all your templates in the same folder, then copy them out of the folder to other folders where you want to create new documents.

Now try this:

4. Repeat step 3 to create another copy of the file on the Desktop.

Ah ha. You see the following dialog box because Windows won't let you create a copy where a file with the same name already exists.

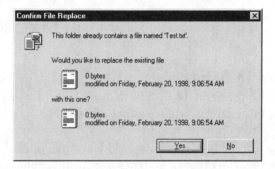

Note that the dialog box contains information about both files. In our example, we're comparing two empty files that were created at the same time, but normally, you'll be able to use the date and size information to decide how to handle the situation. Choose Yes to copy over the existing file or No to cancel the copy operation. Often, you'll try to copy a file and discover that another file with the same name already exists. Just cancel the copy, rename one of the files, and try it again.

Using Drag-and-Drop in Windows Explorer

Windows Explorer provides a unique side-by-side view in which you can select your source files in the right pane and locate the destination in the left pane. The following exercise demonstrates the process by showing you how to copy files in a folder to another folder. The steps outlined next are meant to demonstrate how you can work in Windows Explorer's left and right pane. As always, you can adapt these steps to fit your own needs.

1. Open Windows Explorer, then click + next to Drive C to expand the folder view for that drive.

2. Scroll down the list of folders in the left pane if necessary until you see the Windows folder. Click the + next to the folder.

3. Now scroll down the list further until you see the Media folder.

   If you don't see the Media folder, sound files were not installed at setup, so choose a different folder, such as Fonts or Command. We're just exploring the steps here, so the folder you select doesn't matter.

4. Click the Media folder to select it. A list of files inside the Media folder appears in the right pane.

5. Now scroll the list of files in the right pane until you see the Temp folder.

6. Right-click and drag any file in the right pane to the Temp folder in the left pane and choose Copy Here from the shortcut menu.

A copy of the file now exists in the Temp folder. Since this was just an exercise, you can delete the file at any time.

The Send To Option

You can use the Send To option to quickly send a selected file to another location. For example, right-click a file, then choose Send To | 3 ½ Floppy to copy a file to floppy disk.

The best thing is that you can add your own options to the SendTo folder. For example, you can create a folder called Archive where you copy files that you want to remove from your computer but back up to another disk. After you copy files to the Archive folder, you back up the Archive folder. In this exercise, we show you how to create the Archive folder on the desktop, then create a Send To option for Archive so you can quickly send any selected file to the folder.

1. Right-click the Desktop and choose New | Folder. When the folder appears, rename it Archive and press ENTER.

2. Now open the SendTo folder window. It's in the Windows folder, which you can access by opening My Computer, then Drive C, then Windows, and finally SendTo.

3. Right-click the new Archive folder and drag it into the SendTo folder, then choose Create Shortcut(s) Here.

Archive now appears on the Send To menu because you added it to the SendTo folder. Now when you right-click on any file, you can choose Archive on the Send To menu to copy the file to the Archive folder.

You can use the Find utility to select files located anywhere on your computer. Find will look in different folders to find files that match your search criterion. You can then select the files in the Find window that you want to copy, move, delete, or perform some other operation on. The following example locates sound files (with the .WAV filename extension), but you can adapt this procedure to find any other types of files.

1. Click Start | Find | Files or Folders.
2. Type ***.wav** in the Named field, then click the down arrow button in the Look in field and choose Drive C.
3. Click Find Now.

In a moment, you see a list of files similar to the following. Files from many different folders are displayed in the file list. You can click and drag any of these files to a new folder or drive. You can also delete, rename, and view properties for any of the files.

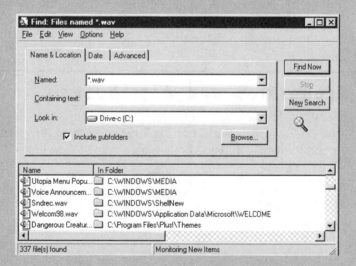

> **NOTE:** When sending to other drives, files are copied. When sending to a folder on the same drive, files are moved.

The Desktop as a Holding Area

The Desktop can be thought of as a *holding area*—a temporary place to put things until you figure out what to do with them.

Think about rummaging through your desk. You place interesting stuff you find on the top of the desk, then find a new cubbyhole and place all the rummaged stuff in it. That analogy explains how you can use the Windows 98 Desktop to reorganize your filing system or gather files together that you want to copy or move to another location. Just drag objects you've found to the Desktop. When you've gathered up all the files you need, create a new folder and drag them into it.

Remember to use move or copy techniques as appropriate for what you are doing. If you are trying to gather up old files you don't want on your system, move them to a new folder. If you're just collecting some interesting files to send to a friend, copy them.

File Properties and Attributes

Now let's look at the properties of files. Right-click any file of your choice on the Desktop or in Windows Explorer and choose Properties from the shortcut menu to display a dialog box similar to the following:

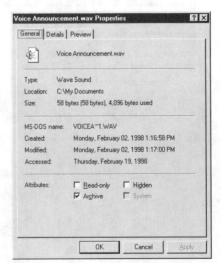

This is where you can get information about a file's size, creation date, and the last time it was accessed. Note that this dialog box is for a sound file and it has a Details tab that displays information about the recording method and a Preview tab that has control features for playing the sound.

Assume you somehow manage to have two files of the same name, but in different folders. Perhaps someone returned a revision of the file after you sent it to them and you stored the revision in a different place. Perhaps you created a copy on your own system and made changes to it, but now you don't know which is the original and which is the copy. One way to find out which file is more recent or has been changed is to compare their Properties dialog boxes. Since both Properties boxes can be on the Desktop at once, you can easily put them side by side and compare the Date and Size fields.

The Properties dialog box is where you change the attributes of a file, as discussed here.

- **Read-only** If you mark this box, the file cannot be changed or deleted until the Read-only field is unmarked. Use this option to protect files from accidental deletion or from being changed. If you need to make changes to a file you've marked as a Read-only file, temporarily disable this option, or duplicate the file and edit the copy.

- **Hidden** Enable this option to hide a file and prevent it from appearing in a folder list. You hide files to protect them from being accidentally deleted or altered. The operating system hides some files.

- **Archive** When a file is first created, or when it is altered, its Archive flag (A) is set on to indicate that the file should be included in a file backup procedure. Backup utilities look at the Archive flag to determine if a file should be backed up. Once the file is backed up, its Archive flag is set off so the file is not included in the next backup. If the file changes in the meantime, its Archive flag is again set on. In most cases, you won't need to worry about the Archive flag, but there may be times when you want to manually set the flag so you can include a file in a special backup. Simply click the field to include the selected file in a backup.

- **System** Files marked System (S) are DOS files that are hidden in DOS file listings.

TIP: While files may be marked as hidden, you can change a Windows 98 configuration option so the operating system shows all files, even hidden and system files. Click Start, then select Settings | Folder Options. Click the View tab on the dialog box and enable the option called "Show all files."

Working with Folders

You can create new folders and files anywhere in the Windows 98 file system. All folders and files can be moved, copied, renamed, and deleted as described here.

Chapter 9 explored the folder hierarchy of Windows 98 that is set up automatically when you install the operating system. Windows files are installed in the Windows folder and programs are installed in the Program Files folder. The My Documents folder is created for your personal files and many Windows programs will automatically suggest storing files in this folder.

You can create new folders for your personal files anywhere in the file system, but we recommend creating them in the My Documents folder for organizational reasons. One other place to create folders is right on the Desktop. In fact, many people start new projects by creating a folder on the Desktop. When the project is done, they move the folder off the Desktop to another location such as an archive folder or a backup disk.

Creating Folders

In this section, we're going to create a new folder right on the Desktop and then work with that folder. You can follow these steps by creating a folder anywhere you want to, such as in My Documents. Several methods for creating folders are outlined here:

- To create a folder on the Desktop, right-click the Desktop and choose New | Folder from the menu (see Figure 10-2).
- To create a new folder within another folder, open the folder and right-click a blank area, then choose New | Folder.
- You can also create new folders "on the fly" while saving documents. If you choose Save As on the File menu of any application, the following Save As dialog box appears. Click the Create New Folder button to create a new folder.

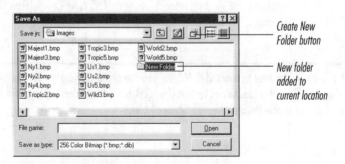

Create New Folder button

New folder added to current location

When you create a new folder, the name is highlighted so you can immediately rename the folder. If you start doing something else without renaming the folder, it retains the default name of New Folder. To rename a folder at any time, right-click it and choose Rename, then type a new folder name.

Duplicating Folders

You can also create new folders by duplicating existing folders. For example, assume you work on a project that restarts every month. The documents for the project include a spreadsheet and a text document to log activities. The spreadsheet includes some predefined rows and columns and the log file has a header for each day of the month. You create these files in advance, then store them in a folder called Project Template. Each month, you duplicate the template folder and rename it with a name like Project June98.

When you duplicate a folder, all the files in it are also duplicated. After duplicating the template folder, you can rename any files within it to match your new project.

The easiest way to duplicate a folder is to use copy and paste techniques:

1. Right-click the folder to duplicate and choose Copy (not Cut).
2. Go to the Desktop or folder where you want to copy the folder.
3. Right-click a blank area and choose Paste.

The folder is copied to the new location. It's that easy. You can also use drag-and-drop techniques to copy folders as discussed earlier under "Copying and Moving Files."

CAUTION: When you duplicate a folder, all the files and folders within the folder are duplicated. If the folder contains a lot of extraneous files, you might use up disk space unnecessarily. Try duplicating only the contents that you need to save disk space.

You can duplicate folders onto other drives or for backup reasons. We regularly copy folders that contain current projects to another computer attached to our network. That way, we've got a backup and another computer we can work on if the original goes down.

This section will show you how to back up a folder by duplicating it to another drive. While you can duplicate a folder to the same drive, it's better to duplicate it to another drive to protect against failure of the first drive. Note the following:

- You can back up a folder to a floppy disk but keep in mind that the floppy disk may not have enough capacity to hold all your files.
- If your system has two hard drives, copy the folder to the second drive.
- If you are connected to a network, copy the folder to another computer on the network.

TIP: Duplicating a folder is just one method of backing up information on your computer. Refer to Chapter 21 for more information about backing up.

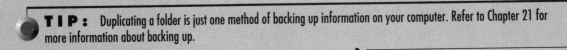

The basic technique for backing up to another drive is the same as duplicating folders, as described earlier. You right-click the folder and choose Copy, then you locate the destination drive and click Paste.

TIP: You might want to create a folder on the destination drive called "Backups" or "Archives" and paste your copied folder into this folder.

Now we're going to tell you about a method we use to back up to another computer, but first we need to tell you about our network setup. The network has a file server called NTserver with shared printers and CD-ROM drives. Network users can access these shared devices. The server also has an extra large hard drive that serves as a repository for backup files. We copy folders from our personal computers to backup folders on the server. Each user has his or her own personal backup folder to prevent name conflicts and provide security. In the following example, we show just one backup folder called "Backups" for simplicity.

To access a backup folder on NTserver, we first create shortcuts on local Desktops as follows:

1. First, open Network Neighborhood as shown in step 1 in Figure 10-4.
2. Next, choose the computer (NTserver).
3. Right-click and drag the Backups folder to the local Desktop.
4. Choose Create Shortcut(s) Here from the menu that appears.

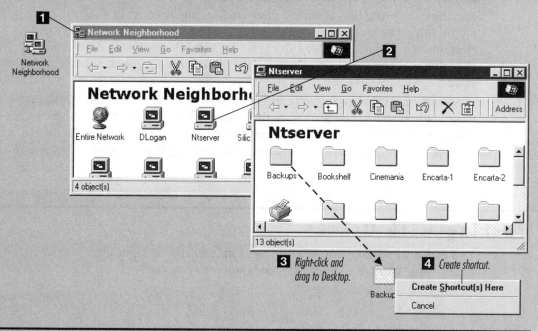

FIGURE 10-4 Create a network folder shortcut

A shortcut to the Backups folder now appears on the Desktop. Now it's easy to drag-and-drop folders and files into the Backups folder.

Since backups must be performed on a regular basis, you'll see a warning message similar to the following every time you attempt to back up over the previous files in the backup folders. You can click Yes to overwrite files, assuming you don't want to save the previous versions of the files.

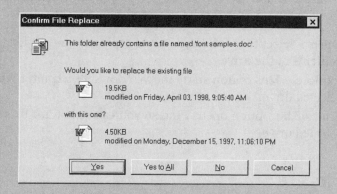

About Moving, Copying, and Renaming Folders

Moving or copying files is simple enough. Moving or copying a folder is another thing entirely. Be aware that you are moving or copying the entire contents of a folder, including all of its files and folders, to the destination. When working with folders, always right-click and drag. Then a menu appears so you can choose exactly what you want to do.

Moving or renaming folders can get you into trouble. If a folder contains program files that are registered with Windows 98, you may not be able to start those programs after moving them since Windows expects the files to be in a specific location. Move or rename these folders only if you are sure it is safe to do so.

Working with Drives

You can work with drives in Windows Explorer. If you right-click a drive in the folder pane, you see a shortcut menu similar to this one:

The options on disk drive menus are listed next. Note that some options are not always available, and some may be grayed out, such as Disconnect, Eject, and Lock, which means they're not applicable for the selected drive.

- **Open**   Select this option to open a separate window for viewing the contents of the drive.
- **Explore**   This option starts the Windows 98 Explorer with a view of the selected drive.
- **Find**   This option opens Find so you can search for files on the selected drive.

- **Backup**   Choose this option to start the Windows 98 Backup program so you can back up files on the drive.
- **Sharing**   Choose this option to share the drive with other network users. This is covered in Chapter 11.

C A U T I O N :   Sharing an entire drive is not normally a good idea for security reasons. Share only the folders that contain files you want other people to access.

- **Add to Zip**   Select this option to add a file or files to a zipped file.
- **Format**   Choose this option to prepare a disk to store files. Normally, you use this option to format floppy disks or new hard drives you've added to your system. Formatting is covered later in this chapter.
- **Create Shortcut**   This option creates a copy of the drive object on the Desktop.
- **Properties**   Choose this option to display the Properties dialog box so you can view and change information and settings for the drive, as discussed in the next section.

If the drive is a network drive or a removable media drive, you will see the following options on the menu as well:

- **Disconnect**   If your system is connected to a network, you may see drive icons for drives that are located on remote network servers. This option will appear on the menu of network drive icons so you can disconnect the drive.
- **Play**   This option appears when a multimedia disk such as an audio CD is in a CD-ROM drive.
- **Eject**   This option ejects a removable disk such as a CD-ROM or hard-disk pack.
- **Lock**   This option locks a removable media disk.

Viewing and Changing Drive Settings

Right-click the Drive C object again and choose Properties on the menu. You'll see a dialog box similar to Figure 10-5. From this dialog box, you can type a new name for the drive in the Label field, view drive statistics, start disk management tools (on the Tools tab), or compress the drive.

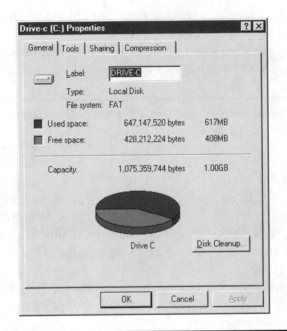

FIGURE 10-5 | Properties for drives

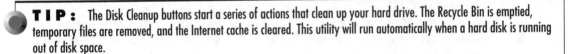

T I P : The Disk Cleanup buttons start a series of actions that clean up your hard drive. The Recycle Bin is emptied, temporary files are removed, and the Internet cache is cleared. This utility will run automatically when a hard disk is running out of disk space.

Click the Tools tab to display the page pictured in Figure 10-6. This is where you go if you want to perform diagnostic checks on the drive, back up the files on the drive, or defragment the drive to improve its performance. Refer to Chapter 21 for more information on these tools.

Click the Compression tab to view information about compressing the files on your drive to obtain more disk space. You will see a dialog box that describes the compression options and the amount of space you will gain when compressing the drive. Compression is also covered in Chapter 21.

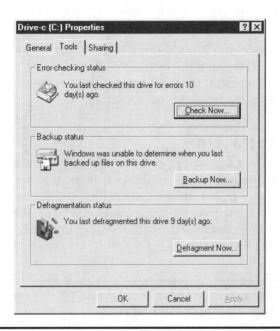

FIGURE 10-6 Disk tools

Deleting Files and Folders

Deleting files is a risky business. If you're using the file selection techniques described earlier, always make sure the selection you've made doesn't include files you want to keep. If you're deleting folders, make sure the folder doesn't include a subfolder that might contain important files.

Windows 98 will display warning messages before deleting files, but stay alert. If you need to make space on a disk by removing files, consider copying the files to a backup disk before deleting them on the current disk.

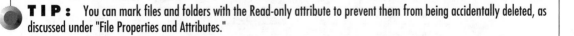

T I P : You can mark files and folders with the Read-only attribute to prevent them from being accidentally deleted, as discussed under "File Properties and Attributes."

To delete a file, right-click it, then choose Delete from the menu. Windows 98 then asks if you really want to delete the file.

To delete a folder, first close it if it is open as a window, then right-click it and choose Delete from the menu. Windows 98 asks if you are sure you want to delete the folder but it does not list the files you are about to delete or tell you that this folder contains another folder.

The Recycle Bin

Fortunately, Windows 98 protects you from accidentally deleting files. The Recycle Bin holds deleted files in a queue that has first-in, first-out characteristics—i.e., as the queue becomes full, the oldest files in the queue are permanently deleted. As long as the queue is large, there is a good chance you can recover files that were deleted days, weeks, or even months ago, depending on how many files you delete.

C A U T I O N : The Recycle Bin has a limited amount of space, so if you delete a folder that has a lot of files, even files that you recently deleted may be dumped out of the queue.

T I P : If you are sure that you will not need to recover files you are deleting, right-click the file or the selected files, and then hold the SHIFT key and choose Delete on the menu. The files are permanently deleted and not sent to the Recycle Bin.

You can open the Recycle Bin to view its contents and recover files. The view looks like any other window. Choose Details on the View menu to list information about files and folders, like their original location and the date they were deleted as shown here.

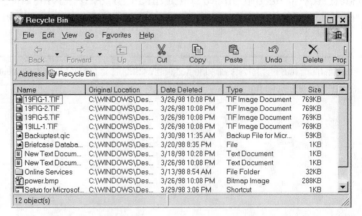

To recover any file, simply click it, then choose Restore from the File menu. The file is restored to its original location. You can also recover files by dragging them out of the Recycle Bin to an appropriate drive and folder.

To clear out all the files and folders in the Recycle Bin, choose Empty Recycle Bin on the File menu or right-click the Recycle Bin icon and choose Empty Recycle Bin. You can also delete individually selected files by choosing Delete on the File menu.

To change the properties of the Recycle Bin, close the window, then right-click the Recycle Bin icon on the Desktop and choose Properties. A dialog box will appear.

Each drive requires space for deleted files. Here, you can adjust the amount of disk space to hold deleted files. The default disk space is 10 percent of the disk drive's total size. You can decrease this value if you are running out of disk space, or increase it if you have a lot of disk space and want to make sure you can recover more files. Settings can apply to all drives or you can adjust each drive independently.

- To adjust the settings for all drives, click "Use one setting for all drives."
- To adjust the settings of each drive independently, choose "Configure drives independently," then click the tab for the drive and adjust its settings.
- Choose "Do not move files to the Recycle Bin. Remove files immediately when deleted" if you don't want to save any deleted files. This removes the ability to recover files using the Recycle Bin.
- Adjust the amount of space required by the Recycle Bin by sliding the arrow button to the left or right. A Recycle Bin of the indicated percentage is created on each drive.

Associating Files and Programs

Most programs automatically add a filename extension to a document when you save the document. In Windows 98, certain extensions are *associated* with programs, so if you click a document with the .DOC extension, for example, WordPad starts unless you've installed another program like Microsoft Word that uses the .DOC extension. In that case, Word starts when you choose the file.

You can create your own associations. For example, you could save letter files in WordPad with the extension .LET, then associate that extension with WordPad. Whenever you double-click a document with the .LET extension, WordPad will start and load the document in its workspace.

Choose Settings | Folder Options on the Start menu to create or edit associations. When the Folder Options dialog box appears, click the File Types tab to display a dialog box similar to the following:

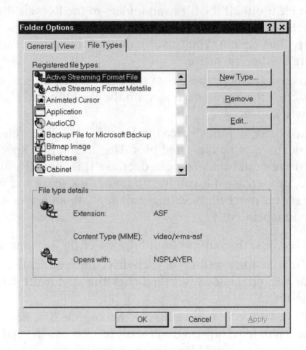

The Registered file types window lists all the current filename extensions and the programs that start when you select a file with that extension. You can click any association, then click the Edit button to change its properties. Click the New Type button to create a new association. For example, to create the WordPad association with the .LET extension or a similar association, follow these steps:

1. Click the New Type button to display the following dialog box:

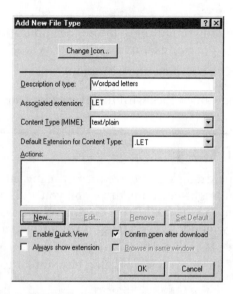

2. In the Description of type field, type a description such as **WordPad Letter**, then type the new extension in the Associated extension field, such as **LET**.

3. In the Content Type field, click the down arrow button and select the type of content the file represents.

4. Click the New button to open the following dialog box, then type **Open** in the action field (Open is the menu option you will see when you right-click a file with this extension).

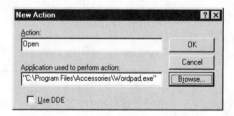

5. Click the Browse button to locate the application associated with the extension. For our example, we locate WordPad.

6. Click OK to complete the operation.

You can now open files with the new extension.

Formatting Disks

You can prepare a disk to receive files by using the Format command. Open My Computer and right-click any drive and you will see the Format command. However, you can't format Drive C while Windows is running, which is good because you would lose everything if you formatted it.

To format a floppy disk, place a disk in the drive, then right-click the drive and choose Format. You see a dialog box similar to the following:

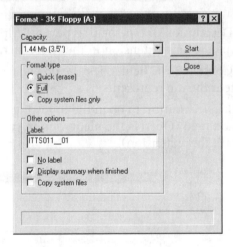

Choose a disk type in the Capacity field (the default type showing in the field is usually appropriate), then set the following options on the dialog box as appropriate:

- **Quick (erase)** This option removes files from a previously formatted disk but does not scan the disk for errors.
- **Full** This option prepares a disk for storing files. If files already exist on the disk, they are lost during the formatting process.

- **Copy system files only**   This option copies the system files to an already formatted disk. System files make the disk bootable.
- **Label**   Type a name for the disk in this field, or choose No label.
- **Copy system files**   Click this option if you choose the Full option to copy the system files to a newly formatted disk, making it bootable.

Now that you know about your local file system, we move on to explain how you can access files and other resources on other computers that are attached to your company's network. Of course, you can skip the next chapter if you're not attached to a network.

11

Your Network Neighborhood

This chapter discusses computer networks for users, not network administrators. We will discuss how to access resources on a network and how to share resources on your computer with other network users.

BASICS

- Learn about computer networks from the users' perspective
- Access shared resources on other computers
- Create shortcuts to shared network resources
- Share resources on your own computer
- Access shared printers and share printers attached to your computer

BEYOND

- Learn about network security and access control methods
- Monitor and manage users who access your computer
- Install a computer-to-computer message system
- Set up a small office or home network

A *network* is a collection of computers that are interconnected with cables or some other data transmission medium. A network may be as small as a few computers in the same room or as large as your company's office building.

Global networks help keep companies connected around the world and with Windows 98, you can dial into your company's network from a remote location and access the network as if you were sitting in your office at work. Some companies are even using the Internet to build intra-city, inter-city, and global networks.

 T I P : The end of this chapter describes some of the basic steps for setting up a small office or home network. See "Setting Up a Network."

About Computer Networks

As mentioned, a computer network links computers on a small or large scale, as shown in Figure 11-1, and allows users to exchange information. You can share files on your computer for other network users to access or you can access shared files on other computers. You can also exchange electronic mail over networks, make phone calls (bypassing normal phone lines), and set up videoconferences that help people save time and travel costs. You can even run collaborative applications over networks that help people work on the same documents at the same time.

As shown at the top in Figure 11-1, most large networks have one or more *servers* that share programs, files, and printers. The servers are dedicated, meaning that no one uses the computer as personal workstations. A network operating system like Microsoft Windows NT is usually installed on the server to manage secure access to files and to provide sophisticated network management tools.

In contrast, small offices and even home users can take advantage of Windows 98's built-in *peer-to-peer networking* features, as shown at the bottom in Figure 11-1. Peer-to-peer means that users share files, CD-ROM drives, and printers on their personal computers with other network users.

One of the big differences between large managed networks and small peer-to-peer networks is the level of security and intruder protection. A Windows 98 peer-to-peer network is usually only appropriate for a small office

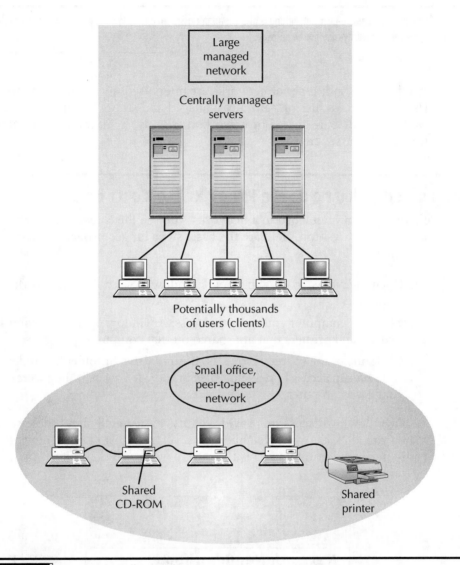

FIGURE 11-1 Large and small networks

where you know and trust other users, but inappropriate for a large corporate office where high levels of security and access control are necessary. That is where Windows NT should be used as a central server.

TIP: Windows 98's peer-to-peer networking is also useful in classroom environments, demonstrations, or other areas where high levels of security may not be an issue.

Of course, both types of networks are often used in corporate environments. Users may access files on centrally managed and secure Windows NT servers as well as files that are shared by coworkers who use Windows 98's sharing features discussed here.

Accessing Shared Network Resources

If your system is attached to a networks, you see the Network Neighborhood icon on your Desktop. Here are the basic steps for accessing a network resource:

1. Open the Network Neighborhood window to see a list of network computers.
2. Click the computer you want to access. A window opens that shows drives, folders, and printers that are shared on that computer.
3. Click one of the shared resources. If it is a drive or folder, a window opens and you can access folders and files in the window as if they were stored on your own computer.

The following discussion provides a little more detail about these steps. When you click Network Neighborhood, you see a list of other network computers similar to Figure 11-2.

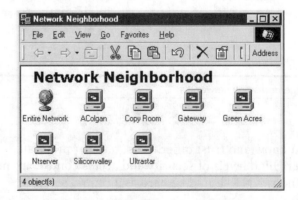

FIGURE 11-2 Your Network Neighborhood

The Network Neighborhood window shows computers that are part of your workgroup or domain as described in a moment. However, other workgroups or domains may exist on your computer. You can access them by clicking the Entire Network icon. A window similar to the following then appears:

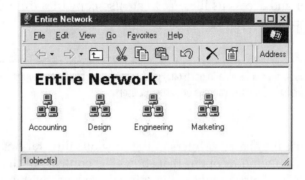

Large networks are divided into workgroups (peer-to-peer networking) or domains (Windows NT Server networks). When you open Entire Network and select a group or domain, only the computers in that group or domain appear. These group and domain categories make it easier to locate other computers. (If a network computer is not on, you will not see it in the Network Neighborhood window.)

Once you open a window on a network computer, you see a list of resources that are shared on that computer similar to the following window, which shows shared folders and printers.

You can't tell in this picture, but some of the folders are shared CD-ROM drives, such as the Bookshelf and the Encarta folders. The folder called "Backup Files" is a folder we use to back up files. As discussed under "Backing Up

Folders to Other Drives" in Chapter 10, we copy folders from our own system into this folder to create backups.

You can treat shared folders like any folder on your own system. Once the shared folders appear in the Network Neighborhood window, just open the folder and access its files. You can also copy files from the folder to your system or copy files from your system to the shared folder.

NOTE: You might not be able to open and/or change shared files even though you can see them in the window. Some network files are locked out to everyone or to specific users.

Note the shared printers in the previous illustration. If you click a shared printer, a window opens that shows the contents of the printer queue, in other words, the current jobs being printed. To work with shared network printers, refer to "Accessing Network Printers" later in this chapter.

You can also access the Network Neighborhood when opening files in your applications. It appears in the Open dialog box—just double-click it to see the list of network computers.

Creating a Shortcut to a Shared Resource

You'll no doubt need to access some network resources on a regular basis. It does not make any sense to open Network Neighborhood and search for the computer and resource every time you want to use it when you can just create a shortcut on your Desktop.

TIP: You can copy files from your system to a network folder by dragging and dropping them onto the shortcut of the folder.

Some network computers contain multiple shared resources. You can create a shortcut on your Desktop for each of those shared resources, but this might clutter your Desktop. A better option in this case is to create a shortcut for the shared network computer itself, then just open it to access any of its folders. For example, you might create a shortcut to a network server since it contains a lot of different shared folders. But if a network user has shared only one folder on her computer, create a shortcut for the shared folder, not her computer.

To create a shortcut:

1. Locate the network computer or folder in the Network Neighborhood window.

2. Right-click and drag the computer or folder to your Desktop.

3. Choose Create Shortcut(s) Here to complete the operation.

About Network Names

The Windows 98 graphical interface makes it easy to access resources on other computers. However, there may be cases where you need to refer to network drives by their actual name.

Files on a computer have a path that specifies the drive and folder where they are located. For example, a file on your own computer called EXAMPLE.TXT in the TUTORIAL folder of Drive C has the following filename:

C:\TUTORIAL\EXAMPLE.TXT

This is the full path of the file. Files located on computer networks have paths that also include the name of the computer that holds the file, along with the folder name and filename.

All Windows computers use the UNC (Uniform Naming Convention) to specify file locations. The UNC format is

*computername**path*

where *computername* is the name of the computer and *path* is the shared folder name and filename. Note the double slashes before *computername*.

Assume that the previous file is located on a network computer called TRAINING. In this case, the UNC would be \\TRAINING\TUTORIAL\EXAMPLE.TXT.

You'll use these names when mapping network drives for older applications, as discussed later.

Sharing Resources on Your Computer

Windows 98 lets you share any drive, folder, or printer on your computer for other network users to access. In most cases, you should never share an entire hard drive since other network users would have access to all of the files on your computer. Instead, share only the folders that you want other users to access.

CD-ROM drives are usually the exception to this rule if they contain discs with reference material. For example, we have a six-disc CD-ROM changer attached to our server that contains reference discs such as Microsoft's Bookshelf and Microsoft Encarta. We share the entire CD-ROM drive so that all users can access these resources. The information is not private and no one can accidentally delete files on a read-only CD-ROM, so we don't need to worry about protecting its files. Also, such discs include a program that requires access to the entire disc.

There are two different resource sharing scenarios for your Windows 98 computer, and each method is described in the following sections.

- **Share-Level Access Control**   You share folders with everybody on a read-only or read-write basis. You control access by giving authorized users a password to open the folders.
- **User-Level Access Control**   This scheme is available if your network has a Windows NT computer that can keep track of individual user accounts. If so, you can grant access to individual users based on their Windows NT user account. For example, you can grant Joe read-only access and Amy read-write access.

Of course, you don't need to restrict access in any way. You can share any resource with everybody and not require that they enter passwords. This might be appropriate for CD-ROM drives, but we recommend sharing folders and using the access controls discussed later.

Which of the previous access control methods is your computer set up to support? To find out, right click any folder and choose the Sharing option. You will see one of the dialog boxes pictured in Figure 11-3. Refer to the following related section for further instructions on how to set up a "share." If your network is managed by a network administrator, you should also discuss sharing options with him or her.

Share-Level Access Control

Here are the steps for sharing a folder if share-level access control is in place:

1. Locate the folder to share, right-click, and choose the Sharing option. The dialog box on the left in Figure 11-3 appears.

2. Click the Shared As button. The current folder name appears in the Share Name field. This is the name that network users will see and you can change it if necessary.

3. Type a description in the Comment field (optional).

4. Click one of the options in the Access Type field as follows:

- **Read-Only**   Users can read but not create, edit, or delete files in the folder.
- **Full**   Users can create, edit, and delete files in the folder.
- **Depends on Password**   Users' access depends on the passwords you type in the two Passwords fields. Give the read-only password to users who should only have read-only privileges and give the full access password to readers who are authorized to create, edit, and delete files in the folder.

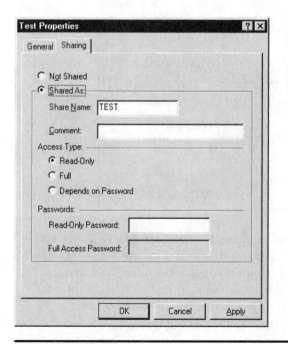
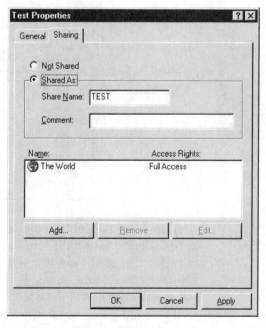

FIGURE 11-3   Share-level (left) or user-level access control (right)

User-Level Access Control

If you are connected to a Windows NT network, chances are your network administrator has configured your system for user-level access control. Here are the steps for sharing folders:

1. Locate the folder to share, right-click, and choose the Sharing option. The dialog box on the right in Figure 11-3 appears.

2. Click the Shared As button. The current folder name appears in the Share Name field. This is the name that network users will see and you can change it if necessary.

3. Type a description in the Comment field (optional).

4. Click the Add button to add a user. The following dialog box appears:

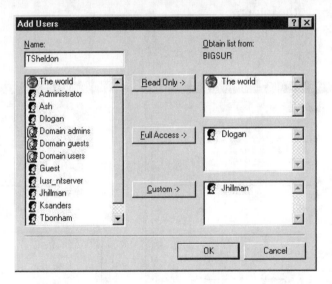

A list of users is obtained from a Windows NT or other type of server and appears in the list on the left. In this example, The world (everybody on the network) has read-only access to the folder, Dlogan has full access, and Jhillman has custom access. To add a user to one of the fields, click the user's name and click either the Read Only, Full Access, or Custom button.

If you add a user to the Custom field, the following dialog box appears when you click OK:

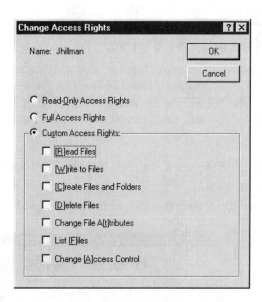

Enabling all of the options under Custom Access Rights is the same as granting someone full access rights. Use this box to grant someone access to create and edit files but not to do other administrative tasks such as change file attributes and access control rights. Here is a common configuration:

- Enable Read Files, Write to Files, Create Files and Folders, and List Files.

- Disable Delete Files, Change File Attributes, and Change Access Control.

T I P : You can find out what each option does by right-clicking it and choosing What's This?.

About Subfolders

When you share a folder that contains subfolders, those subfolders are also shared. In some cases, you want to share the main folder but not the subfolders. Perhaps they contain private information. In other cases, you may only want to share subfolders with read-only access.

To change the sharing options for subfolders, simply go to each subfolder and follow the steps outlined earlier to change the sharing options for each folder you want to change.

Mapping Network Drives

Some applications require that you map drive letters to shared network folders. For example, an application might not recognize a shared folder name such as "Shared files" but only a drive letter such as E or F. To map the shared folder to a drive letter you will need to use the Map Network Drive command. Follow these steps:

1. Right-click the My Computer or Network Neighborhood icons on the Desktop.

2. Choose the Map Network Drive option. The following dialog box appears:

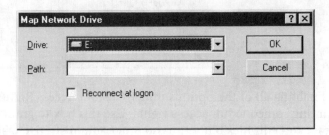

The Drive field contains the next available drive letter. The Path field is where you type the UNC (Uniform Naming Convention) name for the shared resource. Refer to "About Network Names" earlier in this chapter for more information.

3. Type in the Path information.

4. Enable the Reconnect at logon if you want this drive mapping to appear every time you start your computer.

5. Click OK to create the drive mapping.

Now you can open My Computer and see that the new drive mapping appears as a drive icon next to Drive C and other drives. When working in applications, you will see the drive listed next to other drives on the Open and Save As dialog boxes.

Accessing Network Printers

Like any printer, a shared network printer must be installed by Windows 98 before it is accessible to your applications. Your local network is likely to have a number of different shared printers available and you can install as many as you like. For example, one network computer may share a color printer while another shares a laser printer with multiple paper trays that include legal size paper or company letterhead.

To install a printer, follow these steps:

1. Open Network Neighborhood and locate the computer that is sharing the printer.
2. Right-click the printer and choose Install from the menu. The Add Printer wizard appears.
3. You are asked some simple questions about the printer. Click the Next button until you complete the installation.

Once the printer is installed, you can choose it from any Print dialog box as shown in Figure 11-4. Click the down arrow button in the Name field to choose the network printer if it is not already selected. Notice that the UNC path for the network printer appears in the Where field.

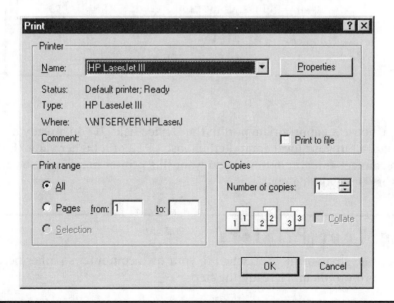

FIGURE 11-4 Network printers can be selected from Print dialog boxes

Setting the Default Printer

You can make any network printer your default printer. First, install the printer as described earlier, then open Printers in the Control Panel, right-click the printer, and choose Set as Default.

Mapping Printers

Some applications may require that you map a printer to a printer port number such as LPT1 or LPT2. Then, when you print from the application, you send print jobs to the ports instead of specifying the printer by name.

To map a network printer to a port, locate the printer in the Network Neighborhood, then right-click the printer and choose Capture Printer from the menu. You see the following dialog box:

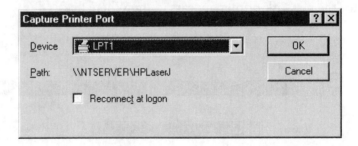

Choose an appropriate port in the Device field. If you already have a printer attached to your local computer, choose LPT2 or a higher value. Enable the Reconnect at logon option if you want this printer mapping to be available every time you log on.

Sharing Your Printers

You can share printers attached to your own computer so other network users can print to them. Here are the steps:

1. Open the Printers folder in the Control Panel.

2. Right-click the printer you want to share and choose Sharing to open the dialog box pictured in Figure 11-5.

3. Enable the Shared As option, then type a name for the printer in the Share Name field.

4. You can restrict access to specific users by typing a password in the Password field. Give the password to people who are allowed to access this printer.

FIGURE 11-5   Sharing a printer

• Monitoring Network Users

If you share resources on your computer with other users, there are two interesting tools that you can use to monitor how they are accessing your system and how much processing time your computer is spending on serving their requests: System Monitor and NetWatcher.

Note that the "server" in the following examples refers to the file sharing processes handled by your computer. It "serves" files to other users. The processes that are used to do that can be tracked apart from other processes handled by your computer.

System Monitor

System Monitor is pictured in Figure 11-6. In this example, we are tracking three processes: the kernel processor usage, the number of bytes read by the server, and the number of bytes written by the server. To start System Monitor, click Start, then choose Programs | Accessories | System Tools | System Monitor.

You configure System Monitor to track just the processes you want to monitor. Here are the steps:

1. Click the Add button to bring up a dialog box similar to the following:

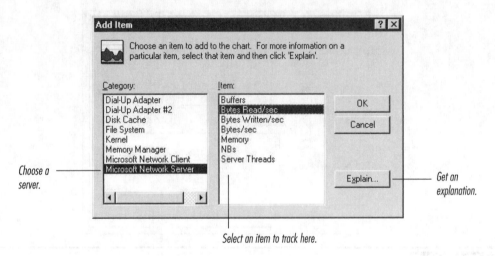

Choose a server.

Get an explanation.

Select an item to track here.

2. Choose Microsoft Network Server in the Category field.
3. Choose an item to track in the Item field.
4. Click Explain to read information about items.
5. Click OK to create the chart.

System Monitor can help you determine whether loss of system performance is due to sharing or some other problem. If sharing is causing the problem, you may need to disconnect some users as discussed in the next section or stop sharing altogether.

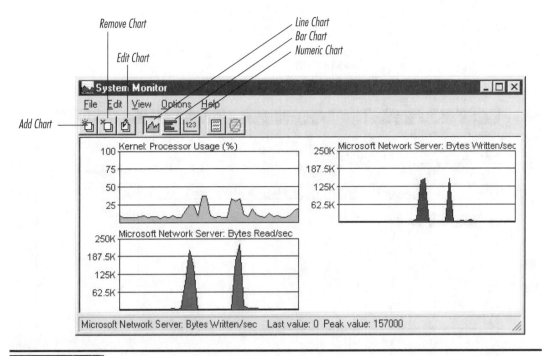

FIGURE 11-6 System Monitor tracks performance

NetWatcher

NetWatcher gives you a view of the users that are accessing your computer, as well as the shared folders and files they are accessing. An example NetWatcher screen is pictured in Figure 11-7. To start NetWatcher, click Start, then choose Programs | Accessories | System Tools | NetWatcher.

Click the Show Users button to find out who is accessing your computer and the name of the computer they are using. Other information is also listed in the window as pictured in Figure 11-7, such as the number of shared files they have open and the time they connected. You can also click the Show Shared Folders and Show Files buttons to get additional information.

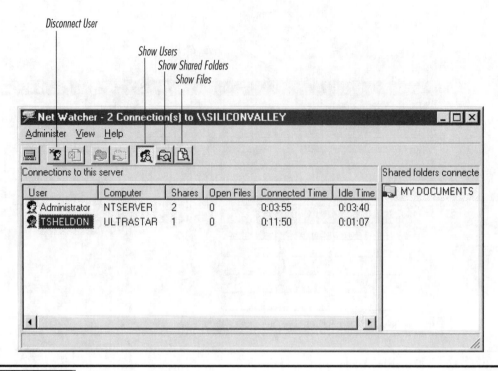

Disconnect User

Show Users
Show Shared Folders
Show Files

FIGURE 11-7 NetWatcher tracks network usage

You may need to disconnect a user from your system at some point. There are several reasons for this:

- The user may have left for the day without removing the connection he or she has to your system.
- You may need to obtain better performance for your own work by stopping users from accessing your system.
- You may need to cut off users who are performing malicious activities on your system.

Select a user, then click the Disconnect user button to stop the user from accessing your shared files. A warning message appears on your computer before the user is actually disconnected. Nothing appears on the user's computer. Also, disconnecting a user does not stop them from immediately reopening a shared resource. You will need to stop sharing the resource to prevent continued access.

T I P :   Before disconnecting users from your system, you may want to call them or send them an email message. You can also use WinPopup to send a message as described next.

Sending Messages with WinPopup

WinPopup is a rudimentary messaging program. You can use it to send a typed message to another user, a computer, or a workgroup. Other types of messages may arrive via WinPopup as well. For example, you may see notification from network printers that a print job is complete.

WinPopup is flawed in one way: a recipient must have WinPopup running to receive incoming messages. If you are part of a small network, you can make sure that everybody on your network automatically runs WinPopup by adding it to their Startup folder as described in a moment. To start and use WinPopup:

1. Click Start, select Run, then type **winpopup** in the Open field, and click OK. The WinPopup dialog box appears.

2. Click the Send button to send a message to another user as shown in Figure 11-8. Choose "User or computer" or "Workgroup" in the To field, then type an appropriate name in the field. Type your message and click OK.

If you are not sure of computer and workgroup names, open Network Neighborhood and inspect the names listed there.

If you like WinPopup, you should add it to your Startup folder so that it starts every time your computer starts. Other users on your network should follow this same procedure as well so you can send them messages that pop up on their screens.

1. Right-click the Start button and choose Open.

2. Open the Programs folder, then the Startup folder.

3. Right-click a blank area and choose New | Shortcut.

4. When the Create Shortcut dialog box appears, type **winpopup** in the Command line field.

5. Click Next and then Finish to create the shortcut.

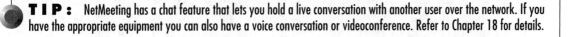
T I P :   NetMeeting has a chat feature that lets you hold a live conversation with another user over the network. If you have the appropriate equipment you can also have a voice conversation or videoconference. Refer to Chapter 18 for details.

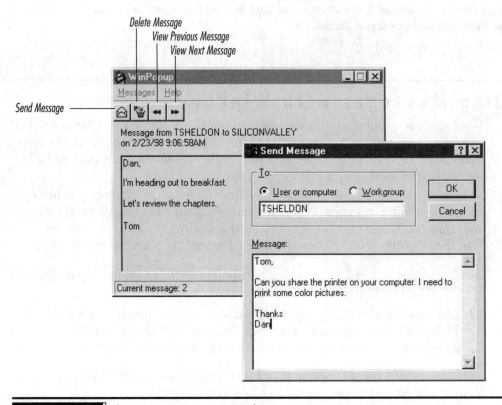

FIGURE 11-8 | The WinPopup messaging utility

Hearts

On the fun side, Hearts is a card game that you can play with up to four people over your network. You might want to try it out just to get a feel for how cool computer networks are.

To start Hearts, click Start then select Programs | Accessories | Games | Hearts. When the program loads, you can choose to be the dealer or just a player in a Hearts game that some other user started.

If you choose to be the dealer, the game waits for others to join. You can call or message your friends and tell them about the game you are starting. Other players then start Hearts and enter the name of your computer to join the game. Once four players have joined (or the computer substitutes for a player), the game begins. Refer to Hearts Help for instructions on playing the game.

Remote Networking

All versions of Windows, including Windows NT and Windows 98, now include dial-up networking capabilities, including the ability to act as a dial-up server. A dial-up server allows remote and mobile users to dial into the computer and access its resources over telephone lines. You can set up your computer to allow other people to dial in and access its resources. You can even dial into your computer while on the road. The modem-to-modem links become a network connection that supports standard network protocols like TCP/IP. The dial-up user perceives no difference between working remotely and working at a computer that is directly connected to the network, except that the performance may be a little slower.

You can refer to Chapter 19 for more information about dial-up networking and remote and mobile users.

Setting Up a Network

This section will outline the procedures for setting up a small office or home network. The purpose is to outline the procedure and point out where network settings are made. Once your computers are connected, you can easily copy files between systems and share printers as described earlier.

The first step is to purchase the network interface cards and cabling. Ethernet is the most popular networking technology and is also very inexpensive. You can buy an Ethernet card for as low as $20. You'll also need cabling and connectors. The best place to go are stores like CompUSA, Radio Shack, and so on. They will have all the equipment you need and help you pick out the components for a complete network.

Now you're ready to install the cards, but you may need to set some switches on the new cards to make sure they don't interfere with other components in your computer. The best way to do this is to configure Windows 98 network settings as if the cards are installed. Windows 98 will recommend the best settings and let you configure the system. Then you can shut down the system, make the appropriate settings on the cards, install them in the system, and reboot.

Note that you need to configure each computer individually as described in the following sections, then attach the cables and restart all the computers before network communication takes place.

Configuring a Network Adapter

This section outlines the steps for installing a network adapter. As mentioned, you don't need to mount the adapter just yet. You can preconfigure it in Windows 98 and let the operating system recommend settings for the board.

1. Open the Control Panel and choose the Network icon. In a moment, the Network dialog box appears as shown in Figure 11-9. (Your component window will be blank if networking has not yet been installed.)

2. Click the Add button to add a new component, then choose the Adapter option and click Add again.

3. Now select the type of network adapter you have and click OK.

4. When you return to the Network dialog box, make sure the new adapter is selected, then click the Properties button. On the Resources page, write down the Interrupt (IRQ) and I/O address range settings. Click OK when done.

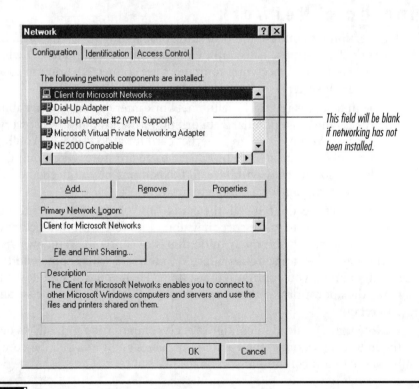

This field will be blank if networking has not been installed.

FIGURE 11-9 The Network utility

CAUTION :   If an asterisk appears in front of these numbers, you'll need to change them by choosing another value from the list.

Now you can install the network adapter in your computer, but first make sure that the settings of the card are the same as what you wrote down. Many adapters can be configured by moving jumpers or setting switches on the boards. Other adapters may require that you run a program on a diskette. Refer to your board manual for more details.

Adding Clients, Protocols, and Services

The next step is to add additional network options like client software, network protocols, and sharing services. We're assuming you've restarted the computer and the network adapter is working properly. Now you can set up the following options:

- Client software lets you access resources on other computers.
- Network protocol software supports data transmissions over computer networks.
- File and printer sharing services allow you to share resources on your computer.

To configure these options, follow the steps outlined next:

1. Open the Network utility in the Control Panel.

2. Click the Add button to open the following dialog box:

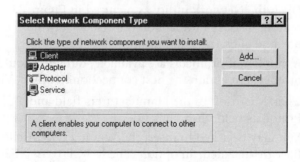

3. Now refer to the following sections to install clients, protocols, and services.

Adding and Configuring a Client

To add a client, choose Client on the Select Network Component Type dialog box and click the Add button. A list of manufacturers (typically Banyan, Microsoft, and Novell) appears. We're going to install the Microsoft client here because it is what you need to access other Windows computers. You can install one of the other clients if you have servers on your network from those manufacturers.

1. Choose Microsoft in the Manufacturer list and click the Client for Microsoft Networks in the Network Clients list, then click OK. You may be asked to place the Windows 98 disc in the CD-ROM drive. The client software is loaded and appears in the Network dialog box.

   If you log on to a Windows NT domain, you need to configure the client. If your network is small, it is unlikely that you need to perform these steps. A network administrator may manage the network and give you advice on these steps.

2. In the Network dialog box (see Figure 11-9), choose the Client for Microsoft Networks option and click the Properties button.

3. In the dialog box that appears, choose Log on to Windows NT domain and type in the name of the Windows NT domain server.

Configuring Network Protocols

This section explains in limited detail how to install network protocols. We're going to install the TCP/IP protocol since it is now the most common and is required to get the most out of Windows 98 networking features. You'll also need it if you plan to connect to the Internet.

1. Open the Network utility as pictured in Figure 11-9 and click the Add button. Choose Protocol on the Select Network Component Type dialog box and click the Add button.

   A number of protocols are available, but you should install the Microsoft protocols to obtain the best connection to other Windows 98 computers.

2. Click Microsoft in the Manufacturers field and TCP/IP in the Network Protocols field, then click OK.

   You may be asked to insert the Windows 98 disc in the CD-ROM. After the files are installed, an option called "TCP/IP -> NE200 Compatible" or something similar appears in the Network dialog box. You may also see a "TCP/IP -> Dial-Up Adapter" option if you have a modem installed.

3. Choose the TCP/IP network adapter option and click the Properties tab. The dialog box shown in Figure 11-10 appears where you can type the IP address for this computer.

   If you are configuring a small network, you can just specify your own IP addresses (an example is given next). If you are connected to a larger network, the network administrator will give you advice on how to set this dialog box. We're assuming that you're configuring your own IP addresses here.

4. Click the Specify an IP address option, then type **192.168.0.1** in the IP Address field and **255.255.255.0** in the Subnet Mask field, and click OK.

Other computers on your network should use an address that increments the last number in the IP address. For example, the next computer should have the address 192.168.0.2. Use the same subnet mask, however. You can go as high as 192.168.1.16. Note that the previous set of addresses are known as the *reserved addresses*. They can be used as examples because they don't conflict

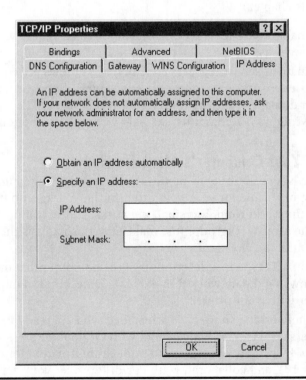

FIGURE 11-10 Setting TCP/IP addressing

with real addresses used on the Internet (in case you ever connect your network to the Internet).

Installing File and Printer Sharing Services

Here are the final steps to configuring your computer for a network:

1. Open the Network utility as pictured in Figure 11-9 and click the Add button. Choose Service on the Select Network Component Type dialog box and click the Add button.

2. Choose Microsoft in the Manufacturers field and File and printer sharing for Microsoft Networks in the Network Services field, then click OK.

3. You are returned to the Network dialog box. Click the File and Print Sharing button and make sure the options to shared files and printers are enabled.

4. Click the Access Control tab on the Network dialog box and enable controls as follows (refer to "Sharing Resources on Your Computer"earlier in this chapter):

   • Enable Share-level access control for basic Windows 98 peer-to-peer networks.

   • Enable User-level access control if a Windows NT computer is attached to a network that manages user accounts. Type the name of the computer or domain where the user accounts are stored. The manager of the Windows NT computer can help you with this option.

Setting Your Computer's Identification

Open the Network utility as pictured in Figure 11-9 and click the Identification tab. Type in a name for your computer. In the Workgroup field, type in the name of the workgroup. For small networks, all the computers are probably part of the same workgroup. Just make sure this name is the same for all computers in the workgroup.

You can also type in a description of the computer that other people will see when browsing the network. For example, a description might be "Tom's computer with color printer."

With networking support now installed, you are ready to communicate with other users. You can exchange email with Outlook Express as discussed in Chapter 14, set up a Web server to publish information for coworkers to view (Chapter 17), and collaborate with coworkers over your network using NetMeeting (Chapter 18).

Web Browsing and Communications

Internet Explorer

12

Web browsing is the process of visiting different sites on the World Wide Web. You can go to a site by typing in a Web site address or clicking a hyperlink button on a page you have already visited.

Web browsing is probably the most intuitive aspect of using computers ever developed. First-time computer users are typically browsing the Web in a matter of minutes after only a few simple instructions.

Web browsers are true multimedia tools. An interesting way to think of Internet Explorer and other Web browsers is as containers for displaying text, graphics, and video; playing audio; and running programs such as Java applications. That is one reason why the Web has been so revolutionary in its impact. Web site managers and program developers now have a single user interface for distributing information and building programs that works on almost every computer on the planet—and users have to learn only one set of instructions.

Basic Web Browsing

We're assuming you already have an Internet account and some kind of connection to the Internet, either by way of a phone connection or connection through your company's network. If you don't, see Appendix B for details about getting connected online.

There are any number of ways to launch Internet Explorer:

- Click the Internet Explorer icon on the Desktop, on the Taskbar, or in the Quick Launch toolbar.
- Type a Web address in the Address field of any open folder window. The window converts to a Web browser and displays Web content.
- On the Start menu, click Favorites and choose a Web page to open (you can add your own Favorites to this list, as you'll see).
- On the Start menu, choose Find | On the Internet to access Web-based search engines.

The first time you launch Internet Explorer, it automatically goes to Microsoft's home page at http://home.microsoft.com (later we'll show you how to change the page that Internet Explorer goes to when you start it).

TIP: Web addresses start with http, as just shown. They are also called URLs (Universal Resource Locators). Appendix B provides more information on Web addressing and other such details.

Try this simple Web browsing example. Type **http://www.yahoo.com** in the browser's Address bar, then press ENTER. Up comes the home page for Yahoo!, as shown in Figure 12-1.

If you haven't heard of Yahoo!, it is one of the World Wide Web's most popular Web sites. As you can tell at a glance, Yahoo! offers a blizzard of links to information on the Internet. Every underlined item is a hyperlink that you click to get to some other page of information. There's also a box where you can type in information you want to search for or you can just browse at your own leisure. You'll quickly discover why the World Wide Web is so appealing—with every mouse click you'll find topics that interest you.

Yahoo! is called a search *directory* because it presents you with a number of subjects you can drill into for information. As we'll see later in this chapter, there are also search *engines* you can use to find information.

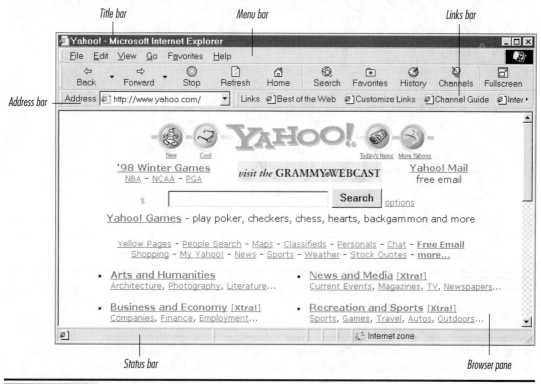

FIGURE 12-1 Yahoo! home page

Let's say you want to browse Yahoo! to find out what information is available on sports utility vehicles. Look at the Recreation and Sports category, which shows Autos as a subcategory.

Clicking the Autos hyperlink brings up the list in Figure 12-2. Note the hyperlinks on the page; Yahoo! breaks its Automotive category into more than 40 subcategories. The Four Wheel Drive category looks most promising for more information about sports utility vehicles.

Clicking the Four Wheel Drive link brings up yet another page of information specific to four-wheel drive vehicles. That's about all there is to it. You browse by clicking hyperlinks that interest you.

Yahoo! offers some related information to help you.

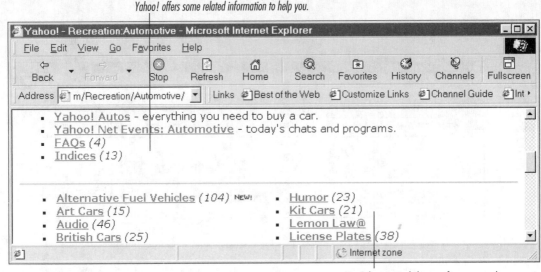

Subcategories help you refine your search.

FIGURE 12-2 | Automotive topics at Yahoo!

WEBLINK: While you're at it, return to the Yahoo! home page and check out the People Search and Chat hyperlinks near the top of the page. You can find friends and acquaintances on the Internet!

Searching on the Web

One of the most important things you will do while browsing the Internet is search for information. There are a number of sites you can check out now. The usual procedure is to type a keyword like **Thunderbirds** and press the search button. A large list of available documents then appears. You click a document to open it. Most sites have instructions for narrowing your searches.

T I P : An interesting search trick is to type "find" right in the Address field, followed by the keyword that you want to search for. Internet Explorer will bring up a list of results. For example, type "find windows" and see what appears.

You can gain quick access to a number of different search sites by visiting Microsoft's comprehensive search page at this address:

http://home.microsoft.com/access/allinone.asp

This site also includes white pages, yellow pages, city guides, and other reference possibilities. Here are the individual addresses for some of the most popular search sites on the Internet:

AltaVista	http://www.altavista.digital.com
Excite	http://www.excite.com
HotBot	http://www.hotbot.com
Infoseek	http://www.infoseek.com
Lycos	http://www.lycos.com
WebCrawler	http://www.webcrawler.com

You can add these sites to your Favorites. Visit the site, then choose Add to Favorites from the Favorites menu. More details about adding favorites are given later.

Viewing Local and Internet Resources

Windows 98 provides integrated access to local file systems, your company network, and the Internet. Try the following now to see how this works. Once again, we're assuming you are connected to the Internet.

1. Browse your local file system by opening My Computer, then Drive C. Note the arrangement of the window toolbars as shown here.

2. Now type the Yahoo! Web address (**www.yahoo.com**) in the Address field and press ENTER.

   The window converts to a Web browser as shown below and shows you the Yahoo! home page. Also note that the window now has the Internet Explorer toolbar configuration.

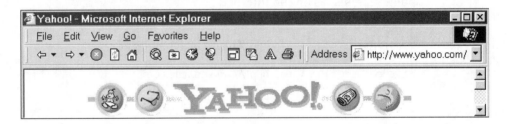

3. Finally, to fully appreciate the Web integration in Windows 98, click the Back button to return to the local file view.

Changing Your View Options

You can change the configuration of the toolbars in Internet Explorer in the same way you change toolbars for folder windows as discussed in Chapter 8. Choose Toolbars on the View menu to open the following menu where you can enable or disable toolbars.

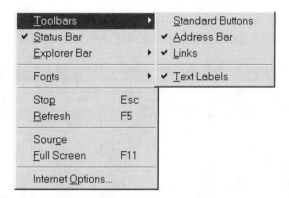

We recommend that you keep the Address Bar and Standard Buttons toolbars always enabled. However, you can disable Text Labels to remove the labels from the buttons and gain a little more room in your Internet Explorer window, which is important if you have a small Desktop. Here's a picture of the Internet Explorer toolbar with and without text labels on the standard buttons:

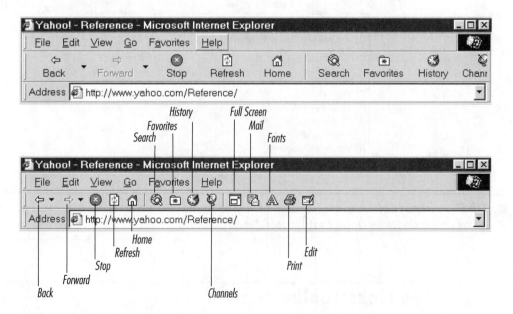

After you get familiar with Internet Explorer and its buttons, you can disable the Text Labels. If you don't know what a button is, just point to it and a description will pop up.

We like to drag the Address bar up to the right of the buttons as shown here. To move a toolbar, click its handle and drag the toolbar to a new position.

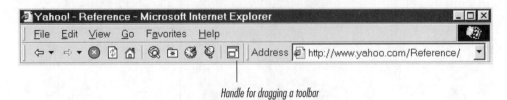

Handle for dragging a toolbar

Experiment with moving toolbars. You can position the Address bar on the Menu toolbar as well, or just drag it down so it is on its own line.

The Address bar is a great place to access sites you've already visited. Click the down arrow button on the right side of the Address bar to see a drop-down list similar to the following:

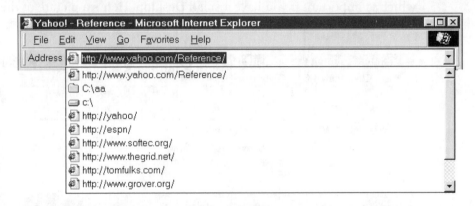

TIP: Toolbars may take up space on a small Desktop, but you can jump between full screen mode and back to window mode at any time by clicking the Full Screen button on the toolbar.

The Links Toolbar

You can also add the Links toolbar to the Internet Explorer window. It provides links to some interesting Web sites, including Microsoft's Best of the Web,

Channel Guide, Internet Start, and Welcome to My Yahoo!. You might enable the Links toolbar for a while to see if you like it. If not, just disable it.

Internet Start and Welcome to My Yahoo! are great places to set up your own personal information page. You can personalize the pages to display just the information you want to see like news, stock quotes, and weather.

You can also add your own links to the Links toolbar or delete links you don't like. To add a new link to the Links toolbar, follow these steps:

1. Go to the Web site you want to add.

2. Click the icon in the Address bar (it looks like a piece of paper) and drag it to the Links toolbar.

3. A vertical position icon appears. Move it left or right and release the mouse button at the position where you want to add the link.

To delete a link from the Links toolbar, right-click the link, then choose Delete from the menu.

The Explorer Bar

There are four Explorer Bar options. When the Explorer bar is enabled, Internet Explorer converts to a two-pane window as shown in Figure 12-3.

To enable an Explorer Bar, choose Explorer Bar from the View menu, then choose one of the following:

- **Search**   Opens the Search pane on the left side of the Internet Explorer window, which lets you use search engines more efficiently. Search results are presented in the Search pane. Clicking on a search result brings up the Web page in the browser window; you can still see the search results in the Search pane.

- **Favorites**   Opens the Favorites pane, where you can choose to jump to one of the favorite Web sites you have added to the list.

- **History**   Opens the History pane, where you can scan through a list of recently visited sites and click a site to jump to it again.

- **Channels**   Opens the Channels pane, providing quick access to a channel. Channels are discussed further in Chapter 13.

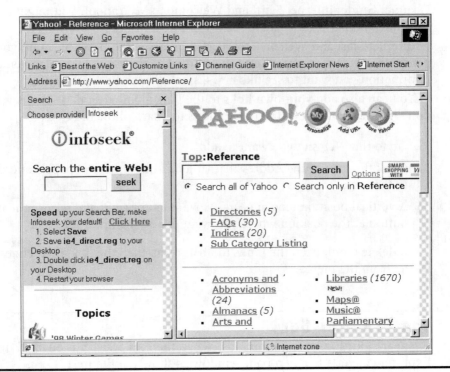

FIGURE 12-3 | Internet Explorer with Search pane open

The Go Menu

If you want to move quickly to other programs and accessories, open the Go menu. A menu similar to the following appears where you can choose any of the options in the lower part of the menu.

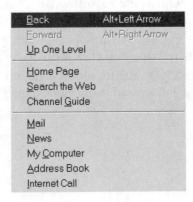

• Tips, Tricks, and Special Settings

Now that you've done some browsing on the Internet, you might be interested in learning about some interesting tips and tricks that can make your browsing easier. Here are just some examples (we describe others in the following sections):

- **Open multiple windows on the Web.**   Need to look at multiple Web sites at the same time? Just open another Internet Explorer window, then go to the other addresses you want to view.

- **Get the latest updates.**   You might need to refresh an open Web page if you think its content may have changed. Click the Refresh button on the toolbar. Internet Explorer will reload all the content for the page. Also, if you stopped a page from downloading earlier, click Refresh to update the page.

- **Change the display font.**   You can reduce or enlarge the size of the fonts that Internet Explorer uses to display information. Reducing fonts lets you see more information in the window. Enlarging fonts makes text more readable. Choose Fonts from the View menu and select an appropriate font.

- **Find information on a page.**   To find specific text on a Web page, choose "Find (on this page)" on the Edit menu. You see the following dialog box where you can type in the text to search for and specify its capitalization and whether you want to match only the words you type.

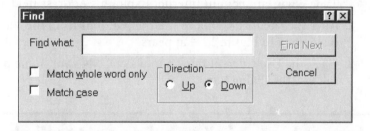

- **Stop loading a page.**   As a page loads, you may decide you don't want to see it. Click the Stop button to stop loading the page. This option is useful if you have two or more Internet Explorer windows open. If all the pages are downloading information, the pages will appear more slowly. You can stop downloading in one of the windows to speed up downloading in another. Later, you can click the Refresh button to reload the Web page.

- **Save a Web page.**   You can save a Web page to your hard drive to look at or print later. Just choose Save As on the File menu and save the page anywhere you want. Note that this option may not save all the content of the page, such as graphic images, in the location you choose.

- **Work offline.** Normally, Internet Explorer will attempt to log you onto the Internet if you start the program and you are not already online. A dialog box appears and asks if you want to log on or work offline. You can also choose Work Offline on the File menu to view subscribed Web sites offline (as discussed in the next chapter), or view Web pages that have already been downloaded.

WEBLINK : For more tips and tricks about Internet Explorer, go to http://home.microsoft.com/ie/.

Changing the Default Home Page

When you start Internet Explorer it connects to the Microsoft home page (http://home.microsoft.com) by default. However, you can make any page on the Web your default page. For example, if you want to catch up on the news of the day, you might make CNN your home page as follows. Remember that you can substitute any Web page for this example.

1. Type **www.cnn.com** in Internet Explorer's Address field and press ENTER.

2. After the site loads, choose Internet Options from the View menu. The dialog box in Figure 12-4 appears.

3. Click the Use Current button to make CNN your home page, then click OK to close the dialog box.

Building a List of Your Favorite Web Sites

Having a handy list of the Web sites you visit regularly will save you a lot of time. In Internet Explorer, these Web sites are called *favorites*. A favorite (called a *bookmark* in Netscape Navigator) is a hyperlink to a Web page. To look at your list of favorites, click Favorites on the Menu bar. You'll see a menu similar

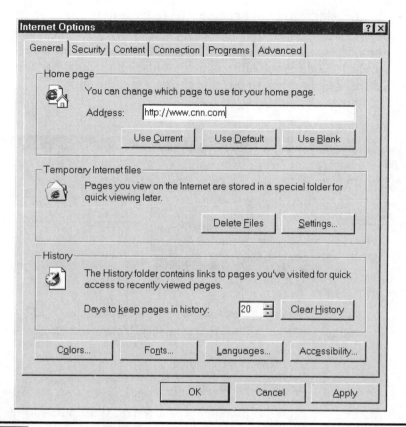

FIGURE 12-4 Internet Options dialog box for setting the home page

to Figure 12-5. Note that Internet Explorer already has some favorites on the menu in the folders called Channels, Links, and Software Updates.

You can also open favorites in Internet Explorer's left window pane. Choose Explorer Bar from the View menu, then choose Favorites on the cascading menu. Your list of favorites is now available for quick access.

It's easy to add a Web site to the Favorites list. Start by going to the Web site. Once the Web page is open in your browser, use any of these techniques to add it to the Favorites list:

• Choose Add to Favorites on the Favorites menu.

- Right-click the page and choose Add to Favorites.
- If you have your list of favorites open in the left pane, just click and drag the Address icon to the pane. The Address icon is the little "e" icon you see on the left side of the Address field. A black horizontal bar appears that you can drag up or down to position the new favorite entry.

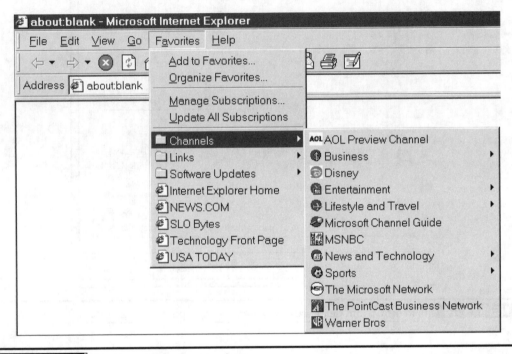

FIGURE 12-5 | Working with the Favorites list

TIP: You can also create shortcuts to Web sites on your Desktop or on the Start menu. Open a Web site, then click and drag the icon in the Address field to the Desktop or to the Start button.

Adding Local Drives and Folders to the Favorites List

As we mentioned, Internet Explorer is like any folder window in that it lets you access files on your local system or on a network. Try this now:

1. Type C: in Internet Explorer's Address field and press ENTER.
2. A list of folders on Drive C appears in the window.
3. Click the Back button to return to your previous Web page.
4. Click the Forward button to return to the Drive C folder view.
5. Now with Drive C visible, add it to your list of favorites by choosing Add to Favorites on the Favorites menu.

You can also open any folder on your local system, or open shared folders on other computers attached to your network, then add them to the Favorites list.

Organizing Your Favorites

After a while, you might create so many favorites that it becomes difficult finding the one you want. You can delete unused favorites or organize them into folders. For example, you might create folders for business and personal favorites, as described here. First, we'll create a Personal and Business folder, then show you how to organize your favorites into the folders. Keep in mind that you can create folders to match your own needs.

1. Choose Organize Favorites from the Favorites menu. This opens the dialog box shown in Figure 12-6.
2. Click the Create New Folder button to create a new folder, then type **Personal** and press ENTER immediately to rename the folder.
3. Click the New Folder button again to create another new folder and name it **Business**.

Now you can begin organizing your favorites into these new folders. You can use the drag-and-drop technique to drag favorites into the appropriate folder, but it may not be possible to see the favorite and the folder in the window at the same time. This is where the Move button comes into play.

4. Click the favorite to move, then click the Move button. A list of folders appears.

5. Click the folder you want to move the object to and click the OK button.

6. Repeat these steps for each favorite you want to move.

T I P : You can get information about any favorite by right-clicking it and choosing Properties.

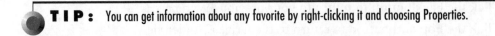

The New Folder button lets you create folders.

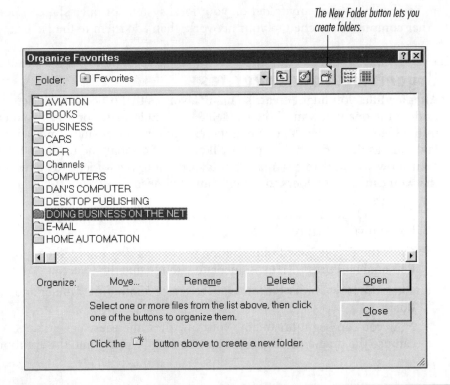

FIGURE 12-6 Organizing Favorites

Once you add new folders to your Favorites list, you will notice that they appear on the Favorites menu. Now when you click Add to Favorites to create a new favorite, you can click the Create In button to display a list of folders and choose the folder you want to add the favorite to as shown here:

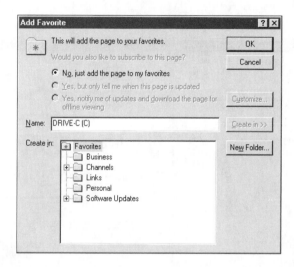

If you have favorites open in Internet Explorer's left pane, you see your new folders listed. You can click and drag the icon in the Address bar to the folders in this pane to add them to the list of favorites.

The History List

Now we're going to revise history. Internet Explorer keeps track of the places you have been on the Web. Later, you can return to any location by choosing it from the History list. The History list makes it easy to find sites you recently visited.

There are two ways to open the History list:

- Click the History button on the toolbar.
- Choose Explorer Bar on the View menu and click History.

In either case, the History list appears in Internet Explorer's left pane as shown in Figure 12-7.

As you can see in Figure 12-7, your recent Web excursions are organized by days, weeks, and months. Click a day and the list expands to display the sites you visited that day. Click on the site and it opens a list of the pages you visited on that site.

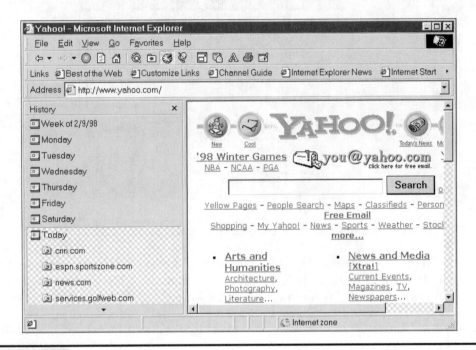

| **FIGURE 12-7** | The History list |

Modifying History Settings

The History list is actually maintained by storing an address file for each site you visit in a folder called History. The History folder is a subfolder of the Windows folder. While maintaining a history of the places you have visited may be beneficial, the history files can begin to use up quite a bit of disk space. Therefore, Windows 98 lets you adjust the number of days that files are maintained in the History list. The default is 20 days but you can change it to as much as 999 days.

To change the History settings, follow these steps:

1. Choose Internet Options on the View menu and make sure the General tab is selected. The dialog box pictured previously in Figure 12-4 appears.

2. In the History field, change the number of days you want to keep history files on your system.

3. Click OK to accept the changes.

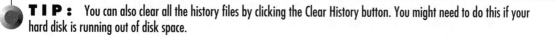

TIP: You can also clear all the history files by clicking the Clear History button. You might need to do this if your hard disk is running out of disk space.

The number of days you keep history files depends on your own needs. If you are working on a long research project in which you visit the Web often, you might want to keep files on hand during the entire life of the project. If you just casually browse the Web, the default setting is appropriate. If you are short on disk space, clear the history files and then change the setting to two or three days.

The Cache

The first time you visit a Web page, all the content of the site, including icons, banners, pictures, text, and other information is downloaded to your computer and placed in a special area called the *cache*. (The cache is located in the Temporary Internet Files folder, which is a subfolder of the Windows folder.) The next time you visit the site, your computer looks in the cache to see if it can use any of the objects it already downloaded instead of downloading them again. This improves performance dramatically.

There's a downside to this caching technique. If the page has changed since it was cached on your computer, you won't know it. However, you can set Internet Explorer to update pages according to your own preferences:

1. On the View menu, choose Internet Options.

2. On the General tab, choose Settings in the Temporary Internet files section. Here you have three choices:
   • Every visit to the page
   • Every time you start Internet Explorer
   • Never
     Choosing Never will give you the quickest page loads, but the page you're looking at may be outdated, which means you'll need to click the Refresh button to ensure you have the latest content. Choosing Every

visit to the page means you always have the freshest content, at the expense of quick loading. The default setting is Every time you start Internet Explorer—an effective compromise between speed and freshness.

You can also adjust how much space Internet Explorer devotes to its cache by adjusting the slider on the previously mentioned dialog box. The larger the cache, the more Web pages can be stored. If you don't have much free space on your hard drive, you'll want to reduce the size of the cache.

In the Temporary Internet files section on the previously mentioned dialog box, you can click the Delete Files button to clear all the files from the cache. This means any page you previously visited will have to reload from the Internet, but you won't have any disk space taken up by cached pages you're not using.

Page Setup Options and Printing Options

You can print any pages you find on the Web by clicking the Print button or by choosing Print from the File menu. Internet Explorer has some interesting features related to printing that you will want to explore.

Choose Page Setup on the File menu to open the dialog box in Figure 12-8. The options are described next. As you change options, the picture of the page in the upper-right corner will provide an approximate view of the changes.

- **Paper**   In the Size field, choose the type of paper you want to use. Since Web pages are often long, you might want to choose legal size paper if your printer supports it. Choose a paper tray in the Source field.

- **Headers and Footers**   You can specify special codes in the Header and Footer fields to control what is printed at the top and bottom of each page. The codes are described in Table 12-1. See "Headers and Footers" later in this chapter for more details.

- **Orientation**   You can set Portrait or Landscape (sideways) mode in this field. If Web pages contain graphics or tables, set Landscape mode to print in the widest mode possible.

- **Margins**   You can change the size of the margins in the field. To print the most information on a page (or to gain more space for printing wide pictures and tables), set the margins to the lowest possible value that your printer supports. A typical laser printer can be set to as low as one-quarter of an inch (.25). You can also set wide margins on the left to accommodate mounting pages in binders.

- **Printer button**   Click this button to change printers or set the properties of a printer. Click the down arrow button to choose a different printer if available and click the Properties button to change the properties of a printer. Refer to "Printing Options" in Chapter 4 for more information about printer properties. Printer setup information is provided in Chapter 20.

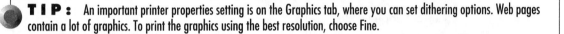

T I P :   An important printer properties setting is on the Graphics tab, where you can set dithering options. Web pages contain a lot of graphics. To print the graphics using the best resolution, choose Fine.

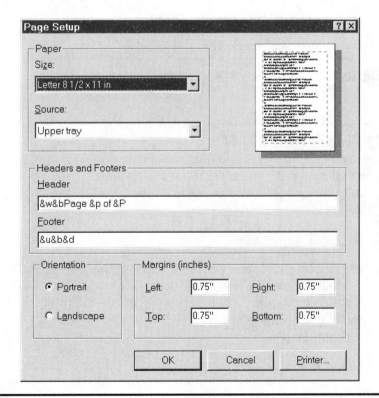

FIGURE 12-8   The Page Setup dialog box

CODE	MEANING
&w	Window title
&u	Page address (URL)
&d	Date in short format as specified by Regional Settings in Control Panel
&D	Date in long format as specified by Regional Settings in Control Panel
&t	Time in the format specified by Regional Settings in Control Panel
&T	Time in 24-hour format
&p	Current page number
&P	Total number of pages
&b	Centered text (following &b)
&b&b	Right-aligned text (following &b&b)
&&	A single ampersand (&)

TABLE 12-1 Codes for Headers and Footers

Headers and Footers

You can change the headers and footers that are printed on your Web pages, although the default settings are usually most appropriate. Let's examine the default header code pictured in Figure 12-8.

The code is

&w&bPage &p of &P

Referring to Table 12-1, &w prints the name of the Web page. This is followed by &b, which centers the text that follows (the word "Page" in this case). The code &p then prints the current page number and &P prints the total number of pages for the Web page.

The default footer is

&u&b&d

which prints the page address (URL), and then centers the date (&b is the center code and &d is the date code).

You can come up with your own Web page headers, but in most cases, these defaults will do. In some cases, you might want to temporarily remove the header and footer codes to print pages without this information.

Printing the Web Page

Once you have your print options set, you're ready to print pages. Choose Print on the File menu to open the Print dialog box pictured in Figure 12-9. Set options in the Print range and Copies field as appropriate.

Notice the Print frames field. This is where you can choose exactly which section of a multiframe Web page you want to print. Some Web pages display actual information in one pane and other extraneous information in other panes, like table of contents lists, Web links, or advertising. You can choose to print just the frame that holds information important to you.

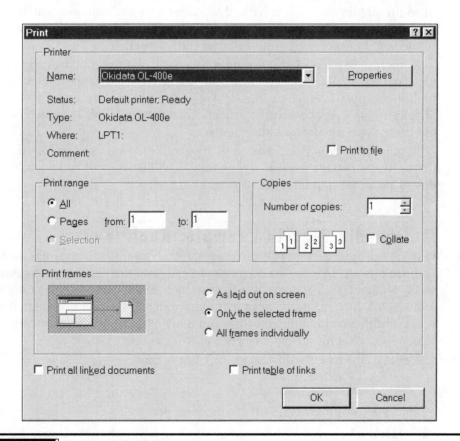

FIGURE 12-9 The Print dialog box

There are three options:

- **As laid out on screen** Choose this option to print all the frames as they appear in the Web browser.
- **Only the selected frame** Choose this option to print only the frame you have selected. If you did not select a frame, close the Print dialog box, click in the appropriate frame, then open the Print dialog box again.
- **All frames individually** Click this option to print all frames, not as laid out in the Web browser, but on individual sheets of paper.

Using Multimedia Options and Add-Ons

Most computers are now equipped with multimedia features and equipment. That's good because the Internet is rapidly becoming a multimedia wonderland. In addition, Microsoft has enhanced Windows 98's multimedia capabilities. With Internet Explorer you can take advantage of text, graphics, animation, sound, and video coming your way over the Internet.

If Internet Explorer doesn't come with a particular multimedia capability, you can install it later as an add-on, plug-in, or viewer. The most popular multimedia plug-ins include RealNetworks' RealPlayer, Macromedia Shockwave, and Adobe Acrobat Reader. There are hundreds more available, but these three are almost indispensable.

In most cases, you don't have to worry about plug-ins until you need them—if a Web page requires a plug-in, you will be asked if you want to download and install it on the spot.

Multimedia Plug-In Example: RealPlayer

One very popular add-on is RealNetworks' RealPlayer. RealPlayer has three components, RealAudio, RealVideo, and RealFlash, that let you access audio, video, and animated content over the Internet. RealPlayer uses streaming audio and video, which means you can listen and watch as the talk show, interview, music or other content downloads—you don't have to save it to your hard drive first, as you did only a couple of years ago.

RealPlayer is free. To download the latest version:

1. Go to http://www.real.com.
2. Click on RealPlayer and fill out the form provided.
3. Click the Download Now button. This will take you to the download and installation instructions.

Once you've downloaded and installed RealPlayer, visit AudioNet (http://www.audionet.com), a popular site where you can use RealPlayer to hear audio programming; you can choose from nearly 200 sources of programming. AudioNet offers music, live events, sports, comedy, speeches, and educational programming. For example, if you like listening to talk shows about computers, you can listen to live or archived shows from across the country. One nice thing about audio programming on the Internet—you can listen while you browse other sites.

Add-Ons, Plug-Ins, and Viewers

Add-ons and plug-ins do much the same thing; add-ons are tools designed for use with Internet Explorer, while plug-ins were originally intended for use with Netscape Navigator. Both add-ons and plug-ins are generally referred to as plug-ins. In this section we'll look at some of the most popular plug-ins.

ActiveX Add-Ons

Add-ons are generally ActiveX controls, which provide active content for Web browsers and the Active Desktop. ActiveX controls can do things that HTML can't, like running an electronic stock tickertape across your screen. ActiveX controls will download and install themselves in the background in Internet Explorer 4.0. Here are some sites you can check.

WEBLINKS: The ActiveX Arena (http://browserwatch.internet.com/activex.html) claims to have links to all the ActiveX controls available on the Internet.

If you want to learn more about ActiveX controls, visit ClNet's ActiveX page at http://www.activex.com/.

Tucows has freeware and shareware browser add-ons at http://tucows.tierranet.com/acc95.html.

Plug-Ins

While plug-ins were originally intended for use with Netscape Navigator, you can also use many of them with Internet Explorer. When you find a plug-in you want to download, click the download link. The following dialog box appears where you can choose to run the program from its current location or download and install it on your system. Internet Explorer stores plug-ins in c:\Program Files\Internet Explorer\PLUGINS.

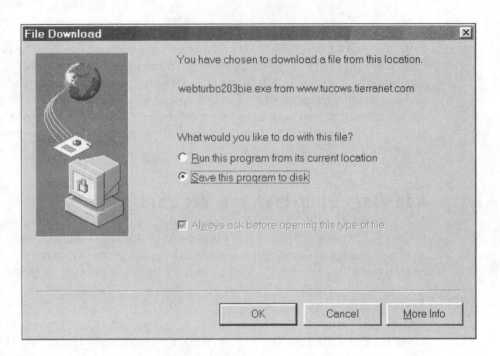

WEBLINKS: Here are some interesting Web sites where you will find plug-ins:

Netscape   http://home.netscape.com/comprod/products/navigator/
                version_2.0/plugins/index.html

Plug-in Plaza   http://browserwatch.internet.com/plug-in.html

Tucows   http://tucows.tierranet.com/plug95.html

Acrobat Viewer

Viewers let you read documents created in particular applications. Adobe Acrobat Reader is probably the best-known viewer. It lets you read, navigate, and print files created in Portable Document Format (the files have a .PDF extension). An Acrobat file looks and prints exactly like the original.

WEBLINK: You can download Acrobat Reader from http://www.adobe.com/prodindex/acrobat/ readstep.html.

Shockwave

Shockwave is another popular plug-in player for viewing graphics and animation as well as listening to audio content.

WEBLINKS: You can download Shockwave from http://www.macromedia.com/shockwave/download/.

For examples of shocked content, try Macromedia's Shockzone (http://www.macromedia.com/shockzone). There are games, music, educational challenges (such as building a dinosaur), animations, movie trailers and more that will entertain and inform you, and spark your imagination for how you can make use of Shockwave or one of the other multimedia players.

Apple QuickTime

Apple Computer's QuickTime allows you to play movies created in the QuickTime format. QuickTime is an Apple Computer multimedia extension that lets you access and control time-based video and audio data that was recorded in the QuickTime format.

WEBLINK: You can download Apple QuickTime from http://www.apple.com/quicktime/sw/sw3.html.

VDOLive Player

VDOLive Player is a free viewer that allows you to see VDO content with your Web browser. VDOLive allows viewing of live and recorded video over the Internet.

WEBLINK: You can download VDOLive Player from http://www.vdonet.com/vdostore/overview.html.

DirectShow

DirectShow is the multimedia player supplied with Internet Explorer. DirectShow plays AVI, MOV, MPEG, WAV, and files in other multimedia formats. When you find a link to a video or sound clip on a Web page, you can play the clip or save it to a drive and play it later.

NetShow

Microsoft NetShow is a free utility that lets you view or listen to content on a NetShow server delivered over the Internet or an intranet. To see what a NetShow program looks like, try the AmericaOne Television Web site. On the site you find yourself in a movie theater; click on the AmericaOne Television logo in the theater and NetShow opens and you're taken to a movie in progress. The image is small, and the audio may not be synchronized with the picture, but it'll give you a glimmer of what you'll be able to do as Web technology improves.

WEBLINK: Check out NetShow at http://www.americaone.com.

VRML

Internet Explorer 4.0 includes a Virtual Reality Modeling Language (VRML) 2.0 browser that lets you view three-dimensional sites. On a 3D site you'll find you can move through the onscreen environment, so that you can look not only ahead, but behind, above, and below you. You can circle objects, zoom back from them, and turn them over. VRML files demand plenty of memory and bandwidth and you may notice a slowdown in your system. But while VRML taxes a modem connection to the Internet, experimenting with the technology will give you a feel for what you'll be able to do on the Internet as more bandwidth becomes available.

WEBLINKS: For more information and to download the latest VRML Viewer, go to http://www.microsoft.com/vrml/toolbar/. The site lists other sites that demonstrate 3D computing.

At Silicon Graphics' VRML site you can play with some feisty animated figures called Floops that may or may not be extraterrestrials. Go to http://vrml.sgi.com/floops/.

• Using Internet Explorer's Security Features

The Internet is a new and wild world, an electronic land of opportunity—and that opportunity extends to various crooks, thieves, and scam artists. Don't assume your activities on the Internet are private and secure. However, recognizing the importance of security and privacy, Microsoft designed Internet Explorer 4.0 with features that let you visit Web sites you may not trust with confidence that your computer will not be exposed to potentially damaging software and inappropriate content. In addition, with digital certificates, you can also safely engage in electronic commerce activities over the Internet.

WEBLINK: Be sure to visit http://www.microsoft.com/ie/ie40/features/ie-security.htm for the latest information about security in Internet Explorer.

Establishing Security Zones

Security zones help protect your computer when you visit unfamiliar Web sites. As the Web becomes more *active* with dancing leprechauns and free downloadable portfolio managers, it also becomes more dangerous. Before active content, the Web was fairly safe because only text and graphics were downloaded to your computer. Today, Web sites will attempt to download executable programs (ActiveX controls, Java applets, scripts, etc.) to your computer without asking and some of those programs could damage your computer. Internet Explorer's security zones are designed to give you the ability to accept or reject the delivery of such content to your system.

However, it is not practical to have Internet Explorer ask you every time something needs to be downloaded to your computer. You might be swamped with verification messages. Therefore, Internet Explorer defines multiple security zones in which you can define Web sites that you trust. If a Web site is defined as a trusted site, Web content is downloaded without asking. You can also define a Web site as somewhat trusted, in which case Internet Explorer will ask you if you want to download. And of course, you can define a site as untrusted, meaning that potentially dangerous content is never downloaded.

The best way to understand security zones is to open the Internet Explorer Security page and explore its options. Choose Internet Options on the View menu, then click the Security tab. You see the dialog box in Figure 12-10.

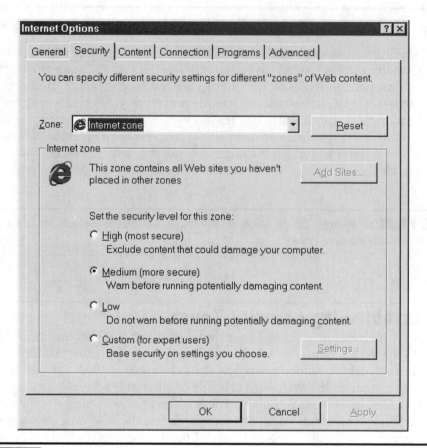

FIGURE 12-10 Setting security zones

First, notice the predefined zones in the Zone drop-down list box. Each zone's default setting is described next. Choose each zone in the Zone field to review its settings as you read through the following sections.

- **Local intranet zone**   This zone is set at medium security level by default and Internet Explorer will warn you before running any potentially damaging content from Web sites configured for this zone. When you select this option and click the Add Sites button, you see the following dialog box. You can disable any of these "general" options and then click the Advanced button to add specific sites to the zone.

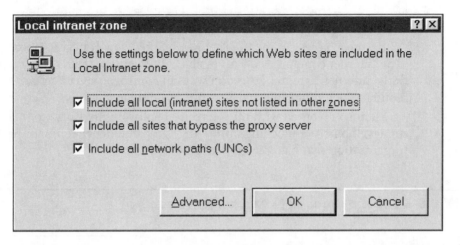

- **Trusted sites zone**   This zone is set at a low security level and Internet Explorer will not warn you before running potentially damaging content. Click the Add Sites button to include specific sites, but use caution when adding sites to this zone because of its trusted nature.
- **Internet zone**   This zone is set at the medium security level and Internet Explorer will warn you before running any potentially damaging content at Web sites on the Internet.
- **Restricted sites zone**   This zone is set at the highest security level and Internet Explorer will not run any potentially damaging content at Web sites defined in this zone.

To add a Web site to a zone, choose the zone in the Zone field and click the Add Sites button. A dialog box appears where you can type an Internet address and add it to a list.

You can also create custom zone settings. Choose a zone in the Zone field, click the Custom option, then click the Settings button. A dialog box appears where you can set how Internet Explorer will handle specific types of content, including access to files, ActiveX controls, scripts, Java applets, and whether sites must be identified with secure authentication (SSL or Secure Sockets Layer).

Blocking Sites

Widespread access to the Internet has sparked new concerns among parents. The Internet contains easily accessible adult content that is not suitable for kids. Internet Explorer gives you ways to control access to certain types of content, including language, sex, nudity, and violence.

Microsoft worked with the Recreation Software Advisory Council (RSACi) to develop its site-blocking utility. RSACi is an independent, nonprofit organization that has created a rating system for Web sites.

WEBLINK: You can visit the RSACi site at http://www.rsac.org/.

RSACi defines five levels that describe Web sites with regard to language, sex, violence, and nudity. When you enable the Internet Explorer content advisor, you can set the level of content that can be viewed with the browser.

You first enable the content advisor system by specifying a password. The password ensures that only you can change the settings. Once enabled, you select one of the categories (language, nudity, sex, and violence) and set the rating level. For example, language can be set to five levels: inoffensive slang allowed, mild expletives allowed, moderate expletives allowed, obscene gestures allowed, and explicit or crude language allowed.

Follow these steps to enable and configure the system:

1. Choose Internet Options on the View menu, then click the Content tab.

2. In the Content Advisor field, click the Enable button, then type the same password in the Password and Confirm Password field and click OK. The following Ratings page appears.

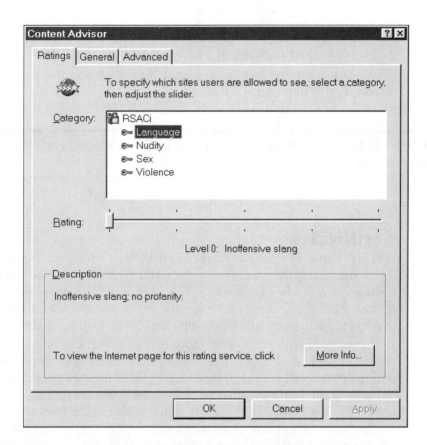

3. Click one of the categories and then slide the Rating button to the level you want.

As you change the Rating slider, a description appears below or you can click More Info to get additional information at the RSACi Web site.

The only problem with the rating system is that not all Web sites use it. That means that, by default, any site that does not have a rating will be blocked. Therefore, your kids might not be able to get into many of the decent sites they like to visit and you will find yourself making compromises. There is an option on the General page called "Users can see sites that have no rating." Normally, this option is disabled, which blocks all sites that do not conform to the rating system. You can enable it and hope that all sites with indecent content use the rating system and are blocked, but so far, that is not the case on the Internet.

We can only hope that this system will improve and that more and more Web sites will implement it.

WEBLINK: If you're looking for more information on blocking software, try Netparents.org (http://www.netparents.org).

Certificates

Internet Explorer takes advantage of *certificates*, which are digital IDs that can be used to verify the identity of people and Web sites and the validity of software. Certificates are used to prevent people from impersonating you and to ensure that Web sites are authentic and not being spoofed by someone who is trying to obtain personal information and credit card numbers.

A personal certificate is something that you obtain from a certificate authority such as Verisign. The certificate authority gathers personal information about you, then binds it to a set of digital keys that can be used for all sorts of things on the Internet, like signing and encrypting electronic mail messages. The certificate authority signs your certificate with its own digital ID so that other people and organizations can verify via the certificate authority's own signature that the contents about you inside the certificate are authentic.

Web sites also have certificates that Internet Explorer uses to verify that the site is authentic when you visit it. Internet Explorer already knows how to verify the authenticity of certificates issued by the most common certificate authorities. When it checks a Web site's certificate, it checks the address stored in the certificate to make sure it matches the site you are visiting.

Software that you download from the Internet can also be verified with certificates. A certificate can prove that the software is from the original source and has not been altered or corrupted in some way.

You enable certificates in Internet Explorer by choosing Internet Options from the View menu, then clicking the Content tab. In the Certificates field, you can do the following:

- Click Personal to add or list personal certificates.
- Click Authorities to specify the types of digital certificates you trust. For example, you can specify that you will trust all sites that use Verisign certificates.

- Click Publishers to specify which certificate authorities you trust.

In general, certificates are a good idea. The Verisign Web site is a great place to get more information about certificates. You can also obtain a free or limited use certificate from Verisign, although its offers may change by the time you read this.

WEBLINKS: You can find out just about everything you need to know about digital IDs by visiting http://digitalid.verisign.com/info_ctr.htm.

For more information about security and Internet Explorer visit the Microsoft Explorer 4.0 site at http://www.microsoft.com/ie/ie40/features/. Choose the Security link on the page, then Security Zones.

Advanced Options

Internet Explorer has a large group of advanced options that you can set as appropriate. In most cases, the default settings for these advanced options are appropriate, but you may want to change them after you've been working with Internet Explorer for a while.

Choose Internet Options from the View menu, then click the Advanced tab. You see a large list of check boxes with some of the boxes checked and some not checked. The trick is to right-click any option and click What's This?. You will then see a description of the option and be able to determine how you want to set it.

Now that you are familiar with browsing the Web and working with Internet Explorer, we move on to the next most important thing about the Internet: Internet electronic mail.

13

Active Desktop, Subscriptions, and Web Channels

The Active Desktop is a place where you can display and run Web content. You can almost think of it as a big Web browser attached to your Desktop. But this Web browser can have multiple panes that display and automatically update news, sports, weather, and other information. To begin, we explain Webcasting, subscriptions, and channels. Then we discuss how to configure Windows 98 to take advantage of these features.

About Webcasting, Subscriptions, and Channels

Webcasting is a term taken from the TV broadcast industry. Television stations broadcast programs. Television viewers tune in to channels of their choice. Webcasting extends this metaphor to the Internet. Web sites can "broadcast" a continuous stream of information that anybody with a Web browser can receive. In Windows 98, you set up a *subscription* in order to start receiving information from these Web sites.

Current Webcasting is done through a little trickery. While it appears like you've "tuned in" to a favorite Web site, what's really happening is that your Web browser periodically visits the sites you've subscribed to and checks to see if there is any new information. Since this happens in the background, information appears to arrive automatically. Of course, you need a permanent Internet connection for best results. If you're connected to a corporate network, you may have a permanent Internet connection and receive information automatically from the Internet as well as corporate Web servers.

That little bit of trickery we just mentioned is called *pull* technology. Pull is exactly what you do when you surf the Web. You visit a site and "pull" information from the site to your computer. The opposite of pull is *push*, the nickname for a technology that is just starting to come into widespread use. Push is true Webcasting because your computer never has to check with the Web site to see if there is new information. The Web site sends out packets of information that you can tune in to receive, just like you tune in to a television station. Information packets have an identification number that associates them with a particular broadcast, such as CNN weather information.

Technically, the packet identification number is called an *IP multicast address* and you'll be hearing more about multicasting as the technology becomes more pervasive. To receive the broadcast, you instruct your computer to receive all packets with the IP multicast address of the broadcast you want to receive.

 TIP: As an analogy, consider newspapers. You can walk down to your local newsstand every day to pick up the paper (pull), or you can have it delivered to your doorstep. In this analogy, true Webcasting (push) is like those free papers that everybody gets, and that you can either read or throw in the recycling bin.

In between pull and push (true Webcasting) is *managed pull* (or *managed Webcasting*, as Microsoft prefers to call it). Managed pull is just like regular pull, but the Web server you visit gets involved in the process by making information more accessible. Web site administrators can choose to enhance their Web sites by adding what is called a Channel Definition File (CDF). A CDF is basically an index of the Web site. When your Web browser visits the site to do a pull, it reads the CDF to learn what the latest updates and additions are at the site. It then retrieves only new information, assuming that your computer already cached other information from previous visits.

Managed pull improves the performance of subscriptions and makes pull more efficient. When a Web site has been enhanced to take advantage of CDFs, it is called a *channel*.

N O T E :   In none of these cases is it necessary for the Web server to maintain a list of recipients in order to distribute information. With pull, you set up your computer to go to the site and get information. Therefore, the target site does not need to know about your computer (although if it does, it can provide custom information). With push, the broadcasting Web site sends out the information for anybody to receive.

In the remainder of this chapter, you will learn about setting up "subscriptions" to Web sites that provide continuously updated news and other information. You subscribe to a Web site by adding it to your Favorites list. Then you define the parameters of the subscription. Internet Explorer can then notify you that it has discovered new content at a site, or it can get the new content and store it for you to browse when you're not connected.

Windows 98 also supports technology for receiving data transmitted over television signals. Anybody with a TV tuner card in their computer can receive these signals. Currently, public broadcast stations (PBS) are including data in part of their transmission signals. Note that you can only receive the data that is transmitted, in much the same way that you receive television programming, but the data you receive is viewable in your Web browser or a component on the Active Desktop.

Taking Advantage of the Active Desktop

In previous chapters, we've used the analogy of a multilayer Desktop to describe the Active Desktop. When Active Desktop is on, you can imagine it as another

Desktop under your normal Desktop. The normal Desktop is then like clear glass through which you can view the Active Desktop. Icons resting on the normal Desktop can be dragged around on top of the clear glass over any content that exists on the Active Desktop.

TIP: You can choose to hide the normal Desktop while you are viewing the Active Desktop and you can turn the Active Desktop on or off at any time.

Another important point is that while the normal Desktop is a place to run applications that were written specifically for Windows, the Active Desktop is a place where you can run Web content such as Active Channel components, ActiveX controls, Java applets, and of course HTML documents (Web pages). If all that terminology sounds confusing, just think of the Active Desktop as a way to make Windows 98 work more like the Web rather than like previous versions of Windows. And with Microsoft's Active Channel technology, discussed later, Web pages you place on the Desktop are automatically updated for you.

So what can you put on the Active Desktop? Here are just a few examples:

- The latest news from Web sites like MSNBC or CNN
- Stocks quotes, weather reports, sports scores, and more
- Pop-up announcements and messages from internal corporate servers
- Notifications for new mail, chat, or public discussion forums
- Any program that was constructed with Web technologies such as ActiveX and Java

Companies can create custom Active Desktop components to place on computers throughout the organization. An example is pictured in Figure 13-1. It includes a news reader, hyperlinks to internal databases and corporate information, and a search box for obtaining technical support from the help staff.

FIGURE 13-1 Corporate Active Desktop

Configuring the Active Desktop

In Chapter 2 under "How to Enable and Disable Active Desktop," we showed you how to enable and disable the Active Desktop. We'll review here to put it into the context of this chapter. To turn the Active Desktop on:

1. Right-click a blank part of the Desktop and choose Active Desktop from the shortcut menu. The following cascading menu appears:

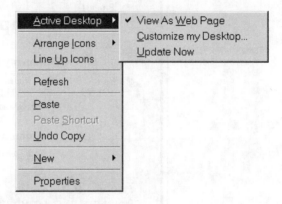

2. If "View As Web Page" does not have a check mark, select it to enable the Active Desktop.

You can repeat this same procedure at any time to turn the Active Desktop on or off. Disable the Active Desktop when you don't care to receive the latest updates or when you don't want the Active Desktop content to clutter your standard Desktop.

T I P : When you're viewing the Active Desktop, you may want to temporarily remove the normal Desktop icons. Right-click the Desktop, choose Active Desktop | Customize my Desktop, then click the Effects tab. Enable the option called "Hide icons when the desktop is viewed as a Web page."

Install Active Components from the Web

There are many sites that provide components for the Active Desktop. Some of these components, such as news feeders, require that you set up a subscription as discussed later. Other components are simply entertaining and do not require updates and subscriptions. Some examples are rotating clocks, mortgage calculators, and animated comics that were created with Web technologies such as ActiveX and Java. You can get them at Microsoft's Web site and other Web sites. We show you how here.

Windows 98 makes it easy to set up a component on the Active Desktop. In most cases, the whole process is automatic. You simply go to a Web site that has components and select a component. The component then installs itself on your Desktop.

1. Right-click the Desktop and choose Active Desktop | Customize my Desktop. The dialog box in Figure 13-2 appears.

2. Note the options in this dialog box. The monitor displays the current layout of the Active Desktop. You see black boxes where existing components are positioned. You can turn the Active Desktop on or off by clicking the View my Active Desktop as a web page field. The lower field displays a list of currently installed components. The Internet Explorer Channel Bar is installed by default. You can disable it by clicking the check box, or you can permanently remove it by clicking the Delete button.

3. Click the New button. A dialog box appears asking if you want to visit the Microsoft Active Desktop Gallery Web site. Click Yes.

4. Windows 98 will automatically connect to the Internet and the gallery site. You will see a security message, asking if you want to download active content. Click Yes to accept content from Microsoft.

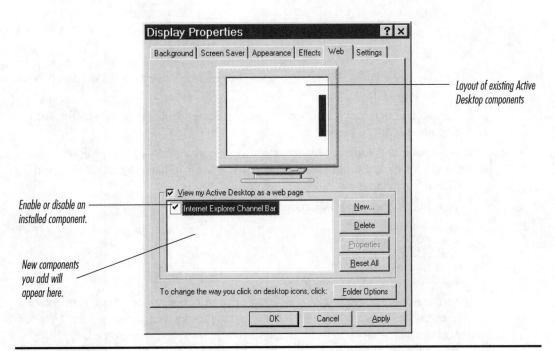

Layout of existing Active Desktop components

Enable or disable an installed component.

New components you add will appear here.

FIGURE 13-2 Customizing the Active Desktop

Previously, you saw how to install an active component on your Desktop. Now we show you how to create your own component and install it on the Desktop. The component is very simple and serves as the basis for a much larger utility if you want to expand it. You'll write the component in HTML, but keep in mind that we're not trying to teach HTML here—we're showing you how to get started creating components. You can refer to Chapter 16 for detailed information about creating HTML pages for your Active Desktop. In particular, refer to "Creating a Desktop Web Page" at the end of Chapter 16.

The HTML file we'll create contains hyperlinked email addresses and will appear on your Active Desktop as shown next. Like we said, it's not too exciting, but what it does is useful: when you click one of the names in the scrolling list, a blank email message opens addressed to the selected recipient. The important point is that you are customizing your Desktop with HTML, the same language that powers Web sites all over the Internet.

1. Start by creating the HTML file on your Desktop. Right-click the Desktop and choose New | Text Document.

2. A new text document icon appears with the name highlighted. Type **EMAIL.HTM** and press ENTER to rename it.

3. Now open and edit the new document: right-click the EMAIL.HTM icon and choose Send To | Notepad. If Notepad is not on the Send To menu, refer to "The Send To Option" in Chapter 4.

4. Type in the following HTML code:

```
<html>
<body>
<p><a href="mailto: address"> name</a></p>
</body>
</html>
```

Replace *address* with the Internet email address of someone that you send mail to often and replace *name* with the name of the recipient. Duplicate this third line for each mail recipient you want to add to your mailing list, changing *name* and *address* as appropriate.

5. Choose Save from the File menu.

Once you've created the HTML file, you're ready to install it on your Active Desktop. Keep in mind that you can go back and edit this file at any time by following step 3. You can also edit this file in FrontPage Express, which has the tools you need to create much more elaborate HTML desktop components. To edit the file, right-click the icon that appears on the desktop and choose Edit from the shortcut menu.

Now you're ready to install the component on the Active Desktop.

1. Right-click the Desktop and choose Active Desktop | Customize my Desktop. The dialog box in Figure 13-2 appears.

2. To add your new mailing list component, click the New button.

3. Click No when asked if you want to download a component from Microsoft's site. Windows 98 then asks where the component is located. Click the Browse button to open a standard Browse dialog box.

4. You saved EMAIL.HTM on the Desktop, so choose Desktop in the Look in field and double-click the EMAIL.HTM file you created previously.

5. Complete the installation by clicking the OK button. Note that when you get to the Display Properties dialog box (Figure 13-2), a check mark appears next to the EMAIL.HTM item indicating that it is enabled.

Now you can move and resize the box like any window on your Desktop. To move the box, point the mouse to the upper part of the window. A Title bar appears that you click and drag to move the window. You can also click any border or corner to resize the window.

If you edit your custom component, you'll need to refresh it on your Desktop. This happens automatically if you reboot, but to see the changes right away, follow step 1 above, then just click OK on the dialog box. The new updates will appear in the Active Desktop component.

Browse the Active Desktop Gallery on your own. You can choose from categories including news, sports, entertainment, travel, weather, and cool utilities. Note that many of these options are subscription services discussed later under "Defining Your Own Subscriptions."

Click the cool utilities section, then click some of the utilities listed. To download any component, click the Add to Active Desktop button. It's automatic from there on. The component is downloaded and installed on your Active Desktop.

To temporarily disable a component, open the Display Properties dialog box pictured in Figure 13-2, then remove the check mark from the component. To permanently remove the component, highlight it and click the Delete button.

WEBLINKS: The following sites provide useful information for Windows users. At the time of this writing, the sites were revamping for Windows 98. Check the sites to find components for your Desktop or references to sites that have components:

http://www.winfiles.com
http://www.windowscentral.com
http://www.halcyon.com/cerelli/
http://www.shareware95.com

Web Site Subscriptions

Many of the Active Desktop components you install will require periodic updating. That is where subscriptions come into play. A *subscription* is basically a schedule that your computer follows to periodically check with a Web site and get new or updated content on your Desktop.

As far as subscriptions go, there are two types of Web sites:

- **Channel-defined sites**   These are Web sites that support Windows 98 channel technology. The sites have a CDF file that provides an index of what is new and changed. Internet Explorer reads the CDF file when it checks the site at the defined intervals and quickly obtains the latest information. It does not need to go through a lengthy process of checking every page at the site to see what has changed.

- **Non-channel defined sites**   If no CDF is available, Internet Explorer must "crawl" the site at the subscribed time intervals. *Crawling* means that Internet Explorer looks at all the Web pages and attached files at the site and compares them with files that already exist in the cache on your computer from the last time the site was visited. New information is then downloaded to your system.

From the user's point of view, there is no difference between the two except that site crawling is time consuming. But, almost any site on the Internet can be crawled so Internet Explorer is capable of getting you the latest information for any site you subscribe to.

Setting up subscriptions is worthwhile for the following reasons:

- Subscriptions automate visiting and crawling of the site on a scheduled basis to check for updated content.
- You are notified when new content is available, either by a "gleam" that appears on your Favorites list or via email.
- New content can be downloaded for *offline viewing*. If you own a laptop computer, you can go on the road with all the latest Web information.

The subscription process starts by visiting the Web site you want to subscribe to and adding it to your Favorites list of Web sites. You then define the parameters of the subscription. Some of these parameters include defining the time schedule, the "depth" of hyperlinks to explore, and whether new information is downloaded or you are simply notified of new information.

An important consideration is the number of levels at which Internet Explorer crawls a site. Some sites may not have enough interesting information to make crawling more than two or three levels deep worthwhile. To alleviate downloading excess information, you can have Internet Explorer download only HTML information and exclude images and other information that may not be necessary and that would take up extra disk space.

T I P : Sites that use CDF files provide the best subscription performance. You may want to encourage the Webmasters of sites you visit often to add CDF files to their site.

Web sites that conform to CDF have many advantages. Webmasters can define logical groupings of information such as sports, news, and financial information in the CDF. You can then have Internet Explorer grab only the type of information that you are interested in. In addition, a Web site can even provide custom CDFs based on your preferences (preferences are found in *cookies*, which are small files on your computer that contain information about your preferences at a specific Web site). In addition, the CDF can provide information about when the next update for the site will take place so Internet

Explorer can check back after the update. This really makes subscriptions efficient and saves bandwidth because it ensures that your system only checks with a site after the date that the new information is supposed to be available.

Defining Your Own Subscriptions

To set up a subscription, follow the steps here. For this example, we show you how to set up and define your own subscription with components available at Microsoft's Active Desktop Gallery, but you can visit any Web site to set up a subscription.

1. Open Internet Explorer and go to the Web site that you want to subscribe to, either on the Internet or on your local intranet.

2. Choose Add to Favorites on the Favorites menu. The following dialog box appears:

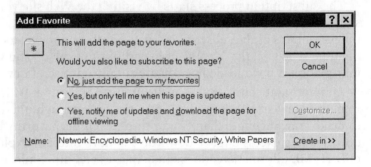

3. Choose one of the following options:

   - *Yes, but only tell me when this page is updated*   Choose this option if you want Internet Explorer to check for new content but not download it. If new content is available, Internet Explorer will add a "red gleam" next to the site name on the Favorites menu. If you click the Customize button, you can also have Internet Explorer notify you of changes via an email message.

   - *Yes, notify me of updates and download the page for offline viewing* Choose this option to download information from the site. If you choose this option, you should change scheduling options to download the site at night if it contains a lot of content.

We'll assume you have chosen the second option just described. It has special options for defining how the subscription is handled as outlined below.

4. Click the Customize button to customize the subscription parameters. The first box that appears is shown here:

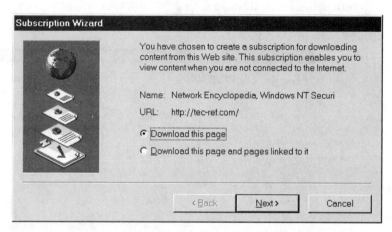

5. Choose "Download this page" if you only want to download the current page listed in the Name field, or choose "Download this page and pages linked to it" to download up to three levels of Web pages from the site.

6. Click Next. If you choose to download multiple pages, you are asked how many levels to download (one through three levels).

7. Click Next, then specify if you would also like to be notified via email about site changes.

8. Click Next again to display the scheduling options pictured next. Choose Scheduled to check the site at a predetermined time, or Manually. If you choose Manually, you can update the Desktop at any time by right-clicking the Desktop and choosing Active Desktop | Update Now.

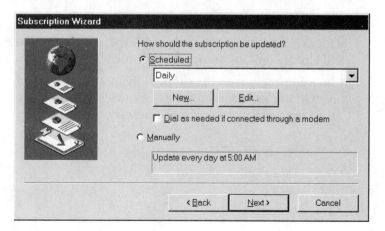

If you decide to set a scheduled subscription, choose the Scheduled option, then click the New button (or Edit button to change a schedule you already created). The following dialog box appears where you can change scheduling options:

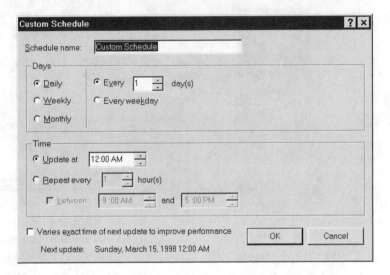

9. Once you've set the schedule, click the Next button. You're then asked to specify a user name and password for sites that require it. Click Finish to complete the subscription.

Managing Subscriptions

Once you've created a subscription, you can view or change the subscription details at any time as follows:

1. Open the Favorites menu, then right-click the Web site you want to work with to open a shortcut menu with various options. (Note the Unsubscribe and Update options on the shortcut menu.)

2. Choose Properties on the shortcut menu to display the following dialog box. On the Subscription tab you can view a summary of the subscription parameters and unsubscribe if necessary.

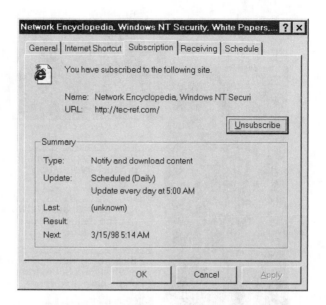

3. Click the Receiving tab to change the following options:

- **Subscription type**   Choose to receive notification that a site has changed or to download the changes to your system.
- **Notification type**   Choose to display a gleam on the Favorites menu or to have a message emailed to you.
- **Advanced button**   Change the number of levels to download and the items to download (images, sound, video, ActiveX Controls, Java, etc.). You can also specify a limit in bytes to download.

4. Click the Schedule tab to change when site information is downloaded.

5. When you're done changing parameters, click the OK button.

Microsoft's Active Channel Guide

The Active Channel Guide, pictured on the right in Figure 13-3, is a quick way to find channels on the Internet that can deliver news and information directly to your Active Desktop. You can open this guide by clicking Channel Guide on the Internet Explorer Channel Bar pictured on the left in Figure 13-3.

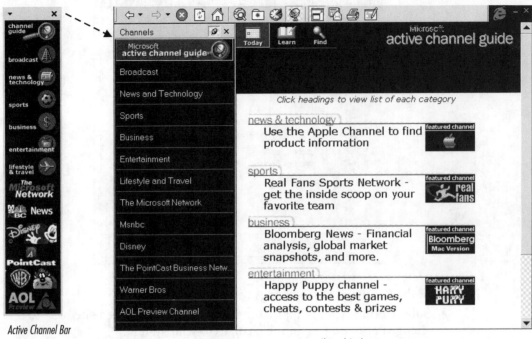

Active Channel Bar   Active Channel Guide

FIGURE 13-3 | Internet Explorer Bar and Guide

NOTE: If you don't see the Active Channel Bar, right-click the Desktop and choose Active Desktop | Customize my Desktop to display the dialog box pictured in Figure 13-2. Enable the option called Internet Explorer Channel Bar and click OK.

The Internet Guide is a full-screen window version of Internet Explorer with icons at the top and a channel bar down the left side of the window. You can click any item in the channel bar to choose from sites that contain active and subscribable content. Explore the sites listed on the guide now. You will find many active components to install on your Desktop as well as many channels that provide news and other information.

In the previous section, you saw how to set up your own subscription to Web sites, especially those that do not support CDF technology. Web sites and active components that do support CDF technology usually have predefined or recommended schedules, so the setup process is a little simpler. Let's revisit the Microsoft Active Desktop Gallery and obtain a weather component that will display the latest weather conditions across the United States.

1. Right-click the Desktop, then choose Active Desktop | Customize my Desktop.
2. Click New to add a new item. When you're asked if you want to visit the Active Desktop Gallery, click Yes.
3. An Internet Explorer window opens and connects with the gallery Web site.
4. Choose the Weather category, then choose MSNBC Weather Map. A description of the weather map appears.
5. Click Add to Active Desktop to download the component and add it to your Desktop.
6. You're asked if you want to add the item to your Active Desktop. Click OK to see a dialog box where you can customize the subscription dates and times as described earlier.

When you're done, the MSNBC weather component is placed on your Active Desktop as shown here and the weather information is automatically updated according to the predefined schedule or the schedule you customized.

To change the receiving and scheduling options, point near the top of the component to open its title bar, then click the down arrow button and choose Properties.

More About Offline Web Browsing

Windows 98's offline browsing feature lets you download the contents of your favorite Web sites at night or any time when you're not using your computer, then view the Web sites at any time without being connected to the Internet. That means, for example, that you can download your favorite sites before leaving on a plane flight, then browse the Web while in flight without being connected.

When working offline, you access Web sites as if you were connected to the Internet. Internet Explorer knows that you are working offline and browses the cache on your computer where downloaded information is stored.

There are many advantages to offline browsing. If you think about it, it doesn't really make much sense to browse Web sites on your own time because it takes so long to download Web pages. Why not do all the downloading while you are asleep. The next day, the pages you've downloaded appear instantly in your Web browser as you explore the contents of a Web site.

Internet Explorer retrieves the Web site contents at the time you specify and puts the pages and associated graphics and other components in a cache on your computer. The contents of the cache can be browsed even if you are not connected to the Internet.

You can set up Web sites for offline browsing in two ways:

- Go to the Web site, then add it to your Favorites list and specify the subscription options in the Add Favorites dialog box.
- Add a Web site to your Active Desktop. Windows 98 automatically adds all Desktop components to your Subscriptions folder.

Channel Broadcasting Enhancements

Microsoft has developed a multimedia Web technology called NetShow that enhances broadcasting with interactive content like audio, illustrated audio (images and sound), and video. NetShow has the following features:

- NetShow lets you use files in the most popular formats such as JPEG, GIF, AVI, QuickTime, and WAV. Now you only need one component to view or hear these files.
- NetShow allows you to play multimedia content while it is still being downloaded to your computer.
- Content producers can create NetShow productions in which graphics, slides, photographs, and URLs can be synchronized with the audio stream.

- NetShow uses multicast technology over the Internet and intranets. Multicasting can deliver information to many users at the same time in a very efficient way.

   With NetShow components installed, Windows 98 is multicast ready. All you need to do is make sure the NetShow Player is installed. To install NetShow, follow these steps:

1. Open the Control Panel and choose Add/Remove Programs.
2. Click the Windows Setup tab, then double-click Multimedia in the list.
3. Check the option called Microsoft NetShow player and click OK, then click OK again to complete the installation. You may be asked to insert the Windows 98 CD-ROM.

WEBLINK :   Audionet provides a variety of NetShow content at http://audionet.com/.

   Network administrators will appreciate most of the benefits of multicasting. The technical details are not important here, but you should know that multicasting will revolutionize broadcasting on the Internet and intranets once network infrastructures are fully configured to use it. Multicasting optimizes network traffic and allows producers to deliver more exciting and dynamic content without burdening the systems.

Television Technologies and WebTV

WebTV for Windows allows your computer to display standard and interactive television broadcasts. With a TV tuner card similar to those discussed next, you can receive:

- **Standard television broadcasts**   TV broadcasts appear in a window or full screen on your computer screen as shown in Figure 13-4. The TV tuner connects to standard TV sources such as Cable TV (CATV), satellite dishes, and video players. You change channels by clicking a channel selector with the mouse and hear sound through your computer-attached speakers. This

FIGURE 13-4 | Desktop TV viewer

capability does not rely on any specific Windows 98 technology since most TV tuner manufacturers supply all their own software to display TV in a window.

- **Interactive television broadcasts** Interactive TV broadcasts include TV and HTML mixed on the same screen. Viewers can watch TV and Web programming at the same time. A company called WebTV developed a box that goes on the top of your TV that provides Web content directly linked to TV shows. A separate computer was not needed. The system provided a Windows-like interface that allows audiences to access the Internet through their televisions. Microsoft bought WebTV and has extended the WebTV concept to Windows 98. More information is available at http://www.webtv.com.

- **Data Broadcasting over TV transmissions** In this scheme, Internet content and other data is delivered over the broadcast television network. No modem or Internet connection is required. Data is embedded in a portion of TV transmissions called the Vertical Blanking Interval (VBI). Microsoft is working with WaveTop, a division of WavePhore, on this technology. Refer to "Data Broadcasting over TV Transmissions" for more information.

TIP: Even if you don't have a TV tuner card, you can still use the WebTV Program Guide to receive television program information from Web sites as discussed in a moment.

TV Tuners

As mentioned, TV tuner cards let you watch TV on your PC, but Windows 98 can help you do much more with your TV tuner. Before discussing those extra features, let's look at TV tuner cards available from ATI Technologies and ADS Technologies.

The ATI All-In-Wonder Pro, pictured in Figure 13-5, is a combination video card that includes 3D, 2D, and video acceleration; video capture; and TV tuner components. It is designed for home and office users. The card includes a CATV-ready "intelligent" DBX stereo TV tuner with Instant Replay 3D acceleration. It also supports DVD quality video playback, still and motion

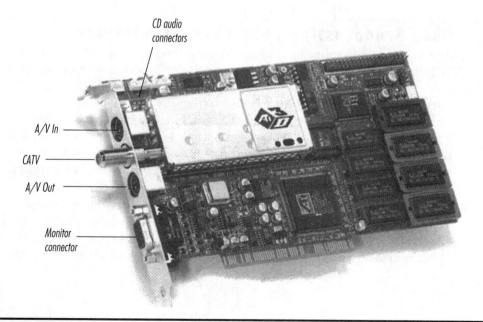

CD audio connectors

A/V In

CATV

A/V Out

Monitor connector

FIGURE 13-5 The ATI All-In-Wonder Pro

video capture, videoconferencing-ready 2D acceleration, and TV set display with S-Video and composite connectors.

WEBLINK: Get more information about ATI video products at http://www.atitech.com.

The ADS Channel Surfer TV card is another tuner card compatible with Windows 98. The card lets you watch TV or video in a scalable window, capture and save video and still images, edit video clips, and more. The product requires that you have a separate video card installed in your system, and so it is much cheaper than the ATI model just discussed, but works with your existing hardware. It has S-Video and CATV connectors.

WEBLINK: Get more information about the ADS Channel Surfer TV card at http://www.adstech.com.

Data Broadcasting over TV Transmissions

As mentioned, Microsoft has integrated the WaveTop broadcast service into Windows 98. WaveTop is a free content delivery service that does not require a modem or an Internet connection. Data streams are embedded into the VBI of television signals that are broadcast from over 264 PBS member stations. PBS stations are part of PBS National Datacast and their signals reach about 99 percent of the homes in the U.S. All you need is a browser and a PC with a TV tuner card to access information, entertainment, and software. For example, while watching the Olympics, you could also view a separate data stream that provides statistics about the games.

Some of the world's leading media companies are taking advantage of WaveTop, including Time Inc. New Media, which publishes online versions of *People, Time, Entertainment Weekly, Money, Fortune,* and *Sports Illustrated.* Other providers include USA TODAY, Wall Street Journal Interactive Edition,

CBS Sportsline, PBS ONLINE, The Weather Channel, Universal Press Syndicate – Comics, and more.

WEBLINKS: For more information about WaveTop and WavePhore, visit the following sites:
http://www.wavephore.com
http://www.wavetop.net (note net, not com)
http://www.wavo.com
http://www.newscast.com

With WaveTop, Windows 98 becomes even more integrated into the home entertainment market. The VBI signal can broadcast a few hundred kilobites of information per second to large numbers of people. But WavePhore has an even bigger plan to broadcast over dedicated channels such as those available with DirectTV. A single dedicated channel can broadcast 32 megabits of data each second. That's enough to download an entire newspaper to your computer every morning.

Of course, if data broadcasting is delivering this amount of content, you'll need lots of hard drive space. Fortunately, 10-gigabyte hard drives have become relatively inexpensive.

You install WaveTop during installation or as follows:

1. Open Add/Remove Programs in the Control Panel and click the Windows Setup tab.
2. Select WebTV for Windows, then click the Details button.
3. Check WaveTop Data Broadcasting and click OK, then follow the instructions on the screen.

You'll need to restart your computer. When it restarts, WaveTop will automatically try to locate channels that are broadcasting information. It takes about 10 minutes to scan 100+ channels. After WaveTop finds channels, it launches the WaveTop browser.

The WaveTop browser is a special version of Internet Explorer that has a channel bar where you can choose to view different types of content. Click GuideTop to get the current listing of WaveTop broadcasts by content category. The list contains the current three-hour brroadcast schedule. Click MyTop to select which providers will supply content for each channel. The other buttons include NewsTop (news, sports, weather), StockTop (stock quotes and business news), and KidsTop (kids-oriented content).

Note that you must leave your PC on to receive content, but after you receive information, WaveTop operates like a standard Web browser. Just click the channel you want to view.

WebTV for Windows Electronic Program Guide

The WebTV for Windows Program Guide is accessible by clicking the Start button, then choosing Programs | Accessories | Entertainment | WebTV for Windows. The WebTV Program Guide appears in full-screen mode similar to what you see in Figure 13-6. The WebTV Program Guide looks quite a bit different from other windows, but you still use a mouse and many familiar controls to access its features.

The Program Guide is basically a listing of local programming in your area, but you must first download the programming to see what's playing. In addition, you must download the programming on a regular basis to get the latest listings. To download programming, follow these steps:

1. Log on to the Internet.
2. Start the Program Guide, then press F10 to open the toolbar. It appears at the top of the window.
3. Choose Channel 97 in the channel selector that appears in the extreme upper-left corner.

   A Welcome message appears and you should hear a voice. If you don't hear a voice, your sound system is not working properly or the volume is reduced.
4. On the Welcome screen, click the hyperlink that downloads the TV listing.

   This takes you to the http://broadcast.microsoft.com/epgdata/ Web site where you specify your zip code to obtain program listings for your area. Just follow the instructions on the screen to download the program listings.
5. Once the program guide has downloaded to your computer, click Next on the Welcome screen and Finish to complete the introductory messages.

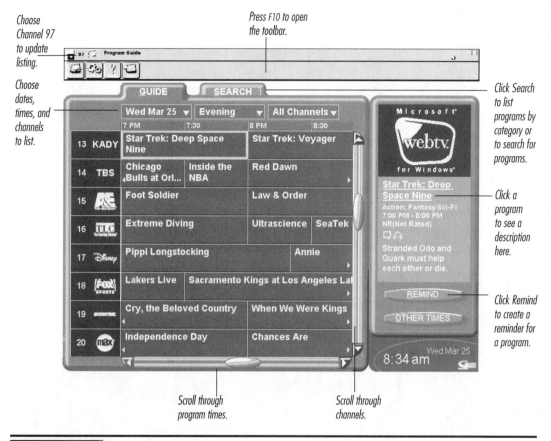

Choose
Channel 97
to update
listing.

Choose
dates,
times, and
channels
to list.

Press F10 to open
the toolbar.

Click Search
to list
programs by
category or
to search for
programs.

Click a
program
to see a
description
here.

Click Remind
to create a
reminder for
a program.

Scroll through
program times.

Scroll through
channels.

FIGURE 13-6 | The WebTV Program Guide

When you're done, the new listing automatically appears in the WebTV Program Guide and you see program listings similar to Figure 13-6. Follow the instructions on Figure 13-6 to access the Program Guide's features. You can access additional help by pressing F10 and clicking the Help button.

TIP: Click a program, then click a hyperlink in the right pane to see a list of sites on the Web that provide information about the program or movie.

We hope the information provided here on broadcast technologies has given you a taste of what the Internet can deliver. Windows 98 with its built-in ability to handle these new technologies is just the operating system you need for the future.

Using Outlook Express

14

BASICS

- Send and receive messages
- Spruce up your messages by formatting them with special fonts, colors, and styles
- Send files, pictures, sounds, and other media to email recipients by attaching them to email messages
- Access Web pages with Outlook Express

BEYOND

- Organize your email into separate folders for later viewing or for archiving purposes
- Import messages and address books from email programs you may have been using prior to running Outlook Express
- Secure your email to prevent eavesdroppers and people other than the recipient from reading the messages

This chapter discusses Outlook Express, which is Windows 98's tool for sending and receiving email messages, participating in newsgroups, and managing address books.

The first time you start Outlook Express, you see the window pictured in Figure 14-1. This initial screen displays icons for the tasks you can perform in Outlook Express. While Outlook Express is primarily designed for communicating via electronic mail, note the Read News icon. It connects you with Internet newsgroups where you can participate in discussions about topics that interest you. Topics include finance, computers, gardening, and things we don't even care to mention here.

Click here to see the overview screen

Choose a folder to see the messages it contains

FIGURE 14-1 The Outlook Express welcome screen

One of the best features of Outlook Express is that it supports HTML formatting and lets you create messages that look every bit as exciting and dynamic as Web pages. You can use special fonts and text styles, and you can insert graphic, sound, and even video right into the messages (instead of just as an attachment). Then you can send your messages to anyone who runs Windows 98 and uses Outlook Express or compatible program. The message recipient will be able to see all the formatting and Web page designs you have placed in your messages.

While Outlook Express is a subset of Microsoft Office's Outlook, many home users and small business users will have little need to upgrade to the advanced versions because Outlook Express has all the features they need to effectively communicate with electronic messaging.

Getting Started

Outlook Express installs automatically when you install Windows 98. You'll find the Outlook Express icon on the Windows 98 Taskbar, or the Outlook Express shortcut on the desktop as shown here:

You can click either to start Outlook Express. You can also start Outlook Express while working in other applications like Microsoft Word. If you're browsing with Internet Explorer or working in a folder window, choose Mail on the Go menu.

If you are starting Outlook Express for the first time, note the following:

- The Internet Connection Wizard helps you enter information about the electronic mail account you have with your Internet Service Provider. Refer to Appendix B or call your ISP for more information about setting up Internet account options.

- You are given the opportunity to import messages from your existing email software (or you can do it later, if you prefer). For example, you can import all the mail folders or selected folders from Eudora Pro, Netscape Navigator, or other email clients. If you need to import messages or address books, refer to the sections at the end of this chapter.

When Outlook Express opens, you see a window similar to Figure 14-1. Click the Inbox icon in the left pane to see a list of messages you have received as shown in Figure 14-2. Note that received messages only appear if you have connected with your ISP's mail server.

Received messages list (double-click a message to open it)

Toolbar (may change depending on the folder selected)

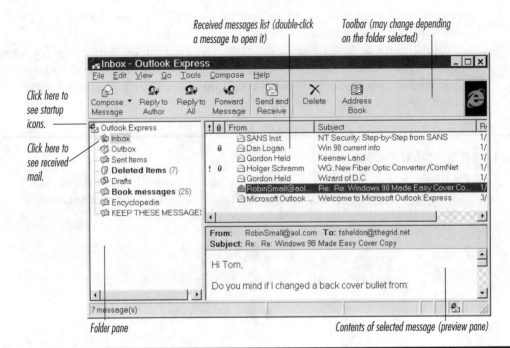

Click here to see startup icons.

Click here to see received mail.

Folder pane

Contents of selected message (preview pane)

FIGURE 14-2 Outlook Express Inbox view

Sending and Receiving Email

The best way to learn about Outlook Express is to send some electronic mail. An interesting exercise is to send a message to yourself. This will give you immediate feedback about how the process works and serve as a test to ensure that your email system is set up. Even though the message is going to you, it will be handled in the same way any email message is: you send your message to a mail server and the server forwards it to the recipient's email address—which just happens to be you. Mail servers are located on your company's network or at your ISP (Internet Service Provider).

Sending a Message

To send a message, click the Compose button on the Outlook Express toolbar. The new message window appears as shown in Figure 14-3.

To start composing a message, you enter the recipient's email address in the To:, Cc:, or Bcc: fields. These fields are described next:

Click here to send message.

Carbon copy recipients

Describe message content.

Type your message here.

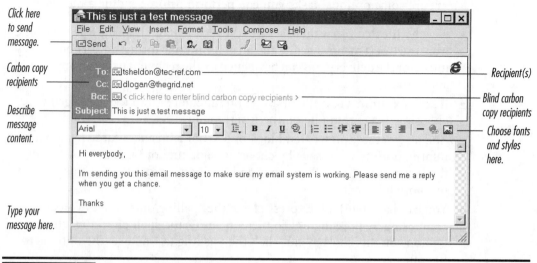

Recipient(s)

Blind carbon copy recipients

Choose fonts and styles here.

FIGURE 14-3 Composing a test message to yourself

- **To:** The main recipient
- **Cc:** Secondary recipients. Recipients listed in this field will receive a message that lists all the other people that received the message.
- **Bcc:** Recipients in this field will receive a message that does not list anyone who received the message that was listed in the To: or Cc: field. You use this option to send a message to someone that should not know who else the message was sent to.

Notice the little address card icon just to the right of To:, Cc:, and Bcc:. Click this to open the Address Book where you can choose one or more recipient names.

After addressing the message, type a subject in the Subject field and then fill in the lower part of the message.

To send the message, click the Send button on the toolbar. The message may be sent immediately depending on the settings of some options that are discussed later. If Outlook Express is not set up to send immediately, the message goes into the Outbox, which gives you a chance to open and edit the message further before sending it.

When automatic send is off, click the Send and Receive buttons to deliver any messages that have accumulated in your Outbox. Outlook Express also checks the mail server and receives any new messages that are addressed to you.

Here are some optional tasks you can perform before sending a message:

- Attach a file that you want to send to the recipient by choosing File Attachment from the Insert menu. The file and all of its internal formatting or coding stay intact for the delivery and can be opened by the recipient using an appropriate application.
- Insert text from a text file or an HTML document into the message by choosing Text From File on the Insert menu.
- Add a signature (prewritten block of text) or a business card (personal information) to a message by choosing Signature or Business Card from the Insert menu. See "Signatures and Business Cards" later in this chapter for more information.
- You can have Outlook Express check the spelling of messages you are composing by pressing F7. To turn on automatic spell-checking, choose Options on the Tools menu, click the Spelling tab, and set the options to fit your needs.
- Insert a priority code by choosing Set Priority from the Tools menu. The priority levels are high, normal, and low.
- Click the Select Recipients button to pick multiple recipients from a list of names in your address book.
- Digitally sign or encrypt the message (see "Securing Your Messages" later in this chapter).

Using InfoBeat

If you like receiving email, you'll like the services offered by InfoBeat, a free service that automatically sends you email with the latest news, sports, finance, weather, and entertainment news. You can sign up by opening Internet Explorer and going to the following Web address:

http://www.infobeat.com/

Once you're at the InfoBeat Web site, you can select exactly which type of information you want emailed to you and when you want it sent. For example, news is available in a morning coffee edition, afternoon edition, or evening edition. Once you're signed up, messages will begin appearing in your Outlook Express mailbox at the time you scheduled.

Checking for New Messages

To check for new messages, click the Send and Receive button on the toolbar. If your mail server has fast turnaround, the message you sent to yourself will be returned right away. Click Inbox in the left pane to view received messages. To read a message, click it to view its contents in the preview pane or double-click it to view the message in a separate window.

Managing Messages

When you receive messages, they automatically appear in the Inbox folder. The following icons indicate the status of messages in the received messages pane.

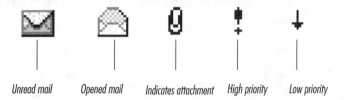

Unread mail   Opened mail   Indicates attachment   High priority   Low priority

If you want to keep your messages for future reference, it helps to organize them into categories, such as Personal and Business. You can create new folders in the left pane of the Outlook Express window, then move your messages into those folders as described under "Creating and Managing Folders" later in this chapter.

One method for moving messages into your special folders is to simply click and drag them by hand, but a more convenient method is to have Outlook Express automatically divert your messages into folders based on the criteria you specify. For example, all messages from your relatives could be moved into a personal folder. This is discussed later under "Filtering Your Mail with the Inbox Assistant."

Eventually, your folders may contain a lot of messages and you may have trouble locating a particular message you want to review. The Find Message on the Edit menu can help you locate specific messages in folders. You can search for messages based on who the message was from, who it was sent to, subject, date, and other criteria.

Replying to Messages

Much of the email you receive will usually require some kind of response. To respond to a message, click the Reply to Author, Reply to All, or Forward Message buttons. Outlook Express then creates a copy of the message with the original text placed in the lower part of the message and a space at the top where you can type your response as shown in Figure 14-4.

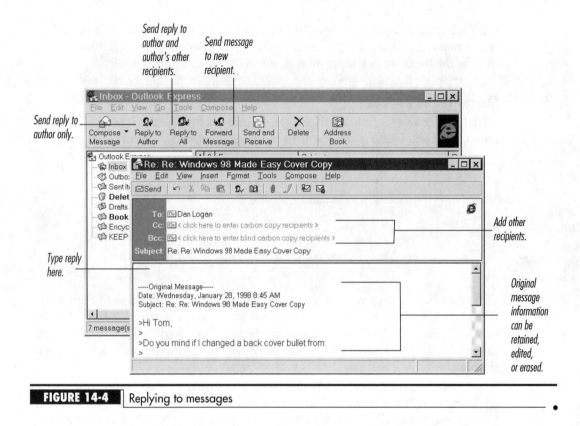

FIGURE 14-4 Replying to messages

TIP: Click Reply to Author to address a reply to the sender of the message. Click Reply to All to address a reply to everyone else that received the message from the sender.

Working Offline

You can use Outlook Express to compose messages and read newsgroup messages while you are offline, that is, without staying connected to the Internet. This can help you reduce connect charges or, if you own a portable computer, let you review messages you have received and write new messages while away from your Internet connection.

- If you start Outlook Express when your computer is not connected to the Internet, Outlook Express may display a dialog box that asks if you want to log on or work offline.

- If you are already online and you want to work offline, choose Work Offline from the File menu. All messages you send are put into the Outbox and delivered the next time you click the Send and Receive button.

- When you are creating a new message and you have the Compose Message window open, you can choose Send Later on the File menu to send the message later.

- To send messages in your Outbox, click the Send and Receive button.

Finding People

You may not always know the email addresses of the people you want to send messages to. You can search for people in your own address book by searching for a name, address, phone number, or other criteria. You can also search for people on the Internet.

Choose Find People on the Edit menu to open the Find People dialog box as pictured in Figure 14-5. Click the down arrow button on the Look in field to see a list of places where you can search. One is Address Book, which searches your own address book. Others include people-finding services on the Internet, such as Four11, Bigfoot, InfoSpace, SwitchBoard, and WhoWhere.

To search your address book, fill out any of the fields pictured in Figure 14-5, then click the Find Now button. To search the Internet, choose one of the services

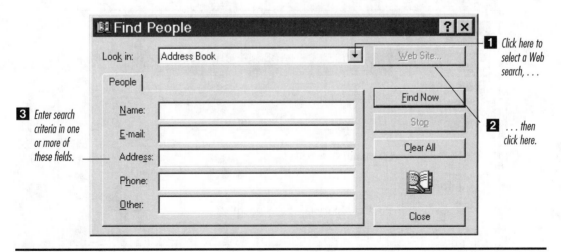

FIGURE 14-5   Finding people in your address book or on the Web

in the Look in field, then fill out the form that appears in the lower field (type a name or email address) and click the Web Site button.

 TIP: You can look for people at any time, even when Outlook Express is not open, by choosing Find on the Start menu, and then choosing People.

Finding Someone's Email Address on the Web

You can send a message to old friends or classmates by locating their email addresses on the Web. Open the Find People dialog box as described previously, then choose Four11 and click Web Site. In a moment, a screen similar to the one shown in Figure 14-6 appears in your Web browser. You can search for people by entering information into one or more of the fields. Four11 may find an exact match or display a list of near matches. You can then get more information on the near matches to identify the person you are looking for.

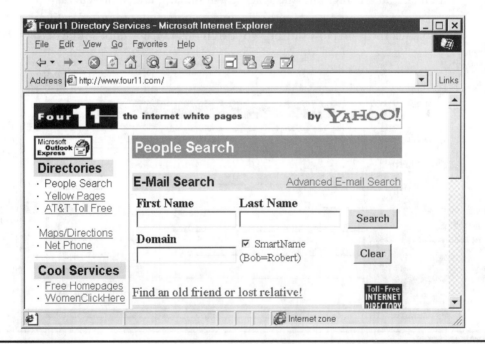

FIGURE 14-6 Searching for people at Four11

WEBLINK: Open Internet Explorer and go to http://www.yahoo.com/Reference/White_Pages/ for more extensive people-searching capabilities.

Formatting Messages and Using Stationery

Outlook Express makes it possible for you to customize the style of your messages with fonts, graphics, and backgrounds. You can customize individual messages, or choose a default style that will be used for every new message you compose.

You can even format messages using HTML, the formatting language of the Web. That makes it more likely that just about anyone will be able to view any special formatting you place in your messages. In addition, your messages can take on the appearance of dynamic and active Web pages if you fully take advantage of Web-like features.

NOTE: Some recipients might not be able to read HTML formatting. Instead, they will receive the message as plain text with an attached HTML file that they can view in a Web browser.

To include Web-like content in your email messages, set HTML as the default format as follows:

1. Choose Options on the Tools menu and click the Send tab.
2. Enable HTML in the Mail sending format and News sending format fields.

Choosing Stationery

One of the easiest ways to format your messages is to choose one of the predefined stationery options. To select stationery, click the down-arrow button next to the Compose Message button. This opens a drop-down list box where you can choose stationery options such as "Formal Announcement," "Holiday Letter," and "Baloon Party Invitation." Another way to select stationery is to choose the option called New Message Using on the Compose menu.

WEBLINK: To find additional stationery, go to Microsoft's Greetings Workshop at http://greetingsworkshop.msn.com.

If you're already composing a message and you want to apply stationery, choose Format on the Menu bar of the Compose Message window and then choose Apply Stationery. Select one of the backgrounds available.

Once you've selected a stationery, you can edit the message and the stationery elements in it any way you like by following the steps outlined under "Formatting Messages" later in this chapter.

Setting Default Stationery

You can choose a default stationery that will be used for all outgoing messages. You're not locked to the default stationery however, since you can still choose different stationery (or none) when the new blank message appears. To set default stationery, choose Stationery from the Tools menu. The dialog box in Figure 14-7 appears.

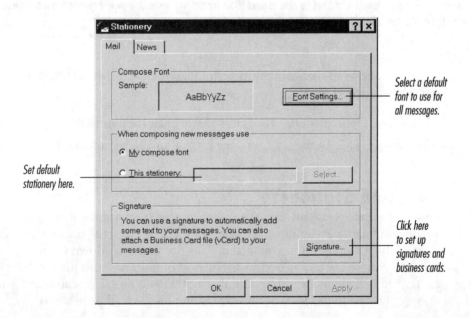

FIGURE 14-7 Setting stationery options

Creating Your Own Stationery with FrontPage Express

You can create your own stationery by using FrontPage Express. To edit any of the stationery supplied with Windows 98, follow these steps:

1. Choose Stationery from the Tools menu.

2. Click the "This stationery" option, then click the Select button to open the Select Stationery dialog box.

3. Choose any of the stationery examples listed as a starting layout for your own stationery.

4. Click the Edit button to automatically open FrontPage Express.

   The stationery you selected opens in the FrontPage Express window, ready for editing. Refer to Chapter 16 for more information about editing HTML documents with FrontPage Express.

5. After editing the stationery, make sure to save it with a different name than the example stationery you selected to edit.

Signatures and Business Cards

A signature is a *message* that you insert on some or all of your outgoing email. The message appears at the bottom of your email. A *business card* is an *attachment* that contains personal information about you, such as your phone number, address, and other information. You can define a signature or a business card, then choose to insert it in any message, or have Outlook Express attach it to every message by default.

To create a signature or business card, open the Stationery dialog box as pictured in Figure 14-7, then click the Signature button. The dialog box in Figure 14-8 appears.

If you click Text, type your message in the Text field, otherwise, click File and specify the name of the file that contains a message.

Click New to create a business card. This opens the address book where you can fill out personal information. When done, choose your name in the Card field.

TIP: The Signature dialog box has options for placing the signature and business card on every message. If you do not enable these options, you can still choose to insert a signature or a business card when composing any message by choosing Signature or Business Card from the Insert menu on the Compose Message Menu bar.

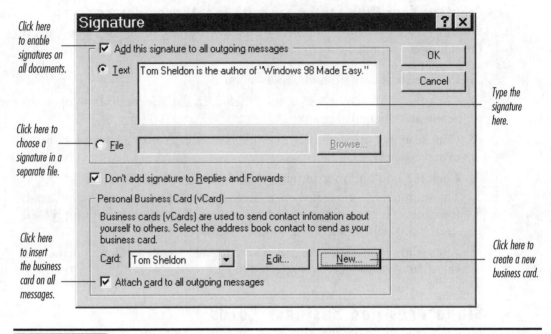

Click here to enable signatures on all documents.

Click here to choose a signature in a separate file.

Type the signature here.

Click here to insert the business card on all messages.

Click here to create a new business card.

FIGURE 14-8 Setting Signature options

Formatting Messages

You'll set most formats when composing messages. Even if you choose stationery, you can still edit what you've typed on a message or change any of the objects that were inserted by the stationery.

NOTE: To format messages as described here, make sure HTML is enabled. Choose Options on the Tools menu, then click the Send tab. Enable "HTML" in the "Mail sending format."

The Compose Message window includes a Formatting toolbar as shown in Figure 14-9. Choose a format before you start typing, or change formats by selecting text and/or paragraphs and clicking a format button. You can also choose Select All from the Edit menu to highlight all of the text and format it.

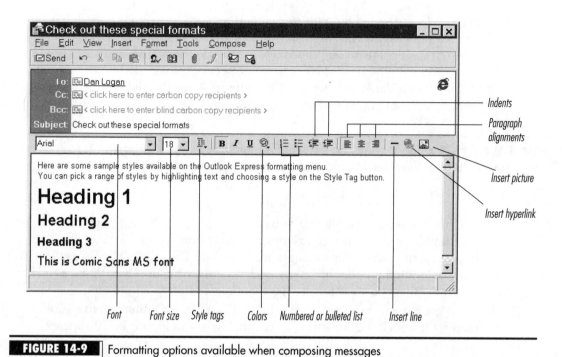

Font   Font size   Style tags   Colors   Numbered or bulleted list   Insert line

Indents

Paragraph alignments

Insert picture

Insert hyperlink

FIGURE 14-9 | Formatting options available when composing messages

TIP : Choose Format | Background | Picture to insert a background picture.

Securing Your Messages

When you read a message from a friend, you assume that the message is really from your friend. But what if someone faked the message to get you to do something or to just play a trick? How can you be sure you are reading legitimate messages? Likewise, how can you provide assurance to your email recipients that the messages you send are really from you? In addition, how can you prevent someone from intercepting a private message and reading its contents?

Outlook Express provides several security features that can help you secure your electronic mail by using digital IDs and encryption techniques. The primary security features are outlined in the following sections. A *digital ID* is a certificate that helps verify the identity of people, Web sites, and companies.

Digital IDs are issued by *certificate authorities* such as Verisign, which has set up an arrangement with Microsoft to issue digital IDs to Windows 98 users. Verisign requires that you prove your identity to them. The company then issues you a digital ID that you can use to secure your messages. The digital ID is signed with Verisign's own ID. Computer systems throughout the world recognize Verisign's ID and use it to verify your ID.

WEBLINK: Digital ID technology is more involved than the simple explanation just given. You are encouraged to visit Verisign's Web site at http://www.verisign.com to learn more about digital IDs.

Once you receive a digital ID, you can use it to sign and encrypt your messages. In addition, you can trust signed messages from other people because Outlook Express verifies that their messages are legitimate. Digital IDs are also used for electronic commerce on the Internet. They verify to vendors who you are and help you verify that you are connected to a legitimate vendor.

To get more information about digital IDs, choose Options on the Tools menu, then click the Security tab. The dialog box in Figure 14-10 appears.

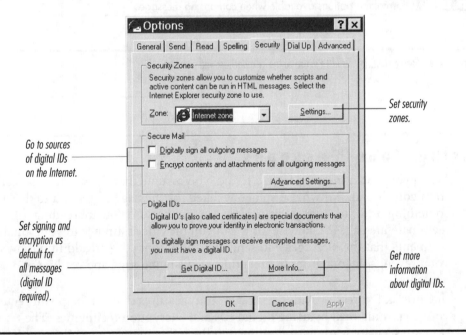

FIGURE 14-10   Security features

Click the More Information button to learn about digital IDs, then click the Get Digital ID button to connect with Microsoft's digital ID information site and a certificate authority.

Once you have a digital ID, you can have Outlook Express sign and encrypt all of your messages by enabling the Secure Mail options on the Security page. Alternatively, you can choose to sign or secure messages on an individual basis by choosing Encrypt or Digitally Sign on the Tools menu when composing a message.

• Setting Special Features and Options

Now that you are familiar with the basic operation of Outlook Express and possibly have had some time to get used to its features, you're ready to customize it. Choose Options on the Tools menu to display the Options dialog box. As shown in Figure 14-11, it has seven tabs on which you can alter Outlook Express' mail-handling capabilities to meet your needs:

- **General**   Sets general options.

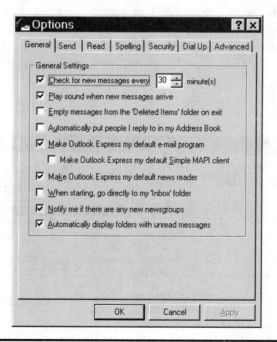

FIGURE 14-11   The Options dialog box

- **Send**   Sets options for how messages are composed and delivered.
- **Read**   Sets how messages are downloaded and displayed for reading.
- **Spelling**   Sets language and options for spelling.
- **Security**   Sets security options.
- **Dial-up**   Sets options for dialing the mail server.
- **Advanced**   Sets options for dispensing with messages and compacting files.

You should look over each option very carefully to determine which settings are best for your needs. You can get a better description of each option by right-clicking it with the mouse, then clicking the "What's This?" option.

Here are some tips for setting the general presentation of the Outlook Express window and how messages are displayed:

- To change the way received mail is presented, choose Layout from the View menu, then try each of the layout options that are presented on the dialog box.
- Message information is listed under columns such as From, Subject, and Received. You can add other column headings such as Sent, Size, and To or remove columns you don't use. To change columns, click Inbox, then choose Columns from the View menu. The Columns dialog box appears as shown in Figure 14-12. Click an option in either pane, then click Add or Remove.
- You can sort on any column in a message list by clicking the button above the column. Click once for ascending order and once again for descending order.

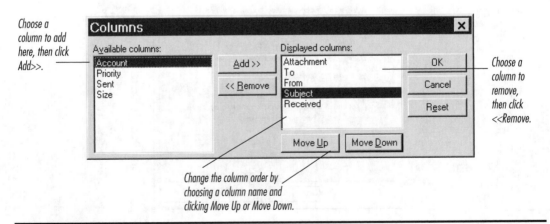

Choose a column to add here, then click Add>>.

Change the column order by choosing a column name and clicking Move Up or Move Down.

Choose a column to remove, then click <<Remove.

FIGURE 14-12   Setting columns

• Organizing and Managing Messages

Once you start getting email, messages begin to accumulate in your Inbox. While many messages can be deleted, important messages can be saved in special folders where you can access them at a later date. To organize your messages, you create new folders in the left pane and then click and drag your messages into appropriate folders. For example, if you look at Figure 14-1, you will see two custom folders called "Book Messages" and "KEEP THESE MESSAGES." These are folders we created for our own needs.

You might belong to a newsgroup mailing list that provides ongoing discussions about topics you are interested in. When someone sends either a new message or a response message, the message is sent to everyone in the list. For example, you might belong to a car club that has a mailing list discussion group. After signing up to be included in the mailing list, you start to receive messages. If you want to keep these messages for later reference, create a folder called "Cars" and move the messages to the folder. You can move messages manually or use Outlook Express' Inbox Assistant to automatically move messages to a folder based on the email address of the sender, the subject header, or other criteria, as discussed later.

Creating and Managing Folders

Outlook Express automatically sets up several folders, including the Inbox and Outbox. These folders appear in the left pane of the Outlook Express window. To create a new folder, choose Folder from the File menu, then select New Folder. Type a name in the dialog box, then choose the folder that will hold the new folder. You can nest one folder within another, which allows you to create hierarchies of folders. To create a new folder at the top level, make sure Outlook Express is highlighted in the folder hierarchy.

Once you've created the folder, you can simply click and drag email messages from one folder into another. For example, click Inbox, then drag the latest messages you've received into your new folder.

Here are some other folder options you can take advantage of:

- Save disk space by compacting mail folders. Choose Folder from the File menu, then select either Compact or Compact All Folders.
- Hold the CTRL key, then select multiple messages to move or copy into other folders. After selecting messages, choose Move To Folder or Copy To Folder from the Edit menu. You can also just click and drag, but the menu option is useful if the target folder is hidden.

- Save messages as files by selecting a message and choosing Save As on the File menu. You might save messages before deleting or moving them from a folder.

Filtering Your Mail with the Inbox Assistant

You can filter messages using the Inbox Assistant on the Tools Menu. Filtering is particularly handy if you receive lots of messages, but not all of them have the same priority and you don't need to read them immediately. Filtering enables Outlook Express to manage your mail for you, eliminating much of the time-consuming, message-by-message culling. Inbox Assistant automatically routes messages to the folders where you want to store them. You can send unwanted mail to the trash. Or, if you have multiple email accounts—one at home and one at work, for example—you can create filters that move the messages from each account into the folders of your choice.

To configure the Inbox Assistant, choose Inbox Assistant on the Tools menu, then click the Add button to create a new filter. Figure 14-13 illustrates an example. All messages received from Dan Logan are diverted to a folder called Book messages.

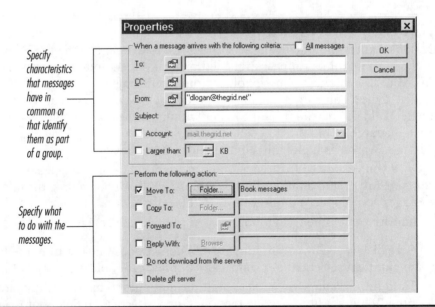

<table>
<tr><td>Specify characteristics that messages have in common or that identify them as part of a group.</td></tr>
<tr><td>Specify what to do with the messages.</td></tr>
</table>

Properties

When a message arrives with the following criteria: ☐ All messages

To:

CC:

From: "dlogan@thegrid.net"

Subject:

☐ Account: mail.thegrid.net

☐ Larger than: 1 KB

Perform the following action:

☑ Move To: Folder... Book messages

☐ Copy To: Folder...

☐ Forward To:

☐ Reply With: Browse

☐ Do not download from the server

☐ Delete off server

OK

Cancel

FIGURE 14-13 Filtering Mail with Inbox Assistant

Searching for Messages

The Find Message utility allows you to search for a message in a folder and its nested folders. You can search by the sender, recipients other than yourself, the subject of the message, text in the message, or specific attachments. You can also search for messages that will fall within a range of dates. To use the Find Message utility, select a folder to search, then choose Edit | Find Message.

TIP: Choose a folder in the left pane before starting a search. You can search through old messages by choosing the Sent Items or Deleted Items folder.

Managing Your Address Books

The Outlook Express Address Book allows you to store a wide range of information about your email recipients, such as addresses and phone numbers, but you need enter only as much information as you want to. You can use the Address Book not only to manage email addresses, but also as a personal information manager.

Open the Address Book by clicking on the Address Book icon on the Outlook Express toolbar. This will bring up the Address Book dialog box similar to Figure 14-14. You can click one or more email addresses (hold

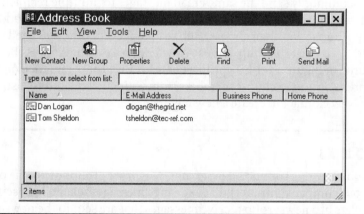

FIGURE 14-14 The Address Book

CTRL while selecting multiple addresses), then click the Send Mail button to send a message addressed to those recipients.

> **TIP:** When composing a message, you can open the Address Book by clicking the little card icon to the right of the To:, Cc:, and Bcc: fields.

To add a contact to the Address Book, click New Contact to open the Properties dialog box. Type information in the Name and E-Mail Addresses field, and then click the Add button. Optionally, you can click the tabs for Home, Business, Other, NetMeeting, and Digital IDs to type in other information.

> **TIP:** When you are addressing a message, you can use the nickname you've entered in your address book, and Outlook Express will provide the email address.

You can also click the Find button on the Address Book toolbar to locate people on the Internet. Refer to "Finding People" earlier in this chapter for more information about Web sites that help you locate email addresses and other information about people and organizations.

Creating Mailing Lists for Groups

If you commonly send the same email messages to multiple recipients, you should create a group that includes all of those recipients. Then you can address the mail to the group rather than choose each recipient every time you need to send email to them. To create a group, choose New Group from the Address Book toolbar pictured in Figure 14-14. Type in a name for the group, and then click the Select Members button to choose members from your current address list. You can also click New Contact to create a new member.

Newsgroups

Outlook Express supports *newsgroups*, which are groups of people on the Internet (or your company intranet) that exchange messages related to specific topics. All members of a newsgroup receive messages that are sent to the newsgroup, either as a new topic or a response to someone else's message. Refer to Chapter 15 for more information about Outlook Express newsgroups.

15

Newsgroups and Discussion Groups

A newsgroup is a public discussion group in which members of the group communicate with one another by exchanging email messages. The term is a bit of a misnomer because it seems to indicate that only news is exchanged. While that may be true with some newsgroups, most are ongoing discussions on a wide range of topics.

You can use Outlook Express to participate in newsgroups. When you participate in a newsgroup, you receive all the messages that are sent to the newsgroup by its members. You can send your own messages and replies to the newsgroup and/or to individual members of the newsgroup. Think of a newsgroup as a mailbox that many different people can access. The mailbox is located on a server somewhere on the Internet or on your company's network. Your Internet Service Provider has a server that keeps track of all the newsgroups and that helps you sign up for and receive messages from newsgroups.

Don't confuse newsgroups with chat rooms and mailing lists:

- *Chat room*   A live (real-time) discussion in which active participants type comments that are immediately displayed for all to see. Comments eventually scroll off-screen, never to be seen again. They are only visible to people in the chat room. Microsoft NetMeeting has chat room capabilities.
- *Mailing list*   This is similar to newsgroups, except that your name is added to a list of message recipients. When someone submits a message, the mail list server forwards a copy of the message to everyone on the list. You receive messages directly in your Inbox.
- *Newsgroup*   Messages sent to a newsgroup are posted to a list. Messages are grouped into *threads* that include an original message and all responses to it. Members can choose to view any message or message thread. Messages are usually removed from the list after a period of time.

T I P : Refer to Chapter 18 to learn about other Windows 98 collaboration tools.

There are well over 20,000 newsgroups on the Internet, and more come into existence every day. There are newsgroups devoted to such topics as adoption, Egyptian culture, education, figure skater Oksana Bayul, health care, music, religion, sports, and video laserdiscs, to name but a few (you really have to browse a news server's list of newsgroups to believe the variety available).

You can just view the messages in a newsgroup or you can take an active role in developing new messages and responding to other people's messages. People who view but don't contribute are affectionately called *lurkers*. People who take an active role in answering people's questions and providing useful information are called "experts" and are sometimes offered book contracts. Then you never hear from them again in the newsgroup because they are too busy trying to meet their contract schedules!

• Subscribing to Newsgroups

The best way to learn about newsgroups is to subscribe to one. During this process you'll see exactly how vast and useful newsgroups can be.

The following discussion assumes you don't have any newsgroups currently installed, but you can follow along even if you do. You must also be signed up to the Internet and have access to a news server. Your ISP can help you with the setup. Refer to Appendix B to learn about connecting to the Internet and working with ISPs.

Start Outlook Express and choose News from the Go menu. If this is the first time you are accessing newsgroups, Outlook Express may ask you to supply the following information:

- Your name
- Internet email address
- News server (NNTP) name (your ISP will supply you with this name)
- Friendly name (this name will be given to a folder that appears in the left pane of Outlook Express).
- Connection method (choose dial-up modem or other methods)

Once you've made the settings, a connection is made to your ISP's news server and you see the following message:

> *"You are currently not subscribed to any newsgroups. Would you like to review available newsgroups?"*

Click Yes to start downloading the names of available newsgroups. The initial download may take a few minutes, so be patient. Note that only the names are downloaded and you'll be able to search through those names to find the groups you want to access. Also, your ISP may not keep track of all the available newsgroups on the Internet, so be sure to ask them if they can recommend a more complete news server.

Figure 15-1 illustrates the process of subscribing to newsgroups. Once you subscribe, click the name of the subscribed group in the left pane to make the messages for that group appear in the right pane of Outlook Express. In this example, I subscribed to the alternative architecture group (alt.architecture.alternative).

To subscribe to another group, click the news folder in the left pane, then click the News groups button on the toolbar. This brings up the Newsgroups subscription window, as shown in Figure 15-1A, with the list of available newsgroups you downloaded in the previous steps. You can then scan through the list to find a newsgroup, or use the *keyword search method*. A keyword search displays the names of all newsgroups that contain the letters or words you type in the top field of the dialog box. In Figure 15-2, note that you can type two separate words to display only newsgroups that contain those words.

Once you narrow a list, you can subscribe to multiple newsgroups before closing the Newsgroups dialog box. Click a group, then click Subscribe. Repeat the process for another newsgroup. A newspaper icon appears next to the newsgroups you have subscribed to. To unsubscribe from a newsgroup, click the Unsubscribe button.

WEBLINK: You can use the Web to find out more about newsgroups. DejaNews (http://www.dejanews.com/) lets you browse newsgroups by category. Best of all, you can also search by keywords, and DejaNews will search the messages in all the groups available to it for that keyword.

The Go to Button

If you want to preview a newsgroup, select the group in the Newsgroup list, then click the Go to button. This will download only the message headers that currently exist in the group without downloading the complete text of each message. You can then determine if the group has the kind of content and

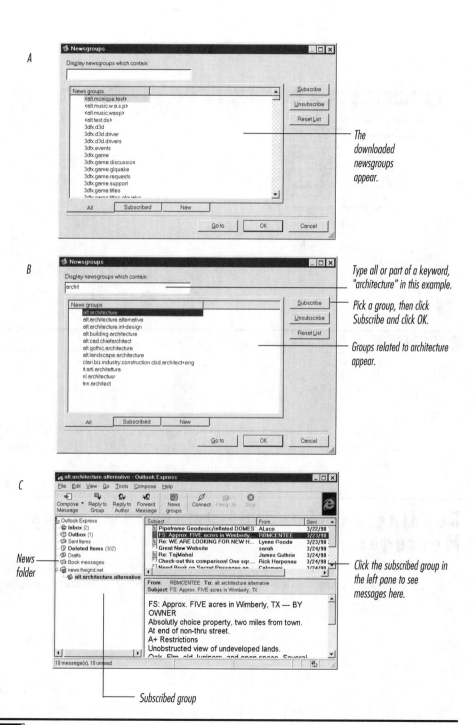

A

The downloaded newsgroups appear.

B

Type all or part of a keyword, "architecture" in this example.

Pick a group, then click Subscribe and click OK.

Groups related to architecture appear.

C

News folder

Click the subscribed group in the left pane to see messages here.

Subscribed group

FIGURE 15-1 Newsgroup subscription process

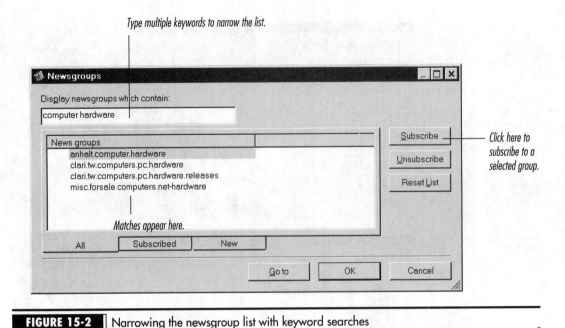

Type multiple keywords to narrow the list.

Click here to subscribe to a selected group.

Matches appear here.

FIGURE 15-2 Narrowing the newsgroup list with keyword searches

message activity you want. Some newsgroups are very busy while others are almost inactive. Using Go to will help you determine which newsgroups are useful.

Reading and Responding to Newsgroup Messages

After you subscribe to a newsgroup, the messages that are currently available for that group are downloaded to your computer. The message appears in the right pane of Outlook Express when you select the subscribed newsgroup in the left pane. Figure 15-3 illustrates four different newsgroups in the left pane. Other features of the newsgroup window are also illustrated.

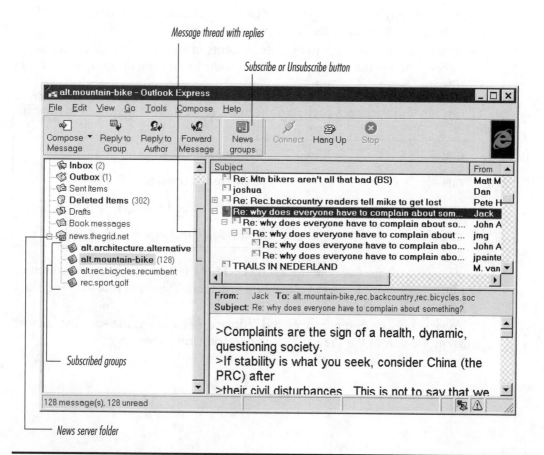

FIGURE 15-3 Reading newsgroup messages

> **TIP:** Threads are messages with one or more replies. A plus sign appears in front of threaded messages. Click the plus sign to view the replies.

Assuming you are still online, you can browse and read messages in two ways:

- Scroll through the message list or click any message that interests you. The selected message appears in the preview pane.
- Double-click a message to read its contents in a separate window. In this mode, you see the handy toolbar with some interesting options, as shown in Figure 15-4.

You can also use these keyboard shortcuts to view other messages in the list:

CTRL->	View next message
CTRL-<	View previous message
CTRL-U	View next unread message
CTRL-SHIFT-U	Jump to next message thread

You can sort the messages in the list by clicking the buttons above the column heading. Click once to sort in ascending order; click again to sort in descending order.

To view only unread messages and reduce the size of the message list, choose Current View from the View menu, then select Unread Messages.

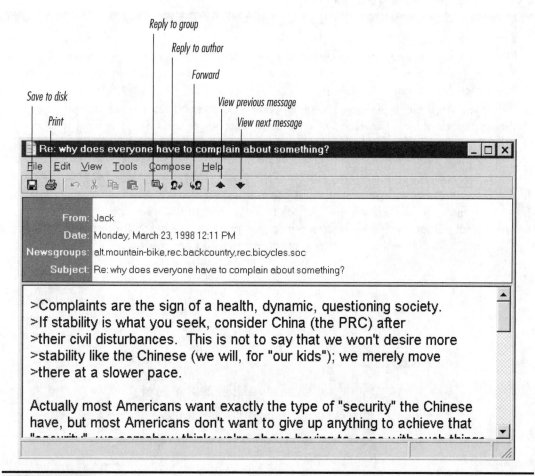

Reply to group

Reply to author

Forward

View previous message

View next message

Save to disk

Print

> Re: why does everyone have to complain about something? _ □ ✕

File Edit View Tools Compose Help

From: Jack

Date: Monday, March 23, 1998 12:11 PM

Newsgroups: alt.mountain-bike,rec.backcountry,rec.bicycles.soc

Subject: Re: why does everyone have to complain about something?

>Complaints are the sign of a health, dynamic, questioning society.
>If stability is what you seek, consider China (the PRC) after
>their civil disturbances. This is not to say that we won't desire more
>stability like the Chinese (we will, for "our kids"); we merely move
>there at a slower pace.

Actually most Americans want exactly the type of "security" the Chinese
have, but most Americans don't want to give up anything to achieve that

FIGURE 15-4 Read a message in a separate window by double-clicking it

When you are online, you can choose to download messages for any newsgroup by simply selecting the group. The message headers and the body text are downloaded as soon as you click the message.

If you work with a dial-up connection, you probably don't want to stay connected for long periods of time. Downloading and reading messages can take some time, so Outlook Express can download only the headers of messages and then lets you mark the messages you want to read. When you reconnect to the Internet, Outlook Express retrieves the text of the messages you have marked. You can then log off and read messages at your leisure. This option is useful if you are taking a trip with a portable computer.

The first thing to do is set how Outlook Express handles downloads for a selected newsgroup. Right-click the newsgroup in the left pane as shown here and choose Mark for Retrieval. Select New Headers to retrieve only the newest headers from the list.

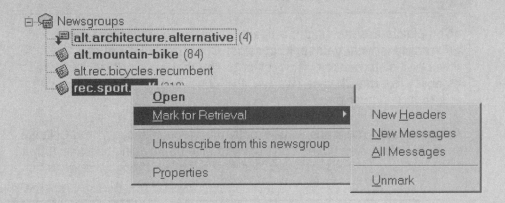

Now you are ready to download message headers for review. Open the Tools menu and choose one of the following options:

- *Download <name of news server>*   Downloads all subscribed newsgroups.
- *Download "This Newsgroup"*   Downloads only the selected newsgroup. This option displays the following dialog box where you can set download options.

Download Newsgroup   ✕

☑ Get the following items:

  ⦿ New headers

  ○ New messages (headers and bodies)

  ○ All messages (headers and bodies)

☐ Get marked messages

OK

Cancel

- *Download All*   Downloads newsgroups and other email.

Once you've downloaded messages, review the message headers and mark the messages you want to read. To mark a message, right-click it, then click Mark Message for Download. When you're done marking, choose one of the download options on the Tools menu as just described.

Posting New Messages

As you browse a newsgroup message list, you'll become familiar with the kind of discussions that members engage in and you may want to contribute your own message or reply to a message. Newsgroup members often hope to contribute a message that will result in a long discussion with contributions and replies from other members. The discussion may generate multiple branching message threads, each with a related but different topic. For example, a discussion about mountain biking in Sedona may branch off into another discussion about other great places to bike in Arizona.

To create your own message and submit it to the newsgroup, first make sure you are in the correct newsgroup, then click the Compose Message button. You'll see a new message similar to Figure 15-5 with the name of the

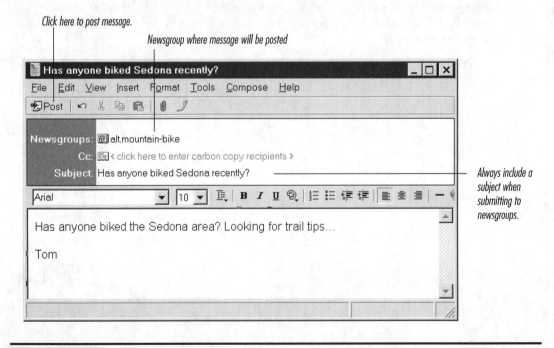

FIGURE 15-5 | Posting a new message

newsgroup listed as the recipient of the message. You can also click Cc to send a copy of the message to someone else. Fill out the message as you would any other email message, then click the Post button.

If you want to cancel a message, choose Cancel Message on the Compose menu. You can also use special fonts, styles, and stationery, or insert a signature and/or a business card on your messages as described in the previous chapter under "Formatting Messages and Using Stationery."

Each newsgroup has its own etiquette conventions. Ignore these conventions and you're likely to get *flamed*—that is, people will send nasty messages to the newsgroup about your missteps—and sometimes they're *really* nasty. If you don't like the idea of being flamed, read the FAQs (*Frequently Asked Questions*) provided on most newsgroups, and read the mail for a few days to get a sense of what flies and what doesn't before you send your first message to the group.

Replying to Message Threads

When you see a message you want to reply to, click one of the following buttons on the Outlook Express toolbar or the toolbar of the message you are reading:

- *Reply to Group*   Send a reply that appears in the newsgroup for all members to read.
- *Reply to Author*   Send a reply as a private message to the author of the message you are viewing.
- *Forward Message*   Send the message to a recipient of your choice, even non-newsgroup members.

About Message Properties

Note that some message authors do not provide their true names or their email addresses. You may only be able to send a reply message to the newsgroup and not directly to the author. There is good reason for this. A number of people and companies compile email address lists by scanning the From header in newsgroups messages, then send junk mail to everyone on the list.

You can view detailed information about messages by clicking a message and choosing Properties from the File menu. You can also right-click a message and choose Properties. On the Properties dialog box, click Detail. This From line may indicate the source of a message, although the author may have specified a bogus email address.

You can also hide your email address as described later under "General Newsgroup Properties."

Finding Messages

Your newsgroup folders may contain a large number of messages. You can sort the messages by clicking the buttons above any of the columns. This may help you locate messages written by a particular author or with a specific subject.

By far the best way to find messages is with the Find Message dialog box. Select the newsgroup folder that you want to search, then choose Find Message on the Edit menu. This dialog box appears:

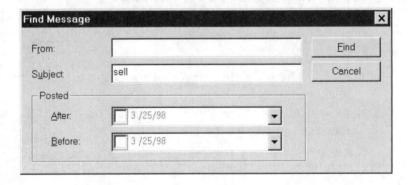

In this example, we're looking for bike equipment to buy, so we enter keywords such as "sell" or "for sale" in the Subject field. You can also enter a sender's name in the From field or specify date ranges in the Posted field. Click OK to start the search, then click F3 to continue searching if a found message is not what you wanted.

Filters

Newsgroups are freewheeling conversation centers where truth, accuracy, good taste, and sensitivity are sometimes in short supply. Messages often test the limits of free speech in many different ways. If you set out to read newsgroup messages, be prepared to be offended.

You can filter newsgroup messages to block messages by newsgroup, sender, subject, size, or how long it has been posted. Choose Newsgroup Filters from the Tools menu to open the dialog box pictured in Figure 15-6. Click Add to add a new filter.

TIP : Notice the underlying box in Figure 15-6. It illustrates a good use of a filter. We got tired of viewing ads for used equipment in the mountain biking newsgroup, so we had it filter out all messages with "sell" or "sale" in the subject line.

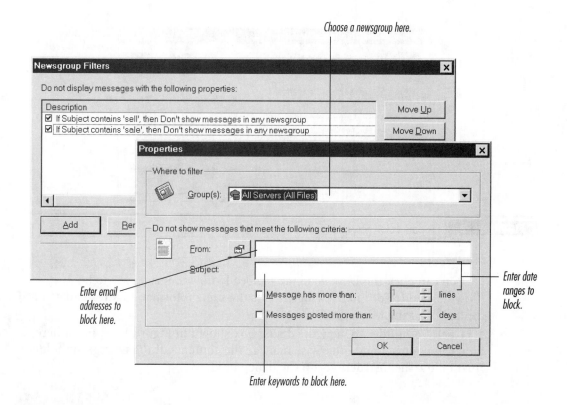

Choose a newsgroup here.

Enter email addresses to block here.

Enter date ranges to block.

Enter keywords to block here.

FIGURE 15-6 Filtering newsgroups

When you click the Add button on the Newsgroup Filters dialog box, the Properties box appears so you can define a new filter. Choose a newsgroup in the Group(s) field, then specify your criteria in the lower fields as outlined. If you want to filter for multiple keywords in the subject line, you need to create multiple filters.

Managing Newsgroups

You can manage your newsgroups by right-clicking a group in the left pane and choosing Properties. The Properties dialog box pictured in Figure 15-7 appears. You can see information about the number of messages in the newsgroup.

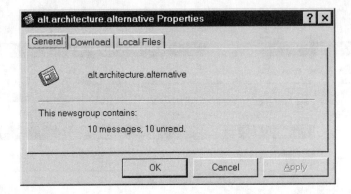

| FIGURE 15-7 | Properties for newsgroups |

You can click the Download tab to specify how messages are to be downloaded for offline viewing. This is the same information already discussed under "Viewing Messages Offline."

Click Local Files to view the dialog box shown in Figure 15-8. From here, you can compact and otherwise manage the contents of the newsgroup folder. Just follow the instructions on the dialog box.

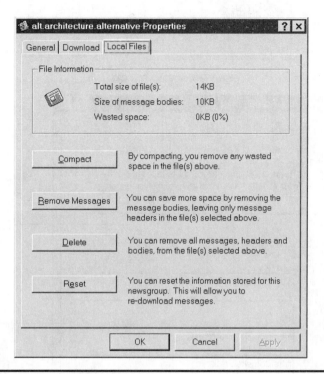

TIP: You can also choose Clean Up files on the File menu.

General Newsgroup Properties

Choose Accounts on the Tools menu, then click the News tab, choose an account, and click the Properties button This opens the dialog box shown in Figure 15-9.

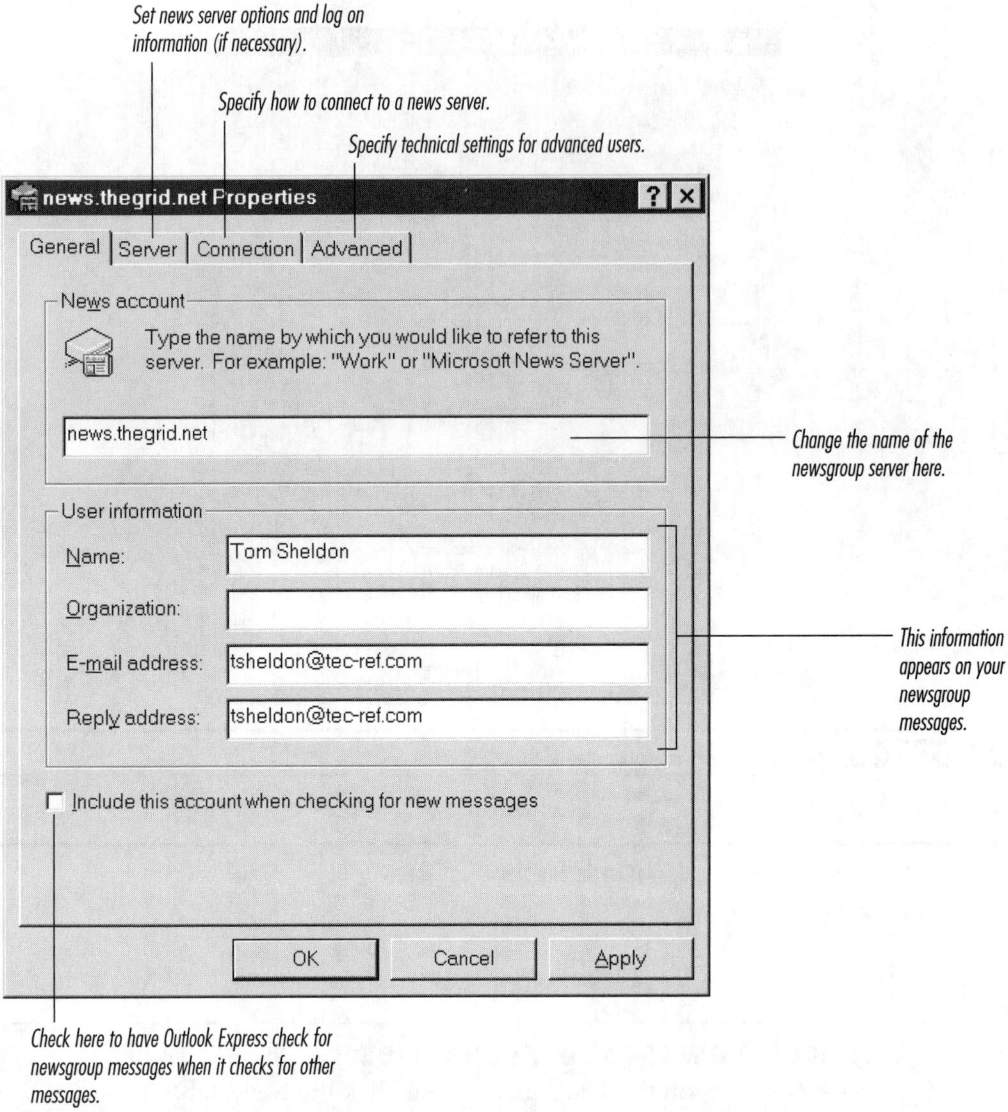
Set news server options and log on information (if necessary).
Specify how to connect to a news server.
Specify technical settings for advanced users.
news.thegrid.net Properties
General
Server
Connection
Advanced
News account
Type the name by which you would like to refer to this server. For example: "Work" or "Microsoft News Server".
news.thegrid.net
Change the name of the newsgroup server here.
User information
Name:
Tom Sheldon
Organization:
E-mail address:
tsheldon@tec-ref.com
Reply address:
tsheldon@tec-ref.com
This information appears on your newsgroup messages.
Include this account when checking for new messages
OK
Cancel
Apply
Check here to have Outlook Express check for newsgroup messages when it checks for other messages.

FIGURE 15-9 Managing general newsgroup properties

The information in the User information field appears in your outgoing messages and replies. If you wish to hide this personal information from people who gather names and addresses for junk mail, enter bogus information in these fields. Type your initials in the Name field and email addresses such as anonymous@nodomain.com in the address fields. This prevents automatic programs from extracting your real email address. The only downside is that newsgroup members will not be able to reply to you directly since your return address will not be part of the message. However, you can include a note in the message such as "Send all personal replies to tsheldon@tec-ref.com."

T I P : If you are not sure what any option on the dialog box is, right-click it to display the "What's This?" option, then click the option to get a short description.

16

Publishing Web Pages with FrontPage Express

B A S I C S

- Learn how Web publishing works on intranets or the Internet
- Create a home page and other pages for your Web site
- Edit pages and insert special options like horizontal lines, tables, graphics, video, and sound
- Create hyperlinks to marks in the same document, to other Web pages at your site, or to Web pages on the Internet

B E Y O N D

- Create thumbnail hyperlinks
- Create forms to collect information from visitors
- Add Web pages to your Active Desktop

Corporations, small businesses, schools, churches, and government organizations maintain Web sites to provide information about their products, services, philosophies, and beliefs. You too can be a part of this information revolution by publishing information about yourself, your job, your company, the services you offer, or the products you sell. This chapter will show you how to publish Web pages with FrontPage Express.

The Web Publishing Process

Let's put Web publishing into context. Figure 16-1 illustrates the different ways that you might publish your Web page.

- In example A, Joe publishes a Web page on his own computer, which is connected to a company network. Joe's coworkers can access his Web page by using their Web browser.
- In example B, Joe publishes information on his company's Web server rather than his own computer. Company policy may require this for security or performance reasons. Also, the company's Web server may be connected to the Internet and allow Joe to publish his page to the world.
- In example C, Joe sends his completed Web pages to his Internet Service Provider (ISP), which publishes his pages on their server.

Windows 98 includes two programs that help you create and publish Web pages:

- **FrontPage Express**   An easy-to-use package for creating Web pages.
- **Personal Web Server (PWS)**   A software program that "serves up" Web pages.

PWS is discussed in Chapter 17. With it, you can set up an HTML Web server on your computer and publish Web pages for other people in your company to view.

The process of publishing Web pages is outlined here.

- Plan your Web pages to include a home page and other hyperlinked pages, such as a bio page, a family page, a page about your work, or other types of pages.
- Create your Web pages by typing the HTML code using a text editor (Notepad, for example), by using FrontPage Express (or the full edition of FrontPage, available from Microsoft).
- Test your Web pages to make sure that layouts and hyperlinks work the way you want. PWS is a great tool for testing your Web pages. It allows you to publish pages and see how they will look on other users' computers.
- Publish your completed Web pages.

T I P :   You can also publish your Web pages by adding them as the background to a shared folder (as discussed in Chapter 8).

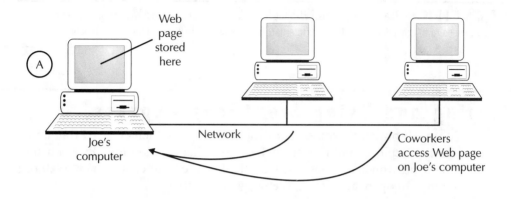

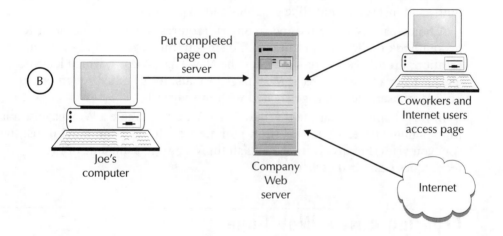

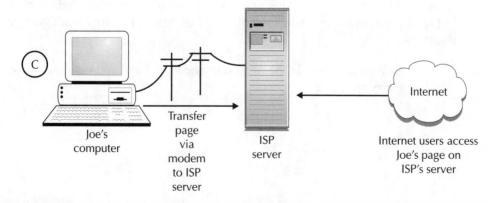

FIGURE 16-1   Methods for publishing Web pages

WEBLINK: The following Yahoo! Web site has links to information about Web design and layout: http://www.yahoo.com/Computers_and_Internet/Internet/World_Wide_Web/Page_Design_and_Layout/.

Starting and Using FrontPage Express

To start FrontPage Express, click the Start button, then choose Programs | Internet Explorer and FrontPage Express. What you see initially is a blank screen, but you can choose New on the File menu to create a new Web page or Open to open an existing Web page for editing.

FrontPage Express makes creating Web pages as simple to use as writing documents with a word processing program. You lay out the page, add special fonts, and insert elements like graphics and hyperlinks.

A home page is a creative endeavor that requires some trial-and-error to make it look the way you want it to. To smooth the process of home page creation, FrontPage Express includes the New Page Wizard, which lets you choose from a variety of basic Web page formats. Joe's home page in Figure 16-2 is an example of a page created with this wizard.

In this chapter, you'll use the New Page Wizard to create a Web page similar to Joe's home page. Then we'll show you how to edit the page to get it just the way you want. Finally, you can publish the Web page using one of the techniques described earlier.

Creating a New Web Page

We're going to show you how to create a home page using the FrontPage Express New Page Wizard. This process is so simple, it hardly needs explaining, but we'll point out a few subtle details and interesting features as we go through the steps.

1. Choose New on the File menu to start the New Page Wizard. The following dialog box appears:

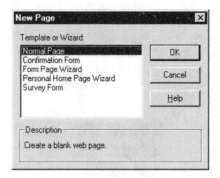

2. For future reference, click each item and read its description in the Description field.

   As you can see, FrontPage Express makes it easy to create not only a personal Web page, but also special forms. Note that the Normal Page option creates a blank page that you can edit yourself.

3. Choose Personal Home Page Wizard in the template list and click OK.

FIGURE 16-2   A sample home page

Now the "sections" page appears as shown next. This is where you create hyperlinked sections, similar to what you see listed under "Contents" in Figure 16-2. The hyperlinks transfer users to different parts of the same page, not another page (although you can create hyperlinks to other pages, as discussed later).

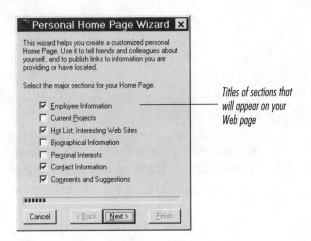

Titles of sections that will appear on your Web page

4. For this exercise, go ahead and choose all of the sections to see what they produce on your Web page. You can always delete anything you don't want when you edit the page later.

   The wizard now leads you through a series of questions to determine what you want to include in the sections you selected. For example, for the section titled "Employee Information," you can include information about your job title, key responsibilities, department, or workgroup. For the section titled "Current Projects," you can include information about the projects you are working on.

5. Proceed through the wizard by answering the questions and clicking the Next button.

   If you selected the "Comments and Suggestions" section, you see a dialog box similar to the following, where you choose how data collected from users is stored for later viewing:

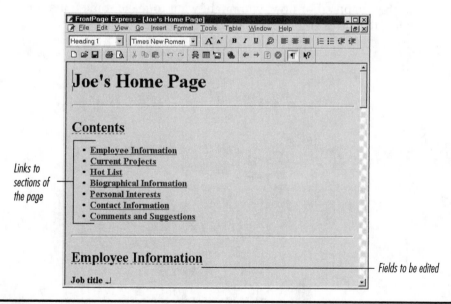

Personal Home Page Wizard

In the Comments and Suggestions section, readers will be able to tell you what they think about your Home Page.

Do you want to use a form that collects input and stores it in a file, or a special kind of link that causes most web browsers to send you e-mail?

Collected data can be viewed with Notepad.

Data is sent to the email address typed in the field.

Collected data can be viewed with a Web browser.

Click here to finish and create the page.

○ Use form, store results in _data file
○ Use form, store results in _web page
⦿ Use link, send _e-mail to this address:

Joe@tec-ref.com

Cancel   < _Back   _Next >   _Finish

On the final dialog box, click the Finish button to create the page. It appears in the FrontPage Express window for editing as shown in Figure 16-3. Note the similarities between this editing window and how the final product appears in a Web browser as shown in Figure 16-2.

FrontPage Express - [Joe's Home Page]
File Edit View Go Insert Format Tools Table Window Help

Heading 1 ▾ | Times New Roman ▾ | A A | B I U | 🔍 | 🔳 🔳 🔳 | ⋮≡ ⋮≡ 🔲 🔲

Joe's Home Page

Contents

Links to sections of the page

- **Employee Information**
- **Current Projects**
- **Hot List**
- **Biographical Information**
- **Personal Interests**
- **Contact Information**
- **Comments and Suggestions**

Employee Information

Job title ⏎

Fields to be edited

FIGURE 16-3 Wizard-created page in FrontPage Express, ready for editing

Editing the New Page

Once you've create a page with the New Page Wizard, all you really need to do is edit the text to fit your own needs and make some other minor changes. You can also use the new page as the basis for creating a more complex Web page that includes multimedia elements, hyperlinks to other Web sites, and forms.

If you scan down the page, you will notice that FrontPage Express has inserted friendly comments and instructions that guide you in the development of the page. Your job is to type over the comments and instructions with your own text. In doing so, the text you type takes on the formatting and properties of the examples.

While some elements of the page are simple text, other elements have unique properties. For example, if you right-click one of the titles such as "Hot Links," the shortcut menu pictured in Figure 16-4 appears. This menu has a whole set of options for changing the properties of various page elements such as the page layout, paragraphs, fonts, and the hyperlink you pointed to. Right-clicking elements is an important aspect of using FrontPage Express.

We discuss general editing options under "Page Editing Techniques" later in this chapter. For now, you might want to make some minor changes to the page, then save and test it as described next.

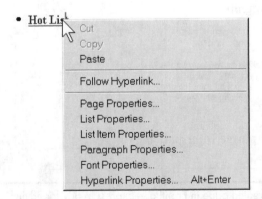

FIGURE 16-4 | Right-click an object to edit its properties

Saving and Testing Your New Page

A well-designed page often takes shape over a period of days or weeks, so you may find yourself going back into FrontPage Express to edit the page often. During this editing phase, you can open the page in a Web browser to see how it looks. You can even put it up on a Web site as an "under construction" page and have people try it out and give you feedback.

1. To save the page for the first time, choose Save As from the File menu.

   A dialog box similar to the following appears. This dialog box lets you specify a location for the page, such as a Web server on your company intranet or even a Web server on the Internet as discussed under "About Saving Pages and Posting Them on Web Servers." For this example, save the page on your computer's Desktop for further editing and testing.

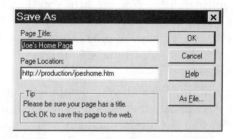

2. Click the As File button, then choose a location in the Save in field (the Desktop for this example) and type **HOME.HTM** in the File name field.

   By choosing As File, the Web page is saved as an HTML file on your computer. At any time in the future, you can open this page and edit it by right-clicking the file on the Desktop and choosing Edit from the shortcut menu. The page will open in FrontPage Express.

3. Click the page now to view it in your Web browser and see it as other people will see it.

   Experiment with the page by clicking the links under "Contents." Jump to "Comments and Suggestions," then click "send me mail." Outlook Express will open a blank message with the email address you specified (presumably your email address).

   Notice that most sections still require some editing (i.e., FrontPage inserted suggestions on what you should put in each section). Keep reading for more instructions on how to further edit this page.

About Saving Pages and Posting Them on Web Servers

One aspect of FrontPage Express that may be confusing is how it saves pages. On the Save As dialog box pictured earlier, you can "post" a page by typing a URL in the Page Location field, or you can save the page by clicking the "As File" button. When you post a page, all of its attached objects (images, sounds, videos) are automatically posted to a server. In contrast, you typically save a page to your own system so you can edit it further, or just use the page as a background for a folder or some other local requirement. If you are still working on a page or set of pages, save them to your local system until you are ready to post them.

If you are running Personal Web Server as discussed in Chapter 17, FrontPage Express will suggest posting the page to the Web publishing folder on your computer. The folder is usually located at \Inetpub\wwwroot by default, but it goes by an alias name that is the name of your computer. Look at the Save As dialog box pictured earlier. You see http://production in the Page Location field. "Production" is the network name of the computer in question. When network users access the computer (by typing **http://production** in the Address field of their Web browser), they are actually accessing files in the \Inetpub\wwwroot folder of the computer.

If you are running PWS on your computer, you will see your computer name in the Page Location field as the suggested location for saving the files. Just remember that the files are actually saved in the \Inetpub\wwwroot folder. Refer to Chapter 17 for more information on this process.

Page Editing Techniques

The FrontPage Express New Page Wizard automatically creates a page layout that you can edit as shown in Figure 16-3. As mentioned, it inserts comments and suggestions that you type over or erase. It also includes suggested hyperlinks and other elements. This section discusses the tools and techniques for editing pages you have created with the New Page Wizard or pages that you create from scratch.

The FrontPage Express Toolbars

One of the first things to do is make sure the FrontPage Express toolbars are enabled. Click View on the Menu bar and enable the Standard toolbar, Format toolbar, and Forms toolbar.

Figure 16-5 describes the buttons on the toolbars. In most cases, you simply highlight some existing text and click an option. For example, to expand the page title's font size, click it, then click the Increase Font Size button. You

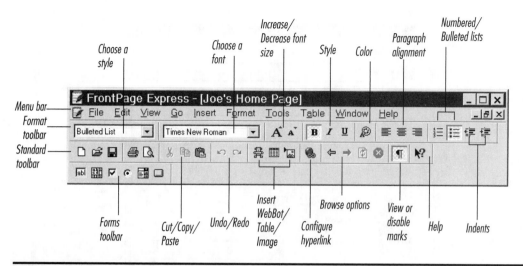

FIGURE 16-5 FrontPage Express toolbars

can also center any selected paragraph by clicking the appropriate paragraph alignment button.

All of the elements of the page can be edited using the same techniques you use to edit text in a word processor such as WordPad.

Web Page Objects and Properties

Note that each item on the page is an object. If you right-click an object, you see a shortcut menu similar to what was previously displayed in Figure 16-4. Here are some of the options for changing properties that may appear on the menu:

- **Page**   View and change properties of the Web page itself.
- **Paragraph**   View and change properties of the selected paragraph.
- **Font**   View and change properties of the selected text.
- **Hyperlinks**   View and change properties of hyperlinks and bookmarks.
- **Horizontal Lines**   View and change properties of separator lines.
- **List**   View and change properties of bulleted and numbered lists.
- **Table**   View and change properties of tables.

For example, to view and change page properties, right-click the document and choose Page Properties, or choose Page Properties on the File menu. The dialog box in Figure 16-6 appears. Here you can view and change title and location information, background sounds, and other information. Click the

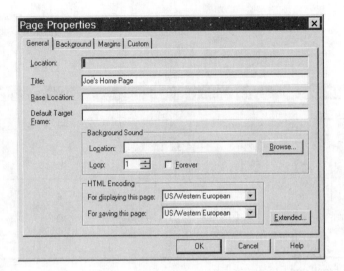

The General Page Properties dialog box

Background tab to change the background image and colors. Click the Margins tab to specify the size of the margins, and click the Custom tab for additional options.

Formatting Fonts and Paragraphs

Formatting characters with a special font or changing the properties of a paragraph is fairly straightforward. You highlight the part of the document you want to change and click the appropriate buttons on the Format toolbar as shown in Figure 16-5.

However, the Format menu has some interesting options that you should know about:

- **Font** Choose Font on the Format menu. This dialog box has two pages. On the first page, you set fonts, styles, and sizes. On the Special Styles page, you can set special options such as blinking text and vertical character positions (superscript/subscript).

- **Bullets and Numbering** Select this option on the Format menu to choose among four different bullet options and six different numbering options. You can also set the starting number for bulleted lists.

Inserting Objects, Text, Images, Components, and Links

The Insert menu has the most important options available in FrontPage. You use the options to insert pictures, video, sounds, files, components, moving text, hyperlinks, and other options. Just click the Insert menu to get an idea of the number of options available. These options make it easy to create great-looking Web pages without any previous experience with the HTML coding language. A description of each option follows. Some options are covered in more detail later in the chapter.

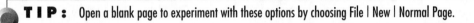

TIP: Open a blank page to experiment with these options by choosing File | New | Normal Page.

- **Break**   Opens the Break Properties dialog box where you can choose line break styles that start a new line without creating a new paragraph (thus you can start a new line without adding white space under it). Breaks are useful for addresses or listings.
- **Horizontal Line**   Inserts a page-width horizontal line. Use these lines to start new sections.
- **Symbol**   Brings up the Symbol dialog box shown next, where you can choose a special symbol to insert on your page. After inserting the symbol, you may change its font size.

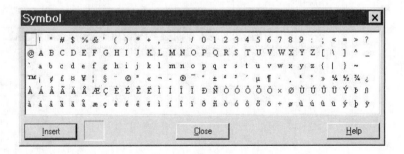

- **Comment**   Inserts text that can be seen in FrontPage Express but not by a Web browser.

- **Image** Inserts an image or piece of clipart. You may obtain clipart from a number of sources on the Internet. The Yahoo! link given earlier is a good start for finding "Web art."
- **Video** Inserts a video file from a drive or from the Web.
- **Background Sound** Inserts a sound file.

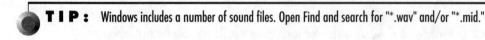

T I P : Windows includes a number of sound files. Open Find and search for "*.wav" and/or "*.mid."

- **File** Inserts the contents of a text file after converting it to HTML. Use this option to insert information that you have obtained elsewhere or typed in a word processor.
- **WebBot Component** WebBots are small applications that automate various tasks as described under "Using WebBot and Other Components" later in this chapter.
- **Other Components** Places ActiveX controls, Java applets, JavaScript, and plug-ins in the document. See "Adding Active Components" later in this chapter.
- **Form Field** Provides a choice of elements for creating forms. Refer to "Working with Forms" later in this chapter.
- **Marquee** Creates scrolling or sliding text. Point to where you want to create moving text, then choose Marquee from the Insert menu. The following dialog box appears where you can specify the characteristics of the moving text.

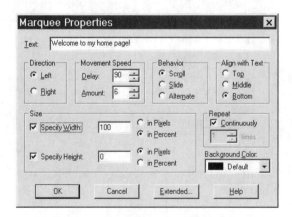

- **HTML Markup**   Inserts HTML-coded text at the current location of the insertion point. You can use this option to insert newly developed HTML tags on a page.
- **Script**   Use this option to insert Visual Basic, Java, and other scripts. You can use these scripts for forms processing, games, access counters, guestbooks, image maps, and other tasks.
- **Hyperlink**   Lets you create hyperlinks to other places on the same page, or to other pages (at your site or on the Internet. See the next section for more information.

Working with Hyperlinks

While some people can fit all their information on a single page, you might be better off putting your information on multiple-hyperlinked pages. FrontPage Express makes it easy to create the following types of hyperlinks:

- Hyperlinks to bookmarks on the same page (i.e., when creating a table of contents)
- Hyperlinks to your other pages
- Hyperlinks to pages at other Web sites (i.e., when creating a list of your favorite Web sites).

You have two choices when creating hyperlinks. One is to hide the URL (Web address) behind some text or a picture. In the following example, the descriptive text is the hyperlink:

Go to Yahoo!

In the next example, the URL is the hyperlink. The advantage of using this second method is that users can see the URL and write it down for future reference. Most important, if users print the page, the hyperlink address will appear on the page.

Go to Yahoo! from my page: http://www.yahoo.com

With this in mind, you create a hyperlink by first highlighting some existing text that you want to convert into a hyperlink, or just click a blank spot where you want to insert a URL hyperlink as in the previous second example. The following steps illustrate converting text to a hyperlink.

1. Type some text like **Click here to jump to my other page**.

2. Highlight the part of the text you want to appear as a hyperlink, such as the word "jump" or the whole phrase.

3. Choose Hyperlink from the Insert menu. The following dialog box appears:

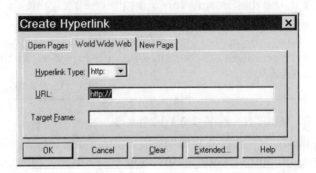

TIP: To create a hyperlink in which the actual URL appears on the page as the hyperlink, just click a blank area where you want the hyperlink to appear and choose Hyperlink from the Insert menu. You see the same dialog box as previously pictured and when you're done, the hyperlink itself will appear in that spot.

The Create Hyperlink dialog box has three tabs as described here. These tabs correspond to the three different types of hyperlinks you can create.

- **Open Pages**   Use this page to create a hyperlink to a bookmark on the same page or to another page that you have currently open in FrontPage Express. A bookmark is just a marker on a page that is the target of a hyperlink. A table of contents is the usual place to create bookmarked hyperlinks. Look at Joe's Home Page in Figure 16-2. When you click "Employee Information," for example, you jump to a section on the page that has been bookmarked as "Employee Information."

- **World Wide Web**   Create hyperlinks that lead to locations on another Web server, either on your local intranet or the Internet. Refer to "Creating Internet Links" next for more information.

- **New Page**   Click this section to create a hyperlink to a new page. FrontPage Express will lead you through the steps of creating a new page. Refer to "Creating New Page Links" for more information.

The following sections provide more information about creating and using hyperlinks. Each page has a different set of options, so you should read further before clicking OK on the Create Hyperlink dialog box to create the hyperlink.

Creating Internet Links

To create a hyperlink to a site on the Internet, type the text to describe the link, highlight the text, then choose Hyperlink on the Insert menu. When the Create Hyperlink dialog box appears, click the World Wide Web tab to display a page where you can type the target URL (this page is pictured earlier). Here are the steps for creating the hyperlink:

1. Choose the type of link in the Hyperlink Type field. (See Table 16-1.)
2. Type the address of the link in the URL field, or copy it from your Web browser (assuming it is pointed at the target page).
3. If the page consists of multiple frames of information, indicate the appropriate frame in the Target Frame field.
4. When you're done, click OK to complete the Internet hyperlink.

Create an Email Link

If you want readers of your Web page to send you an email message, choose mailto: in the Hyperlink Type box, then type your email address in the URL field. When readers view your page and click the mailto hyperlink, a blank

TYPE	FUNCTION
File	Opens a designated file on a local or network hard disk
ftp	Downloads the designated file using the File Transfer Protocol
Gopher	Connects to a Gopher site, which organizes information in a hierarchical set of programs and documents
http	Opens another Web site
https	Opens a secure Web site
mailto	Sends email to the recipient designated in the URL field
News	Opens the designated newsgroup server
telnet	Connects to another computer to allow remote operation of that computer
wais	Performs a search of a Wide Area Information Service server on the Internet

TABLE 16-1 Types of Hyperlinks

email message opens on their screen with your email address inserted in the To field.

Creating New Page Links

When you choose to create a new hyperlinked page, a hyperlink is created on the current page that links to a new page at your Web site. The New Page Wizard then runs to help you create the new page. Follow the steps here to create the new page. Note that you can also insert a picture, then use this same technique to make the picture a hyperlink to another page, as discussed later.

1. Click the spot on the current page where you want to insert a new page hyperlink.

2. Type some text that describes the link, such as **My Favorite Photos**.

3. Highlight the text, then choose Hyperlink on the Insert menu. When the dialog box appears, click the New Page tab to see the following dialog box:

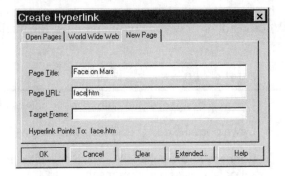

4. Type a title for the page in the Page Title field. FrontPage Express recommends a name for the HTML file in the Page URL field. You can accept this name or type a new one. Refer to "About Saving Pages and Posting Them on Web Servers" earlier in this chapter for more information about page URLs.

5. Click OK to start the New Page Wizard. The New Page dialog box appears where you can choose a template as described earlier under "Creating a New Web Page."

If you choose Normal Page, a blank page appears in FrontPage Express that you can edit on your own. After you create and save the new hyperlinked page, test it by opening the page that contains the hyperlink in a Web browser and clicking the hyperlink. Your new page should appear.

Bookmarks and Table of Contents Entries

Bookmarks allow you to create hyperlinks to other locations on the same page. If you look at Joe's Home Page, the links under "Contents" are bookmarks. You can click on "Employee Information" to jump to the section with the same name. Each bookmarked section also includes a "Back to Top" bookmark that returns to the table of contents.

A *bookmark* is a name that you assign to a section of a Web page. The steps for creating a bookmark are simple. First, go to the section on a page that you want to hyperlink to and add the bookmark, then go back to the top and add a hyperlink to the bookmark.

You can try this now on Joe's Home Page by following the steps here. For this example, we'll first create a new section on the page, so the first few steps below are specifically about setting up this new section.

1. Go to the place on the page where you want to insert the new section. There you will see a hyperlink in the previous section called "Back to Top." Place the blinking cursor at the end of this line.

2. Choose Horizontal Line on the Insert menu. The horizontal line is inserted after the previous section.

3. Press ENTER to insert a new blank line.

4. Type the title of the new section and press ENTER several times to insert some new blank lines.

5. Select the title (highlight it), then change its font style and size as necessary to match your other titles. For example, choose Heading 2 on the Format toolbar.

6. Choose Bookmark from the Edit menu to open the Bookmark dialog box as pictured here:

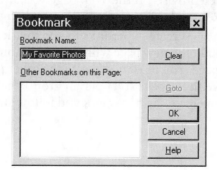

7. The suggested bookmark name is the name of your title. Click OK to accept it or type a shorter name if you prefer.

8. Now go to the place on the page where you want to create a hyperlink to this bookmark, type the text of the hyperlink, then highlight the text and choose Hyperlink from the Insert menu.

9. Click the Open Pages tab on the Create Hyperlink dialog box to display the following dialog box.

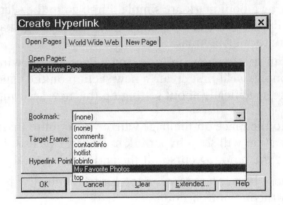

10. Make sure your current page is selected in the top field, then click the down arrow button on the Bookmark field and choose the bookmark you just created.

11. Finally, click OK to create the hyperlink to the bookmark. Now save the page and the changes you have made.

To test the new bookmark, open your Web browser, then load the Web page. If you saved the Web page to your Desktop, just click its icon to load the page in your Web browser. If the Web page was already open in your Web browser, click the Refresh button to get the latest changes.

You can also create hyperlinks to bookmarks on other pages. When users click the hyperlink, the new page will open and jump to the bookmarked section on the other page. You must first create the other page, add the bookmark, and save the page. With the page still open in FrontPage Express, go to the page where you want to create the bookmark and follow steps 8 through 11.

Adding Graphics, Video, and Sound Elements

You can add graphics to your Web page to make it more interesting, or to provide a visual hyperlink. While graphics will make your page more exciting, you need to keep some things in mind:

- Graphics take time to download, increasing the time it takes someone to see your page (they may go elsewhere before it completely downloads). Video clips take even longer to download.

- You can create your own images, purchase images, or obtain them for free at some Web sites.

- The graphic must fit on the viewer's screen, so it's best to keep images within the 640 by 480 pixel range.

- Minimize the number of colors used. Some users may only run 16-color displays.

- The usual graphic file format for Web pages is GIF and JPEG. These files have the filename extension .GIF and .JPG.

- Graphic elements are stored in separate files. If you move your Web pages to another directory on your system or to another computer such as a Web server, you'll need to move the graphic images with them.

- To add a sound, choose Insert Background Sound from the Insert menu, or refer to "Web Page Objects and Properties" earlier in this chapter.

WEBLINK: The Yahoo! site listed here has links to Web sites that have free clipart and images: http://www.yahoo.com/Computers_and_Internet/Internet/World_Wide_Web/Page_Design_and_Layout/Graphics/.

The following example will demonstrate how to insert a simple graphic image into your Web page. We'll use one of the GIF images that come with Windows 98 for this example, but you can use your own image if you prefer.

First, you need to find a GIF image and then copy it to the Desktop where your Web pages are located. The Windows folder contains some images you can "borrow."

1. Open the Windows folder and locate the file called HLPGLOBE.GIF. Right-click and drag it to the Desktop (or the folder that holds your Web pages), then choose Copy.

2. Now return to FrontPage Express and place the cursor at the position in the Web page where you want to insert the image.

3. Choose Image from the Insert menu to open the Image dialog box.

4. Click the Other Location tab, then click the Browse button and use standard file open techniques to open the file called HLPGLOBE.GIF that you just copied to the Desktop. When you find the file on the Desktop, click Open to complete the operation.

The image now appears on your Web page similar to the following. Add some descriptive text before or after the image to describe it. You can also make the image a hyperlink, so you might want to type some text that describes what the hyperlink opens.

Images may have a background that differs from your Web page background, thus causing them to appear in a box of a different color. If you want your images to blend into the background, edit them so they have the same background as your Web page. Alternatively, you can change the Web page background to match the image color. Choose Page Properties from the File menu, click the Background tab, and change the color of the Background field.

You can go through this same procedure to add any image, such as a scanned picture of yourself or your family, a corporate logo, a map, and so on. Some small images, such as the globe, are good to use as hyperlink buttons or even bullets for your paragraphs.

It is common to show thumbnails of large images. Then visitors to your site can see a preview of the image before downloading it. Figure 16-7 illustrates an example of a Web page with a thumbnail image that hyperlinks to a larger version of the image.

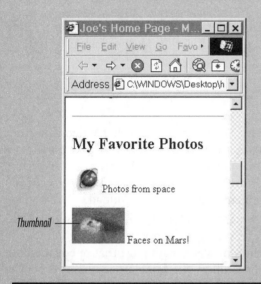
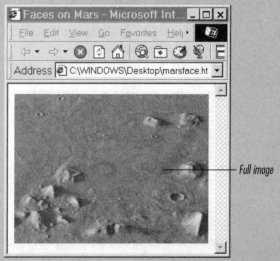

Thumbnail

Full image

FIGURE 16-7 Creating thumbnail images

To create thumbnail hyperlinks, you'll need two separate images, one small and one large. Many graphics editors have commands that create thumbnail images for you. In this example, we just cut out a small part of the image and saved it as a separate GIF file.

1. Insert the thumbnail on your main page.
2. Highlight the thumbnail and choose Hyperlink on the Insert menu.
3. When the Create Hyperlink dialog box appears, click the New Page tab.
4. Fill out the New Page tab and click OK.
5. When the new page dialog box appears, choose Normal Page.
6. A new blank page appears in the FrontPage Express window. Insert the large graphic image on this page. You can include descriptive text if necessary.

Hyperlinking the Image

While text hyperlinks are useful, it's much more interesting to use images as iconic hyperlinks. Here's how:

1. Highlight the image you just inserted.

2. Choose Hyperlink on the Insert menu to open the Create Hyperlink dialog box.

3. Click an appropriate tab based on the type of hyperlink you want. Refer to the section "Working with Hyperlinks" earlier in this chapter for more information.

About Video Clips

You can also add video clips to your Web page by choosing Video from the Insert menu. Keep in mind that videos can be large files that take a while to download. If your Web site is connected to an internal corporate network, this may not be a problem, but if users are connecting over the Internet via dial-up connections, a video clip can take many minutes to download.

You should put video clips on separate Web pages. As of this writing, they tend to play automatically when the Web page is opened (not a good idea for your home page). Create a hyperlink on your main page that opens another Web page containing the video clip. Follow the same procedure as described under "Creating Thumbnail Links to Large Images," except insert your video clip on the new page.

Adding Tables

Tables help you present information in a format that makes it easier for viewers to read and understand. Figure 16-8 illustrates a table under construction and the settings in the Insert Table dialog box that were used to create it.

To create a table, follow the steps here. Note that the initial settings you specify, such as the number of rows and columns, can be changed at any time.

1. Position the cursor where you want to put the table, then Choose Insert Table from the Table menu. The Insert Table dialog box appears similar to what you see in Figure 16-8.

2. Specify the number of rows and columns in the Size field, then set the other options. (See Table 16-2.)

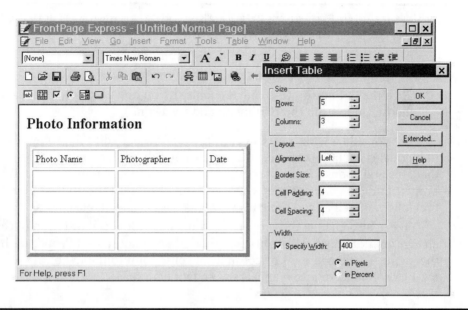

FIGURE 16-8 Creating a table

OPTION	FUNCTION
Alignment	Where the table appears on the page—either left, centered, or right.
Border Size	The width of the border surrounding the table.
Cell Padding	The number of pixels between the cell text and the cell walls. Increasing this option gives the table a more open look and better readability.
Cell Spacing	The number of pixels between adjacent cells. Increasing this value makes the table grid "fatter."
Width	You can specify an exact width for the table by clicking "in Pixels" or a variable width by clicking "in Percent." The "in Percent" option is usually best since users will be displaying the page on screens with different widths. Use this option to widen a table beyond the sum of its characters.

TABLE 16-2 Table Options

T I P : Blank tables are "squashed" until you type text in the cells. The table width increases as you type text in fields. The exception is when the table has the width you specify in the Width field.

3. Click the OK button to create the table. If you don't like what appears, choose Undo from the Edit menu and try again.

Once you add a table, you can edit its properties or edit the properties of individual cells. For example, you can change cell border colors. Right-click the table and choose Table Properties from the drop-down menu. The Table Properties dialog box appears where you can change all the options described previously as well as add table backgrounds and change table colors.

You can also change the properties of any individual cell or group of cells. To change an individual cell, right-click the cell and choose Cell Properties from the menu. To change rows or columns of cells, point to the left of the row or top of a column. An arrow appears as shown here.

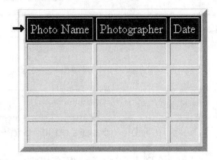

Click to select, then drag to select multiple rows or columns. After highlighting a group of cells, right-click the group and choose Cell Properties to display the Cell Properties dialog box where you can change most of the properties already discussed, but for only the selected cells, not the entire table.

There are a number of other edits you can make to tables, as outlined next. We recommend that you create a "dummy" table and experiment with each of these options to see how they work.

T I P : To select a single cell to be included in a formatting operation, click the cell, then choose Select Cell from the table menu.

- **Insert rows or columns**   Click the row or column where you want to insert a new row or column, then choose Insert Rows or Columns from the Table menu. Specify the number of rows or columns to insert and whether to insert them above or below the current selection.
- **Insert cell**   Point near where you want to insert a cell and choose Insert Cell from the Table menu.
- **Insert a table in a cell**   Interestingly, you can insert a table inside of another cell. Click the target cell, then choose Insert Table from the table menu.
- **Merge cells**   You can combine the contents of two separate cells into a single cell. Click and drag through the cells to be combined, then choose Merge Cells from the Table menu.
- **Split cells**   You can split an existing cell into multiple rows or columns. Click the cell, then choose Split Cell from the Table menu. In the dialog box that appears, specify rows or columns and the number of rows or columns. The new cells fill the existing cell space and any text that was in the cell remains in the first cell.
- **Insert a caption**   Choose this option to insert a caption either above or below the table.
- **Delete cells**   Click the cell to be deleted, then choose Select Cell from the Table menu. Press the DELETE key on the keyboard.

Using WebBot and Other Components

A WebBot is a small application that will carry out a specific task automatically. FrontPage Express includes three WebBots that perform the tasks outlined next. However, WebBot components can only be used on Web servers that support FrontPage server extensions, so you will need to check with your ISP or network administrator before using these components. Refer to the FrontPage Express Help system for more information about components.

To insert a WebBot component, position your cursor, then select WebBot Component on the Insert menu and choose one of the following components:

- **The Include WebBot**   The Include WebBot will insert material from another Web page. If that Web page changes at any time, the material in the current Web page is automatically updated with the changes. On a server running FrontPage extensions, whenever the inserted file is modified, the files in which it is inserted will also be changed. This means you have to change only one file in order to effect a change common to many of the pages on your site. When you choose this option, you are asked to type the URL of the Web page to include.

- **The Timestamp WebBot**   Timestamp inserts the date (and time, if desired) when the page was last edited or automatically updated. Choosing Timestamp from the list of WebBot components brings up a dialog box where you can modify the date and time formats.

- **The Search WebBot**   The Search WebBot adds a search engine to the page that visitors can use to locate information on any of the pages at your site that are linked to your home page. Adding this component includes a field where visitors can type keywords to search for. It also includes a Start Search button and a Reset button.

Adding Active Components

You can add ActiveX controls, Java applets, JavaScript, and plug-ins to your Web page by choosing Other Components on the Insert menu. On the cascading menu, choose one of the following options:

- **ActiveX Control**   Microsoft has included a number of ActiveX controls with FrontPage Express. ActiveX controls add live content and interaction to your Web site.

WEBLINK: To download other ActiveX controls and find out more about ActiveX controls, try ClNet's ActiveX page at http://www.activex.com/.

- **Java Applet**   These are small applications written in the Java programming language that you can make available for visitors to run in their Web browsers.

WEBLINK: The HTML Tutor at http://html.cavalcade-whimsey.com/index.html offers information on running Java applets and JavaScript.

- **Plug-In**   Like Java applets, plug-ins are small applications that you can add to your Web browser to enhance its functionality. A plug-in might let you use certain types of audio or video file formats, to name only a couple of possibilities. The Plug-In Properties box lets you identify the location of the plug-in.

WEBLINK: Plug-ins are available at Dave Central Software Archive at http://www.davecentral. com/audplug.html.

- **PowerPoint Animation**   PowerPoint is Microsoft's graphics presentation (slideshow) software. You can insert PowerPoint animations on your page, and visitors with the free Microsoft PowerPoint Animation Player will be able to run your presentations via the Internet.

WEBLINK: Microsoft posts the PowerPoint Animation Player pages at http://www.microsoft.com/ powerpoint/internet/player/installing.htm, and there are sample presentations at http://www.microsoft.com/ powerpoint/internet/player/gallery.htm.

Working with Forms

A form is a Web page that users fill out with information that is submitted back to you. Some common forms include guest books, surveys, and registration pages. You can create forms that aid your business marketing and sales efforts.

FrontPage Express' Form Page Wizard lets you build forms from scratch, but it also comes with templates you can use to create two types of forms: surveys and confirmation forms. The best way to create any form is to start by creating them with the Wizard and then change them to fit your specific needs.

When you finish the form, you must post it to a server that runs the FrontPage Extensions. The Personal Web Server (PWS) discussed in Chapter 17 is a FrontPage-enabled Web server that comes with Windows 98. If PWS is running on your system, FrontPage will recommend posting Web pages to this server. Talk to your ISP or network administrator if you need to post forms on other Web servers.

Creating a Basic Form

In this section, we show you how to use the New Page Wizard to create a basic survey form. You'll see how to set up forms that collect contact information, account information, product information, ordering information, personal information, and more.

1. On the File menu, click New to bring up the New Page Wizard.

2. Click Form Page Wizard, then click OK. An opening page appears with some information you can read. Click Next and you are then asked to verify the page title and URL.

3. Click Next. You see an Add button on the next page. Click the button to open the following dialog box:

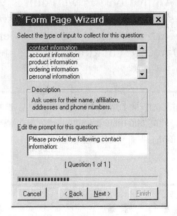

4. Choose the type of input you want to collect from visitors, then select the Next button. Each type has a different set of options. For example, if you choose "personal information," the following dialog box appears. Fill out the options as appropriate.

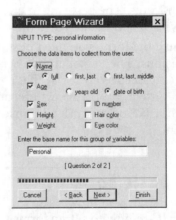

5. Click the Next button to accept the changes. You can then click the Add button to add more items.

6. When you're done adding options, click the Next button to set presentation options, then click Next again to get to the following dialog box:

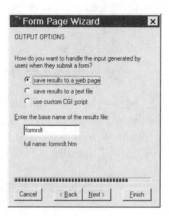

7. This is where you specify how information collected from users is handled. You can save the information in a Web page or a text file, or you can process it with a custom CGI script. Choose an option and click Next, then Finish.

The new form appears in the FrontPage Express window so you can edit the page.

Editing Forms

Each of the input fields you selected appears on the form. Change any of the field names, field widths, security options, and validation options to fit your needs. You can also add other fields by clicking the buttons on the Form toolbar. Point to any button to see a description of what it does.

Right-click on any form section in the Web page and choose Form Properties. The following dialog box appears. Note the different form handlers in the drop-down list box. The basic form you just created uses the WebBot Save Results Component to save information entered by users into a file.

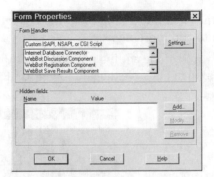

Click the Settings button to open the dialog box pictured next. This is where you can specify the name and location of the results file and the file format. You can also include additional information in the results file by clicking the options in the lower part of the dialog box.

Post the Page

After you finish editing the page, you're ready to post it to your Web server. Click Save As on the File menu to open the Save As dialog box. If PWS is installed, the Page Location field should show a URL similar to the following:

http://*yourcomputername*/form.htm

where *yourcomputername* is the name assigned to your computer. If PWS is not installed, enter the URL for the Web server where you want to post the page.

Viewing Submitted Information

After posting your page, Web users can access your form and fill it out. When they click the Submit button, the form is processed and information is stored in a file that you can view at any time.

How this information is collected depends on the settings you made earlier in step 7. If you chose to store the information to a Web page or text file, FrontPage Express stored the information in a file called FORMRSLT.TXT in the \Windows\TEMP folder. If you chose the CGI option, forms processing depends on your custom script. Refer to a book on CGI for more information.

Other Forms Options

The FrontPage Express New Page Wizard includes two other form templates. In addition, you can add individual form fields and buttons to your Web pages by clicking the options on the Forms toolbar.

Confirmation Form

You can return a confirmation to visitors who fill out your forms. Here are the steps to creating a confirmation form:

1. Choose New on the File menu, then click Confirmation Form and OK. The confirmation form appears immediately.
2. Post it to your Web site by choosing Save As on the File menu.
3. Next, open the form that will send the confirmation to people who fill it out.
4. Right-click in any part of the form area and choose Form Properties. On the Form Properties dialog box, click the Settings button.
5. On the Settings dialog box, click the Confirm tab and type the location of the form in the URL of confirmation page field.

The URL you type is the same location where you posted the confirmation in step 2.

Survey Form

The FrontPage Express New Page Wizard will create a survey form that has many interesting options for collecting information from people. It is a form that will require a lot of editing on your part, but overall, the form created by the wizard will save you a lot of work when compared to creating it manually.

1. Choose New on the File menu, then click Survey Form and OK. The Survey form appears immediately.
2. Edit the form as necessary.
3. Save the form by choosing Save As on the File menu and specifying the destination Web server in the Page Location field.

You use your Web browser all the time to gather information on the Internet. In the process, you hyperlink from one place to the other and send messages to people. Why not put this same functionality right on your Active Desktop by building a Web page similar to what you see in Figure 16-9?

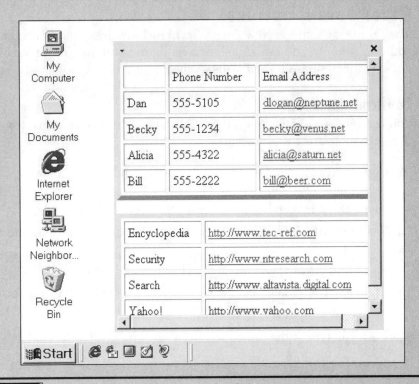

FIGURE 16-9 Putting a Web page on the Active Desktop

In this example, we'll create a Web page with FrontPage Express that contains hyperlinked mail addresses and Web site addresses. When you click on an email address, Outlook Express opens with a message addressed to the recipient. When you click a Web address, Internet Explorer opens and takes you to that address.

Of course, you can employ all of the other FrontPage Express features to spruce up the Web page you put on your own Desktop. For example, you might want to include icons that hyperlink to graphic images or document files on your own system or on network servers. You could even create a calendar that includes your most important appointments. When you click on an appointment, a Web page or document opens that includes information about the appointment.

To create a Web page similar to Figure 16-9, follow these steps:

1. Open FrontPage Express, click on File and New to create a new Normal Page.
2. Follow the steps described under "Adding Tables" to create the tables for your names and addresses.
3. Add the text to the table, then convert each address to a hyperlink. Highlight the email address or URL and press CTRL-C to copy it to the Clipboard. Choose Hyperlink from the Edit menu, then paste the address in the URL field and click OK.
4. Once the page is complete, choose Save As on the File menu, click the As File button and save the page on your Desktop.

   Now you need to add the page as an item on your Active Desktop.

5. Right-click the Desktop, then choose Active Desktop | Customize My Desktop from the menu.
6. Click the New button to add a new item. You may see a message asking if you want to connect with a Microsoft Web site. Click No.
7. You are now asked for a filename. Click the Browse button and specify the name and location of the Web page you just created.

The Web page appears on your Desktop. If you point to it, you can resize its borders or move it around. Click any of the hyperlinks to make sure they work.

In the next chapter, you learn more about Personal Web Server, a desktop Web server utility that lets you publish the pages you create in FrontPage Express on your own computer for other users to see.

Personal Web Server

17

BASICS

B A S I C S

- Create Web Pages without any knowledge of HTML
- Publish a personal home page and other hyperlinked pages
- Make non-HTML documents available at your Web site for others to download
- Monitor activities at your site and track performance
- Add hyperlinks to other documents on your system or other systems

B E Y O N D

- Create a guest book and review its contents
- Collect messages and other information from visitors
- Publish pages created in FrontPage Express

Personal Web Server (PWS) is a tool for publishing Web pages on your own computer (as opposed to just creating Web pages as you can do in FrontPage Express). The software lets you publish electronic information to share with other people in your company or even on the Internet. PWS is basically a desktop Web server.

PWS includes a wizard that helps you create a home page. In addition, it includes features that make it easy to manage a Web site, such as:

- Configure a guest book and message drop box. Visitors can leave personal information and comments or messages that you can read later.
- Make any type of file available to visitors, not just published Web pages. You can include hyperlinks to Word documents, Excel spreadsheets, and other types of documents. When visitors click the hyperlink, they can choose to open or save the documents on their computers.
- Add new documents to your Web site by simply dragging and dropping them to the PWS icon on the Desktop.
- Use PWS as a test platform for developing other Web sites. With PWS, you can try out pages that you are developing to post on other Web sites. You can check to make sure the links, scripts, and other features work properly.

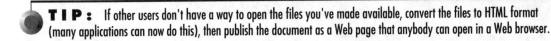

TIP : If other users don't have a way to open the files you've made available, convert the files to HTML format (many applications can now do this), then publish the document as a Web page that anybody can open in a Web browser.

Installing and Starting Personal Web Server

Personal Web Server is an optional program that you install by loading its software from the Windows 98 CD-ROM. It is not installed automatically by Windows 98 setup.

To load the software click Start, then choose Run. Type the following command in the Open field, replacing d with the drive letter of your CD-ROM:

   d:\add-ons\pws\setup.exe

During the installation, you are asked a few questions about how you want to set up PWS. In most cases, use the defaults. If you are familiar with more advanced details about Web servers, you may choose to set custom options, but otherwise, the default settings provided should be sufficient.

PWS will be available on your local network with an address that includes your computer. For example, if your computer's name is Greenacres, visitors will type **http://greenacres** in the address field of their Web browser to access your PWS Web pages. This assumes that a WINS (Windows Internet Naming Service) server is located on your network to translate the computer name into an appropriate IP address. Your network administrator can tell you about

WINS. If a WINS server is not available, visitors can type the IP address of your computer in the Address field of their Web browsers.

After you install PWS, the following icon appears on your Desktop:

Publish

You can click this icon to open the Personal Web Manager as shown in Figure 17-1. Note that you can also drag-and-drop documents you want to publish onto the Publish icon as described later.

The Personal Web Manager is pictured in Figure 17-1 with the Main page visible. The Main page has the features described here:

*   It displays the URL where the home page is available to other users. In this case, the URL is http://production.

*   The Stop button makes your Web pages unavailable until you click Start. You can stop the Web server for maintenance purposes or because it is reducing the performance of your local applications.

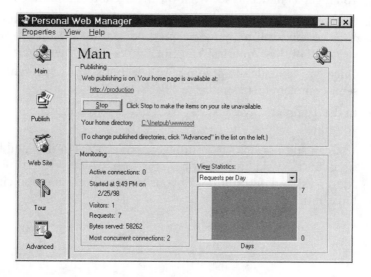

FIGURE 17-1 The Personal Web Server main screen

- The Monitoring field provides statistics about the number of visitors and requests to your site.
- You can click any of the icons on the left to view or manage other aspects of PWS as described in a moment.

Creating a Home Page

Personal Web Manager has a wizard that helps you create a home page. The wizard steps you through the process and eliminates the need to know anything about programming or writing HTML code. Keep in mind, however, that you can also create Web pages by using other tools such as FrontPage Express or by writing your own HTML code in a word processor. We show you how to use the PWS home page wizard here, but later, we show you how to publish pages you have created in FrontPage Express.

To create a Web page, follow these steps. When you are done, the complete Web page will be available to anyone visiting your Web site.

1. Click the Web Site button in the left pane of the Personal Web Manager. This starts the Web Page wizard.

2. Click the arrow button to begin stepping through the wizard. On the first page that appears, you can choose a template. Just choose Journal for now. You'll get a chance to see what the other choices look like in step 4.

3. Click the arrow button to continue on. In the next few boxes, you're then asked if you want to include a guest book and a message drop box. Answer yes to all of these queries. You can always undo them later.

   Once you've made the preliminary selections, you're presented with a semi-complete form similar to Figure 17-2.

4. In the Template Style box, try each of the styles and choose the one you like.

5. You can add hot links to your favorite Web sites in the "add links" section (look for the Add Link button on the form). Just type the URLs (Web site addresses) and descriptions of your favorite Web sites and click the Add Link button.

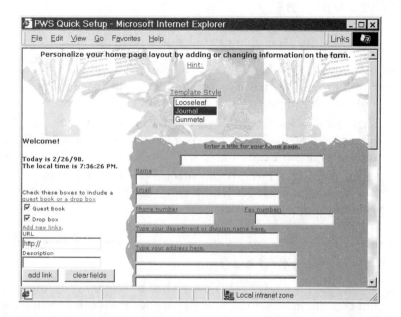

FIGURE 17-2 Semi-complete Web page form

6. Fill in the remaining boxes as appropriate. The form contains extra headings if you need them. If you don't type text in the fields, nothing appears in that spot when the complete page is viewed in a Web browser.

7. When you're done, click the Enter New Changes button at the bottom of the form.

In a moment, your new home page appears in the Internet Explorer window. This is how visitors to your Web site see the page, so look over the features and edit the page further if necessary, as discussed next.

TIP: For future reference, PWS does not actually create an HTML Web page during this process. It stores the field options you typed in a file called MYINFO.XML in the \Windows\SYSTEM\inetsrv directory. When visitors access your Web site, a template called DEFAULT.ASP is displayed and the settings in MYINFO.XML are applied to it.

Other Options

Editing your home page is easy. Open the Personal Web Manager, then click the Web Site icon. The right pane now lists three options:

- **Edit Your Home Page**   When you click this option, you return to the Web page form as shown in Figure 17-2. You can choose a different template style, fill in additional fields, and add other Web links.
- **View Your Guest Book**   If you enabled the guest book, you'll choose this option on a regular basis to view information left by users. Refer to "About the Guest Book" next.
- **Open Your Drop Box**   If you enabled the drop box, you'll choose this option to view messages left by users. Refer to "Opening Your Drop Box" later in this chapter for details.

About the Guest Book

If you enabled the guest book option when setting up your home page, visitors to your site will be able to view and sign your guest book. A hyperlink appears on the Web page called "Read my guestbook." Visitors click this option to view a page similar to Figure 17-3 where they can sign the guest book and leave a

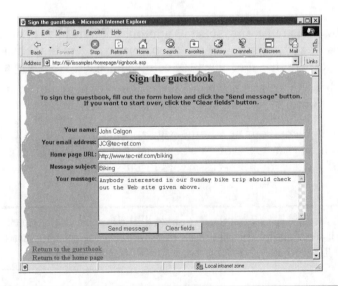

FIGURE 17-3   Visitors' view of signing the guest book

message, then click the Send message button to post the message to your guest book.

After a number of messages have been posted, the guest book looks like what you see in Figure 17-4. Visitors can view a list of who else has visited the site and read a message by clicking on it. The list can also be sorted by date, author, or subject.

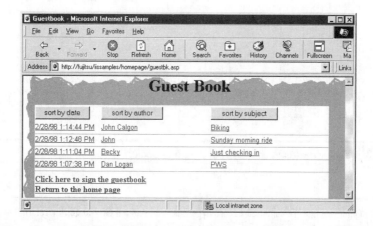

FIGURE 17-4 | Visitors' view of guest book entries

As the Webmaster of your site, you can view the guest book in Personal Web Manager. Click the Web Site icon in the left pane, then click View Your Guest Book to see the box in Figure 17-5.

Here, you can specify exactly which messages you want to see by changing any of the options. For example, in the MessageDate field, you can specify all messages before, after, or on a specific date. In the MessageFrom field, you can specify text that appears in the name left by the visitor. In Figure 17-5, I am searching for all messages that have John in the MessageFrom field. In the MessageSubject field, type text to find in the subject of a message.

Click the Submit Query button to see a list of messages that match the query parameters you specified. A list of entries similar to Figure 17-4 appears. You can choose any entry to read it. More importantly, you can delete any entries that are undesirable for whatever reason.

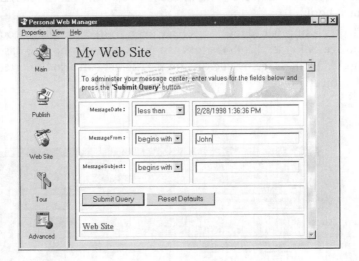

FIGURE 17-5 Your view (as Webmaster) of the guest book

T I P : The email address and Web site address are hyperlinks that make it easy to quickly return a message to the guest or visit his or her Web site.

Opening Your Drop Box

Visitors to your Web site can also leave a private message for you. An option called "Leave a Private Message" appears on your home page. When visitors click this option, a message screen appears similar to Figure 17-3 where they can type personal information and the message. When users click the Send Message button, the message goes in a private mail box (drop box). Other visitors cannot see messages dropped in the box.

You can view these messages by opening the Personal Web Manager. Click the Web Site icon in the left pane, then click the Open Your Drop Box option. You see a list of messages that you can sort in date, author, or subject order.

Publishing Documents

You probably have documents that you need to share with other people in your organization. Some of these documents are easily converted to HTML format so that anybody can view them with a Web browser. However, some documents can only be opened by specific applications, such as Microsoft Word and Microsoft Excel.

PWS lets you create hyperlinks on your home page to any document stored on your computer. When visitors click a hyperlink to a file, the following dialog box appears on their system:

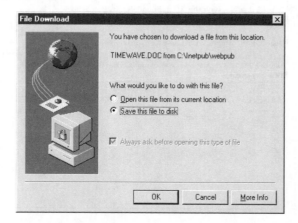

If the visitor clicks the first option, the file is opened in an application that is associated with the document type. If the visitor clicks the second option, a Save As dialog box appears so a folder and filename can be selected. The file is stored and can be opened later.

There are two ways to publish documents on your Web site:

- Open Personal Web Manager if it is not already open and click the Publish button.
- Drag-and-drop a document onto the Publish icon that appears on your Desktop.

In either case, the Web Publishing Wizard starts and you see the dialog box pictured in Figure 17-6. The steps for publishing a document are outlined here:

1. Type a document path and name in the Path field, or click the Browse button to search for the file.
2. Type a description in the Description field. Visitors read this description to determine if the file is what they want.
3. Click the Add button to add the file to the publishing list.

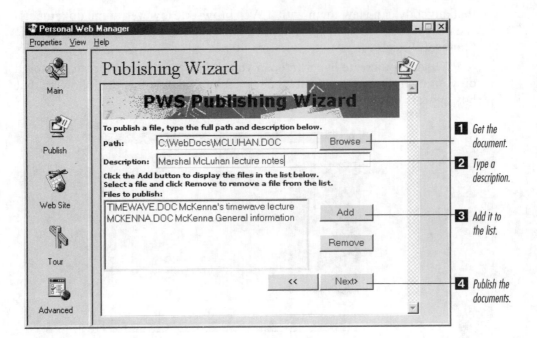

FIGURE 17-6 | Publishing documents

Now you can repeat steps 1 through 3 to add more files to the publishing list. You can change the description at any time by clicking a file in the publishing list and typing a new description. You can also click a file and click the Remove button to remove it from the list.

4. To publish the files in the publishing list, click the Next button.

After posting documents, an option called "View My Published Documents" appears on your Web page. When visitors click this option, the browser window displays your list of published files similar to what you see in Figure 17-7. Each filename is a hyperlink that opens or downloads the file when selected.

Here's what happens when you publish files in this way: The files are copied from their original directory into the webpub directory (discussed in the next section). This directory is accessible by visitors to your site and all the files you've published are kept together within it. If you change one of the files you have published, you will need to refresh its copy in the webpub folder.

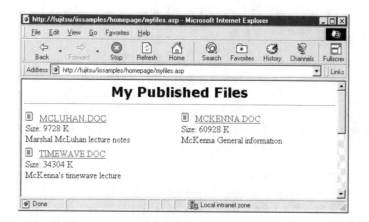

FIGURE 17-7 How visitors see your published documents

To manage your published files, click the Publish icon in the Personal Web Manager. The options pictured in Figure 17-8 appear. Click the Add option to publish more files, click the Remove option to remove some of your published files, click the Refresh option to recopy files for which the originals have changed, and finally, click the Change option to change the description of any published files.

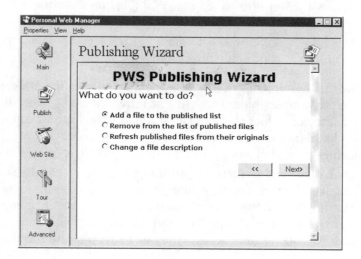

FIGURE 17-8 Adding, updating, and removing published documents

About Publishing Directories and Web Documents

When you install PWS, it sets up a number of folders to hold your home page and other files. The PWS program files and some of the templates used by PWS exist in the Windows\SYSTEM\inetsrv folder. The folder of most interest to you is called Inetpub and it is located at the root of the drive where you installed PWS. The Inetpub folder contains a set of its own folders, the two most important of which are

- **wwwroot** This folder is the home directory for your Web site by default. It contains the home page that people see when they visit your Web site. If you create your own home page (rather than use the one PWS helps you create), put it in this folder.
- **webpub** This folder holds a copy of files that you publish as discussed under "Publishing Documents" earlier in this chapter. Note that the webpub folder is marked read-only to protect its contents from visitors who might try to change your files.

Virtual directories are folders located elsewhere on your hard drive that can appear to visitors as if they are part of the home directory. Virtual directories take on an *alias* name that represents the folder. For example, assume you created a folder called Special Projects in your My Documents folder that contains a group of documents you want to publish. You can do two things:

- Follow the steps described under "Publishing Documents" to copy the documents into the webpub folder.
- Make the Special Projects folder a virtual directory that appears to be a subfolder of your home directory (wwwroot).

The first example may seem easier, but you'll end up with copies of the files in the webpub folder that must be refreshed as the originals in the Special Projects folder change. The second method is best when you already have a lot of files in an established folder. Users access the original versions of the files instead of a copy, so no refreshing of the copies is necessary.

You assign a virtual directory an alias name that is usually short and easier to type than the real directory name. The alias also disguises the real location of your directory for security reasons. For example, assume your computer name is Greenacres and you add a virtual directory with an assigned alias name of Back40. Visitors access your site by typing **http://greenacres** in their

Web browser. To access the Back40 alias, they type **http://greenacres/back40/**. Even though they are accessing a directory at some other location, it appears the virtual directory branches directly from greenacres.

Creating Virtual Directories

In this section, we show you how to create and manage virtual directories and how to set other special features. Open Personal Web Manager and click the Advanced icon in the left pane. The Advanced page is pictured in Figure 17-9. This is where you set special options as described next.

The Virtual Directories field shows the current virtual directories. Click on any directory and the Edit Properties button to see where the original directory is located.

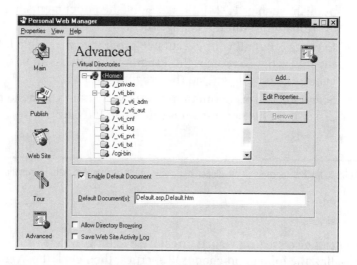

FIGURE 17-9   Personal Web Manager advanced settings

1. Click the Add button to create a new virtual directory. You see the following dialog box where you can click the Browse button to locate a directory:

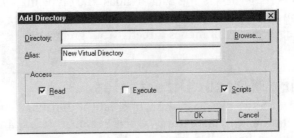

2. Type a short descriptive name in the Alias field.

3. Now set an option in the Access field as follows:

- **Read**   Set this permission on directories that contain information to publish, such as HTML files or published documents. Users can read or download files but not change them.

- **Execute**   Put all your executable programs in a single folder and assign the folder the Execute right. Programs can then run in the folder, but visitors cannot download the program files.

- **Scripts**   Set this permission to enable a script engine to run in the directory. This permission is safer than Execute.

NOTE: Refer to the PWS documents mentioned at the end of this chapter for more information on these permissions.

You can also create a virtual directory by going directly to the folder. Right-click the folder and choose Properties, then click the Web Sharing tab and select "Share this folder." The Web Sharing tab only appears if PWS is installed.

Default Documents

The Enable Default Document field on the Advanced page is where you set the name of the document that is displayed when visitors access your site. Two documents are already set in the field and PWS will display whichever one is available in the folder. The order of names in the field determines which document is displayed first. For example, in Figure 17-9, DEFAULT.ASP would be displayed before DEFAULT.HTM if both documents exist.

You can specify your own home page in this field. For example, if you create a new set of Web pages in FrontPage Express and call the main page HOME.HTM, you would type **HOME.HTM** as the first entry in this field. See "Creating a Home Page with FrontPage Express" for more details on how to do this.

Directory Browsing and Activity Logs

The bottom of the Advanced page has two interesting options as described here:

- **Allow Directory Browsing**   This option allows visitors to view a list of files in the directory they are accessing. Each file is listed with a hyperlinked name so if you click on a file, the file is either opened or downloaded. For example, assume as before that users access your Web page by typing **http://greenacres/**. If you enable this option and a visitor types **http://greenacres/ webpub/**, they will see a list of files in the webpub directory. This can be beneficial for folders in which the file list is quite long and users know what they are looking for. In most cases, it's not a good idea to enable this option since users may see files at your site that should not be seen.
- **Save Web Site Activity Log**   Enable this option to maintain a log of visitors to your site. The log collects information about visitors, the time they visited, and what they did at your site. You can use this information to track user activities, see what is popular at your site, check for malicious activities, and so on. Refer to the PWS help files and documentation for more information.

Creating a Home Page with FrontPage Express

Chapter 16 discusses how to create Web pages with FrontPage Express. You can save your FrontPage Express pages in the wwwroot folder and build a complete Web site with them. Once you add the pages, you need to specify your new home page as the default document for your Web site. You do this by typing the name of the new home page in the Default Document(s) field on the Advanced page in Personal Web Manager (see Figure 17-9).

For example, assume you create a new home page with FrontPage Express called HOME.HTM. It includes three hyperlinks that open other HTML pages. The home page and the additional pages must all be saved in the wwwroot folder, along with any graphic elements or other inserts you added to the page (unless you specified in your Web page the exact path where those files are located).

To save your work to the wwwroot directory in FrontPage, click the Save As option on the File menu. You will see a field called Page Location that contains the name of your Web server ("http://production" would appear using our earlier example). Basically, FrontPage Express knows all about PWS and is ready to save your Web pages in the PWS default directory (wwwroot). Just click OK to save your Web pages. FrontPage will ask you if you want to save the attached files into the directory as well. Note that you still need to save each page individually, but FrontPage does most of the work of putting everything into the right directory.

Finally, go to the Advanced page in Personal Web Manager and add the name of your home page as the first entry on the Default Document(s) field. Be sure to insert a comma after the name if other names are in the field.

That's it. Now visitors will see the much more dynamic pages you can create in FrontPage Express.

Getting More Information on Personal Web Server

Hundreds of pages of information for using Personal Web Server can be found by opening the Personal Web Manager and choosing the Help option on the menu. PWS is quite extensive and there are many more features than introduced here. If you need to take advantage of Web publishing beyond these basics, we encourage you to read through the documentation. Help information appears in your Web browser in a hyperlinked format that makes it easy to locate just the information or help you need.

Here are some of the additional topics you'll find in the documentation:

- Creating your own pages with text editors.
- Building interactive forms that visitors fill out and submit to you.
- Viewing and working with information submitted by visitors.
- Changing the home directory to a different folder.
- Troubleshooting information.

In addition to the previous documentation, you should obtain a suitable text that explains Web publishing in intranet environments and on the Internet.

This chapter and the last chapter conclude our exploration into building your own Web pages and Web sites. We hope that you find these features useful in communicating information to your coworkers or people on the Internet.

Collaborating with NetMeeting

18

B A S I C S

- Talk with others as if you were on a telephone
- Videoconference with people on your intranet or the Internet
- Set up chat sessions with multiple users
- Set up a whiteboard in a conference call to create drawings that multiple users can see
- Transfer files in the background while carrying on the other activities
- Share applications and work on documents with multiple users

B E Y O N D

- Manage multiparty conferences
- Set special options to fine-tune NetMeeting
- Collaborate by letting multiple users work in the same application

NetMeeting is a conferencing and collaboration tool that lets you talk to other people over computer networks, set up videoconferences, and collaborate with other people by sharing applications. You can connect with coworkers over the Internet or an intranet to discuss projects and actually work on documents online.

A typical NetMeeting session is pictured in Figure 18-1. This figure looks confusing at first. On your own system, you can pull the whiteboard, chat, and video windows off to the side to make things less confusing.

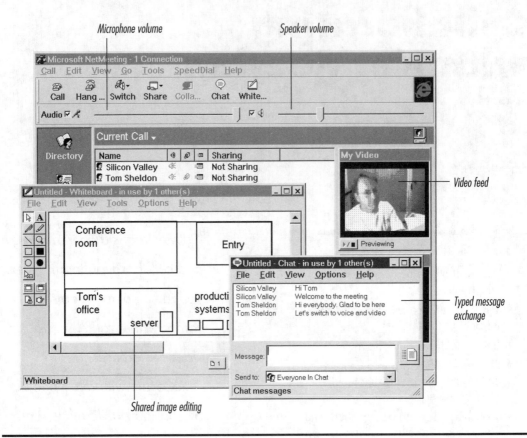

FIGURE 18-1   NetMeeting session running Whiteboard and Chat

Since NetMeeting works over the Internet, you can set up conferences with anyone in the world without incurring long-distance charges. NetMeeting is not only a great tool for business, it can also bring family members together. Also, you don't need to have all the prescribed hardware to use NetMeeting. If you don't have a camera, you can still use the voice component to talk with people over the Internet and if you don't have a microphone and speakers, you can use the whiteboard and chat features.

Keep in mind that Internet telephony (making phone calls over the Internet) and videoconferencing haven't yet reached a high level of sophistication, but it's getting there. The bandwidth of the Internet is increasing everyday and that means that sound quality and video resolution will only improve. In just a few years, a videoconference over the Internet will probably have TV-like quality. Still, NetMeeting is an interesting tool that has real-world applications now, and if your company has a high-bandwidth network, you'll be able to communicate with coworkers over that network at much higher resolution than is available over dial-up lines.

WEBLINK: Microsoft maintains a NetMeeting Web site at http://www.microsoft.com/netmeeting/.

• The Equipment You'll Need

Making phone calls and videoconferencing over the Internet require some specific hardware. A sound card, microphone, and speakers are required for basic voice calls. Most computers today come with sound cards and speakers. All you may need to add is a microphone. You might prefer a headset because they add privacy and background noise reduction. Headsets can be plugged into sound cards in place of the microphone and speakers. To videoconference, you'll need a camera.

Audio and video demand a lot of bandwidth. If you use NetMeeting over a phone connection to the Internet or to a directly dialed user, the minimum acceptable dial-up equipment is a 28.8 kbps modem. Use a 33.6 or 56 kbps modem if your ISP supports them. ISDN lines can provide 128K or better performance. You should also have a Pentium class computer with 32MB of RAM or better.

If you want to get into videoconferencing you'll also need a camera. The Connectix QuickCam shown in Figure 18-2 is the most popular camera for home videoconferencing. The size of a golf ball, the QuickCam is available in a grayscale model (about $60) and color models ($99-150). The QuickCam plugs into your computer's parallel port.

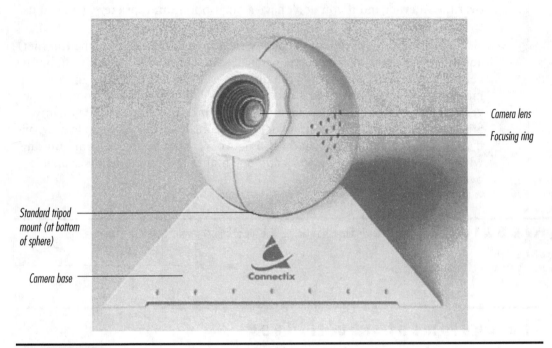

Camera lens

Focusing ring

Standard tripod
mount (at bottom
of sphere)

Camera base

FIGURE 18-2 Small and popular Connectix QuickCam

More and more manufacturers are coming out with competition for the
QuickCam. Panasonic sells the EggCam, which uses its own PCI video capture
board rather than the parallel port, making it somewhat faster than the parallel
port models. The EggCam sells for under $200.

WEBLINKS: Connectix has a lot of information on videoconferencing at http://www.connectix.com.
The PanasoniWeb site is at http://www.panasonic.com/PCSC/PCPC/.

About NetMeeting Calls

This section provides an essential overview of the NetMeeting call process.
There are two types of NetMeeting connections:

- A dial-up modem connection in which you directly call the other party's computer
- Intranet and Internet connections in which you must locate the person you want to call on the network

The first option is easy. Each party sets up a modem and one person calls the other. If you have multiple phone lines, you can even talk over a normal phone while you set up the video conference. Then you can hang up the phone and continue your session with NetMeeting. If you're connecting over an intranet or the Internet, you first connect to the network, then locate the computer of the party to connect with.

If you know the address of the party you wish to connect with, you type in the party's address and establish a NetMeeting-to-NetMeeting connection. If you don't know an address, you can use the Internet Locator Server services discussed next. Once you find an address using this method, you can add the address to your SpeedDial list as discussed later.

About Internet Locator Servers

NetMeeting takes advantage of Internet Locator Server (ILS) services to help you locate other parties to call or to help other people find you. An ILS is a service put together by Microsoft that provides a directory of other people who are currently using NetMeeting. Several different ILS services exist. Some are business-oriented and others are personal and family-oriented. One way to think of an ILS is a place where you can meet with others to establish NetMeeting sessions at prearranged times. You can also leave your name with the ILS so that other people can find and make calls to you. Your computer will alert you when someone from an ILS attempts to call your system, but only if you're online at the time of the call.

Microsoft's primary ILS service is located at http://ils.microsoft.com. Other ILS servers are also available, such as http://ils1.microsoft.com. If a lot of users are checked into a particular server, it may have poor response. Try checking into one of the other ILS servers available in the ILS listings.

Microsoft currently maintains most of the available ILS services, but as NetMeeting grows in popularity, it is expected that ILS services will pop up everywhere—in local communities, at corporate sites, and for special interest groups.

WEBLINK: For more background on Internet Locator Servers, visit Microsoft's ILS Web page at http://www.microsoft.com/netmeeting/ils/.

The process is simple. You connect to the Internet, then start NetMeeting and connect with an ILS service. A list of people currently using NetMeeting (or who have left their address on the server) appears and you can attempt to connect with anyone in the list. You can prearrange with your business associates and friends to meet in a particular ILS, thus making multiparty calls easier to arrange. The ILS you choose may simply depend on how busy other ILS services are on a particular day.

Another advantage of ILS services is that you can connect with other NetMeeting users to experiment with NetMeeting's features. To learn more about NetMeeting, we encourage you to connect with other people and try out the system.

T I P : You can prevent your name from appearing in the ILS, but still access its list of users by changing a setting as discussed later You can also control the information that is displayed about you in the ILS listing.

Starting NetMeeting for the First Time

Launch NetMeeting by going to the Start menu and choosing Programs | Internet Explorer | Microsoft NetMeeting. If you plan to use NetMeeting often, create a shortcut on the Desktop. See "Shortcuts" in Chapter 4.

When you start NetMeeting for the first time, a configuration wizard walks you through the process of configuring NetMeeting. The steps of this configuration are outlined next.

T I P : Someone may have already configured NetMeeting for you. You can change the configuration at any time by choosing Options from NetMeeting's Tools menu.

1. NetMeeting asks if you want to connect with an ILS server by displaying the following dialog box. Choose a server from the drop-down menu. At first, accept the default ILS server (ils.microsoft.com), but later, you can try connecting to other servers.

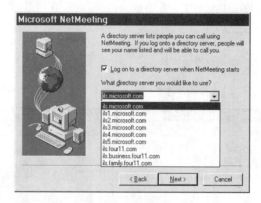

2. Click the Next button, then fill out the user information screen. You must type information about yourself such as your first and last name, email address, and city. You don't need to fill out every field if you want to keep the information private; however, the email address is essential if you want other people to get in touch with you later via email.

3. Click the Next button, then select how you want to categorize your user information on ILS servers. The options are personal, business, and adult-only use. Business or adult-only use will restrict the number of users you see listed. You can change categories at any time.

4. Click the Next button, then choose the type of connection you are using: 14400 bps modem, 28800 bps or faster modem, ISDN, or Local Area Network. NetMeeting will automatically adjust its audio and video settings to provide the best audio and video quality for the transmission speed selected.

5. Click the Next button, then perform the final setup step, which is to adjust the microphone and speaker volume. The Audio Tuning Wizard will lead you through this process.

On the last screen of the Audio Tuning Wizard, you can click the Finish button to complete the setup. In a moment, the NetMeeting window appears on your Desktop.

Making Calls and Using NetMeeting

When you start NetMeeting, it will try to connect with the Internet and your default ILS service. If the connection is successful, a list of users appears in the directory window similar to what you see in Figure 18-3.

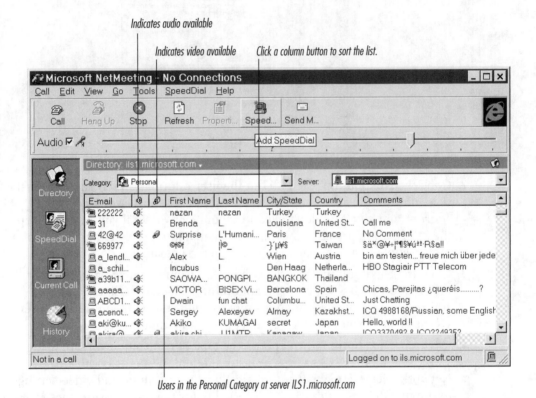

Indicates audio available

Indicates video available　*Click a column button to sort the list.*

Users in the Personal Category at server ILS1.microsoft.com

FIGURE 18-3 | NetMeeting's directory listing

The NetMeeting window includes the following icons in the left pane:

- **Directory**　Click here to see a directory listing and connect with other users.

- **SpeedDial** Click here to see the list of users you have added to your personal SpeedDial list. To add a user to this list, click the user in the Directory window, then click the Speed button on NetMeeting's toolbar.
- **Current Call** Click this button to return to your current call session.
- **History** Click this button to see a call history list.

Note that if you use an ILS, it might take a minute or so to log on to a service. You can see the progress of the connection in the right corner of the status bar at the bottom of the screen. If a lot of users are logged on to the same ILS, you may not be able to access it at the moment. You can keep trying, or log on to a different server.

The best way to learn NetMeeting is to connect with another user and experiment. Try the following:

1. Click the down arrow button in the Server field to connect with a different server.

2. Click the down arrow button in the Category field to choose a different category, such as business or personal.

3. When the list of users appears, select a user and click the Call button on the NetMeeting Toolbar. A dialog box similar to the following appears.

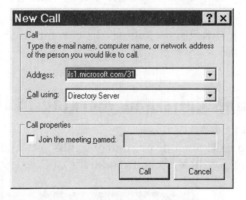

Note the contents of the Address field. It shows the name of the server followed by the "handle" or name of the person you selected.

4. Click OK to make the connection.

You can also double-click any name in a list to connect with the caller. NetMeeting will attempt to connect with the user. If the connection is successful, you can start your session. If the connection was unsuccessful, NetMeeting asks if you want to send the person an email message.

Note that it is often difficult to make a successful connection with someone in the list. Just because a name is in the list doesn't mean the user is standing by and waiting for a call. The list retains names for a long period after the user has signed off, but if someone in the list has their computer on and is standing by, they will hear or see an alert that you are trying to contact them.

User Information and Options

You can get information about any user by right-clicking the user's name and choosing Properties. You see the information they supplied in the User Information dialog box during setup. Other people will see similar information about you. To change this information, choose Options on the Tools menu, then click the My Information tab.

When you right-click a name in the directory list, you can also choose these options:

- **Call**   Call and make a connection with the user.
- **Add to SpeedDial**   Add the user to your SpeedDial list.
- **Send Mail**   Send the user an email message.
- **Refresh Directory**   Refresh the current directory list (or just press F5 at any time).

Accepting Calls and Working in the Current Call Screen

When you call someone or someone calls you, the following dialog box appears on the screen. Click Accept to take the call.

The view in the NetMeeting window changes to the Current Call window similar to what you see in Figure 18-4. In this example, we are connected over a local network. Both of us have audio capabilities, so we can hold voice

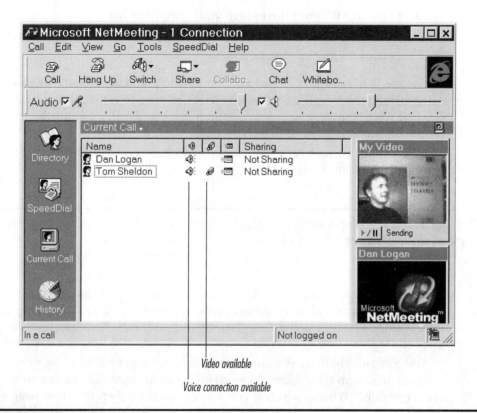

Video available

Voice connection available

FIGURE 18-4   Taking a call

conversations. Only Tom has video hooked up, so Dan gets to see what Tom is doing but not the other way around.

There are several things you can do while working in the Current Call window. You can right-click a user and choose one of the following options:

- **Stop using audio and video**   Click this option to work in NetMeeting with Chat, Whiteboard, and file exchange capabilities as discussed later. Use this option when you want to gain some privacy, the light makes video impractical, or your environment is too noisy for audio.
- **Send File**   Send the user a file. A Browse dialog box appears so you can select a file to send.
- **Send Mail**   Send the user an email message.

- **Add SpeedDial**   Add the user to your SpeedDial list.
- **Remove from Meeting**   Drop the selected user from the current meeting.
- **Properties**   View information about the user.

You can also click Call to call another person and add them to the meeting. After making a new call, click the Current Call icon to return to your call session. When multiple people are participating in a call, click the Switch button on the toolbar to switch to that user.

At any time during a call, you can share applications, run the Whiteboard, or run the Chat utility as discussed later.

TIP: You can have NetMeeting automatically accept all incoming calls. Choose Options on the Tools menu, then enable "Automatically accept incoming calls" on the General page.

When you're working in the Current Call window, you can move the My Video and Remote Video windows around the Desktop. Double-clicking on either window will detach it from NetMeeting; you can then drag it where you want it. Double-clicking it again returns it to the right side of the window.

You can quickly mute the microphone by clearing the check box next to the microphone symbol, or mute the speakers by clearing the check box next to the speaker symbol. This is handy if you don't want the other person to hear what you're saying, or if someone comes into the room and you want to talk with them without interruption of the NetMeeting audio.

TIP: If you're videoconferencing, the video's bandwidth demands can degrade the audio. Click the Pause button on the video image to temporarily stop sending video.

Connecting with Intranet Users

You can also call another user on your local intranet. Click the Call button on the NetMeeting Toolbar to open the New Call dialog box. Choose Network

(TCP/IP) in the Call using field and type the name of the other person's computer in the Address field. In the following illustration, the computer named Production is called.

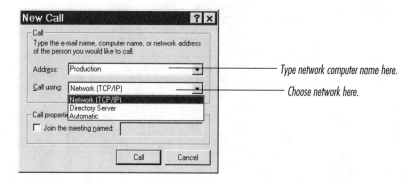

If you don't know the computer name, you can open the Network Neighborhood to find out the name of another computer. If you still can't tell from that list, call the user and have him or her do the following to find out the name of his or her computer:

1. Click Start | Settings | Control Panel.
2. Open the Network utility.
3. Click the Identification tab.

The name of the computer is in the Computer name field. Of course, you can always give the user the name of your computer and have him or her call you.

Using Your SpeedDial Personal Phone Book

SpeedDial is NetMeeting's version of your little black book. SpeedDial makes it easy to dial people you call often; you simply click on the name of the person you want to call. One of your goals in using NetMeeting is to add as many people as possible to your SpeedDial list. This allows you to bypass ILS services.

To add a new SpeedDial entry, click the Directory icon, then the SpeedDial button on the toolbar (or choose Add SpeedDial from the SpeedDial menu). The following dialog box appears:

Type an address in the Address field. This may be an ILS address or a computer name on your in-house network. If it is a network computer, choose Network in the Call using field.

TIP: It's usually easier to add a SpeedDial entry while you are connected with the user. Then NetMeeting does all the typing. Right-click the user's name in the Current Call window, then choose Add SpeedDial.

You can send your NetMeeting connection information to other users. Fill out the Address and Call using fields with your information, then click the Send to mail recipient option. When you click OK, NetMeeting opens your mail program and a message appears containing the information that you can send to someone.

Fine-Tuning Your Settings

You can quickly change many of your NetMeeting settings by opening the Tools menu and choosing Options. The General page on the Options dialog box is pictured here.

Most of the options on this page are self-explanatory. You can also right-click the text of any option and choose What's This? to get a description. We give some general tips here.

- **Set startup and call acceptance options.** In the General field, you can set how NetMeeting starts and whether it automatically accepts incoming calls. The last item puts the Intel Connection Advisor icon on the Taskbar. The Connection Advisor displays information about your audio and video setup.

- **Adjust the bandwidth setting.** If you move up to a faster modem or network connection, choose a bandwidth setting in the Network bandwidth field on the General page.

- **Change file transfer settings.** You can change the location where transmitted files are stored by clicking the Change Folder button on the General page. You can also click View Files to view files you've already seen.

- **Change your personal information.** Click the My Information tab on the Options menu to change your personal information. This information appears in the ILS service listing, so you may want to be discreet with what you enter. You can also set a default category for where your name will be listed.

- **Change ILS directory settings.** Click the Calling tab on the Options dialog box to change the default ILS service that NetMeeting connects with upon startup.

- **Hide your name in ILS listings.** Click the Calling tab on the Options dialog box, then enable the option called "Do not list my name in the directory."

- **Change the default SpeedDial settings.** Click the Calling tab on the Options dialog box. You can have people you call automatically added to the SpeedDial list. You can also set SpeedDial refresh options.

- **Enable Duplex Audio.** Click the Audio tab on the Options dialog box. Click the Enable full duplex audio option if you want to speak while receiving audio. You will need a headset to prevent feedback if you select this option.

- **Manually adjust microphone sensitivity.** Click Audio on the Options dialog box and choose the Let me adjust sensitivity myself option. Then move the slider appropriately. The automatic setting is normally recommended.

- **Call a telephone.** You can call a telephone with NetMeeting by going through an H.323 gateway. Click the Audio tab on the Options dialog box and enable the Use H.323 gateway option.

- **Automatically send or receive video.** You can have NetMeeting automatically send or receive video upon startup by setting the Sending and receiving video options on the Video page. You can also adjust the size of the video image on this page.

- **Adjust fast video versus high-quality video.** The Video page has a slider where you can adjust the video for more speed or more quality.

- **Set up cable-connected local computers.** Home users and small office users can run NetMeeting between directly attached computers where the computers are in adjacent or nearby rooms. Click the Properties tab on the Options dialog box and enable the Null Modem option.

Taking Advantage of Chat

Chat is a funny little tool. You type a sentence or message, press the ENTER key, and the other people in the conference see your words. They can type chat messages at their own computer that everyone else sees. But why do all that typing when you can use the phone? One reason is to create and save a log of the meeting conversation. Another is to use Chat if you don't have audio capabilities, or when you mute audio for privacy reasons. In fact, any user that does not have video or audio capabilities can use Chat to participate in the meeting.

To start Chat, click the Chat icon on the NetMeeting toolbar. All participants in the current meeting will see a Chat window appear on their screen, similar to Figure 18-5.

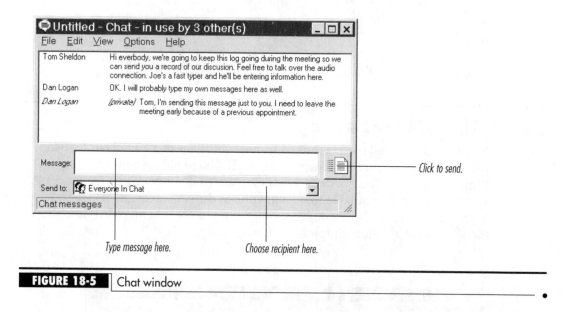

FIGURE 18-5 | Chat window

You type a message in the Message field, then click the Send button. The message immediately appears in the window of all members of the chat session, assuming that you choose the "Everyone in Chat" option in the Send to field.

TIP : You can send a private message to anyone in the chat session by choosing a name in the Send to field.

The Chat File menu has options for saving and printing Chat sessions. You can also copy and paste text (Edit menu), change the viewing options (View menu) and change the Font (Options menu). To change message display and format options, choose Chat Format on the Options menu to open the following dialog box. Set these options as appropriate for your Chat session.

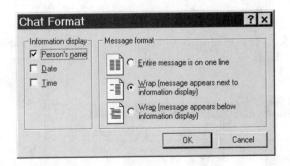

Using the Whiteboard

NetMeeting's Whiteboard is the electronic equivalent of a whiteboard where you can sketch pictures and express yourself while holding a meeting. Whiteboard looks and operates much like Microsoft Paint. (See Chapter 5.) A variety of tools are available that let anyone in the session create images related to the conversation. For example, someone might create a map that describes the location of a building project as shown in Figure 18-6.

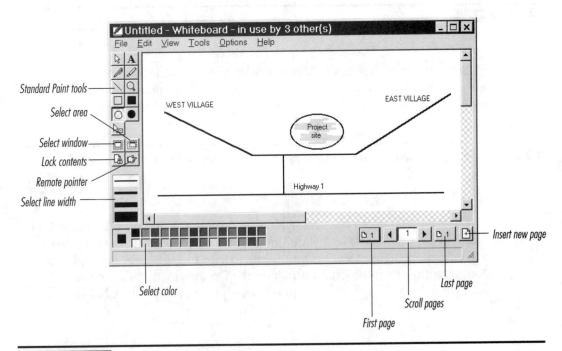

FIGURE 18-6 | NetMeeting's Whiteboard

To start the Whiteboard, click the Whiteboard button on the toolbar. Any party can start the Whiteboard and it becomes available to everybody in the session.

You're not limited to a single page on the Whiteboard. You can open multiple pages and scroll through them. You can erase the contents of a page by going to the page and pressing CTRL-DEL.

To prevent anyone from making further changes to the Whiteboard's contents, click the Lock Contents button in the toolbox.

You can also save Whiteboard sessions with the standard Windows File | Save As procedure. The file will be saved with a .WHT extension.

Transferring Files During A Call

NetMeeting makes it easy to transfer files to any or all of the members of your session. The quick way to send a file is to simply click and drag the file into the NetMeeting window. The file is then delivered to all participants.

Users can click Open to view the file immediately or Close to close the window. Click the Delete button to remove the file.

If files are not visible so you can drag-and-drop, choose File Transfer on the Tools menu. A cascading menu opens where you can choose to send a file, cancel a file that is being sent, cancel a file you are receiving, or open the folder that contains received files. Received files are saved in the Program Files\NetMeeting\Received Files folder.

Sharing Applications

NetMeeting lets participants share applications, folders, and even the operating system across the Internet or an intranet, even if only one person has the application. Note that application sharing as discussed here is about one person opening and working in an application while other meeting participants watch what happens. Collaboration, as discussed next, is about allowing other people to take control of and make changes in shared applications.

To share a Windows application:

1. Start the application on any computer that is participating in the meeting.

2. Click the Share button on the NetMeeting toolbar.

3. Choose which currently open application to share.

Collaborating With NetMeeting

NetMeeting's collaboration feature takes application sharing a step further by allowing NetMeeting participants to take control of the pointer, make changes in documents, or open folders and files on the other computers.

To use the collaboration feature, follow these steps:

- Start your NetMeeting session.
- Once people have joined your session, start the application you want to share and click the Share button on the toolbar.
- Click the Collaborate button.

Users can view and work in the open application and use the remote pointer. Any participant can take control by double-clicking in the application. To cancel collaboration, press the ESC key.

You'll find that collaborating in NetMeeting teaches you new NetMeeting skills. Because each of us has grown used to having complete control over the mouse, watching it move one way when you are telling it to go another can be annoying. So you battle for control, double-clicking furiously. Adding to the confusion, it might seem a bit difficult to figure out who has control at any given moment; however, the initials of the participant who is in current control are shown on the pointer. The Current Call window also shows who has control.

To minimize the control problem, establish some ground rules. For example, the participant with control might move the pointer to a designated spot on the screen that signals he or she is done for the moment.

The Advantages of NetMeeting

NetMeeting is a wonderful tool and it is bound to get better as computer and communication technologies get better. While currently restricted by bandwidth limitation, NetMeeting provides a way for people to exchange ideas over internal networks and the Internet in new and unique ways. That overused term "productivity" comes to mind. As it becomes easier for people to work together without picking up everything and moving to a physical meeting site, productivity will increase. Electronic mail has already done this on a small scale compared to what collaboration is bound to do.

It has useful applications in the product-support environment as well. Support people can literally show users how to use applications without traveling from their office. That makes their use of time more efficient and ensures that more users get help.

NetMeeting also benefits home users. Families can communicate with one another no matter where they have traveled. And people at home can use NetMeeting to meet and communicate with people all over the world. ILS services list users in almost every country along with things they are interested in.

We hope you use NetMeeting and take advantage of its many features.

Mobile and Remote Computing

19

B A S I C S

- Learn about the mobile features in Windows 98
- Use deferred printing while on the road
- Use Direct Cable Connect to exchange files between your desktop computer and your mobile computer
- Use the Briefcase for files synchronized between your desktop computer and mobile computer
- Learn about Windows CE handheld computing devices
- Use Dial-Up Networking to dial into other computers

B E Y O N D

- Manage the power requirements of your mobile computer
- Use hardware profiles to configure your system for desktop use and mobile use
- Use Dial-Up Server to make your computer available to mobile users, including yourself

With its full support for mobile computing, Windows 98 is the ideal operating system for portable or remote-access computers. It helps you stay connected with your home or office computer and your company's network. This chapter covers what you need to know if you take Windows 98 on the road.

The Mobile User's Dilemma

These days, many people are connected to networks and have access to data and devices like printers on other computers. They also communicate with others via electronic mail and share information like schedules and documents. With Windows 98, going on the road does not mean giving up these contacts and connections.

If you use a portable computer or you use a computer at another location, you probably fall into one or more of these categories:

- You move from office to office in the same building to attend meetings, give presentations, or work with other people on projects.
- You need to take your work home in the evening or over the weekends.
- You work on the road and at client sites but need to connect with the home office to access databases and other resources.

The only problem with going on the road or switching to another computer is that you loose your local computing environment, such as connections to network servers, email systems, printers, fax machines, and other devices. In addition, files on mobile computers become "out of sync" with files on desktop computers and network servers. You must track changes in files you take with you and update the home office files when you return. Sometimes, it's hard to tell which files are the most up to date.

Windows 98 Mobile Support Features

Fortunately, Windows 98 has features that support your on-the-road activities. It supports docking stations for laptop computers so you can quickly attach or detach your laptop to and from your desktop connections. A typical docking station provides power, network attachments, video connections to high-resolution monitors, and slots for additional plug-in boards. Windows 98 can automatically detect whether your computer is docked or not and change its internal configuration to match the docked or undocked state.

TIP: Port replicators are not docking stations. They simply add extra ports to your laptop, but do not provide the extensibility and Plug-and-Play features of a true docking station. Be careful about what you buy.

For example, when connected to a docking station, your computer may have a network connection and use a high-resolution monitor. When you undock, Windows must release the network connection and revert to your laptop's display resolution. Windows 98's ability to perform this task relies on two features:

- **Hot-docking capabilities**   *Hot-docking* is an industry term that refers to the ability to remove a portable device from a docking port without first turning the system off.
- **Plug-and-Play**   This is a Windows 98 feature that automatically detects new devices and peripherals attached to your system and installs the appropriate software drivers to support those devices.

When Windows detects a hardware change, it rebuilds its configuration and loads or unloads drivers as necessary. For example, assume you are working on a presentation for a meeting. You finish at the last minute, undock your laptop, and move to the meeting room where another docking port is available. You don't even need to shut down your applications, power down the computer, or reboot with some laptops because Windows 98 is capable of handling this mobile transition.

N O T E :   The Eject PC option on the Start menu undocks a laptop computer from its docking station. It signals to Windows 98 that the hardware configuration is changing.

Different hardware configurations are handled by a Windows 98 feature called Hardware Profiles. You can have multiple profiles, for example, one for mobile use and one for each docking station you need to attach to. This is discussed under "Using Hardware Profiles" later in this chapter.

In 1996, Intel announced a chipset called the 380 Dock Set which laptop vendors could use to create a truly mobile platform when combined with the Intel 82430MX Mobile PCIset and a Pentium processor. The 380 Dock Set was the first PCI chipset to enable true "hot-docking." With this setup, a laptop computer running Windows 98 can dynamically configure system resources when docked or undocked. A nonvolatile memory interface stores docking identification and laptop configuration information to speed up dynamic configuration. When docked, for example, the system can execute a pre-programmed user sequence such as uploading and downloading electronic mail, synchronizing files, or sending faxes.

Other Mobile Features

Here are some of the other mobile computing support features available in Windows 98:

- **Power Management**   Windows 98 works with your computer to help save battery power. It starts powering down the CPU and peripherals after periods of nonactivity.
- **Direct Cable Connection Support**   Windows 98 lets you directly connect with another computer and exchange information by using serial or parallel cables.
- **Dial-Up Networking**   Create a dial-up configuration for connecting to your office desktop computer, your company LAN, or your Internet Service Provider. You can even run a dial-up server on your desktop computer, then dial into it and use the desktop computer as if you are sitting at it.
- **PC Card Support**   The PC Card (PCMCIA) is a credit card-size plug-in peripheral such as a network card, modem, disk drive, or other device. You can add and remove the cards at any time.
- **My Briefcase File Synchronization**   The Briefcase helps you keep files on your desktop computer and laptop computer synchronized.
- **Deferred Printing and Faxing**   This is a convenience feature that lets you print documents even when you're away from your printer. The printers stack up files in a queue and print when you reconnect with the printer.
- **Handheld PC and Palm Computer Support**   Windows 98 fully supports small computing devices such as handheld and palm computers. It can fully synchronize with and update information on the devices when you connect with a cable.

WEBLINKS: To learn more about mobile computing in general, check out Mobile Computing Online Magazine at http://mobilecomputing.com. You'll find plenty of links for anything having to do with wireless and mobile computing at http://mobilecomputing.com/lx/genlink.htm.

Power Management Features

When you're on the road, a critical concern is optimizing the battery life of your computer. There are a number of things you can do short of turning your system off every time you stop using it for a few minutes.

TIP : Much of the information in this section applies not only to saving energy on mobile computers, but also to so-called "Green Desktop PCs" that have energy-saving features.

Power management features refer to the ability of your computer and the operating system to control energy consumption. If no activities occur on the computer for a set period of time, the power management system can drop it into sleep mode. When some activity occurs on an input device like the mouse, keyboard, or joystick, the system wakes up. A unique feature is to have a call from an attached modem wake up the system. This way, your office computer can go to sleep until you call it from a remote location with your laptop computer.

Windows 98 has a standby/suspend feature that really saves battery life. You can activate it manually, or have your system automatically go into suspend after a period of non-activity. To manually suspend the system, click Start, then choose Shutdown and click the Suspend option. For desktop systems, suspend is really a power-saving standby mode. On many laptop systems, suspend actually shuts the system off after first saving all information in memory to disk. When you turn the system back on, the Desktop is quickly restored to its pre-suspend mode.

A power-saving tip is to reduce the brightness of your display. You should also consider increasing the memory of your system. If you have less than 32MB of memory, your system may need to store and retrieve more information in the disk-based virtual memory system. Not only does this reduce performance, but it requires frequent disk access that draws battery power. Still another tip is to disable features that use power unnecessarily. For example, make sure the infrared port is not running if you don't need it. Open Infrared in the Control Panel and disable infrared communications.

Advanced Configuration and Power Interface (ACPI)

Many new computers support a power management feature called Advanced Configuration and Power Interface (ACPI). ACPI-compliant PCs can describe their device configuration and power control hardware interface to Windows 98. A Windows 98 feature called OnNow then manages the power requirements of the system. It can turn on and off devices such as CD-ROMs, network cards, hard disk drives, and printers.

To take full advantage of Windows 98's power management features, your computer must have a system BIOS chipset that supports ACPI. ACPI initializes during system startup, then hands off control to Windows 98. Older BIOS chipsets cannot hand off full control to Windows 98. Therefore, power management must be controlled by configuring the BIOS as discussed later.

If your computer supports ACPI, Windows 98 will detect it during setup and install the appropriate power management controls, which are accessible through the Control Panel.

NOTE: Some ACPI systems might not be properly detected. Check with your computer vendor for instructions on getting ACPI configured for Windows 98.

Advanced Power Management (APM)

Advanced Power Management (APM) is a specification that allows the system BIOS to control power management. You set timers in the BIOS that determine when devices go into sleep mode. The BIOS then sends a command to Windows 98 that it should prepare to "put the PC to sleep." Windows 98 then suspends the PC. APM BIOS also monitors battery status and initiates suspend mode when the battery gets low.

While APM is an older power management interface that has some limitations, it has useful power-saving features that should be used if you need to conserve the battery life of your computer.

BIOS Power Saving Features

You must set the power-saving features in the BIOS of your computer to use those features. When your computer starts, you'll see a message that says "To run Setup, press the Del key" or some other key such as F2. When you do, a BIOS configuration screen appears. Not all BIOS screens are the same, so we can only talk in general terms here. You'll need to refer to your owner's manual for specific information.

On the BIOS setup screen, go to the option that refers to power management setup. You'll see a lot of settings that may look a little daunting, but the first option typically lets you choose minimum or maximum options that change all the other settings. For example, the minimum option puts the system to sleep after one hour of non-activity while the maximum option puts the system to sleep after only a few minutes of non-activity.

Some BIOS menus will have an option called "PM Control by APM." Choose this to enable your BIOS to communicate with Windows 98 about power events. You may see a similar control for ACPI. Always enable ACPI if it is available.

You will see power-saving modes called doze, standby, and suspend. These are progressive modes in which the system goes to doze first, then standby, then suspend. According to the "User Guide to Power Management in PCs and Monitors" (http://eande.lbl.gov/EAP/BEA/LBLReports/39466/), the following modes and energy savings are possible:

- **Doze Mode**   The CPU is slowed or stopped, but other devices stay active. There is about a 25 percent power savings.
- **Standby Mode**   The CPU is stopped and other devices move into their first power-saving mode. The power saving is about 30 percent for PC and about 60-90 percent for monitors.
- **Suspend Mode**   The CPU is stopped, and other devices are powered down if possible. The power saving is up to 45 percent.
- **Hard Disk Power Down**   You can usually enable the hard disk to spin down separate from the other power-saving features. Note that the disk electronics remain on to provide quick recovery, so the power saving is usually only about 10 percent. However, spinning down the disk on many systems can really reduce the noise level!
- **Hibernation**   This mode is common on laptop computers. The system goes into full shutdown mode and all memory contents and system state information are saved to disk. Check your computer manual for more information on this mode.

Be sure to set some type of power-saving mode. If you leave your system on when it is running on battery power, you might return to find your batteries drained, just when you need to use it in battery mode.

The Power Management Utility

Now we get to the Power Management utility. Open Power Management in the Control Panel to see a dialog box similar to Figure 19-1. Note that the dialog box options may be different, depending on whether your system is running on battery power or plugged in.

In the Power schemes field, you can choose a different set of power scheme options. An option called "Portable/Laptop" should already be selected if you have such a computer. You can create your own custom power scheme setting. First, change any of the options on this dialog box, then click the Save As button and save the changes under a new power scheme name.

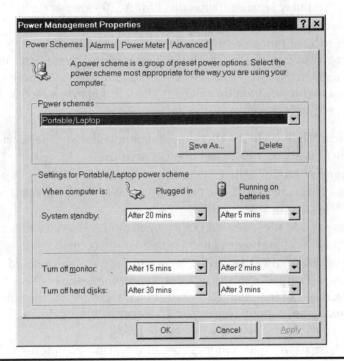

Note the System standby fields in the middle of the box. This is where you can set the time of non-activity that passes before the system goes into power saving standby modes. There are settings for when the computer is plugged in and when it is running on batteries. Obviously, the battery setting has a lower wait time.

You can also adjust the time for the monitor and hard disk spindown in the lower boxes.

- **Alarms**   Click the Alarms tab to configure the type of alarm that occurs when the battery power drops to a specified level. The default is that a message is displayed when the battery drops to 5 percent. An audible alarm option is also available. You can also specify what the computer will do when the alarm goes off, such as go into standby mode or shut down.

- **Power Meter**   Click this tab to see information about the batteries installed in the system. For example, you can view power state before leaving on a trip to ensure that batteries are fully charged.

- **Advanced** Click this tab to enable or disable the power meter on the Taskbar and to set a password that is required to restore the computer from standby mode.

Using Hardware Profiles

With hardware profiles, you can run Windows 98 with different hardware configurations. While this is not normally necessary for desktop computers, mobile users will often find themselves in situations where the system must be started without network support or without an external monitor. When multiple profiles are enabled, you'll see a menu similar to the following, before Windows 98 even begins to load, where you can choose which profile you want to start with:

```
Select one of the following configurations:

1. Docked

2. Undocked

3. None of the above

Enter your choice:
```

To set up hardware profiles, follow these steps:

1. Open System in the Control Panel and click the Hardware Profiles tab. You will see a list of current startup profiles.
2. Click Copy to create a new profile, then rename the profile appropriately.
3. Click the Device Manager tab and locate the device that you don't need in the new configuration.
   We'll assume you want to disable the network interface in this example.
4. Double-click Network Adapters (or whatever type of hardware you want to disable) in the list, then double-click the adapter you want to disable. The Properties dialog box for the adapter appears.
5. Place a check mark by the option called "Disable in this hardware profile" or if you want to remove it entirely in the profile, place a check mark by "Remove from this hardware profile."

The next time you start Windows, it presents you with the list of profiles to start with. Enter the number of the profile and press ENTER.

> **TIP:** By using multiuser profiles as discussed under "Profiles for Multiple Users" in Chapter 6, you can create different Desktop configurations, say one for the road and one for your office. Pretend that you have multiple personalities, one for the road and one for your office and set up a profile for each. On the road, you would then log in as your mobile personality to gain access to the mobile desktop.

Deferred Printing

Deferred printing is a Windows 98 feature that lets you send print jobs to a printer, even when you're away from the printer. The print jobs accumulate on disk, then print as soon as you reconnect to your printer.

To defer printing, follow these steps:

1. Choose Settings from the Start menu.
2. Choose Printers to open the Printers window.
3. Click the printer to which you want to defer printing (refer to Chapter 20 for instructions on installing new printer drivers, if necessary).
4. Choose Work Offline from the File menu.

These steps "gray out" the printer to indicate that printing has been deferred. Note that it's not critical to set the Work Offline feature. If you don't and the printer is disconnected, Windows 98 will still queue up your print jobs. However, it will constantly remind you that the printer is not connected. To avoid this reminder, use the Work Offline feature.

If you're traveling to another location and you want to print on a printer at that location, install the driver for the printer before you leave. During your travels, you can create print jobs, then print them on the printer when you arrive.

Using PC Card (PCMCIA) Cards

PC Card is an industry standard for small, credit card-size devices that slide into slots on the side of laptop computers (and desktop systems, if you have a

PC Card docking device). Network adapters, modems, hard drives, memory cards, and other peripherals are available in the PC Card format. You can even add ports to your laptop for CD-ROM drives, joysticks, MIDI music devices, and video capture and playback.

Windows 98 fully supports the PC Card through its Plug-and-Play technology. That means you can insert and remove PC Cards without powering down your system (this is true in most cases, but check your system's manual for any precautions).

There are Type II and Type III PC Cards. Type II cards are thin and most laptop computers have slots to accommodate two Type II cards. Type III cards are thicker than Type II cards. Hard drives usually take this format. A Type III card occupies the two Type II card slots on most laptops.

PC Card services are installed automatically by Windows 98 setup if your system has a PC Card slot. You can open the PC Card (PCMCIA) utility in the Control Panel to view information about your PC Card devices. A dialog box similar to the following appears:

About the only thing you really need to do in this dialog box is to stop Windows 98 from using a card before you physically remove the card from your computer. Select a card, then click the Stop button. This assumes the computer is already on and has already installed support for a card. If the computer is off, just remove the card and boot the system. Windows 98 will start without support for the card.

> **NOTE:** PC Cards that support hot-docking do not require that you go through the Stop route described earlier. Just remove the card at any time. Be sure to check your PC Card and computer manuals before doing this since hot-swapping is not always supported.

Direct Cable Connection

Direct Cable Connection, or DCC as we'll call it here, is a great way to exchange information between your laptop computer and your desktop computer. Basically, DCC lets you build a network of two computers by connecting them with serial or parallel cables. If your desktop computer is already connected to a network and your laptop computer has a network card that you can plug into the same network, you probably don't need DCC since you can do all your file transfers over the existing network.

As we mentioned, DCC operates like a network connection. You use the same folder-sharing techniques discussed in Chapter 11. One computer, usually the desktop system, becomes the host and the other computer becomes the guest. In addition, if the host computer is connected to a network, the guest computer can access that network through the host.

> **NOTE:** If Direct Cable Connection does not appear on your system, refer to "Adding and Removing Windows 98 Components" in Chapter 6.

Cable Requirements

Direct Cable Connection requires either a serial or parallel cable connection between two computers. The best connection is with ECP (Enhanced Capabilities Port) parallel ports found on relatively recent computers. When special "active" cables are used, throughput rates in excess of one megabit per second are possible over parallel links. Refer to your computer manual to see if it has ECP ports. You may need to enable ECP support on the port by accessing your system's BIOS setup.

> **WEBLINK:** Parallel Technologies has a line of "DirectParallel" cables. You can access the company's Web site at www.paralleltech.com.

Note that the serial cable is a standard null-modem cable which is available in most electronics stores. The parallel cable may be harder to find, but as mentioned, provides the best transfer rate. Some stores will have so-called Laplink parallel cables that work fine. You can also buy an adapter that converts the printer end of a standard printer cable into a 25-pin mail connector. This is often called a Laplink adapter. The wiring scheme for a parallel cable is presented here just in case you need to make one. It requires a male 25-pin D connector at each end:

```
One end        Other end
pin 2 <----> pin 15
pin 3 <----> pin 13
pin 4 <----> pin 12
pin 5 <----> pin 10
pin 6 <----> pin 11
pin 15<----> pin 2
pin 13<----> pin 3
pin 12<----> pin 4
pin 10<----> pin 5
pin 11<----> pin 6
pin 25<----> pin 25
```

DCC Setup and Configuration

Since DCC operates like a network, you'll need to install network protocols on both systems ahead of time. If your host desktop system is already connected to a network, it may already be running a protocol like TCP/IP. You can then install TCP/IP on your guest system. Some of the finer details of installing TCP/IP, like specifying an IP address, are discussed at the end of Chapter 11.

To make things easy, we recommend that you just install the NetBEUI protocol on both the host and the guest system if you don't already have protocols installed. NetBEUI is a small "lite" protocol that requires no configuration after setup and you can install it on your desktop system even if that system is already running another protocol like TCP/IP.

DCC requires that you have these networking components installed:

• Client for Microsoft Networks (or optionally, Client for NetWare Networks).

• A dial-up adapter (or support for any other type of network adapter). A dial-up adapter will be installed for you the first time you run DCC if it does not already exist.

- File and printer sharing for Microsoft Networks (or optionally, file and printer sharing for NetWare Networks).
- A network protocol. We recommend NetBEUI for the reasons mentioned earlier, but you should choose TCP/IP if any other computers you connect to use it.

We will demonstrate the bare-bones steps in this section. If you already have a network card or Dial-Up Networking installed, some of these steps are not necessary. We're assuming that no networking components are installed on your system.

1. Click the Start button, then choose Programs | Accessories | Communications | Direct Cable Connection. The following dialog box appears:

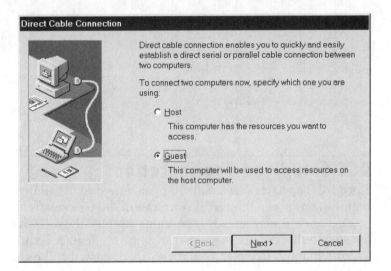

2. Choose Host if this is your desktop computer and/or the computer that is also connected to your in-house network. Choose Guest if you are working on your laptop/portable computer.

3. Click Next. If networking support is not installed, a message appears to inform you that Microsoft Dial-up Adapter must be installed. Click OK to start the installation. You may need to insert the Windows 98 CD-ROM during this part of the installation.

4. In a moment, a message appears informing you that system settings have been reconfigured. Click OK, then open Network in the Control Panel.

You will see Dial-Up Adapter and TCP/IP->Dial-Up Adapter (DCC installs TCP/IP by default). You still need to add the NetBEUI protocol, a network client, and file and printer sharing.

5. Click the Add button, then choose Protocol in the list and click the Add button. Choose Microsoft in the Manufacturers list, then choose NetBEUI in the Network Protocols list and click OK. You are returned to the Network dialog box and you should see NetBEUI->Dial-Up Adapter added to the list.

6. Click the Add button again, then choose Client. In the Manufacturer list, choose Microsoft and in the Network Clients list, choose Client for Microsoft Networks. Click OK.

7. You are returned to the Network dialog box. Click the File and Print Sharing button and check mark both options for sharing files and printer, then click OK.

8. Click OK to complete the configuration, then click Yes when asked to restart your system.

9. When your computer restarts, click the Start button, then choose Programs | Accessories | Communications | Direct Cable Connection. You see the Direct Cable Connection dialog box pictured earlier. Choose Host or Guest once again and click Next.

10. This time, you're asked to select the port to use, either an LPT port (parallel) or a COM port (serial). Make a selection and click Next, then click Finish to complete the connection.

Repeat these steps on the other computer. If everything goes well, you're ready to establish a connection. When you click Finish after installing the second system, the connection will take place automatically. At any other time in the future, start the host first, then start the guest.

Using the Connection

When a successful connection is made, DCC looks for shared folders on the hosts and displays a window of those shared folders. You may want to share other folders at this time. After sharing new folders, go to the shared folder window on the guest system and choose Refresh on the View menu to update the list and see the new folders. To learn more about shared folders, refer to Chapter 11.

TIP: The next section about the Briefcase shows you how to create an automatic synchronization between files on connected computers.

The guest computer is literally a network extension of the host computer. It can access all the same network resources that are available on the host computer. You can go to the guest computer and open the Network Neighborhood. A window then opens that shows all the computers on the network that are sharing resources. You can access any of these resources from the guest computer. If those resources are part of a Windows NT domain, you'll probably need to log on to access each folder. To overcome this, enable domain logon in the Network utility of the guest computer. See your domain administrator for more details.

Synchronizing Files with the Briefcase

If you're like most mobile users, you have a computer (or file server) at your office and a computer that you take on the road, or you travel to locations where other computers are used. When you get ready to go on the road, you probably copy files from the desktop computer to the portable computer. But when you edit those files while you're on the road, they become "out of sync" with the original files on your desktop computer.

The Windows 98 Briefcase solves this problem by helping you work with copies of the same files that are located on two different computers as illustrated in Figure 19-2. The briefcase metaphor is appropriate. When you are ready to go on the road, you copy files into the Briefcase, then copy the Briefcase to your mobile computer. When you're on the road, you open and edit the files in your Briefcase. This makes them out of sync with the files on your desktop computer, but when you return to your office, you copy the Briefcase back to your desktop computer. At that point, the Briefcase will indicate which files are out of sync with the originals on your desktop computer.

Note the following:

- You can click and drag files from any location into the Briefcase. The Briefcase will keep track of their original location.
- After returning from your trip, Briefcase automatically updates the files that have changed in their original location. You don't need to copy the changed files to their original location.
- If you have just a few files in the Briefcase, copy the Briefcase to a floppy disk and transfer it to your laptop computer.

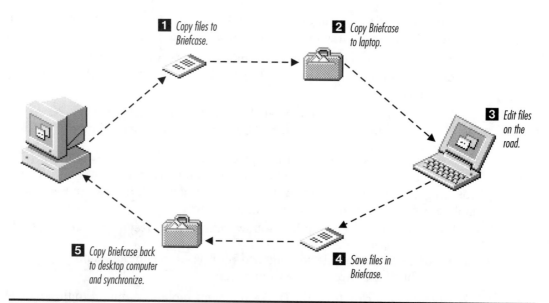

1 Copy files to Briefcase.

2 Copy Briefcase to laptop.

3 Edit files on the road.

5 Copy Briefcase back to desktop computer and synchronize.

4 Save files in Briefcase.

| **FIGURE 19-2** | Transferring files with the Briefcase |

- If you routinely transfer a lot of files, set up a Direct Cable Connection as discussed earlier (or use a network connection if available) along with the Briefcase.

Creating a Briefcase

In most cases, you need only one Briefcase to carry files between two computers, but you can create any number of Briefcases to fit different needs. We recommend using a single Briefcase, but if you work with a lot of different types of files, you may want to create a Briefcase to hold each file type.

In this section, we'll demonstrate how to transfer the Briefcase over a Direct Cable Connection. This method also applies if your desktop and mobile computers are connected via a network.

1. To access the Briefcase from your mobile computer (the Guest), you'll need to put it in a shared folder. Create a folder on the Desktop called Mobile Files (or choose any folder that is already shared). Share the folder as outlined in Chapter 11.

2. Open the folder, then create a new Briefcase. Right-click a blank part of the folder window, then choose New | Briefcase from the Shortcut menu.

3. Now copy files you want to take on the road into the shared folder. You can use the click-and-drag method or copy-and-paste method.

4. Now go to your mobile computer and make sure it is connected to the desktop computer and that the Direct Cable Connection is activated as described earlier.

5. You should see the shared folder that contains the Briefcase. Open it, then click and drag the Briefcase to the Desktop of your mobile computer.

Now you can disconnect your mobile computer and hit the road. All the files you need to work with are in the Briefcase, which is really just a folder. When you dragged the Briefcase to your Desktop, you moved all the files in it to your mobile system. Now you can edit them in any way.

When you return to your office, follow these steps to resynchronize your files:

1. Reconnect your mobile computer to your desktop computer and re-establish the Direct Cable Connection.

2. Drag the Briefcase from the Desktop of your mobile computer to the shared folder on your desktop computer.

3. Go to the desktop computer and open the Briefcase in the shared folder. The Briefcase window will look similar to the following (choose Details on the View menu).

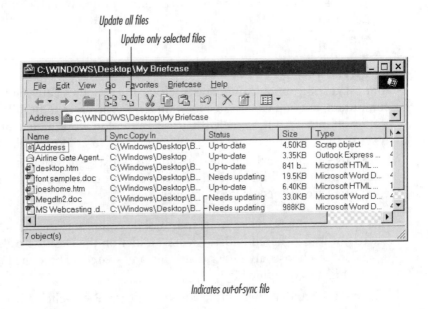

Update all files

Update only selected files

Indicates out-of-sync file

Note that changed files show "Needs updating" in the Status field. Also note the Sync Copy In field, which shows the original location of the file that Briefcase will synchronize with.

4. Click the Update All button to synchronize all the files in the list, or select a file in the list and click the Update Selection button. A dialog box similar to the following appears to help you with the update.

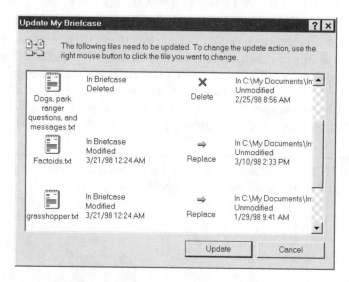

5. Click the files to update and click the Update button.

When you're ready to go back on the road, you'll need to update your Briefcase. It retains a copy of the files you put in it, even when you're working at your normal Desktop. When you change your desktop computer files, the Briefcase files go out of sync. To update files already in the Briefcase, simply open the Briefcase window and choose Update all on the Briefcase menu. You'll see a dialog box that indicates which files need to be updated and you can choose the files you want to update, then click the Update button.

In some cases, both the original files and the Briefcase files change. Perhaps someone has used your computer while you were gone and changed one of the files. If the files are stored on a network server, then other network users may have changed the file. At any rate, the Briefcase will not update files automatically. The Update dialog box will indicate that both files have changes and you must determine how you want to handle the update.

TIP: Many Windows 98-based applications provide special "reconciliation handlers" that can track the differences in files and merge them should this problem occur.

• Going Mobile with Windows CE

Handheld PCs (H/PCs) and palm computers are the latest rage. They are small, light diskless devices that use the Windows CE operating system. Windows CE is a slimmed-down version of the Windows 98 interface designed to run on small devices. Best of all, H/PCs and palm computers connect directly to desktop PCs and automatically synchronize files and other shared information with one another. Figure 19-3 illustrates Casio Cassiopeia H/PC and E-10 Palm computers, as well as a prototype palm computer from Microsoft.

WEBLINKS: Weblinks The Microsoft CE home page is at http://www.microsoft.com/windowsce. For information about the Casio Cassiopeia, visit http://www.casiohpc.com/.

FIGURE 19-3 Handheld PCs and palm computers

Windows CE devices run "pocket" versions of popular applications such as Microsoft Excel, Word, Internet Explorer, and email programs. An example Windows CE Desktop is pictured in Figure 19-4.

Pocket applications can automatically exchange files and other information with their desktop versions. The whole process is automatic and handled through a software component called ActiveSync. The Windows CE devices come with software that installs on your Windows 98 desktop computer. This software helps your desktop applications share information with the handheld device. When you connect the Windows CE device to a desktop computer (using the supplied serial cable), the software automatically detects the connection and initiates synchronization.

The software can also automatically back up the information held in the memory of the handheld device, a useful feature since the devices don't have their own disks.

ActiveSync automatically synchronizes information on H/PCs with Windows-based computers. You must install Windows CE Services on desktop computers that you will connect with your H/PC. Just connect the devices using a variety of methods, including direct connect cable, network links, cellular links, modem links, and infrared connections. *All* of your information is synchronized—email messages and attachments; contacts, calendar, and tasks data; Word, Microsoft Excel, and PowerPoint files; and group scheduling requests.

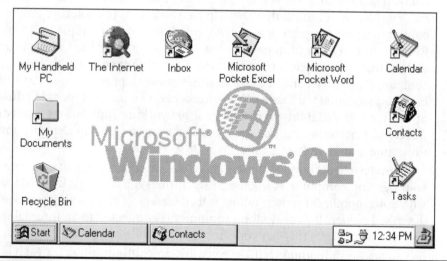

FIGURE 19-4   Windows CE Desktop

Your desktop system that runs Windows CE services includes a Mobile Devices Folder. After you connect your H/PC device to the desktop system, the icons on the H/PC desktop appear in this folder window. You can access the utilities and folders as if you were working directly on the H/PC. Synchronization starts on its own.

Note the following:

- Files can be moved, copied, and automatically converted between the H/PC and the desktop computer. All you need to do is drag-and-drop them on the folders that appear in this window.
- You can add and remove programs using this same window.
- You can create a backup file on your desktop computer that includes all the files, databases, Pocket Outlook data, RAM-based programs, and other information on your H/PC.
- A folder called Synchronized Files exists in the My Documents folder on both the desktop and H/PC device. Files in this folder are automatically synchronized.

For more information about handheld devices and the Windows CE operating system, refer to the Web sites given earlier.

Dial-Up Networking

Dial-Up Networking lets you connect with other computers using dial-up modems. But don't think that Dial-Up Networking is just another modem communication program. It is much more. It supports a unique protocol called PPP (Point-to-Point) protocol that lets you send networking protocols over dial-up lines. That means you can make a direct connection with your company's network using TCP/IP or other network protocols and gain all the benefits associated with using these protocols. The benefits include efficient use of the line and the ability to run all your networking applications as if you were directly connected to the network. You can even run multiple applications over the connection at the same time.

If you have a desktop computer and a mobile computer, you can even set up your desktop computer as a dial-up server, then connect to it from the road with your mobile computer, taking full advantage of networking protocols as described earlier. If your desktop computer is connected to an internal network, you can even access that network from your mobile computer.

You set up individual Dial-Up Networking configurations for each system or service you want to dial into. You probably already set up a Dial-Up

Networking configuration to connect with your ISP and establish an Internet connection. In this section, we show you how to use Dial-Up Networking to dial into another computer, such as your own desktop computer from your mobile computer.

NOTE: If Dial-Up Networking components do not appear on your system, refer to "Adding and Removing Windows 98 Components" in Chapter 6. Dial-Up Networking and Dial-Up Server are listed in the Communication section of the Windows Setup page of the Add/Remove Programs dialog box.

Here are two preliminary procedures for setting up a computer to support both Dial-Up Networking and Dial-Up Server:

- Install a modem on your system. The procedure is outlined under "Setting Up Communication Equipment" in Chapter 20.
- Once a modem is installed, you can install a networking protocol such as TCP/IP. This protocol will bind itself to the modem and create what is called a dial-up adapter. To set up network protocols, open the Network utility in the Control Panel. The procedure for installing these protocols is outlined at the end of Chapter 11.

Configuring Dial-Up Networking

To create a Dial-Up Networking connection, follow these steps:

1. Open My Computer, then open the Dial-Up Networking folder.
2. Click the Make New Connection option.

   The Make New Connection Wizard appears to guide you through the process. You must answer the following questions as you step through the wizard:

   - Specify a name for the connection and choose a modem on the first screen.
   - Enter the telephone number of the service or computer you want to dial.
3. Click Finish to create a new Dial-Up Networking icon.
4. Right-click the icon and choose Properties. On the General tab, edit the phone number and modem settings if necessary.
5. Click the Server Types tab to open the following page and edit the options as described next:

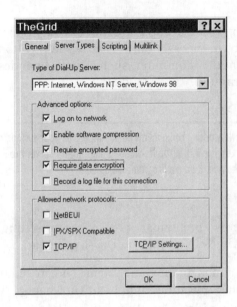

- **Type of Dial-Up Server** Choose the communication protocol that is supported by the system you are dialing. Choose the PPP option if you are connecting to your own server, then choose PPP when configuring the server as discussed later.
- **Log on to network** Enable this option if you want to log onto the network attached to the server you are dialing.
- **Enable software compression** Enable this option to speed data transfers. You might disable it if you have communication problems.
- **Require encrypted password** For security reasons, some servers only accept passwords that are encrypted. Enable this option if that is the case. If you are setting up Dial-Up Server as discussed later, you can also enable this option on the server.
- **Require data encryption** Enable this option for better security, but it may not work unless the other system supports Microsoft Dial-Up Networking.
- **Record a log file for this connection** Enable this option to create a file that keeps track of session activities. Use this option for troubleshooting.
- **Allowed network protocols** Enable the protocol you want to use over the dial-up connection. If you enable TCP/IP, click the TCP/IP Settings button and configure the following options:
  - **Server assigned IP address** Some dial-up servers automatically assign your computer an IP address. Enable this option if that is the case.

- **Specify an IP address** Enable this option and type the IP address you want to use for the connection. Refer to a network administrator for information about IP addresses.

- **Server assigned name server addresses** Name servers convert user-friendly names (such as www.microsoft.com) into numeric IP addresses that are required to access servers on TCP/IP networks like the Internet. Enable this option if the system you are dialing assigns the address of its name server; otherwise, enable the next item.

- **Specify name server addresses** If you know the IP address of your name servers, enable this option and type in the IP addresses.

- **Use IP header compression** Enable this option to optimize data transfers. Disable it if you experience communication errors.

- **Use default gateway on remote network** Enable this option to route IP traffic to the connection.

When you're done setting options, click the OK button. For convenience, you can right-click and drag the new Dial-Up Networking option to the Desktop to create a shortcut. Click the new icon to make a connection.

Configuring Dial-Up Server

If you want to dial into your own computer from another location or have other people dial into it using Dial-Up Networking, set up the Dial-Up Server as outlined here. As mentioned earlier, you need to first install a modem and the appropriate network protocol support before going through these steps:

1. Open My Computer, then open the Dial-Up Networking folder.

2. Choose Dial-Up Server on the Connections menu. A dialog box similar to the following appears:

3. Enable the Allow Caller Access button, then click the Change Password button to add a password. Note that on systems attached to Windows NT computers, you may be able to select from a list of users that can log on.

4. Click the Server Type button to change the following options:

   - **Type of dial-up server**   Choose the PPP option in most cases.

   - **Enable software compression**   Enable this option to improve performance. If you choose this option, dial-up users should also set the option on their Dial-Up Networking options.

   - **Require encrypted password**   Enable this option to encrypt the password used during logon for security reasons. As earlier, this option should also be used by dial-up users.

When you click OK to complete the setup, your system is ready to accept calls from dial-up users, including yourself when you're on the road.

Dial-Up Networking and other Windows 98 mobile features help free you from the confines of your office. Take your computing environment on the road or home with you. By taking advantage of these features, you can set yourself free of your office and maybe even become more productive.

Configuration and Management

Managing Windows 98 Software and Devices

20

BASICS

- Install devices
- View, manage, and troubleshoot device settings
- Set up and configure printers
- Set up and configure modems
- Install high-bandwidth Internet connections such as ISDN (Integrated Services Digital Network)
- Set up and configure multimedia devices

BEYOND

- Learn about special modem settings to improve your Internet connections
- Increase your communication line bandwidth with PPP Multilink modem aggregation feature
- Install and work with new and emerging technologies such as DVD (Digital Video/Versatile Disc), Multiple Display support, and high-speed modem communications
- Set up the Multiple Display feature to create a virtual desktop with up to nine monitors

This chapter discusses how to install and configure standard devices on your computer, such as printers, modems, and multimedia equipment. Once a new device is attached, special software called "drivers" must be installed to tell Windows 98 how to use the devices. Fortunately, the whole process is fairly automated, as you'll see.

Installing and Managing Peripherals and Devices

The Control Panel is the central place where you install and configure new devices for Windows 98. The Add New Hardware utility starts a wizard that guides you through the installation of new hardware and matching device driver software.

Windows 98 implements Plug-and-Play, which automatically detects new installed hardware (in most cases). After installing new devices, you start your computer and Windows 98 should detect the hardware and help you install the appropriate software drivers and make other settings.

When you add new adapters to a computer, you must make sure that the adapters do not conflict with other devices already installed in the computer. Each internal device is assigned a special IRQ (interrupt request line) and I/O (input/output) address, usually by setting switches or jumpers on the card.

In some cases, you can install a new adapter in a computer without configuring any switches. If you're lucky, Windows 98 will detect the new card, install new drivers, and everything will work just fine. However, conflicts may occur. If so, Windows will request that you resolve the conflicts. That involves several steps in which you shut down Windows 98, pull out the card, change the settings, put the card back in, and restart Windows 98.

There is a better way. What we are going to show you here is a way to install the driver software for a new adapter before you ever touch the hardware. This process will help you determine exactly which IRQs and I/O addresses are available that don't conflict with those used by other adapters. You then make the appropriate settings on the card, install it in your system, and start Windows 98.

Follow the steps here, which guide you through installing a network adapter, but these steps also work for other types of adapters. Keep in mind that we're installing the software for a device before we install the device in this example, but also keep in mind that the owner's manual for a device will usually have the most appropriate installation procedure.

1. Open the Control Panel and start the Add New Hardware utility.
2. Click Next on the opening screen, then Next again. A dialog box appears where Windows will recommend searching for the new hardware. Note that Windows 98 might find devices that are not completely configured and display a list of those devices. Choose "No, the device isn't in the list" and click Next. The following dialog box appears. You can install those other devices later on your own.

In most cases, you can choose the Yes option to search for new hardware. Many printers, monitors, and other peripherals do not require any special IRQ or I/O settings. You simply plug them in and have Windows detect the new hardware and install the appropriate drivers. But for this example, we're assuming you need to make IRQ and I/O settings and the hardware is not yet installed. We're going to let Windows 98 recommend the best settings to us.

3. Choose "No, I want to select the hardware from a list" and click Next. The following dialog box appears:

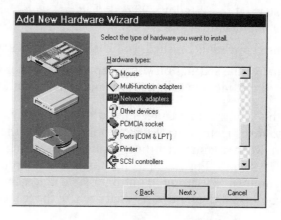

4. Choose the type of hardware you want to install from the list and click Next. In this exercise, we choose Network adapters and click Next.

5. Now you see a list of manufacturers and models. Make the appropriate choice from the list and click OK.

6. If you don't see the appropriate device, click Have Disk and insert the driver disk that comes with the device. If you didn't get a driver disk, obtain a driver by contacting the hardware vendor or by downloading it from the vendor's Web site.

In a moment, a dialog box appears with some recommended settings for the device similar to the following. In this case, the recommended I/O setting is 240 (drop the leading zero) and the IRQ is 12.

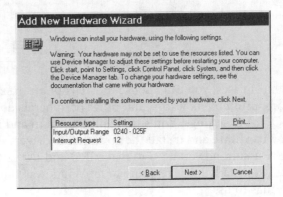

7. Click next to accept the recommended settings. Windows 98 may ask you to insert the Windows 98 CD-ROM so it can copy the drivers to your system. If the Windows 98 disk does not have the driver, insert a disk from the manufacturer.

8. Once copying is finished, you click Finish and shut down your computer.

9. Change the settings on your adapter card to the settings that Windows 98 recommended, install the card, and restart Windows.

At this point, your adapter should work properly. If it doesn't, you might need to investigate your system settings a little further as discussed in the next section. Keep in mind that the recommended settings given by Windows may not always work. For example, it's possible that your hardware cannot be set to the recommended setting. It's also possible that a conflict may not arise until after you install the hardware. That's where the System utility can help.

TIP: The "Viewing Computer Resources" section later in this chapter shows you how to view a list of resources that are currently in use so you can avoid using those same settings on new adapters.

The System Utility

The System utility provides information about the internal operation of your system and can help you install devices. Choose System in the Control Panel, or right-click My Computer and choose Properties from the shortcut menu, then click the Device Manager tab. The dialog box in Figure 20-1 appears.

You use Device Manager to view the current settings of installed devices and resolve conflicts. You click the plus sign to expand a list of devices. In Figure 20-1, the network adapter section has been expanded. You can then select a device and click Properties to view its settings. You can also click Remove to remove a device from your system.

Resolving Conflicts

Note the exclamation point over the NE2000 Compatible network card in the list. This indicates a problem with the device. To view information about and resolve such problems, select the device that has problems and click Properties.

| FIGURE 20-1 | The Device Manager |

The Properties dialog box for the device appears with a message that warns the device is not working properly.

Click the Resources tab to view a dialog box similar to the following. Here you see the resources that have been allocated for the device. Note that this device has been set to IRQ (Interrupt Request) 7, which conflicts with another device as indicated by the message in the lower field.

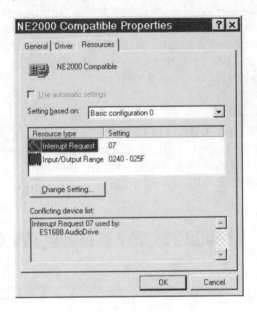

You can change the current settings by doubling-clicking any of the options in the resource list. For this example, we double-click Interrupt Request to open the following dialog box:

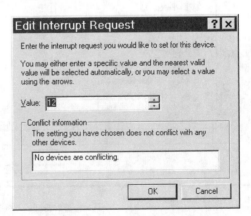

Change the Value field and watch the Conflict information message box. When you find a value that does not conflict with another device, click OK. You must then close the Device Manager, shut down your system, change the hardware settings, and restart Windows 98. That should solve the conflict.

The prior discussion illustrates one way to use the Device Manager. You can also use it to temporarily disable some hardware components, view driver information and update drivers, insert special startup commands, perform tests on devices, and so on. Take some time to explore each of the devices in the Device Manager list.

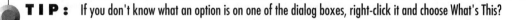

T I P :   If you don't know what an option is on one of the dialog boxes, right-click it and choose What's This?

Viewing Computer Resources

You can view a consolidated list of resources (interrupt request lines, input/output settings, and other settings) on the Computer Properties dialog box. Open System in the Control Panel, then click the Device Manager tab. Highlight Computer at the top of the list, then click the Properties button (or just double-click Computer in the list). The following dialog box appears.

Click any of the buttons at the top to see a list of resources that are in use for that category. The illustration shows the current interrupt requests in use. Note that IRQ 9 and 10 are not in use, so you can tell from this list that those interrupts can be used for any new adapters you might need to install in your computer.

Other Device Options

The Control Panel has a number of other device configuration options. Many of these were already discussed in Chapter 6.

- **Display**   See "Changing the Display Characteristics" in Chapter 6.
- **Game Controllers**   Open this option to select and calibrate joysticks and other gaming devices.
- **Mouse**   See "Customize Your Mouse" in Chapter 6.
- **Network**   See Chapter 11.

In addition, all tools related to configuring, optimizing, and managing disk drives are covered in Chapter 21.

There is also a System Information tool that provides troubleshooting and other information about your system. You can open it by clicking Start, then choosing Programs | Accessories | System Tools | System Information. System Information is covered in Chapter 22.

The System utility in the Control Panel discussed earlier also has a page called Performance where you can change the performance settings of various hardware components. These are covered in Chapter 22 as well.

Printer Setup and Management

When you buy a new printer and attach it to your system, you must install driver files that let all of your Windows applications know about the printer. You can install multiple printers on your system and then choose which printer you want to use when printing. You can also add printers that are attached to other computers on your network as discussed in Chapter 11. In this section, we discuss printer installation and how to configure the settings that are unique to every printer.

To install or manage printers, open Printers in the Control Panel. You see a dialog box similar to the following with an Add Printer icon and icons for the currently installed printers.

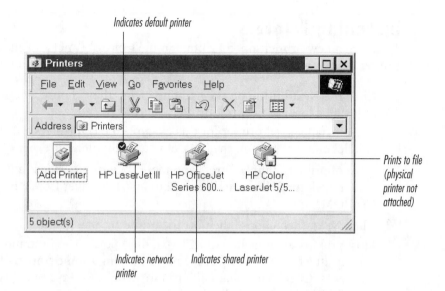

Indicates default printer

Prints to file (physical printer not attached)

Indicates network printer

Indicates shared printer

Notice the installed printer icons. The HP LaserJet III has a check mark to indicate that it is the default printer. In addition, the cable underneath it indicates that it is a network printer attached to some other computer. The HP OfficeJet printer is shared for other network users to access, as is indicated by the hand. The HP Color LaserJet prints to a file, as indicated by the diskette. Printing to files is discussed next.

Printing to Files

You can install a printer driver for any printer in the world, even if the printer is not physically attached to your computer. When you print to this "phantom" printer, the print job is directed to a disk file. Why do this? Say you want to print documents on one of those expensive, high-resolution color printers down at your local copy shop. You'll need to create the documents and prepare them on your own computer before you get to the copy shop. This is best done by setting up your computer as if it actually had the printer attached. But instead of printing to an actual printer, you print to a file that acts like the printer. Then you can take the file down to the copy shop. The file contains all the codes and commands that are needed to print directly to the copy shop's printer. By using this technique, you don't need to copy your actual working documents to the copy shop's computer and then reformat them to print on the copy shop's printer. You can do all the document setup and formatting in the comfort of your own office.

Installing Printers

To install a new printer, open Printers in the Control Panel and choose the Add Printer icon. A wizard starts that helps you select and configure a new printer.

1. Click the Next button on the opening menu, then choose whether you want to install a local or network printer.

   We'll install a local printer for this example. Local printers attach to the parallel or serial port on the back of your computer.

2. A list of printer manufacturers and models appears. Choose a printer in the list, or click the "Have Disk" button to install a driver from a floppy disk or CD-ROM.

3. Click Next, then choose the port the printer is attached to.

   Most printers are attached to LPT (parallel) ports. Mice and modems are usually attached to COM (serial) ports, although some printers have serial interfaces. Check your manual for more details. Choose File if you want to set up this printer as a "phantom" printer and send print jobs to disk files.

4. Click Next and answer the next few questions. You are asked to name the printer and asked whether you want to print a test page.

5. Click Finish to complete the installation.

That's it! In a moment, the printer appears in the Printers window. Now when you choose the Print option in your applications, you'll be able to choose this printer. If you have access to multiple printers, you can make one of them the default printer. This and other options are discussed next.

Managing Printers

If you right-click any printer, you see the following shortcut menu:

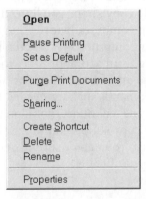

Most of the options are self-explanatory; just remember that they are available on this menu. In particular, note the following:

- **Open**   Open a list of print jobs waiting to be printed on the printer.
- **Pause Printing**   Temporarily stop printing so you can change paper, replace ink, or just temporarily mute the printer.
- **Set as Default**   Make the printer the default printer that will be used when you print documents.
- **Purge Print Documents**   Remove all print jobs that are waiting to print on this printer.
- **Sharing**   Share the printer on your network with other users. See Chapter 11.
- **Properties**   Set special options for the printer as discussed next.

If you choose Properties, a dialog box similar to the following appears, but keep in mind that the options on this dialog box will differ for every printer. The general features are similar, however.

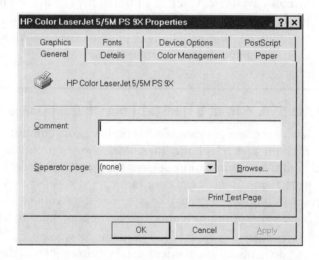

Most printers' Properties dialog boxes will have the General, Details, Paper, and Graphics tabs. Additional tabs include Fonts, Color Management, Device Options, and PostScript. Each page has a collection of options that you can learn more about by right-clicking the option and choosing "What's This?"

- **General**   Type comments about the printer for your own benefit or for the benefit of other network users who might access this printer. Comments can include a description of the printer, what it does, who is supposed to use it, what kind of paper is loaded in the trays, and so on.

- **Details**   This page is where you can change the printer port (or specify printing to a file), update the printer driver, and change other connection settings.
- **Paper**   Choose paper sizes and types, portrait (vertical) or landscape (horizontal) printing mode, the number of copies, collation methods, and related features.
- **Graphics**   Specify the printer resolution, halftoning methods, negative image printing, scaling, dithering, and intensity options.
- **Fonts**   Select which font cartridges are installed (if any) and how TrueType fonts are handled.
- **Color Management**   Windows 98 can provide an almost exact printed rendition of the colors you see on your screen, assuming that proper color management settings are made. Graphic artists may need to make these exact color matches. Use this page to add a color profile that matches your system.
- **Device Options**   Set printer-specific options, such as the amount of memory available, whether optional paper trays are in use, and so on.
- **PostScript**   This option appears if a printer supports the PostScript printer language. In most cases, the default settings are appropriate, but you may want to change them in certain cases.

Setting Up Communication Equipment

Modems are communication devices that allow computers to transmit information over telephone lines. Windows 98 supports most industry modems and digital communication devices such as ISDN (Integrated Services Digital Network) units, which can communicate at speeds of 64 or 128 kilobits per second. Windows 98 even allows *modem aggregation*, which lets you combine the bandwidth of multiple modems and phone lines to increase throughput.

Most modems, even external modems, now support Plug-and-Play, so all you need to do is install the modem and Windows 98 will detect it and help you install the right drivers. If the modem is an internal model, you still need to make sure that your modem uses a port, IRQ, and I/O address that does not conflict with other devices. If it's an external model, you'll need an available serial port.

Modem setup and configuration is handled by the Modems utility in the Control Panel. Once installed, any communication programs can use the modem.

The procedure for installing a modem is to first determine what COM ports are available. You may have a mouse attached to COM1 but nothing attached to COM2. If you are installing an external modem in this situation, you connect the modem cable to the COM2 port on the back of your computer, start your system, and run the Modems utility as discussed later.

If you are installing an internal modem, you'll need to set the modem to a COM port that is not in use, such as COM3 or COM4. However, if you already have devices on COM1 and COM2 such as a mouse, you'll need to adjust the interrupt (IRQ) settings as follows:

- **COM1 vs. COM3**   COM1 and COM3 both use IRQ 4. If you already have a device on COM1 and COM2 is in use, set your modem to COM3 and change the interrupt setting on the modem adapter to a setting that is not in use.

- **COM2 vs. COM4**   COM2 and COM4 both use IRQ 3. If you already have a device on your COM2 port and you can't use COM1 or COM3, set the modem at COM4 and change its interrupt setting to an IRQ that is not in use.

Refer to "Viewing Computer Resources" earlier in this chapter for instructions on how to find available interrupts.

N O T E :   Serial ports are identified by their I/O address: COM1=3F8, COM2=2F8, COM3=3E8, and COM4=2E8.

Running the Modems Utility

Once your modem is installed, you can start Windows 98 and the modem should be detected by the operating system. A wizard then runs to help you install the proper drivers. If the wizard doesn't start, you can run the wizard yourself as described here.

1. Open Modems in the Control Panel. The Install New Modem Wizard appears. You can choose to select the modem yourself by clicking the Don't detect my modem option, but we recommend that you click Next to run automatic detection.

   Windows 98 does a scan of the COM ports, then queries the modem it finds on a port. In a moment, it displays the name of the modem it found. If this is not the correct modem, click the Change button and select your modem from the list, or click the Have Disk button to install a driver on a disk supplied by the modem vendor.

2. Click Next to continue. In a moment you see a message indicating that Windows 98 has installed the software. Click Finish to complete the operation.

That's it! The Modem Properties dialog box appears as shown in Figure 20-2 so you can view or change the configuration of the modem as described next.

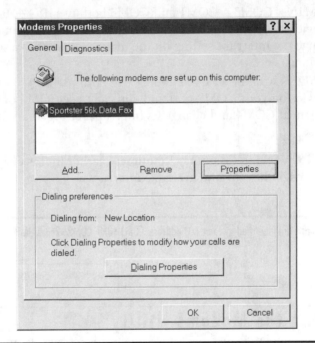

FIGURE 20-2 Modem Properties dialog box

Configuring a Modem

You can view and change a modem's configuration by opening the Modems utility in the Control Panel. The Modem Properties dialog box appears as shown in Figure 20-2 with your modem listed. Select the modem, then click the Properties button to open the Properties dialog box similar to the following:

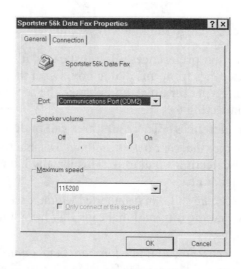

TIP: The settings you make here will be the default settings for the modem. When you set up a dial-up networking configuration as discussed in Chapter 19, you can set custom options for the configuration.

On the General page, you can change the COM port used by the modem if necessary, adjust the speaker volume, and change the speed of the modem. Adjust the speed down only if you have an older, slower computer that is exhibiting communication errors.

Click the Connection tab to display the Connection page pictured here:

Here you can change the following settings:

- **Connection preferences**   In most cases, it's not a good idea to change these settings from this dialog box. Open the application you are using, such as HyperTerminal, and change the settings to match the computer you are connecting to.
- **Call preferences**   There are three call preference options:
  - *Wait for dial tone before dialing*   Disable this option if your modem is not detecting a dial tone. This usually happens when you are out of your own country.
  - *Cancel the call if not connected within x secs*   Increase this value if you are making international calls that have long delays before the call is connected.
  - *Disconnect a call if idle for more than x mins*   Increase this value to stay connected to a service for a longer period of time, even if you are not actively using the service.
- **Port Settings**   Click this button to adjust the size of the receive and transmit buffers. There is little reason to change these options unless you have an older, slower computer that is exhibiting communication problems.
- **Advanced**   Click the Advanced tab on the Connection page to access the Advanced Connection Settings dialog box pictured here:

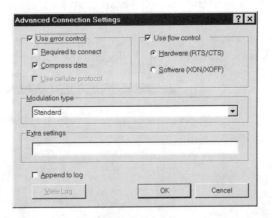

This is where you set error control, flow control, and modulation settings as described here.

- *Use error control*   Enable this option if you have a newer modem that eliminates errors caused by noisy telephone lines. Most modems now support this feature. If you have connection problems, try disabling this feature.

- *Required to connect*   Enable this option if your modem should only connect with another modem that uses error control. If the lines are always noisy in your area, you may want to enable this option.

- *Compress data*   Most newer modems support data compression, so you should enable this option to boost throughput. If you have connection problems, try disabling this option. Note that some data may already be compressed before it reaches the modem and this may cause problems if your modem is also compressing.

- *Use cellular protocol*   Enable this item to use protocols that reduce errors over cellular connections. Disable this option if your call is going over normal lines.

- *Use flow control*   Enable this item for all external modems to avoid data loss. Click the Software option in most cases. If your modem is connected with a special cable in which the RTS and CTS wires are connected, then click Hardware. Check with a technician for more details.

- *Modulation type*   You can choose between Standard (the default) and non-standard (Bell, HST) modulation types in this field. Use Standard unless the modem you are connecting to uses one of the other settings.

- *Extra settings*   In this field, you can specify initialization sequences and setup commands that are sent to your modem before it dials another system. These strings might be required to connect your modem with another system. If you are connecting with an Internet Service Provider, call and tell them what type of modem you have. They may have a command you need to type in this field. It is not necessary to include the "AT" prefix in this box.

- *Append to log*   Click this box to record the commands and responses to and from your modem. The log information is stored in a file called MODEMLOG.TXT in the Windows folder. Use this option to debug modem problems. Click the View Log button to view the log previously discussed.

As mentioned, many of these settings are also available when you create a dial-up configuration as discussed in Chapter 19. The settings you make in the Modems dialog box are system-wide settings for the modem, while the settings you make in your dial-up configuration are specific to the service you are dialing. This is especially important with options like "Extra settings", in which an ISP gives you a special string to connect with the types of modems they use. The extra settings are usually only necessary to connect with that type of modem and no other.

Setting Up ISDN Devices and Services

ISDN is a digital telephone service provided by the telephone companies that works over existing copper telephones lines. While most of the phone company's backbone network is all-digital, the wire that runs from the phone company to your home or office is still a voice-grade analog line. ISDN converts this line to digital.

A basic rate ISDN connection consists of two lines that run at 64 kbps (kilobits per second). You can use either line for voice calls or data communications. While you're talking on one line, you can connect with the Internet on the other. Best of all, you can combine the two lines into a single 128 kbps data channel. The fastest analog modem connections are only 56 kbps and only in one direction. Not only does ISDN provide faster service, it is also less susceptible to line noise and can therefore dedicate more of its throughput to sending actual data. The only drawback is that ISDN is relatively expensive and difficult to get in some areas. Newer DSL (Digital Subscriber Line) services are appearing in many areas that offer cheaper and faster service than ISDN.

Another interesting feature of ISDN is that you can connect up to eight different devices to a single ISDN line. For example, you could connect an ISDN phone, fax, and computer network equipment in a daisy-chain configuration to the line. ISDN then arbitrates the use of the two B channels among the devices and routes incoming calls appropriately.

TIP: Older analog telephones and equipment are also supported by ISDN. The analog signals are converted to digital for transmission over the digital line.

ISDN connections are made by installing either an external ISDN modem or an internal ISDN adapter. Since the external modem connects to the serial port on your computer, its speed is limited to 115 kbps. An ISDN adapter connects directly to the system bus and is capable of providing full ISDN throughput. Therefore, you should use an internal ISDN adapter if possible.

When you sign up for an ISDN line, the telephone company can help you select the type of equipment you will need at your home or office. The phone company should recommend the type of equipment that is necessary to connect to its line. They will also assign you one or two phone numbers, depending on how you plan to use the ISDN connection. With two phone numbers, you can receive calls on each of the 64 kbps channels that make up the ISDN connection. In the United States, the phone company will also supply you with a SPID (Service Profile Identifier) that you will use when configuring your equipment. Note that each device you plan to connect to the line requires its own SPID so that calls can be routed to the appropriate device. A SPID is like an extension to your phone number that identifies each of the devices on the line.

WEBLINK: For more information about ISDN, check Microsoft's ISDN Web site at http://www.microsoft.com/windows/getisdn.

To install ISDN, follow the steps here. We assume you have obtained ISDN service from your telephone company, that the ISDN lines are installed at the location of your computer, and that you have appropriate ISDN connection equipment for your computer.

1. Open Network in the Control Panel.
2. Click Add, then choose Adapter.
3. Locate the manufacturer and model of your ISDN adapter and click OK, or insert the driver disk from the manufacturer.

The ISDN Wizard starts to help you install the ISDN adapter. It will ask for the information that you should have obtained from your ISDN provider, such as the switch protocol, phone numbers, and SPID numbers. For each phone number you enter, you must also enter the corresponding SPID that identifies the communication device attached to that line.

Once the ISDN device is installed, you can configure dial-up networking to use the device as discussed in Chapter 19. You can also refer to the next section for information about configuring the PPP Multilink protocol to work with your ISDN lines.

Configuring Multilink Modem Connections

Multilink is a method for aggregating (combining) multiple communication links into a single high-speed link. The most common use of multilink is with ISDN connections. Multilink will combine the two 64 kbps B channels into a single 128 kbps data channel. You can also use multilink to combine multiple standard modem and analog telephone lines into a single channel to obtain data transfer rates that are higher than the current highest rate of 56 kbps.

Note that the service you are dialing must also support multilink and must have matching equipment. If you are aggregating four modems, the service you dial must also have four dial-in lines with modems attached to each that are configured to support multilink. Contact your ISP or the service you plan to connect with and ask them if they support PPP Multilink.

It's easy to set up Multilink with ISDN. You create a dial-up networking connection to your service provider or other service and specify that you want to be able to combine the two B channels.

1. Obtain two or more analog phone lines.
2. Connect a modem to each line.
3. Install and configure each modem in Windows 98.
4. Create a dial-up networking configuration that uses PPP (Point-to-Point Protocol) and enable multilink to combine the modems.

If you use analog modems, the connection setup requires a few more steps. Set up the phone lines, connect the modems, then follow these steps to configure PPP Multilink:

1. Open My Computer, then open the Dial-Up Networking folder.
2. Double-click Make New Connection and follow the procedure outlined in Chapter 19 for creating a dial-up connection. Be sure to specify PPP as the connection type. Configure the new connection with the first modem in the group you plan to aggregate.
3. When the new dial-up networking icon appears in the folder window, right-click it and choose Properties on the shortcut menu.
4. Click the Multilink tab, then click the Add button to open the Edit Extra Device dialog box shown here.

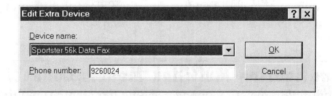

5. Choose one of the modems you already installed in the Device name field and type a dial-up phone number in the Phone number field.

The phone number may be the same or different, depending on the service you are dialing. Most ISPs will have a single phone number and all incoming calls to that number are routed to different modems that answer the call. In other cases, the location you are dialing may have a different phone number for each modem.

6. Click the Add button for each modem you want to aggregate, then click OK when done.

If you ever need to change the multilink configuration, open this dialog box again and use the Add, Remove, and Edit buttons to change the configuration.

Now test the connection by double-clicking the Dial-Up Networking icon. The primary number is dialed first and once a connection is made, the other numbers are dialed to complete the aggregate connection. To view the status of the connection, double-click the "communicating computers" icon in the Taskbar.

Multimedia Device Configuration

Windows 98 is a multimedia operating system that fully supports graphics, video, and sound in a variety of formats that enhance the multimedia experience, whether you are creating, displaying, or playing multimedia titles.

The multimedia features of Windows 98 include Microsoft DirectX and the Media Control Interface. DirectX includes support for two-dimensional and three-dimensional graphics, accelerated animation, gaming over modem and network links, and integrated graphics, audio, and video production capabilities. The Media Control Interface (MCI) provides applications with the ability to control media devices such as compact disc (CD) audio players, digital audiotape players, image scanners, MIDI (Musical Instrument Digital Interface) sequencers, videocassette recorders/players, videodisc players, animation players, and digital waveform-audio playback devices.

The following table lists the different types of multimedia files you are likely to encounter and the associated filename extensions. You can play these files with Windows 98 utilities such as CD Player, Sound Recorder, and Media Player as discussed in Chapter 5.

FORMAT	FILENAME EXTENSION
Digital video	.AVI
Waveform audio	.WAV
Moving Picture (MPEG)	.MPG
Apple QuickTime	.MOV
Musical Instrument Digital Interface (MIDI)	.MID

To change multimedia settings, open Multimedia in the Control Panel. You see the following dialog box where you can configure multimedia options as described next.

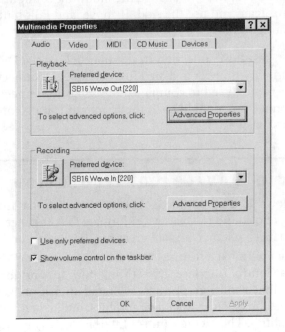

- **Audio**   Some computers have multiple audio playback and recording devices. Choose the device you want to use by default on this page. If you click Advanced Properties in the Playback field, you can choose speaker types such as quadraphonic or surround-sound speakers.
- **Video**   Choose the size at which you want to play back digital video files. You can choose full screen or several different window sizes.
- **MIDI**   Configure MIDI devices. Refer to "More About MIDI" next for details.
- **CD Music**   Use this page to set the default volume for CD music that is played from a CD-ROM drive. If you have more than one CD-ROM drive, choose which drive is used for CD Music.
- **Devices**   The Devices page is where you can view the device drivers used by your multimedia computer system. There is not much you can do on this page except view the drivers, their version numbers, and disable them if necessary. Check the Video and Audio Compression Codecs (coder/decoders) section to see what compression options you have installed on your system.

More About MIDI

MIDI is a serial interface standard that lets you connect electronic musical instruments to each other and to computers. MIDI defines how instruments are interconnected and how music and sound are encoded and transmitted among devices or stored on disk. A MIDI file contains playback information, not actual recorded sounds, that instruct MIDI devices on how to play back recorded music. The MIDI device generates the actual sounds based on notes, keystrokes, and other recorded information in the MIDI file.

Most sound cards now include a MIDI interface that also doubles as a game port connector.

The MIDI page on the Multimedia Properties dialog box is where you can redirect MIDI channels. MIDI commands can be sent over up to 16 channels. That means you can create a MIDI score that has 16 tracks and the sounds in each track can be directed to a device that is connected to a channel. For example, you can attach a MIDI drum machine to your computer and direct Channel 10 to the external drum machine.

Most sound cards include their own synthesizer or sound-generating circuitry. By default, most of your MIDI channels will be directed to the sound card. If you do install other MIDI equipment, click the Custom configuration option, then click the Configure button. Choose a channel, then click the Change button and select a target device in the instrument list where you want the channel redirected to.

DVD (Digital Video/Versatile Disc)

DVD is a new high-capacity optical disc standard that can store full-length motion pictures and other digital information for playback on your computer. DVD is a technology that bridges the computer and the home entertainment industry. A typical DVD disk contains a movie and multimedia information that can be played on a computer. There is so much room on DVD discs (typically 4.7Gb) that producers often include video with different screen formats (letterbox, pan, and scan), different soundtracks, multiple languages, and different ratings.

The hardware required to run DVD in your Windows 98 computer includes a decoder card and a DVD drive. The decoder card contains hardware that converts video compressed in the MPEG-2 format into full-motion video. Many computers are not capable of doing this on their own. DVD drives will read existing CD-ROM formats.

Because of its capacity and acceptance by the home entertainment industry, it is expected that DVD will catch on in a big way. Many computer vendors already offer computer systems with DVD drives. DVD recordable drives that provide an excellent backup medium for massive amounts of data are also available. No doubt, there is a DVD drive in your future.

Installation of DVD is fairly automatic. You install the drive and Windows 98 detects it upon rebooting. The drive may contain its own VCR-style control application, similar to what you see in Figure 20-3.

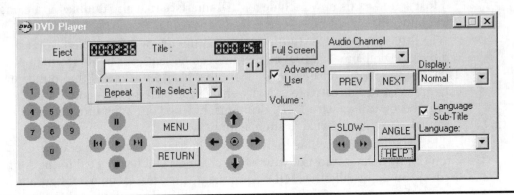

| **FIGURE 20-3** | Windows 98 DVD Player |

At the time of this writing, we were testing the Creative Lab's PC-DVD Encore Dxr2 system (but waiting for Windows 98 drivers). It appears to be an excellent package that includes DVD player output to your computer screen or TV and support for Dolby Digital (AC-3) surround sound. Check www.soundblaster.com for more information.

Multiple Display Support

Windows 98 lets you connect up to nine monitors to your computer, all of which can display the Windows 98 Desktop. Imagine a *virtual Desktop* that is the size of a 3-by-3 grid of monitors! Of course, you can use as few as two monitors, which still provides a greatly expanded Desktop as shown in Figure 20-4. The Desktop on both monitors always touch each other to provide the illusion of a seamless Desktop. This allows the mouse to move from one screen to the other without getting lost.

In order to use Multiple Display, you must install a video card for each display and install appropriate drivers for both the video card and the monitor

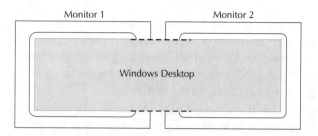

FIGURE 20-4 Multiple Display Desktop

that is attached to it. The resolution, color depth, and position of each monitor can be adjusted separately.

Multiple Display is configured with a primary display and one or more secondary displays. The primary display can use any PCI VGA video card that has a minidriver using a linear frame buffer and a packed (non-planar) format. Check with your vendor for more details. The video card for the secondary display must be one of the following at this writing:

- S3-ViRGE series, S3-Trio64V+, S3 Aurora
- Cirrus 5436, 5446, 7548
- ET6000
- ATI Mach64, Rage I, II
- Imagine i128(2)

Place the primary video card in your lowest-numbered PCI slot since that is how the BIOS picks which display will be primary.

To configure the system for multiple monitors, follow these steps:

1. Install the video cards and their drivers, then make sure the proper display drivers are installed for the displays attached to each video card.

2. Open Display in the Control Panel and click the Settings tab.
   An image of the Desktop appears on the window with a frame to indicate each monitor attached to the system.

3. Click Frame 1 (the primary frame), then select the display adapter and set its color depth and resolution.

4. Click the next frame and repeat the procedure.

5. Click OK when you are done configuring each frame.

You can open Display in the Control Panel at any time to adjust the Multiple Display configuration. Keep in mind that each monitor provides a view of the underlying virtual Desktop. The primary monitor has coordinates 0,0 for its upper-left corner and x,y for its lower-right corner, where x,y depends on the screen resolution. For example, if the resolution is set at 1024 by 768, the lower-right x,y coordinates are 1024,768.

As mentioned, the Control Panel is the primary place to add and configure new devices. In the next chapter, we look at ways to optimize and troubleshoot your system.

Managing Drives and Data

21

Microsoft has improved some familiar system tools and added several new utilities to Windows 98 which can help to keep your system running smoothly. Although Windows 98 practices preventive maintenance, the system can sometimes crash. Windows 98's utilities will often identify the problem when the system is restarted and fix it immediately.

523 •

• Accessing Disk Utilities

This chapter is about disk-based utilities. You find most of the utilities under the System Tools menu as pictured here. Click Start and choose Programs | Accessories | System Tools.

> **N O T E :** If you don't see all these utilities, refer to "Adding and Removing Windows 98 Components" in Chapter 6 for installation instructions.

You can also start disk utilities by right-clicking any drive and choosing Properties. On the Drive Properties dialog box, choose Tools to display this page:

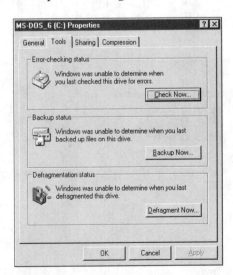

Windows Maintenance Wizard

Windows 98 has several tools that can perform certain disk housekeeping tasks at times when you're not normally using the computer. The Maintenance Wizard schedules the following tasks:

- **Speed up programs**   Runs the Disk Defragmenter utility, which rearranges the way programs are stored on your hard disk.
- **Scan hard disk for errors**   Runs the ScanDisk utility, which scans for and fixes hard disk errors.
- **Delete unnecessary files**   Runs Disk Cleanup, which finds unnecessary files and removes them to free up disk space.

Disk Defragmenter, ScanDisk, and Disk Cleanup are separate utilities that you can run on your own at any time. They are discussed in more detail later in this chapter. Maintenance Wizard helps you schedule these common tasks.

To run the Windows Maintenance Wizard, choose Maintenance Wizard from the System Tools menu pictured earlier. A wizard starts, offering two options:

- **Express**   Choose this option if you want to use the default settings. You then specify when you want to perform the maintenance—at night, in the middle of the afternoon, or in the evenings.
- **Custom**   Choose this option to set special options and run times for the Maintenance Wizard. We guide you through these steps.

If you choose the Custom option, the first dialog box that appears is where you set when the Maintenance Wizard runs. You can select nights, days, evenings, or a custom schedule. You then click the Next button to proceed through the wizard and set scheduling options for Disk Defragmenter, ScanDisk, and Disk Cleanup.

Here's an example of the dialog box that appears for scheduling Disk Defragmenter:

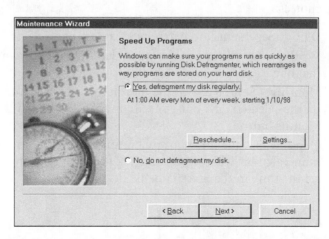

You can choose Yes to run Disk Defragmenter or No to skip it for this scheduled session. If you choose Yes, click the Reschedule and Settings buttons to change the defaults if necessary. Refer to "Rescheduling a Task" for more details. Note that each task has its own Reschedule button.

Click the Next button to work your way through the wizard. When you're done, the tasks will then run at the scheduled times.

Rescheduling a Task

Click the Reschedule button to open the following dialog box where you can set custom time options:

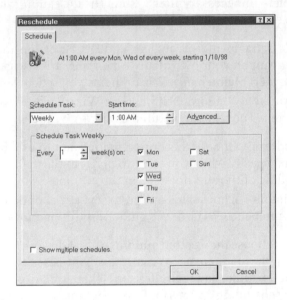

The first thing to do is choose an option in the Schedule Task field. The other options in the dialog box change depending on what you select. Here are the choices:

- **Daily** Set the task to occur every x days at a selected start time.
- **Weekly** Set the day of the week that the task runs and the start time for that day.
- **Monthly** Set the day of the month that the task runs. It runs every month on the selected day, but you can disable any month by clicking the Select Months button.
- **Once** Click the down arrow button in the Run on field to show a mini-calendar where you can click the day you want to run the task, then set the time in the Start Time field.

- **At system startup**   Select this option to run the task when the system starts. This option is not practical for prolonged tasks like Disk Defragmenter, especially if you restart your system often.
- **At login**   Select this option to run the task when you log on. You can bypass the task by clicking Cancel at the Logon dialog box.
- **When idle**   This is a good option if you leave your system on often. You can choose how many minutes of idle time must pass before the task starts.

The Daily, Weekly, Monthly, and Once options have an Advanced button. If you click it, you can schedule the task to repeat at intervals of minutes or hours and until a time you specify or for a specific amount of time.

Disk Cleanup

Disk Cleanup is a handy utility that can give you some instant relief if you're in a crunch for disk space. Disk Cleanup will get rid of temporary Internet files, downloaded program files, files in the Recycle Bin and other temporary or unnecessary files.

To run Disk Cleanup:

1. Click the Start button, then choose Programs | Accessories | System Tools | Disk Cleanup.
2. Select the drive you want to clean up, then click OK. The utility calculates the amount of space you can free up and then displays the Disk Cleanup dialog box pictured in Figure 21-1.
3. A list of files to delete appears. Click each file type to see what the files contain in the Description field. You can also click the View Files button to see a list of files for each category that will be deleted.
4. Mark each group of files you want to delete.
5. Click OK to start the cleanup, or refer to the following section.

Other Disk Cleanup Options

Disk Cleanup can also help you remove other files that may not be necessary on your system, and you can set an option that automatically runs Disk Cleanup if you run low on disk space.

Click the More Options tab to display the dialog box pictured in Figure 21-2. On this dialog box, you can choose to do the following:

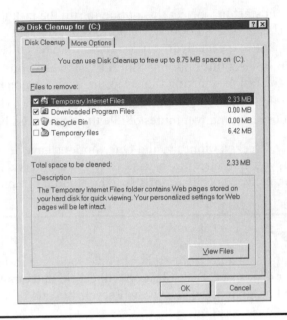

FIGURE 21-1 | Disk Cleanup utility

- **Remove Windows components** Removing optional Windows components you don't use will open up disk space.
- **Remove installed programs** Removing programs you rarely use will free disk space.
- **Convert the drive to FAT32** Converting to FAT32 makes more efficient use of the space on the drive, leaving more space available.

ScanDisk

ScanDisk monitors your hard disks and floppy disks to locate errors that could cause data loss. If ScanDisk finds a problem, it corrects it. One way that disk problems can occur is if you turn your computer off without going through the Windows 98 shutdown procedure. The next time you boot your system, ScanDisk detects an improper shutdown and automatically scans your disk for files that are improperly stored, corrupted, or no longer necessary.

In most cases, you won't cause serious damage by turning off your computer, assuming you have already saved the files you had open and closed your applications. However, doing so causes ScanDisk to run when you reboot, which takes time when booting, so you're better off shutting down properly.

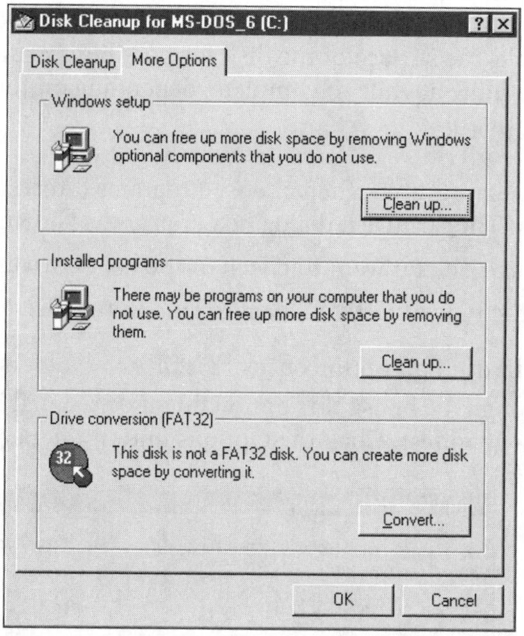

FIGURE 21-2 More disk cleanup utilities

If you turned your system off or it crashed while you had files open, then be prepared for possible data loss. What ScanDisk does is try to recover your files in the best shape possible so you can reopen them and continue on with what was salvaged.

ScanDisk also checks for files that may have data in bad sectors. A *sector* is a unit of data storage and a typical file will usually require many sectors. What ScanDisk does is mark bad sectors so they can't be used in the future, then replace the data in your file that occupied the bad sector with zeros. ScanDisk cannot recover data in these bad sectors but it will fix your file so you can at least open it. When you open the file, you may see a blank section where the data was, but the rest of the file should be OK. What you need to do then is fix the part of the file that was corrupted and continue on. Hey, it's better than retyping the whole file!

TIP: Older disks are more likely to have corrupted sectors. If you notice disk errors are increasing and know that the disk is already old, replace the disk.

ScanDisk provides two types of disk scans. The *Standard* scan checks the files and folders on a disk for errors. The *Thorough* scan checks the files and folders, and also checks the surface of the disk for possible corruption. The Thorough scan can take quite a while to complete, depending on the size of the disk.

To run ScanDisk:

1. Click the Start button, then choose Programs | Accessories | System Tools | ScanDisk. The ScanDisk dialog box appears as shown in Figure 21-3.

2. Select the drive you want to check in the list of drives.

3. Choose the type of test you want to run on the disk as described here:

   - **Standard**   This option checks the files and folders on the disk for errors.
   - **Thorough**   Choose this option on an occasional basis to give your hard disk a good test. Click the Options button to open this dialog box:

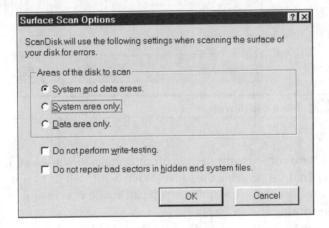

   - *System and data areas*   Normally, you would choose this option to have the entire disk checked, but if you're strapped for time or know about a potential problem in the system or data area, choose either the System area only or the Data area only option.
   - *Do not perform write-testing*   A write test provides a very thorough examination of your drive, but takes time, so you may want to check this option to disable write-testing. A write test reads data from sectors and then writes it back immediately to ensure that a sector can be both read and written to. If the sector is bad, the data is written elsewhere and the sector is marked as unusable.
   - *Do not repair bad sectors in hidden and system files*   Older copy-protected programs will not operate if they are moved out of the

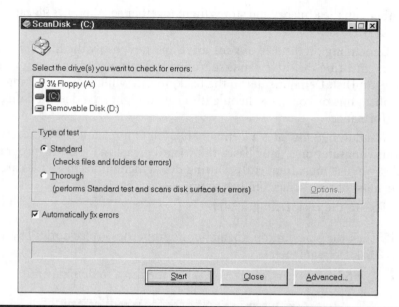

FIGURE 21-3   The ScanDisk utility checks your disk for errors

sectors they occupy. You should enable this option if you run such programs, although today very few programs use this method.

4. To fix errors automatically, check the Automatically fix errors box, or leave this option disabled to set your own options on how you want errors fixed. If you disable this option, click the Advanced button to set custom fix options. On the dialog box that appears, right-click each option and choose What's This? to see a description of the option.

5. Once you've set all the options, click Start.

ScanDisk starts running and shows you its progress. You can click Cancel at any time to stop the process.

Disk Defragmenter

Files are divided into pieces and stored in sectors on disk. When a file is deleted, the sectors become available for storing other files. But if new files are large, they may need to be broken up (fragmented) and placed in sectors that are scattered throughout the disk, which will slow disk read performance. Disk Defragmenter gathers up these pieces and stores them together so Windows 98 can read the files faster.

Depending on the size of your drive and how badly the files are fragmented, defragmenting the drive can take from a few minutes to an hour or more. You can run Disk Defragmenter in the background while you're working in other applications or you can schedule it to run at night so it does not affect system performance.

Windows 98 includes a Defragmentation Optimization Wizard. As you use your computer on a daily basis, the wizard creates a log of the programs and files you use most frequently. During defragmentation, these files are placed in the most optimal place on disk to improve access.

To run the Disk Defragmenter:

1. Click the Start button, then choose Properties | Accessories | System Tools | Disk Defragmenter.

2. A window appears where you select the drive to defragment:

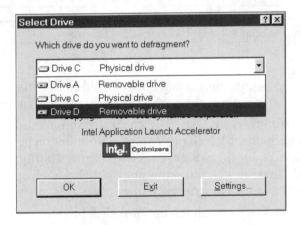

3. Click the Settings button to change the following options:

- *Rearrange program files so my programs start faster*   There is little reason not to enable this option. It improves the performance of your drive.
- *Check the drive for errors*   When this option is enabled, the defragmentation process may take longer. If you've recently checked for errors, you can disable it.
- *This time only*   The settings you choose are used only for the current session.

- *Every time I defragment my hard drive* The settings you choose are used until you change them again.

4. Make the necessary changes to the settings, then click OK. You are returned to the Select Drive box, where you can click OK again to start defragmentation.

The following dialog box appears during defragmentation. You can stop or pause the process at any time. If you're working on your system, defragmentation may pause while you perform some activities, then resume a little later.

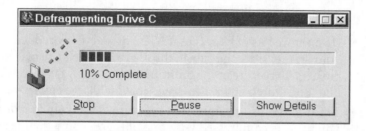

TIP: Click the Show Details button to see an interesting view of the disk defragmentation process. You see each of the data clusters (groups of sectors) on your drive and can watch as the program moves clusters around to optimize their position on the drive. Click the Legend button to see a description of the data clusters.

Using FAT32

FAT (File Allocation Table) is the file system that has been used in Microsoft operating systems since DOS (Disk Operating System) was introduced in the early 1980s. FAT basically keeps track of where files (or pieces of files) are stored on disk. It allocates space on disk for new files, handles deleting files, and keeps track of free space.

Windows 98 includes a newer and more efficient upgrade to FAT called FAT32. FAT32 is an option that you can choose to install, but we recommend that you read through this section before deciding.

FAT32 can improve disk performance and provides these other features:

- You can format a drive larger than 2Gb as one drive, without having to partition it. The older FAT required that you split a 4Gb drive, for example, into two partitions of 2Gb each.

- You can choose smaller cluster sizes, meaning the space on large drives is used more effectively when saving small files.

The smaller cluster size is the most important feature. Not only does it help improve performance, it also lets you maximize the space on the disk and store more files. With the older FAT, the smallest amount of space (by default) that you could store a file in was 8,000 bytes. If you had a small file that was only 2,000 bytes, then 6,000 bytes of disk space would go unused. With FAT32, the smallest amount of space is 4,000 bytes, which makes for more efficient use of disk space.

There are some disadvantages to FAT32:

- If you store lots of large files, FAT32 may actually reduce performance on your system since the data in the files will have to be placed in many smaller clusters. Large streaming multimedia files such as video and audio may be better off stored on FAT16 drives in which large cluster sizes are enabled.
- Third-party disk compression software is unlikely to work with FAT32; if your disk is compressed with one of these, you won't be able to convert the disk to FAT32.
- Older anti-virus software may see the changes FAT32 makes to the master boot record as evidence of a virus.
- Older versions of disk utility programs that use FAT16 may not work with FAT32 disks.
- If you have a dual boot system that runs Windows 98 with Windows 95 version 4.00.950, Windows 3.x or Windows NT 3.x or 4.0, you won't be able to dual boot if you convert to FAT32 with Drive Converter (FAT32).
- While Windows 98 includes a utility to convert FAT16 to FAT32, it doesn't include a utility to convert a FAT32 system back to FAT16, if you want to do so. You'll have to repartition and reformat your FAT32 drive before you can use FAT16.

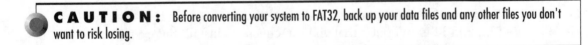

CAUTION: Before converting your system to FAT32, back up your data files and any other files you don't want to risk losing.

You can see if your drive is already set up with FAT32 as follows:

1. Click My Computer on the Desktop.

2. Right-click the drive in question and choose Properties.

3. On the General tab, the File system entry tells you whether the drive is FAT or FAT32.

Running the FAT32 Conversion Utility

To use the Windows 98 utility for converting FAT disks to FAT32:

1. Click the Start button, then choose | Programs | Accessories | System Tools | Drive Converter (FAT32).

2. When the Drive Converter (FAT32) window opens, you can click Details to read more information about FAT32, or you can click Next to continue on with the conversion.

3. When you click Next, you get to choose the drive you want to convert.

4. Click Next to continue. A message may appear to tell you that you have anti-virus software on your system and to remove it because it is not compatible with FAT32. Click OK. The utility will check for any incompatible programs. Click Next if there are none.

5. Follow the steps to create a backup before you convert.

After the backup completes, the utility will restart your computer to begin the conversion process.

Checking for Software Viruses

Windows 98 does not include its own virus scanning software. Third-party virus checkers for earlier versions of Windows may or may not work with Windows 98, and even if one finds a virus it may not be able to clean it from the system.

WEBLINKS: We recommend either of the following anti-virus checking software programs because Symantec and McAfee are reputable companies with the financial resources and customer commitment to keep their products as up to date as possible. This is especially important since new viruses appear almost everyday. Check the Web sites listed for more information:

Norton AntiVirus from Symantec (http://www.symantec.com)

McAfee VirusScan from Network Associates (http://www.networkassociates.com)

Compressing Disks to Save Space

To make the most of the storage space available on your drives, Windows 98 includes the DriveSpace 3 utility (for compressing FAT16 drives only). DriveSpace compresses files and makes megabytes of space available. A compressed drive may run a little slower than a non-compressed drive, but unless you're accessing your disk constantly, you probably won't notice any difference. Compressed drives are also an excellent place to store archived files that you access infrequently.

You can even compress floppy disks! A 1.44MB floppy disk will provide up to 2.56MB of space after compression.

When you compress a disk, DriveSpace 3 creates what is called a "host" drive for the original drive letter. The original drive is then compressed and the resulting file information is stored as a volume on the host drive. You only need to know that this new drive is related to disk compression.

Instead of compressing an entire drive that already contains files, DriveSpace 3 can also use any existing free space on an uncompressed drive to create a new, empty compressed drive. Your original files remain uncompressed. For example, if you have 100MB of free space, DriveSpace will create a new 200MB drive. This is a useful feature if you are not sure whether existing files will benefit from compression and it can help you gain additional space immediately if your drive is starting to run out of space.

To run DriveSpace, click the Start button, then choose Programs | Accessories | System Tools | DriveSpace. The DriveSpace 3 window appears as shown here:

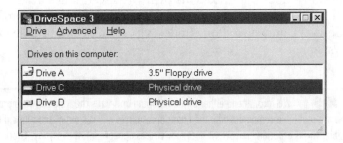

Here are some of the things you can do in DriveSpace 3:

- **Compress the whole drive**   Choose the Compress option on the Drive menu to compress the drive you select.
- **Create a new compressed drive**   Choose the Create Empty option on the Advanced menu to create a new compressed drive with nothing in it.
- **Uncompress a drive**   Choose the Uncompress option on the Drive menu to uncompress a drive.
- **View the properties of a compressed drive**   Choose the Properties option on the Drive menu to look at information about the drive you select.
- **Upgrade a compressed drive**   Choose the Upgrade option on the Drive menu to reformat a drive that uses the DoubleSpace or DriveSpace format into a DriveSpace 3 compressed drive.
- **Mount and unmount compressed drives**   Choose the Mount or Unmount option on the Advanced menu to connect the compressed volume file to or disconnect it from the drive you select.
- **Delete a compressed drive**   Choose the Delete option on the Advanced menu to delete a compressed drive.
- **Change a drive's compression ratio**   Choose the Change Ratio option on the Advanced menu to compress files more tightly or decompress them.
- **Adjust the free space on a compressed drive**   Choose the Adjust Free Space option on the Drive menu to move free space between the host drive and compressed drive.
- **Change Letter**   Choose the Change Letter option on the Advanced menu to change the letter identifying the compressed drive.
- **Tune and adjust compression settings**   Choose the Settings option on the Advanced menu to modify the compression settings to free up more space or speed operation.
- **Format a compressed drive**   Choose the Format option on the Drive menu to format the drive and remove all files.
- **Update the drive window**   Choose the Refresh option on the Advanced menu to be sure the Drive window shows the current status of the drives.

Compression Agent

If you are using a drive compressed with DriveSpace 3, you can use Compression Agent to improve the compression on the drive. It can only be used on drives that have already been compressed with DriveSpace 3.

Compression Agent basically lets you compress existing compressed files even further. The compression options are

- **Standard compression**   This is the standard compression provided by DriveSpace 3.
- **HiPack**   This option compresses files even further but not enough to adversely affect the speed at which the files can be opened on slow systems.
- **UltraPack**   This option provides the most compression. Files are packed in a format that takes more time to open (although this may not be noticeable on fast systems). You should use UltraPack on files that you don't access often, or when creating archives.

To start Compression Agent, click Start, then choose Programs | Accessories | System Tools | Compression Agent. When the Compression Agent opens, you click the Settings button to specify the following:

- You can choose either HiPack or UltraPack compression.
- If you choose UltraPack, you can have it UltraPack only files that have not been used in the number of days you specify.
- You can exclude specified files from being compressed by clicking the Exception button.

Once you've set the options, click the Start button to start the compression. The utility may run for a while and affect the performance of your system. You may want to start the compression when you are not using your system.

You can look at the statistics for compressed drives. Right-click the drive and choose Properties, then click the Compression tab. The following shows the statistics for a compressed floppy drive in which some of the files were packed using UltraPack compression:

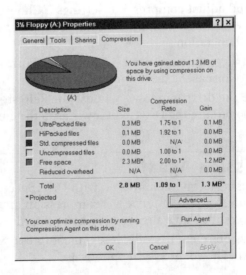

Backing Up Drives and Data

Backing up files is an important part of using computers. We know someone who had a hard drive failure. In an attempt to recover the files on his drive, he actually bought a duplicate drive and moved the circuit board from the new drive to the old drive. Unfortunately, this didn't solve the problem so he sent the drive to a very expensive service that specializes in recovering files from broken drives. After about a week, he finally got his files back, but only after spending a lot of time and money. Also, he had to re-type some files that he needed while the disk was being recovered.

By creating backups and storing them in a safe place, you always have a way to quickly recover from some catastrophic event or system failure. A typical procedure is to back up your entire system once a week, then back up all the files that have been added or changed on a daily basis. For added protection, you might want to carry backups to another location to protect them from local events like fire or burglaries.

Our favorite backup method is now CD-R (compact disc recordable). The drives and writeable discs are now so inexpensive that it makes more sense than backing up to tape or other mediums. In addition, CD-R discs can be read in any CD-ROM drive. That means you can go to a friend's or coworker's system and access your files without having to go through clumsy steps to restore your files to another hard drive. You're back in business in no time, assuming you have access to another computer.

Of course, backups can't help you recover files that you were working on when your system failed or that you didn't have time to add to your latest backup set. We like to keep a floppy disk handy and copy our latest files to it. Then at the end of the day, we also include the files in our daily backup.

Here are some tips for protecting your system with a minimum of time and effort.

- **Perform incremental backups.**   Back up the files that change each day—it doesn't take much time and it minimizes the amount of data you'll lose.
- **Perform major backups.**   Do major backups of your system weekly or monthly, depending on use. Follow a regular schedule so you know what is on your backups.
- **Back up the Windows registry.**   Periodically back up the Windows registry files, which are where your critical Windows settings are stored. The Windows 98 Backup utility discussed next helps you do this.
- **Decide what to back up.**   Evaluate whether you should back up your entire system rather than only your data files. Reinstalling software and

settings could be a time-consuming task—and you'd be doing it under the pressure of getting back into operation.

- **Consolidate files.** Group your files into folders so you can back up entire folders in one operation.
- **Test your backup procedure.** Try restoring your backed up files as a test.
- **Keep backups protected.** Store a set of your backed up files away from your office or home for maximum safety. If you have a safe deposit box, put a backup set there.
- **Schedule backups for down time.** Set up a schedule to back up your files when the computer isn't being used.
- **Back up to other drives.** If you're connected to a network, ask your network administrator about backing up important files to drives on other computers over the network.

The last point is especially convenient. We have an in-house network with a server that sports a very large hard disk. Our printers and CD-ROM drives are connected to this server and available for everyone to use. In addition, everyone has an allocated amount of disk space on the server where they can copy important files on their system. Backing up then becomes as simple as clicking and dragging a folder full of important files to the network server.

The Windows 98 Backup Utility

Windows 98 has its own Backup utility that gives you a lot of flexibility in choosing how, when, and where to back up your files. The Backup utility is pictured in Figure 21-4.

Backup provides a painless way to back up any combination of files, folders, or drives to a variety of media, including floppy disks, hard disks, network drives, and, of course, traditional streaming tape media (QIC or quarter-inch cartridge). You can compress files to save space, restore selected files, and even rebuild your operating system setup.

Running Your First Backup Job

Let's try doing a backup. Because Microsoft Backup has an interface that's consistent with the rest of Windows 98, you'll quickly grasp how it works. Note that you will need some backup device, such as another drive, a tape drive, or a network drive.

1. To start Backup, click Start, then choose Programs | Accessories | System Tools | Backup. A Welcome box appears where you can choose to create a new backup set.

2. In the Welcome dialog box, choose Create a new backup job and click OK. The Backup Wizard starts to help you create a backup. You can start the Backup Wizard at any time in the future by choosing Backup Wizard from the Backup utility's Tools menu.

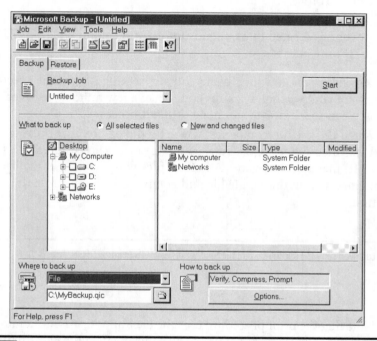

FIGURE 21-4 Windows 98 Backup utility

At this point, the Backup Wizard guides you through the backup process. You can make the following selections:

- Back up your entire computer or selected files. If you choose to back up selected files, a Browse dialog box appears where you can choose drives, folders, and files in a hierarchical tree. You expand parts of the tree by clicking the plus sign, then you check mark the items you want to include in the backup.

- If you choose drives and folders (which contain groups of files), you can have Backup only back up files that are new or changed within the groups.
- Choose the destination for the backup. You will see a list of devices available on your system, such as floppy drives, hard drives, tape drives, and network drives.
- You can have Backup compare the backup with the original to verify integrity, but this takes more time. You can also choose to compress files to maximize the space on the backup medium, but compression also adds time to the backup process.
- Finally, you must name the backup session. Every time you back up, a new session is created that contains information about what was backed up and how to restore it.

Depending on how much data you are backing up and the speed of the hardware you're using, backups could take a few minutes to several hours. As you can see, however, it's not a difficult process.

When the backup completes, you see a dialog box that provides messages and statistics about the backup session. The backup is stored as a file with the QIC filename extension. All of the files you included in the backup are contained within this single file and compressed if you chose the compression option.

TIP: You can even copy the backup session file to other disks at this point.

Note that the prior procedure uses the Backup Wizard. As mentioned, you can start the Backup Wizard at any time by choosing it on the Backup utility's Tools menu. You can also work directly with the options on the Backup window to create a backup. Looking again at Figure 21-4, note the Backup and Restore tabs. Click Backup, then follow these general steps:

1. Choose the drives, folders, or files to back up in the What to back up field.
2. Choose the destination where backed up files will be copied in the Where to back up field.
3. Change the settings for the backup by clicking the Options button in the How to back up field. See "Fine-Tuning Your Backup Job Options" later in this chapter for more details.
4. Click Start to begin the backup.

Choosing a Destination

You can back up your files to any of a variety of media. Each has its advantages and disadvantages.

- **Backing up to a floppy disk**   Although floppies have limited space, Backup will back up to a series of disks to handle space requirements. Be sure to choose the compression options to maximize the space on the disks. Be sure to label and number the disks in the appropriate order.

- **Backing up to a Zip-type drive**   You can back up your files to an Iomega, SyQuest, or other popular parallel or SCSI device.

- **Backing up to another hard drive on your system**   If you have two or more hard drives on your system, you can back up to another drive, but you will still need to create another backup that you can carry off-site. Use this option if you are clearing off another drive or rearranging files, or if you just want to create duplicates on the local system to protect against failure of the original drive.

- **Backing up to another computer on the network**   You can back up to another computer on your network. In Network Neighborhood, click the computer you want to back up to, then select the shared folder where you want to put the file.

- **Backing up to a tape drive**   The Windows 98 backup utility supports the QIC-113 format standard and can read tapes made with backup software that supports the standard.

- **Backing up over the Internet**   A growing number of companies are offering remote backup storage where you can back up your files to servers on the Internet. However, if you have only a modem connection to the Internet, this will be slow.

WEBLINK: As an example of remote backup storage, Visto Briefcase (http://www.visto.com) will automatically encrypt and upload your files to a secure server.

Fine-Tuning Your Backup Job Options

To refine the settings that Backup uses, click the Options button in the Microsoft Backup window. The Backup Job Options dialog box appears as shown here:

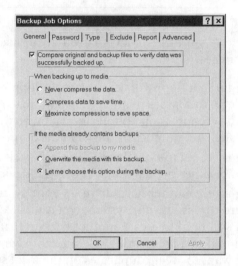

The dialog box has six pages that are described in general below. You can get more information about specific options by right-clicking a field and choosing the What's This? option.

General

- **Verify successful backups.** Compare your original and backup files to assure they have backed up properly.
- **Save space by compressing your data.** Choose to compress data and save space, or not compress and save time.
- **Overwrite or save previous backups.** You can choose to append the backup to the media, or overwrite what is already on the media.

Password

- **Protect your backups from prying eyes.** You can assign your backup a password to prevent unauthorized access.

Type

- **Specify the backup procedure.** Choose to back up all selected files, or choose to do differential or incremental backups of the new or changed files.

Exclude

- **Exclude files you don't want included in the backup.**   Click on the Add button to exclude files with registered or custom file extensions from being backed up.

Report

- **Create reports on your backups.**   You can obtain reports on which files were backed up or not backed up, errors and warnings that occurred during the backup, and messages and prompts that appeared during unattended backup.
- **Perform an unattended backup.**   When this option is set, Backup does not display message boxes or prompts that must be answered by an operator. It performs a complete backup on its own based on the information you supply. See "Running an Unattended Backup" later for more information.

Advanced

- **Back up your Windows registry files.**   Keep a copy of the Windows registry, which is the central storehouse for all your critical Windows settings. Back up the registry whenever you make settings changes you wouldn't want to have to reconfigure later if you had a system failure. You can use your emergency startup disk and backup files to recover from a catastrophe.

Restoring Backed Up Files

We hope you are never in a situation where you need to restore your backups, but just in case, the steps are described here. As an example, we can think of two possible restoration scenarios which assume that your previous system was lost due to fire or theft:

- After acquiring a new computer, you perform a complete restore from your backup set. This option restores Windows 98 completely the way you had it configured on your previous system.
- You rebuild your system and install Windows 98 from the original disk, then restore only data files from your backup sets. This option does not restore your previous Windows 98 setup, just the data files, but it lets you restart with a fresh system setup.

The second option provides more flexibility but requires more knowledge of what you are doing. It assumes that your new system does not have the same hardware components such as video cards and disk drives as your previous system.

 N O T E :   You can restore your entire system from previous backups by starting with the emergency startup disk you created when you installed Windows 98.

Here's how a typical restore session is handled. You might want to test restoring your backup files on another drive or on another computer just to make sure everything works the way you planned.

1. Start Microsoft Backup, then click the Restore tab to see the window pictured in Figure 21-5.

2. Place the media with the backup file into the appropriate drive device (for example, if it's a floppy disk or tape).

3. Choose Restore Wizard on the Backup utility's Tools menu.

4. In the Restore from field, click the folder icon to open the Restore from dialog box where you can choose the backup file you created in a previous backup session. Choose the file and click Open.

5. Click Next to open the Select Backup Set dialog box where you can click the name of the backup set you want to restore and click OK.

6. The Restore Wizard now displays a dialog box where you can select exactly which files you want to restore. You can check mark the entire set, or click the + boxes to expand the file lists and choose just the files you want to restore. Once you've selected files, click Next.

7. Now the Restore Wizard asks you where to restore the files. You can choose to restore to the original location, or browse to an alternate location. Once you've selected a location, click Next.

8. In the How to restore field, choose how you want Backup to restore files that already exist: ignore them, replace if the files on your computer are older, or always place the files on your computer.

9. Click Start to start the restore.

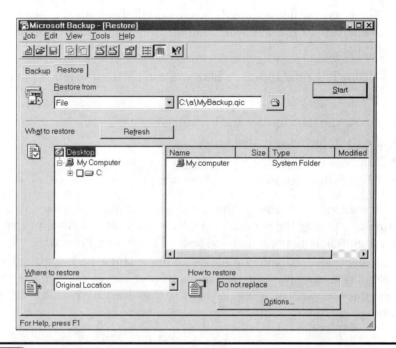

FIGURE 21-5 | Restoring files from backup sets

Running an Unattended Backup

Backups take time, but you don't have to surrender your computer during working hours in order to back up your files. The Scheduled Tasks Wizard can run your backup without your having to be there.

To run Backup automatically:

1. Click the Start button, then choose Properties | Accessories | System Tools | Scheduled Tasks.

2. In the window, click Add Scheduled Task, then click Next.

3. When asked which programs you want Windows to run, click Backup, then click Next.

4. Type a name for the task in the text box, such as **Evening Backup**, then select when you want it performed and click Next.

5. If you choose a daily, weekly, or monthly backup, Microsoft Backup will ask you to schedule a time. Select the time, then click Next.

6. The wizard will schedule the task and ask if you want to see the Advanced Properties for the task when you are finished. Click this option, then click Finish.

A dialog box now appears where you can change the following options for the task:

- Revise the schedule for the backup.
- Control the time allotted for the backup.
- Alter the backup time if the computer is in use.
- Change the backup process if the computer is on battery power.

You can view and change the settings on this dialog box at any time in the future by opening the Scheduled Tasks window as described in step 1 earlier, then right-clicking the scheduled task and choosing Properties.

As mentioned, backing up files is an important aspect of using computers. It's almost as important as putting gas in your car, or more to the point, changing your tires on a regular basis so you don't have a blow-out on the freeway.

Optimizing, Updating, and Troubleshooting

22

BASICS

- Check the performance status of your system
- Adjust file system performance
- Adjust graphic system settings to overcome problems
- Optimize virtual memory settings
- Learn troubleshooting techniques

BEYOND

- Learn how to update Windows 98
- Use Microsoft System Information Utility and its associated tools
- Use System Monitor to track performance problems

Windows 98 includes many features to optimize performance and troubleshoot problems. Fortunately, Windows 98 will dynamically configure itself for the best performance in most cases. This chapter discusses ways you can change the optimization settings that Windows 98 uses and troubleshoot problems.

Optimizing Performance

Performance is relative. It depends on what you are used to and the type of programs you run. If you've just upgraded from a vintage 1980s PC, you're going to see a big performance improvement with Windows 98 running on a fast Pentium system. But if you've just upgraded from a 1995-era Pentium 90 to a Pentium system running at 200 to 300 MHz, you might have trouble perceiving exactly where the performance improvement is.

In our own experience, we have found that upgrading to faster processors and video systems and installing more memory provides nowhere near performance gains that we get when upgrading to high-performance disk storage devices. While many magazines provide performance tests that seem to show incredible speed improvements by upgrading to new faster processors, you might have trouble noticing those improvements unless your computer is crunching numbers or generating complex graphics on the screen. But upgrading to a fast disk can improve startup time, application loading, and disk-intensive tasks like a database search.

A typical hard disk like those supplied with most off-the-shelf PCs will read data at about 1 to 2MB per second. A carefully selected high-performance drive can read data at 5 to 8MB per second! That's a vast improvement. If you're buying a new system, ask for Ultra-ATA IDE drives or SCSI drives with the so-called "fast and wide" interface. Another speed enhancer is the spin rate of the disk, which allows data to be read much faster. A typical off-the-shelf drive spins at 5,400 revolutions per minute while new fast drives spin at 10,000 revolutions per minute.

TIP: Chapter 21 discusses utilities for improving disk performance. To learn more about system optimization and troubleshooting, and to obtain useful utilities for these tasks, purchase the *Windows 98 Resource Kit*, a Microsoft publication available in bookstores.

Checking Performance Status

Beyond improving disk performance, there are a few things you can do to monitor and possibly improve overall system performance. To check your system's current performance status, follow these steps:

1. Open the System utility in the Control Panel (or right-click My Computer and choose Properties).

2. Click the Performance tab.

The dialog box shown in Figure 22-1 appears to show your current system resource settings and how they are being used.

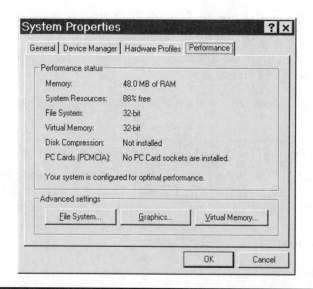

FIGURE 22-1 Check performance status in the System Properties dialog box

The percentage of free system resources is an important indicator of system performance. As you open applications and perform other tasks, system resources such as memory, system variables, data values, and cache space are used. When you close applications, Windows 98 should free those resources and make them available for other applications to use. When resources are freed up properly, you can open more windows, use more fonts, and run more applications simultaneously.

During normal usage, system resources may drop to about 50 percent free. Under heavy loads, it may drop to as low as 25 percent free. If your system seems to run slow, track this setting for a while. If it remains below 50 percent under normal usage, you may be using an application that needs to be upgraded to work with Windows 98 or you may have other problems that require troubleshooting.

If the Performance page indicates that *real-mode* components are being used, you should upgrade the drivers for the listed components. Microsoft strongly recommends that you use 32-bit, protected-mode drivers whenever possible. Most vendors now make these drivers available for their products and you may need to obtain them by contacting the vendor. To upgrade a device driver, follow these steps:

1. Open the System utility in the Control Panel.
2. Click the Device Manager tab on the System Properties dialog box.
3. Select the device that needs upgrading and click the Properties tab.
4. Click the Driver tab, then click the Update Driver button and follow the on-screen instructions.

Refer to Chapter 20 for more information about the Device Manager.

Adjusting File System Performance

You can adjust the performance settings of your file system on the System Properties dialog box (see Figure 22-1). Open the System utility in the Control Panel as previously described, then click the File System button to open the dialog box shown in Figure 22-2. The dialog box has five tabbed pages that are discussed next.

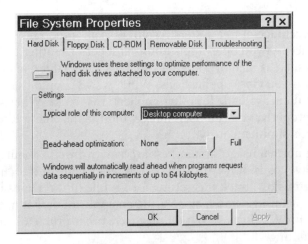

FIGURE 22-2 File System Properties dialog box

CAUTION: Most of the settings on this dialog box are preset for optimum performance by your computer. Only change the settings if you have reason to do so or if you are following instructions provided with a device or by a technician.

TIP: Right-click any options and choose What's This? to get a description.

- **Hard Disk**   Here you can change the role of the computer (desktop computer, laptop, or network server). You may need to change the role of a computer to Network Server to give network users better performance, but keep in mind that this may reduce performance for the local user (yourself?). The Mobile or docking system option should be selected for portable computers that run on battery power. The mobile setting writes information in the cache to disk more often to protect the data from battery failures. The page also has an adjuster for read-ahead optimization. When data is being read from disk, the system can read more blocks into memory than were requested. Performance is improved if those blocks are requested in the next read request. You should set this option high unless your system has less than 16MB of memory (refer to the Performance page as shown in Figure 22-1).

- **Floppy Disk**   Here you can enable an option that has Windows 98 look for a disk in the floppy drive when it starts and read its directory. This may be a nuisance.

- **CD-ROM**   Here you can change the type of CD-ROM drive in your system and the size of the cache allocated to it. The CD-ROM type is related to its speed and your system should have detected it properly, so there is little need to change these settings. However, if your system has less than 16MB of memory, you can reduce the cache size to free up more memory for applications. The cache holds information already read from CD-ROM in case it is requested again.

- **Removable Disk**   If your system has removable disk drives such as ZIP and JAZ drives, enable the write-behind caching option on this page, but disable it if the drive has operating problems.

- **Troubleshooting**   The options on this page are used for troubleshooting or to correct very specific system problems. Microsoft points out that re-setting any of these options will seriously degrade system performance. They should only be enabled when recommended by a qualified technician.

Advanced Graphics Settings

The Graphics button on the Performance page of the System Properties dialog box (Figure 22-1) provides an adjustment for changing graphics hardware acceleration. In most cases, the setting will be appropriate for your system and determined by Windows 98, but if you notice irregularities on the screen or system failures, reducing hardware acceleration may solve the problem.

The Advanced Graphics Settings dialog box has four notches. The notch furthest to the right is the Full acceleration setting and should be used whenever possible. The first notch from the right may correct mouse pointer display problems. The second notch from the right may correct certain display errors. The lowest notch removes all driver acceleration support from the display system and should be set if the system frequently stops responding to input.

T I P : If your display problem is solved by adjusting the slider downward, you might have a problem that requires a hardware or software upgrade. Contact the display adapter manufacturer to obtain possible fixes or updates.

T I P : If you receive an error message at system startup stating that an application caused "an invalid page fault in module," use the lowest notch until you can resolve the problem with the adapter manufacturer.

Virtual Memory Settings

Windows 98 uses a virtual memory system to allow your computer to use more memory than it actually has. A virtual memory swap file (sometimes called a *paging file*) is created on disk and appears as an extension to your RAM memory. With virtual memory, you can run many programs at the same time. The virtual memory manager temporarily frees memory by swapping unneeded information to the paging file on disk. If the swapped information is needed again, it is quickly reloaded and other information in RAM memory that is not needed is moved to the swap file.

The important point is that the swap file acts like RAM memory, although it is not as fast as RAM memory. All swapping activities happen in the background automatically. If you notice a lot of disk activity while running multiple applications, then you know that virtual memory swapping is probably taking place. However, since virtual memory is slower than RAM, you might want to add more RAM if virtual memory swapping takes place often.

Note that the Windows 98 swap file is dynamic and can shrink and grow in size based on how you are using your computer. It is usually best to let Windows 98 dynamically manage the swap file. However, if your system has multiple drives, you might gain performance by placing the swap file on the fastest drive or the drive that is less busy (i.e., the drive that does not contain all your programs and data), assuming that disk has plenty of available disk space. To change the swap drive, do the following:

1. Click the Virtual Memory button on the Performance page of the System Properties dialog box (Figure 22-1).

2. Enable the option called "Let me specify my own virtual memory settings."

3. In the Hard Disk field, choose the fastest drive or the drive that is less busy.

4. Set the Maximum field to the highest number possible. This ensures that the virtual memory system will dynamically manage the size of the swap file.

• Troubleshooting Tools and Techniques

Troubleshooting problems with your system is easier in Windows 98 because the operating system comes with a variety of tools to help you identify problems or work with qualified technicians who can help you troubleshoot problems. We cover some of the more important tools here. Note that this book does not have room to cover nearly all the details of troubleshooting, but the quick introductions you'll find here will get you on the way. For more information, check with the Web sites listed next or obtain a copy of Microsoft's *Windows 98 Resource Kit,* which is available at bookstores.

WEBLINKS: Check the following Microsoft Web sites to get more help with troubleshooting Windows 98:
http://www.microsoft.com/hwtest/
http://www.microsoft.com/kb/
http://www.microsoft.com/support/

Here are some other non-Microsoft sites that can help you with system problems or provide advice about Windows in general. Note that at the time this book went to press, many of these sites still had Windows 95 in their names, but you should be able to go to the sites and get directed to new Windows 98 sites:
http://www.winfiles.com
http://www.windowscentral.com
http://www.halcyon.com/cerelli/
http://www.shareware95.com

Get the Latest Updates

One thing you should do on a periodic basis is make sure you have the latest update of Windows 98. You can do this by going to Microsoft's Web site. All you have to do is choose Windows Update on the Start menu. This takes you to the Windows 98 update site where you can access the Update Wizard, which helps you keep your computer current with the latest operating system software and device drivers. You can also access Microsoft technical support to find answers to your Windows 98 questions.

WEBLINK: If you don't see Windows Update on your Start menu, go to http://www.microsoft.com/windowsupdate.

Microsoft System Information Utility

The Microsoft System Information utility is a central place to get information about your system. The main window, pictured in Figure 22-3, shows system information similar to what you see when you open System in the Control

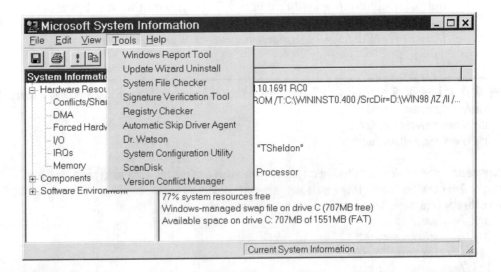

FIGURE 22-3 Microsoft System Information utility

Panel and choose the Device Manager option. If you click the Tools menu, you can access the following tools to help you troubleshoot problems:

- **Windows Report Tool** Use this tool to report problems to Microsoft and get responses from Microsoft technical support.
- **System File Checker** This tool checks system files to see if they are current, restores system files that have been corrupted by a virus or altered for some other reason, and monitors changes in application files.
- **Signature Verification Tool** Choose this tool to determine whether a file has been granted a digital signature and whether that file has been modified after being granted a digital signature.
- **Registry Checker** The Registry Checker is a tool for scanning, fixing, backing up and restoring the Registry and system configuration files. Registry Checker runs each time Windows starts.
- **Automatic Skip Driver Agent** This tool detects devices that prevent Windows from starting. You can use it to detect device drivers or operations that fail at startup.
- **Dr. Watson** Dr. Watson is a debugging tool that detects faults with applications and generates a snapshot of your system when those faults occur. It creates a log file that indicates the program that caused the fault, the program the fault occurred in, and the memory address where the fault occurred. Developers and technicians will help you use this program to reproduce and record faults so that they can diagnose problems.
- **System Configuration Utility** This tool allows you to modify the system startup configuration by enabling or disabling specific startup commands and options. By changing the startup configuration, you can resolve startup problems through a process of elimination.
- **ScanDisk** Use this tool for resolving conflicts between different versions of the same file.
- **Version Conflict Manager** Windows 98 Setup automatically installs a Windows 98 file over a newer file that may be on the hard drive.

System Monitor

System Monitor is a Windows 98 tool that helps you track the performance of the various components of your computer to determine if there are performance problems and decide whether settings require adjustment or whether equipment needs replacing.

System Monitor does not tell you directly if there is a problem. You need to run the program over a period of time and watch patterns of activity under various loads. This is not necessarily an intuitive process. If you are having performance problems, it might be easier just to add more memory or a better hard drive since that is usually the cause of problems in the first place.

However, it might be worth your time to at least experiment with the program. Technically inclined users will certainly gain some insight out of using the program. To start System Monitor:

1. Click Start.
2. Choose Programs | Accessories | System Tools | System Monitor. The dialog box in Figure 22-4 appears.
3. You then configure System Monitor to track specific processes as follows:
   a. Click the Add Chart button to open the Add dialog box.
   b. Choose a category in the Category field.
   c. Choose an item to track in the Item field.
   d. Click Explain to read information about items.
   e. Click OK to create the chart for the item if you want to track it.

With the optimizing and troubleshooting features in Windows 98, speeding up your system and resolving problems is now easier than ever. If you need more assistance, don't forget to access the Microsoft Web sites at the addresses given earlier.

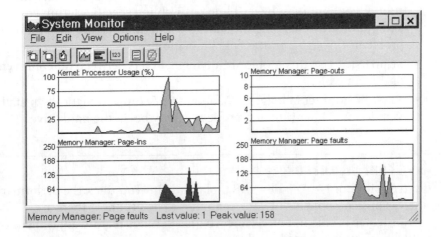

FIGURE 22-4 System Monitor

Setting Up Windows 98

A

Microsoft has improved the installation process with Windows 98. The process takes 30-60 minutes. You spend a few minutes making choices, then installation runs on its own until it's almost complete. You can do other things during the process but occasionally check to see if it needs you to make a choice or change a disk.

• Planning Your Windows 98 Installation

Installing a new operating system requires some decisions about the best way to install it on your system. Do you install it over Windows 95 or do you back up your existing data, erase your hard drive, and install it on a fresh drive? If you've been using your computer for a while, your setup may be too complex to rebuild with a fresh installation, so your options are to install over the old setup or create a dual-boot configuration in which you can still access the old operating system. In any case, back up the data on your system before continuing.

Before going further, you might want to review the information in the readme files on the Windows 98 CD-ROM. These files have information about specific software and hardware issues. A quick review of these files can save you a lot of grief. To read the information files, insert the Windows 98 CD-ROM into your CD player and look at the list of files in the readme folder. You can look at the files from DOS by running EDIT and then opening the files you want to view. If you're running Windows 95, just double-click the files you want to read. Be sure to read SETUP.TXT.

To use Windows 98 efficiently, we recommend a Pentium system with 32MB of RAM, though Windows 98 will run on a 486-66 system with 16MB of RAM.

Windows 98 actually has two sets of requirements regarding hard drive space, one for setting up Windows 98 and the other for running it. Setup needs extra hard disk space for its temporary setup files. You'll also find that the necessary disk space depends on the type of installation and optional components you choose, the hardware you have on the system, and the drivers the hardware requires.

A normal installation will require at least 120MB of hard disk space. If you create a highly customized installation and back up all of your Windows 95 system files during setup, you may need as much as 300MB of hard drive space.

Here are some pointers to guide you through the installation:

- You can configure your system for dual-boot in most cases. That means you can keep your Windows 95 or Windows 3.1 installation and decide at startup which one you want to boot.
- Back up your current data and configuration files.
- If you are connecting your computer to a network, get all the required network connection information from your network administrator (you can also install network support later if you prefer).
- Decide whether you are going to install Windows 98 over your existing installation or on a freshly formatted disk.

- After installing Windows 98, get the latest updates by choosing Windows Update on the Start menu. This takes you to the Microsoft Web site where you can run a program to update your system.

There are three ways to run Windows 98 Setup: from within Windows 95, from Windows 3.1, or from MS-DOS. The method you use depends on the configuration of your system. If you're running Windows 95 and want to retain your current settings, you can run setup from within Windows 95. If your system has an existing operating system such as Windows 3.1, MS-DOS, Windows NT, or OS/2, and you want to retain that operating system, start the installation process from DOS.

To keep from corrupting any system settings, close any programs before you begin the Windows 98 Setup. You will also want to disable or uninstall certain types of programs that could conflict with Setup, such as the following:

- **Anti-virus programs**   Disable or uninstall anti-virus programs before you attempt to install Windows 98. Also, verify that your anti-virus software is compatible with Windows 98. Check the software manual or visit the vendor's Web site for information. You should also disable virus-checking routines that are handled by your system's BIOS. Check your computer manual for more information.
- **Disk-caching programs**   Remove any third-party disk-caching software (though Windows 98 Setup removes most disk-caching software during installation and replaces it with its own disk-caching program).
- **Memory managers**   If you are running a memory manager such as QEMM, Maximizer, NetRoom, or others, read your software user's manual or visit the software vendor's Web site to verify that the memory manager is compatible with Windows 98.
- **Screen savers**   Close all screen savers and other programs.
- **Terminate-and-stay-resident programs**   If you have terminate-and-stay-resident anti-virus software, you will have to modify your AUTOEXEC.BAT, CONFIG.SYS, and WIN.INI files to keep the program from launching.

Installation Choices

When you run Windows 98 Setup, you'll be asked what type of installation to perform. There are basically four choices:

- **Typical** is the default Setup option.

- **Portable** helps you install Windows 98 on a portable computer, including setup of the Briefcase to synchronize files and software and to establish a direct cable connection between two computers.
- **Compact** is best if you are short on disk space and want to trim Windows 98 to a minimal size.
- **Custom** installation lets you choose the components you want to install; it's intended for knowledgeable users who know the options they want.

The Emergency Startup Disk

During Setup you'll be asked if you want to create an emergency startup disk on a 3.5-inch, 1.44MB floppy disk. The disk will provide an alternative way of booting your system if it won't boot from its hard drive. The disk includes utilities that help you recover from problems.

An important reason for creating an emergency startup disk is to assure access to your CD-ROM even if you can't run it from your C drive because of a system failure. The emergency startup disk has a generic ATAPI CD-ROM driver called OAKCDROM.SYS that will let you run many IDE CD-ROM drives, though it won't work with SCSI CD-ROM drives.

While the generic driver may work with your CD-ROM, a better way is to copy the drivers specific to your CD-ROM to your emergency startup disk. Read the documentation that came with your CD-ROM to find out which driver files you should copy and which statements you should add to your CONFIG.SYS and AUTOEXEC.BAT files so that the drivers load when your system starts from the emergency startup disk.

Installing over Windows 95

Windows 98 tries to make it easy for you to retain the settings you used with your previous operating system. This is easiest if you are upgrading from Windows 95, because Windows 98 will use the same settings. Setup will ask you for very little information.

Setup will install Windows 98 in the folder where Windows 95 is installed; if you want to install Windows 98 in a different folder, you will have to use the MS-DOS setup.

To run Windows 98 Setup from Windows 95:

1. Start your computer with Windows 95.
2. Back up your system following procedures outlined in Chapter 21.

3. Close all programs, including anti-virus, disk-caching, and memory management programs.

4. Insert the Windows 98 CD-ROM into your CD-ROM drive. If you don't see a Welcome message, open the Start menu and click Run.

5. In the Run dialog box, type the location of the Windows 98 setup disc. For example, if you're setting up Windows 98 from your CD-ROM, and the CD-ROM drive is your Drive D, you will type **d:\setup**.

6. Click OK to run the Windows 98 Setup Wizard.

Windows 98 Setup will ask you a series of questions about how you want to set up the operating system. After answering these questions, the setup is fairly automatic. The system will reboot several times during the installation as Windows 98 is configured to run over the old operating system.

Installing over Windows 3.1

You can upgrade Windows 3.1 or Windows for Workgroups to Windows 98. Setup will use most of your existing settings in the upgrade, and also configure your previously installed programs. The procedure is outlined here:

1. Insert the Windows 98 CD-ROM into the CD-ROM drive and make it the active drive.

2. Open File Manager and click the active drive.

3. Click File | Run.

4. In the Run dialog box, type the location of the Windows 98 setup disc. For example, if you're setting up Windows 98 from your CD-ROM, and the CD-ROM drive is your Drive D, you will type **d:\setup**.

5. Click OK to begin setup.

Creating a Dual-Boot System

If you want to keep your previous operating system and also install Windows 98, you can set up a dual-boot configuration. Dual-boot configurations are useful when you have programs that will not run under Windows 98 and you don't want to attempt to reconfigure your system in a way that might make those programs difficult or impossible to run. Dual-booting works with Windows 98 and other operating systems such as MS-DOS 5.x or higher,

Windows 3.1, or Windows NT. However, you can't set up Windows 98 and Windows 95 in a dual-boot configuration.

The procedure for setting up a dual-boot system is simple. Start your system as normal and boot the existing operating system. Put the Windows 98 disc in your CD-ROM drive and run the Setup program as previously outlined. When asked for the directory where you want to install Windows 98, do not specify any existing Windows directory. Instead, specify that you want to create a new directory (Win98, for example). Setup will then install Windows 98 in the new directory and allow you to start your old operating system as well.

Performing a Fresh Install

A fresh install refers to installing Windows 98 on a brand new disk or a disk that has been freshly formatted. There is no existing data or system setup information from a previous operating system installation.

The first step is to prepare the hard drive by partitioning and formatting it as a bootable disk. Then you need to install support for a CD-ROM drive and reboot so you can run the Windows 98 Setup program from the CD-ROM drive.

If you just purchased a new system with a blank hard drive or you just replaced the hard drive in your system, you'll need to follow the steps outlined here to partition and format the drive before you can install Windows 98.

All disks must be partitioned with the FDISK command and then formatted with the FORMAT command before you can install Windows 98 on the disk. You use the FDISK command to create one or more partitions on the drive. If you create one partition, that partition will become Drive C (we're assuming you are creating a boot disk). If you create two partitions on the disk, the first partition will be Drive C and the second partition will be Drive D. Of course, you can create additional partitions as well, depending on how you want to split up the drive.

The basic steps for creating a fresh installation are outlined next. Refer to your DOS manual and system manual for more detailed instructions.

1. Boot your system with the DOS floppy diskette.
2. Run the FDISK command and partition the disk into one large partition or several smaller partitions.
3. Run the FORMAT command to format each partition. You must type **FORMAT /S** on the first partition. The /S parameter installs the operating system files so you can boot from the disk.

4. Install the CD-ROM support files on the newly formatted Drive C disk partition, then create CONFIG.SYS and AUTOEXEC.BAT files that automatically load the CD-ROM support files when you boot from the hard drive. The disk that comes with your CD-ROM probably includes an install program that performs all of these steps for you.

5. Reboot the system and make sure that the CD-ROM support files load properly.

6. Place the Windows 98 disc in the CD-ROM drive and run the Setup utility on the CD-ROM.

Now you can follow the onscreen instructions for installing Windows 98.

Working with Compressed Drives

If you have compressed your hard disk with older Microsoft or third-party compression software, you may find you don't have enough space on the host partition for Windows 98's installation needs. After you make more space available, run Setup again.

Here are some ways to free up space for setting up Windows 98 with compressed drives:

- Set up Windows 98 on an uncompressed drive if you can.
- On the host partition, delete those files you don't need.
- If you use DriveSpace or DoubleSpace, free space on the host drive for the compressed drive:
  1. Exit Windows.
  2. Launch DriveSpace or DoubleSpace.
  3. Choose the compressed drive for the host partition where you want more space.
  4. Click Drive, then click Change Size.
- If you are using Windows 3.1 with a permanent swap file, you can reduce the size of the swap file.
- If you have third-party compression software on your system, refer to the software documentation for information about freeing up space.

For more information about compressed drives, see Chapter 21.

• Uninstalling Windows 98

If you want the option of uninstalling Windows 98 later, answer Yes when Windows 98 Setup asks if you want to save your system files. If you don't want the option, click No. Saving the files will require 6-9MB of disk space.

T I P : You won't be given the uninstall option if you are installing Windows 98 to a new folder.

You can save the uninstall files to a hard drive on your system, but not to a floppy disk or network drive.

You can uninstall Windows 98 and restore the system as follows:

1. Click the Start button, then choose Settings | Control Panel.
2. Click Add/Remove Programs.
3. On the Install/Uninstall tab, click Uninstall Windows 98, then click the Add/Remove button.

If Windows 98 doesn't run correctly after you install it, start the computer with the emergency startup disk, then launch UNINSTAL. You can also go to the \Windows\Command folder and run UNINSTAL from there.

Once you have Windows 98 running successfully, you may want to get rid of the uninstall files. To do this:

1. On the Start menu, choose Settings | Control Panel.
2. Click Add/Remove Programs.
3. On the Install/Uninstall tab, select Old Windows 3.1/MS-DOS System Files, then click Remove.

B

Getting Wired—Connecting to the Internet

BASICS

- Learn about the Internet and the Internet Protocols
- Learn about using Internet services
- Install and configure your modem
- Sign up with an Internet Service Provider
- Figure out domain names and IP addresses

BEYOND

- Install TCP/IP
- Install dial-up networking

Setting up an Internet connection is fairly simple, assuming you work with an Internet Service Provider (ISP). Your ISP can provide you with the information and system settings you need to connect your system in a matter of minutes. In this appendix, we explain what the Internet is and the services it provides, then discuss how you can get connected.

Quick Introduction to the Internet

The Internet is a global web of interconnected computer networks—a network of networks in which schools, libraries, businesses, hospitals, federal agencies, research institutes, and other entities can communicate with one another. The Internet spans the globe and includes people everywhere. The underlying connections include the dial-up telephone network, satellite and ground-based microwave links, undersea and overland fiber-optic cable links, and even the cable TV (CATV) network.

All over the Internet are servers that provide information. Government agencies like NASA have Internet sites that publish information about the latest space probes while companies like IBM and Microsoft have sites that publish information about their products. Most Internet sites now publish information using Web technologies. The Web is the overlaying graphical, hyperlinked interface for the Internet. It is what has made the Internet so popular. Anybody can learn to use a Web browser in a matter of minutes because most of what you do is click hyperlinked selections and buttons.

The Internet also provides a communication highway for transmitting electronic mail with anyone on the planet who has an Internet connection. In addition, it serves as the backbone for new emerging technologies such as Internet telephone and multimedia broadcasting technologies. Soon, you'll watch movies and interactive television over your Internet connection.

Internet Protocols

The Internet is a network of physical communication links that join computer systems. But computers must use communication protocols in order to send data to one another. A communication protocol defines the rules for sending and receiving information. If connected computers don't abide by communication rules, chaos would rule as each computer tried to transmit any time it dang well pleased.

The communication protocol for the Internet is TCP/IP (Transmission Control Protocol/Internet Protocol). TCP/IP is perhaps one of the most successful computer technologies ever developed, and if you can believe it, it was created by a government agency. Back in the early days, the U.S. Department of Defense needed a communication system that would interconnect large computer systems at research institutes, military installations, and universities. TCP/IP developed from that work.

As we mentioned, the Internet is easy to use, thanks to Web protocols. You start a Web browser like Internet Explorer and type in the Web address of the site you want to visit. For example, to visit Microsoft's Web site, you type the following address:

http://www.microsoft.com

The *http* part of this address stands for "hypertext transfer protocol." HTTP is a communication protocol that supports hyperlinks and other features that make the World Wide Web so unique. To get to a Web site, just type an address similar to the previous one in the Address field of your Web browser, and in a moment, pictures, text, animations, and other information start appearing in your Web browser.

So how do you get Web addresses? As you browse through magazines, you'll find the Web addresses listed for businesses and other organizations. Just type in the address to get there. Hyperlinking is another method. When you visit a Web site, you'll probably see hyperlinked pictures and/or text descriptions that point you to other Web sites. Just click the hyperlinks.

But not every site is that easy to find and get to, so you might need to do an Internet search. That means going to Web sites like Yahoo! and Digital's AltaVista where you can do keyword searches for Web sites that might interest you. For example, to find all sites that have information about anteaters, just go to AltaVista's site and type **anteaters** on the search menu. Soon you'll see a list of possibly hundreds of sites on the Internet that have information about anteaters.

Refer to Chapter 12 for more information about using the Internet. Also, once you're connected, refer to the following sites for other Internet and Web information:

WEBLINK: The following site has questions and answers to commonly asked questions by new Internet users: http://www.internic.net/rfc/rfc1206.txt.

The Steps in Connecting to the Internet

The Internet has become a playground—and a work arena—for personal computer users. Linking to the Internet via an ISP has been a cumbersome and frustrating experience for many users, so Microsoft took steps in Windows 98 to simplify the process of getting connected.

There are four steps to accessing the Internet:

1. Install and configure your modem (this must be done before you can access the Internet via an ISP).

2. Install TCP/IP and dial-up networking.

3. Identify the ISP you want to use and contact the company to sign up and obtain any necessary software.

4. Run the Internet Connection Wizard.

Step 1: Install and Configure Components

Before creating an Internet connection, you need to set up a physical connection. You can either connect to the Internet through a modem, or go through your company's LAN. If you're going through a LAN, please consult your network administrator. The remainder of this Appendix will assume you are setting up a modem connection from your home or office.

A modem is a device that connects your computer to the Internet, commercial online services, bulletin board services, or directly to other computers. Details about modems and modem configuration are covered in Chapter 20. To check the configuration of your modem now, click the Start button, then choose Settings | Control Panel | Modems. You should see your modem listed in the box. If not, refer to Chapter 20 for instructions on installing the modem.

TIP: If your modem isn't working, try the modem troubleshooter. On the Start menu, click Help. When the Help menu opens, type **Modem**. Click "troubleshooting" under the Modem heading, and then click to run the troubleshooter.

Step 2: Choose an Internet Service Provider

While Windows 98 gives you all the software tools you need to connect to the Internet, you still need to have an account with an ISP that can provide you with a link to the Internet, an email account, and various other Internet-related services. ISPs basically provide gateway services into the Internet. You dial into the ISP's modem banks and after making a connection, the ISP automatically establishes a direct connection between your computer and the Internet. The ISP also has mail servers that store your incoming mail and deliver the mail you send to other people.

There are currently over 4,000 ISPs in the United States; ISPs are generally broken down into regional and national service providers. The national service providers include such names as AT&T WorldNet, MCI EarthLink, and Netcom. There's also the commercial online services such as America Online, Microsoft Network, and Prodigy that offer both Internet access and their own proprietary content that you can access if you're a member. The large providers offer local access telephone numbers in the large cities throughout the country, so if you travel a lot, one of them might be your best bet.

The regional providers serve smaller areas of the country. *Boardwatch Magazine* defines a regional provider as one that serves less than 25 area codes. Regional ISPs tend to offer more personalized service, particularly in setting up your Internet connection, which is sometimes the most frustrating part of the Internet experience.

Here's what to look for in an ISP:

- Be sure to choose an ISP offering a local access number in your area. You don't want to be paying long distance phone charges while you're on the Net.
- Obtain a flat monthly rate. For about twenty dollars a month you can get unlimited Internet access.
- Ask about availability of effective technical support.
- Ask other people who use the service about busy signals and other connection problems.

Where do you find an ISP? The best place is your local Yellow Pages under Internet or Computer Services. If you know people who are already online, ask them about the service they use, or ask them to use their connection to check the following sites (we realize if you're reading this, you must not be online!). You can also go to your local library and try its Internet connection. Take this book along and access the sites listed here:

BOARDWATCH MAGAZINE'S ISP DIRECTORY	HTTP://WWW.BOARDWATCH.COM/ISP/INDEX.HTML
ISP Select	http://home.netscape.com/assist/isp_select
Thedirectory	http://www.thedirectory.org
Mecklermedia	http://thelist.internet.com/

You can use the Internet Connection Wizard that comes with Windows 98 to find an ISP, as we'll see later.

Setting Up an Account with an ISP

Once you've identified an ISP that offers the services and prices you want, contact the company to set up an account and obtain any setup software you'll need.

We're assuming that you're making a basic user connection to an ISP and that you'll become part of the ISP domain. For example, our ISP is THEGRID.NET in San Luis Obispo, California. Because we are part of their domain, our email addresses are tsheldon@thegrid.net and dlogan@thegrid.net. If you need to set up your own domain with your own unique domain name, contact your ISP. They can work with the Internet agency that handles domain setup and obtain a domain name and IP address for you.

To set up a basic Internet account, the ISP will give you the following information that you will need when running the Internet Connection Wizard:

- Your logon name and password
- A local access telephone number
- A personal email address
- The address of an email server and a news server
- At least two DNS (Domain Name System) IP addresses

If you don't need any of these pieces of information, your ISP will tell you so.

The email server is where email sent to you will accumulate when you are not online. When you log on, the email is downloaded to your computer. When you send email to others, it first goes to this email server and is dispatched over the Internet from there. A DNS server is basically an address lookup system. When given a name like http://www.whitehouse.gov, it returns an IP address that your computer uses to access the site.

Step 3: Install TCP/IP

The next step is to install TCP/IP, the communications protocol used on the Internet. You can install TCP/IP during your Windows 98 Setup, or install it later by going to the Control Panel and clicking Network. Assuming that Windows 98 is already installed, but TCP/IP is not installed, follow these steps:

1. On the Start menu, click Settings | Control Panel | Network.
2. On the Configuration tab, click the Add button.
3. Double-click Protocol in the Select Network Component Type dialog box.
4. Click Microsoft in the Manufacturers list in the Select Network Protocol dialog box.

5. Click TCP/IP in the Network Protocols list and click OK.

NOTE: Make sure you have a modem installed as discussed earlier. If you're connecting through your company's network, contact your network administrator.

When TCP/IP is installed, you'll need to reboot your system to complete the protocol installation. Then you can check the installation to make sure it is working:

1. On the Start menu, click Settings | Control Panel | Network.
2. On the Configuration tab, scroll through the list of installed network components for TCP/IP. You should see an option called "TCP/IP -> Dial up network adapter."

This setting indicates that TCP/IP is "bound" to your dial-up adapter, which in this case is your modem (the modem is treated as if it is a network adapter).

Step 4: Run the Internet Connection Wizard

Armed with the information from your ISP, you can use the Internet Connection Wizard to quickly set up your Internet connection.

1. On the Start menu, click Programs, then click the Internet Explorer menu option.
2. Choose Connection Wizard on the cascading menu.

   The Connection Wizard opens and offers you three choices for installing Internet support:

   • **I want to sign up and configure for a new Internet account.**   Choose this option if you want Windows 98 to help you look for and establish an account with an ISP.

   • **I have an existing Internet service through a local area network or Internet service provider. Help me set up my Internet software to connect to this Internet service.**   Choose this option if you already have an account with an ISP or if you are connected to the Internet over your company's LAN.

   • **My computer is already set up for the Internet. Do not show this wizard again.**   This option assumes you have already set up an Internet connection using another technique (i.e., the Dial-Up Networking

Wizard) and you just want to configure the Internet utilities to work with that connection.

We're assuming that you have obtained an ISP and you're ready to create an Internet connection over a phone line.

3. Choose the previous middle option, and click Next. On the next menu, you'll see the following options:

   - Select this option if you are accessing the Internet using an Internet service provider or a local area network (LAN).
   - Select this option if you are accessing the Internet using an online service such as The Microsoft Network or America Online.

   If you choose the second option, you're asked to choose a service in the Online Services folder that exists on your Desktop. We're assuming you need to connect via an ISP, so choose the first option and click Next, then choose the option for setting up a phone line connection.

4. In the next window, you may see a list of existing connections or the window may be blank. If the window is blank, choose "Create a new dial-up connection" and click Next; otherwise, choose "Use an existing dial-up connection" and select one of the connections. We assume you've chosen the former in the rest of these steps.

5. In the phone number window, enter the access number your ISP gave you. If it is a local access number, clear the box that reads "Dial using the area code and country code." Then click Next.

6. In the Username and Password dialog box, type the user name and password your ISP gave you. Click Next.

7. In the Advanced Settings window, click Yes and Next to enter any advanced settings the ISP may have given you. You are given the following choices. Refer to your ISP for more details:

   - Choose a connection type, either PPP or SLIP.
   - Choose a logon procedure: either no logon, manual logon, or logon with a logon script.
   - Choose whether you manually enter an IP address or whether your ISP assigns it to you automatically.
   - Specify the IP address of the ISP's DNS servers.

8. After setting these options, type a name for this Internet connection.

9. Now you're given the opportunity to set up your Internet Mail Account. Fill out each field with the information provided by your ISP and click Next to continue through the wizard.

10. Next, you can set up the Internet News Service by providing the name of the news server located at your ISP. If you're not sure, bypass this option for now.

11. After that, you can set up an Internet directory service account if your ISP gave you the name of an LDAP server (an *LDAP server* keeps a directory of people and company names), or you can do this later by clicking No. If you're not sure, bypass this option for now and obtain more information from your ISP.

12. Click Finish to complete the configuration of your Internet connection.

If you travel, you might have several ISPs or dial into the same ISP with different phone numbers. You can create Internet connections for each of these, so choose a name that fits each connection type.

That's it! Your system should be ready to log you on to the Internet. Start Internet Explorer at this time to test the connection. Windows 98 should automatically connect you to your ISP using the connection you just created. You can also open Outlook Express or other Internet-based programs to make an automatic connection. Refer to Chapter 12 for more information about using the Internet.

Index